the archaeologist was a spy

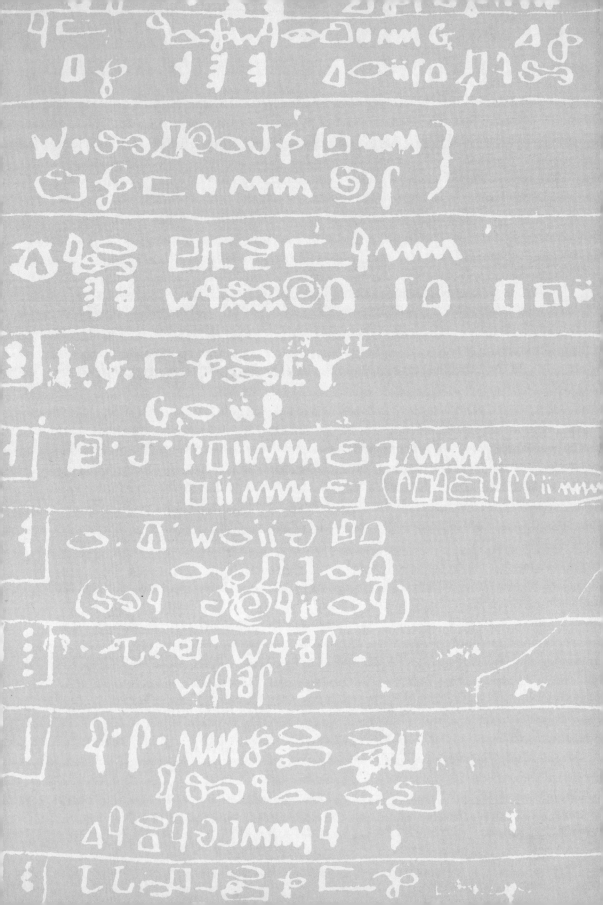

the archaeoLogist was a spy

Sylvanus G. Morley
and the Office of
Naval Intelligence

*Charles H. Harris III
and Louis R. Sadler*

University of New Mexico Press
Albuquerque

Library of Congress Cataloging-in-Publication Data

Harris, Charles H. (Charles Houston)
The archaeologist was a spy : Sylvanus G. Morley and
the Office of Naval Intelligence / Charles H. Harris III
and Louis R. Sadler.— 1st ed.
    p. cm.
Includes bibliographical references and index.
    ISBN 0-8263-2937-3 (cloth : alk. paper)
  1. Morley, Sylvanus Griswold, 1883–1948.
  2. Archaeologists—United States.
  3. Espionage, American—Central America.
  4. Espionage,
German—Central America.
  5. United States. Office of Naval Intelligence.
  6. World War, 1914–1918—Military intelligence.
I. Sadler, Louis R. II. Title.

D639.S8 M67 2003
940.4'8673'092—dc21   2002152230

Body text set in Sabon 11/14.5 pt
Display text set in American Typewriter
Printed and bound by Thomson-Shore, Inc.
Design and composition: Robyn Mundy

Contents

Contents

List of Figures

List of Figures

Acknowledgments

This was one of those monographs that began with the pulling of a thread, longer ago than either of us would like to admit. As a result we must necessarily acknowledge a number of institutions and individuals.

Our research was funded in part by a generous grant from the Weatherhead Foundation; a summer stipend from the National Endowment of the Humanities; and a series of grants from the Arts and Sciences Research Center, New Mexico State University (NMSU).

At the National Archives in Washington we are indebted to Gibson Smith who a quarter century ago first drew our attention to Sylvanus Morley. Subsequently our friend Tim Nenninger (who had produced a finding aid for ONI records) suggested that we must consult with Rebecca Livingston, a naval archivist. We suspect that she often wished that her colleague Nenninger had never mentioned her name. For more than six years Revecca Livingston has answered dozens of queries and repetitively explained the intricacies of the U.S. Navy filing system to two non-military historians. We are enormously indebted to her and without her truly substantial assistance this monograph could not have been written. At Archives II, military archivists Mitchell Yokelson, Rick Cox, George Chalou and the irreplaceable John Taylor were most helpful. In addition, William Walsh, a diplomatic archivist at Archives II, located key documents.

A number of other individuals and institutions facilitated our research. These include: the National Personnel Records Center (Military), St. Louis; the Federal Records Centers at Fort Worth, Texas (the late George Younkin), East Point, Georgia, Denver, Colorado, and Laguna Nigel, California; the Franklin D. Roosevelt Presidential Library (Karen Anson and Raymond Teichman) at Hyde Park, New York; among others Jeff Flannery of the Manuscript Division, Library of Congress; Operational Archives Branch (Sandy Doyle and Bernard Cavalcante), Navy Historical Center, Washington; and the U.S. Army Military History Institute, Army War College, Carlisle, Pennsylvania.

We thank the Keeper and staff, Public Record Office, Kew, for their courtesy to a non-British historian and the staff of the Centro de Estudios de Historia de México, Departamento Cultural de Condumex, Mexico City.

In addition we wish to express our appreciation to the Carnegie Institution, Washington; the Peabody Museum (Susan Haskell and Patricia Kervick), Harvard University; the Harvard University Archive; the Archive of American

Art at the Smithsonian, Washington; the American Museum of Natural History, New York City; and the American Philosophical Society (Robert. S. Cox), Philadelphia; the Elmer E. Rasmuson Library (Caroline Atuk), University of Alaska, Fairbanks; Latin American Library (David Dressing), Howard-Tilton Library (Leon Miller), both Tulane University; L. Tom Perry Special Colletions (Brad Westwood), Harold B. Lee Library, Brigham Young University, Provo, Utah.

Our former graduate student Tyler Ralston assisted us by obtaining a copy of a document in a Mexico City archive. Our friends Ben and Linda Montoya visited a Santa Fe graveyard to check a quotation. Peter and Linda Ditmanson at Cambridge, Massachusetts, were kind enough to house a Latin American historian during our research.

We would like to thank Judith Sandoval of Miami, Florida, and Kornelia Kurbjuhn of New York City for providing us with valuable leads.

Bill Beezley of the Department of History, University of Arizona, is not only an old friend, but he gave us excellent advice during the gestation of this manuscript. Michael Meyer, John Hart, José Garcia, Ricardo Aguilar, Frank Rafalko, David Kahn, and the late Jack McGrew were of assistance during the research and writing. We thank them all.

Tim Lawton, Department of Earth Sciences, NMSU, was helpful in solving a technical problem and obtained the services of a bright graduate student, Risa Madoff, to draw a much needed map. At NMSU University Communications, Darren Phillips digitized photographs for us. We are indebted to them.

In the Department of History, Ken Hammond was most helpful as were emerita faculty Darlis Miller and Joan Jensen. All of our colleagues, we are certain, are delighted that they will no longer have to hear more than they ever wanted to know about Sylvanus Morley.

Three secretaries in the History Department: Juanita Graves (who word-processed our first cut at the manuscript), Patsy Montoya and more recently Stacy Seagraves constantly responded to our cries of help from the technologically illiterate. Our colleague and former student Mark Milliorn, who is technologically brilliant, made absolutely certain that our word processors were up and running. We thank them all.

Betty Harris word-processed the entire manuscript—a number of chapters several times. Our indebtedness to her is enormous and we hope she knows it.

Finally, the Associate Director and Editor-in-Chief of the University of New Mexico Press David Holtby signed a contract with us a number of years ago for a book which for a variety of reasons was never written. We hope this monograph will fulfill our obligation. We could not have found a better editor than David and we thank him, managing editor Evelyn Schlatter, book designer Robyn Mundy, and their colleagues at the University of New Mexico Press.

Preface

In an almost-forgotten cemetery in Santa Fe, New Mexico, a simple two foot by eight inch slab of marble tombstone is unique: at the bottom left there is a cross, and at the bottom right a Maya hieroglyph. The inscription reads:

SYLVANUS GRISWOLD MORLEY

JUNE 7 1883

SEPT. 2 1948

Who was Sylvanus Morley, and why is there a Maya hieroglyph on his grave marker?[1] Because Morley was the most influential Maya archaeologist of his generation. His professional career focused on the study of that splendid pre-Columbian civilization which covered southern Mexico and much of Central America. His decades of research, much of it at the ruined ceremonial center of Chichén Itzá, culminated in his classic work *The Ancient Maya*, published in 1946 by Stanford University Press. The book has gone through five editions in English and one in Spanish. Through more than a dozen printings, the book is still in print almost half a century later, something few scholarly works achieve. Sadly, although *The Ancient Maya* is one of its all-time best sellers, Stanford University Press has seen fit to take Morley's name off the most recent edition.[2] Nor is this all.

Fairview Cemetery, Santa Fe, New Mexico. (Photo by Louis R. Sadler)

The 884-page *Oxford Companion to Archaeology*, published in 1996, has not a single reference to Morley.[3] This of course tells us more about the editor of the *Oxford Companion* than it does about Morley. Yet the fact remains that a whole generation of archaeologists, concerned with revisionist theories, tended to discount Morley as "Mayacentric." But in recent years Morley's reputation has enjoyed a revival. For example, Yale archaeologist Michael Coe, the present-day synthesizer of scholarship about the Maya, admits that on a number of important points Morley "may have been more right than wrong."[4] The current recognition, however grudging, of Morley's scholarly contribution to archaeology is unfortunately not paralleled by a recognition of his accomplishments as an intelligence agent.

Sylvanus G. Morley was arguably the finest American spy of World War I. It has been known for years that Morley did *something* in the wartime Office of Naval Intelligence. One magazine article has him cracking German codes.[5] To his credit, however, Morley's biographer Robert L. Brunhouse devotes a chapter to Morley as "Secret Agent."[6] Writing in 1971 and relying heavily on Morley's diary, Brunhouse accurately sketches the outline—but only the bare outline—of the archaeologist's intelligence-gathering activities in Central America.

This is more than the organization Morley served so honorably—the Office of Naval Intelligence — has done. There is not one word about Morley in Captain Wyman H. Packard's (USN, Ret.) massive study, *A Century of U.S. Naval Intelligence*, published jointly in 1996 by the Office of Naval Intelligence and the Naval Historical Center. Surprisingly, Packard does highlight Morley's assistant, the artist John Held, Jr., as an Office of Naval Intelligence operative during World War I. And in July 1975, the Navy Museum in Washington held an exhibit of the late John Held's artwork.[7] This emphasis on Held is curious; it is roughly analogous to celebrating Operation Sunrise, the World War II surrender of more than 1,000,000 German troops in northern Italy negotiated by Allen Dulles, by honoring Dulles's radio operator.[8]

Heretofore the approach to writing the history of the Office of Naval Intelligence has been to treat it in terms of an institutional narrative focusing on headquarters in Washington, as in the case of Jeffery Dorwart's two-volume study.[9] This approach establishes the institutional framework but, as has been observed, tends to neglect coverage of tactical and strategic intelligence.[10] As Rear Admiral Roger Welles, wartime Director of the Office of Naval Intelligence, put it in 1919:

> the nature of much of the work of the Office of Naval Intelligence during the war was of such a confidential nature that it cannot be told.[11]

But with the declassification of government archives in recent years it is now possible to approach the subject from another perspective—that of the agent in the field. Paul Sullivan utilized some ONI files in his five-page discussion of Morley's clandestine activities.[12] The present authors, however, intend to present a full-blown treatment of Morley's ONI service, thereby giving him his long-overdue due. But this book is about much more than reconstructing an important chapter in the life of this remarkable man.

The study of Morley sheds considerable light on how ONI almost overnight had to confront problems such as recruiting secret agents, creating agent networks, and directing, financing, and communicating with its agents in the field. This treatment also permits examination of topics that are still relevant today, such as the ethical questions posed by the relations between scholarly institutions and the government, and the role of scholars as spies. Since ONI obviously did not operate in a vacuum, that organization must be set within the context of the emerging United States intelligence community. And that community was larger and more effective than many writers on the subject have supposed. There was much more to American intelligence than what appeared on organizational charts.

1. The Intelligence Community

At 1:18 P.M. on the sixth of April 1917, the United States of America declared war on the German empire.[1] Rarely has a great power been so ill prepared for war—particularly since World War I had been raging for almost three years. Furthermore, the likelihood that America would become involved had been apparent since the sinking, by a German U-boat, of the British passenger liner *Lusitania* almost two years earlier, with the loss of 128 American lives.[2]

Indeed, beginning in the fall of 1914, the German government—in the words of the distinguished American historian Arthur Link—had "mounted a massive campaign on American soil of intrigue, espionage and sabotage unprecedented in modern times by one allegedly friendly power against another."[3] German agents carried out so many covert operations in the United States because almost immediately after the outbreak of World War I both the British and French governments contracted with American munitions manufacturers for huge quantities of artillery and small-arms ammunition. In an attempt to halt or slow down the manufacturing process, German intelligence officers carried out a bewildering string of operations ranging from strikes at munitions plants to preemptive purchases of ammunition production, and including attempts to blow up plants. Two of these sabotage operations were spectacularly successful: on July 30, 1916, 34 boxcars loaded with ammunition were blown up on Black Tom Island in an explosion that rocked New York City; an even more sensational operation occurred on January 11, 1917, when German agents set fire to the Kingsland munitions factory near New York harbor and 1,275,000 artillery shells destined for

Russia were destroyed. Moreover, German operatives managed to plant delayed-action incendiary devices aboard freighters carrying war matériel to the Allies.[4] The Germans even engaged in bacteriological warfare by injecting glanders and anthrax germs into horses and mules purchased in the United States that were being shipped to France. Apparently the vials had been mishandled, and the germs were dead. This topic, incidentally, has received little attention from scholars despite incontrovertible evidence of this covert operation.[5]

To cope with this German onslaught the United States initially had only limited intelligence capability. There was of course the venerable Secret Service, the oldest component of American intelligence and seemingly the best prepared to handle counterintelligence. Organized in 1865 at the close of the Civil War to catch counterfeiters of United States currency, for almost half a century the Secret Service was the only government agency staffed with trained detectives. The Treasury Department, the parent agency of the Secret Service, adopted the practice of lending Secret Service agents out to other government departments. Over time the Secret Service developed the techniques of tradecraft—surveillance techniques, mail covers, black-bag jobs, agent-provocateur operations, Alphonse and Gaston interrogation techniques, dead drops, dangle and penetration operations, etc.—that other agencies would copy.[6]

At the outbreak of the Spanish-American War in 1898, the McKinley administration turned to the Secret Service to ferret out Spanish spies, which it did with some degree of success, including an operation in Canada that unveiled a Spanish naval attaché recruiting spies to enlist in the United States Army.[7]

Then, beginning in 1910 with the outbreak of the Mexican Revolution, the Secret Service was handed a new mission, that of monitoring the activities of Mexican exiles in the United States. Because the United States shared a 1,951-mile border with Mexico, and because the upheaval in Mexico originated in its northern states, the Mexican Revolution inevitably spilled over into the United States. For the next decade this Revolution, the world's first great social revolution of the twentieth century, would keep Mexico in turmoil and constitute a major foreign-policy problem for the United States. And American intelligence organizations would hone their skills as they tried to keep abreast of revolutionary developments. At the outbreak of the Mexican Revolution the Secret Service was charged with investigating the activities of the various revolutionary juntas that sprang up in American cities, principally in the Southwest. Besides trying to keep up with the sometimes dizzying combinations and permutations among Mexican exiles, the Secret Service also tried to monitor the printing of fiat currency by the factions.[8]

But increasingly World War I became the first priority, and the Secret Service was ordered to investigate German intelligence operations in the United States. To learn what the Germans were doing, agents succeeded in installing wiretaps on German Ambassador Johann Heinrich Andreas Hermann Albrecht Count von Bernstorff's telephone, boldly purloined a briefcase full of incriminating documents from a German diplomat, and succeeded in identifying the principal German espionage agents in the United States.[9] However, between the American entry into the war and early 1918, the Secret Service was caught up in a classic Washington bureaucratic turf battle, which it lost. As a result, the Secret Service was ordered to leave primary counterintelligence responsibility to the relatively new federal Bureau of Investigation—to be renamed in 1935 the Federal Bureau of Investigation—of the Department of Justice.[10]

Formally organized on July 1, 1908, the Bureau of Investigation (BI) was established by Attorney General Charles Joseph Bonaparte, the grandson of one of Napoleon Bonaparte's brothers, because the Congress passed legislation forbidding the Department of the Treasury from lending more than a handful of Secret Service agents to other departments. The Department of Justice obviously needed investigators to prosecute criminals effectively, so the attorney general, despite congressional opposition, created the Bureau of Investigation without the approval of Congress while that body was in recess.[11]

Initially the Bureau's work was fairly routine, handling investigations for the various U.S. attorneys. By 1910 there was a flurry of congressional interest in prostitution, specifically the importation of women from Europe to staff houses of prostitution. As a result, Congressman James Robert Mann of Illinois introduced the White Slave Traffic Act of 1910, which that year passed the Congress without a dissenting vote, and was subsequently known as the Mann Act. The Bureau of Investigation was given enforcement responsibility for the new statute. As a result, the BI named "White Slave" agents in its various bureaus who had the dubious distinction of pursuing pimps at the national level. It should be noted that it was this piece of legislation that established an expanded precedent for the federal government in prosecuting interstate crime. This ultimately resulted in the BI becoming a national police agency.[12]

The Bureau of Investigation was also charged with enforcing the neutrality statute, which prohibited the use of United States territory for the purpose of attempting to overthrow a friendly government. It was in discharging this responsibility that the BI became involved with Mexican revolutionary activity, for when the Revolution broke out on November 20, 1910, against the long-ruling dictator General Porfirio Díaz, his government was considered friendly by the United States. In its efforts to monitor the Revolution, the BI over the years developed the intelligence and counterintelligence expertise it would later employ against the Germans.

At first the Bureau of Investigation's efforts to deal with rebel activities along the border were severely constrained because only a few agents were available. It took nearly a year for the Bureau to begin to get a handle on the situation.[13] By the fall of 1911, however, the agency had acquired some Spanish-speaking personnel and had hired a number of informants, usually called "special employees," who were providing intelligence about the various factions. The Bureau in San Antonio even succeeded in placing an undercover agent in the inner councils of a faction led by the former Mexican minister of war, General Bernardo Reyes, who was preparing to invade Mexico. The Bureau's work was instrumental in the United States government's smashing the Reyes conspiracy in November 1911.[14]

But it seemed that no sooner was one revolutionary movement contained than another erupted. In February 1912, General Pascual Orozco launched a major insurrection in the border state of Chihuahua. The rebels counted on supplying their army through El Paso. President William Howard Taft, however, imposed an arms embargo, and the Bureau, together with the U.S. Army, was expected to enforce it. By working closely with the intelligence service of President Francisco Madero, who had overthrown Díaz and was now trying to defeat his own former subordinate Orozco, the Bureau was able to suppress most of the rebels' arms-smuggling operations. Largely for lack of war matériel, the Orozco rebellion collapsed by the summer of 1912.[15]

President Madero's efforts to consolidate his rule ended abruptly, though. In February 1913, a military coup in Mexico City overthrew Madero, who was murdered shortly thereafter. The new Mexican strongman was the conservative General Victoriano Huerta. Incoming President

Woodrow Wilson was shocked by these events and refused to extend diplomatic recognition to the Huerta regime. That government soon faced a widespread rebellion encompassing the Mexican border states. Led by Venustiano Carranza, former governor of Coahuila, the rebels professed to be fighting to avenge the martyred Madero. Carranza called his movement the "Constitutionalists," a shrewd choice of name. Constitutionalist activity became frenetic as they intensified the smuggling of weapons despite the arms embargo, organized juntas, recruited volunteers, sought to influence American public opinion, and battled Huerta.

The Mexican Revolution entered its bloodiest phase from 1913 through 1915, causing enormous problems for the Bureau along the border. As of 1913, the Director of the BI, Bruce Bielaski, had only one hundred agents nationwide and a very limited budget for investigating neutrality violations. The Bureau had to make do with what it had.[16] By 1914, although still attempting to enforce the arms embargo, the Bureau was shifting toward providing more political intelligence; although the United States remained technically neutral, President Wilson favored a Constitutionalist victory and, in February 1914, lifted the arms embargo. By the summer, Huerta was in exile and Venustiano Carranza was now the dominant political figure in Mexico. Yet his authority was seriously challenged by General Francisco "Pancho" Villa in the north and General Emiliano Zapata in the south.

It was during this next round of civil war in Mexico that the Bureau was called in to help suppress the most bizarre irredentist movement in twentieth-century American history. In 1915, there surfaced in South Texas the so-called Plan de San Diego, ostensibly promulgated in the hamlet of San Diego, Texas. The document called for a Mexican-American uprising, the execution of all Anglo males over the age of sixteen, the establishment of an independent Hispanic republic in the Southwest, and aiding blacks in establishing a republic of their own in the South.[17] The Plan was initially viewed as a joke, but by the summer of 1915, South Texas was verging on a race war; Mexican-American militants, augmented by raiders striking across the Rio Grande from Carranza-controlled territory, plunged the region into turmoil and produced a deadly Anglo backlash. Not only were troops rushed in to protect the border, but Texas Rangers, county lawmen, and vigilante groups killed without benefit of trial more than three hundred Mexican-Americans suspected of involvement in the Plan.[18] The Bureau's San

Antonio office deployed agents to South Texas as well as hiring additional Spanish-speaking informants. Aspects of the Plan remain obscure, but what is clear is that the Plan of San Diego was used by the Carranza regime as a ploy to secure American diplomatic recognition; within a week after the United States, in October 1915, recognized Carranza as the de-facto president of Mexico the raids into Texas stopped.[19]

Within six months events took a turn that had important consequences for the Bureau. Outraged by Carranza's triumph and by American recognition of Carranza, Pancho Villa struck back. On March 9, 1916, he led some 480 guerrillas in raiding the small New Mexico border town of Columbus. Eighteen Americans died and much of the town was burned. It was a poor man's Pearl Harbor. Bowing to an infuriated American public, President Wilson dispatched Brigadier General John J. Pershing and the Punitive Expedition into Mexico to pursue Villa.[20]

In the immediate aftermath of the Columbus raid, BI agent E. B. Stone, based in El Paso, rushed to Columbus where he began to gather intelligence. He picked through the debris of the raid, interviewed captured *Villista* prisoners as well as an American woman who had been Villa's captive, and recovered a saddlebag full of *Villista* documents, whose contents he reported to Washington. His efforts were hampered because the army permitted the curious to roam at will over the battlefield collecting souvenirs. One of these sightseers, Morris Nordhouse, collected an impressive amount of loot, to the point that Bureau agents acting as a technical intelligence team at Columbus alerted their superiors. The Bureau launched a manhunt across the Midwest, finally locating Nordhouse in Kansas City and seizing two trunks full of his souvenirs. The items were dispatched to the army at Columbus. Although they yielded little of intelligence value, this incident was noteworthy as perhaps the first instance of the Bureau acquiring technical intelligence. And despite clashes of jurisdiction between the Bureau, the army, the State Department, and the Customs Service, the Bureau was able to provide both the army and the Department of State with accurate post-raid intelligence.[21]

The principal result of the Columbus raid and the consequent dispatch of Pershing's Punitive Expedition into Mexico was that relations between Washington and Mexico City rapidly deteriorated. The nationalist president of Mexico, Carranza, denounced the Punitive Expedition as an invasion of Mexico and demanded its recall. By the summer of 1916, Carranza revived Plan of San Diego raids into Texas, and there occurred clashes between Mexican and American troops. In June the two countries were on the verge of full-scale war.

This war crisis resulted in the Bureau of Investigation, for the first time in its history, launching what in the future would be called a "Major Bureau Special"—an all-out augmentation and reinforcement of Bureau personnel, this time at the border. The Bureau would have been unable to provide additional personnel for budgetary reasons, had it not been for the secret transfer of funds from the Department of State to the Justice Department. More than forty agents and "special employees," some undercover, and "informants" were recruited, assigned solely to gathering intelligence, and deployed along the Mexican border; in addition, agents were assigned to monitor Mexican developments from New Orleans.[22]

Bureau personnel, acting both as intelligence and counterintelligence agents, performed admirably during the crisis. One "special employee," former Texas Ranger Captain Tom Ross, developed information about an imminent raid by Plan of San Diego supporters against a cavalry detachment bivouacked downriver from Laredo. When the attack came, the army had reinforced the unit, and the raiders were repulsed with heavy losses.[23] Ross was also involved in a rather unsavory operation. He located at Laredo a black Plan of San Diego recruiter, a physician from Oklahoma who sported a commission as a major in the Carranza army. Ross arrested the man, Jesse Mosley, seized his papers, and had him jailed. Ross released Mosley from jail but evidently arranged for two local thugs to dispose of him, which they did by beating his brains out. Ross weathered the resulting flap, and a charge of murder against him was eventually dropped. Despite Ross's notoriety, and his serious drinking problem, the Bureau considered him such an asset that he was promoted from special employee to special agent. However, by the end of the year Ross's bosses' tolerance for his drinking had worn thin. As a result, on New Year's Day 1917, he was ordered to San Antonio where Special Agent in Charge R. L. Barnes fired him.[24]

Ross's actions were not the only time that BI special agents operating on the border sought to play as rough as their targets in Mexico. In two specific cases Bureau agents suggested to their superiors what the CIA would coyly refer to as "termination with extreme prejudice" operations. Bureau Special Agent E. B. Stone, in El Paso, had recruited two Japanese residents of Mexico who were acquainted with Pancho Villa and his brother Hipólito. The agent asked the two Japanese informants if they would be willing to kidnap Villa and bring him to the border or kill him and bring his body to the border. There is no extant record that Stone's superiors responded to the suggestion.[25]

Stone, who seemed to have a penchant for termination with extreme prejudice operations, had nine months earlier sought to broker a much more substantial venture of that type. In late October 1915, as a result of two major attacks near Brownsville by Plan of San Diego units, Special Agent in Charge Barnes went to Brownsville with Agent Stone to determine if the Bureau could assist the United States Army in stopping the raids.[26]

Barnes and Stone talked with Captain Frank McCoy, the army's intelligence chief in the Lower Valley, who advised them that the U.S. Army, officials in Hidalgo County near Brownsville, and a former U.S. Customs mounted inspector had four informants across the river who would be willing to kill or capture the leaders of the Plan of San Diego, Luis de la Rosa and Aniceto Pizaña, for a suitable reward. Agent Stone, after conferring with all of the appropriate officials, advised Barnes that since the governor of Texas had posted a $1,000 reward each for de la Rosa and Pizaña, dead or alive, a similar reward might work. Indeed, for that sum of money one informant declared he would cut off de la Rosa and Pizaña's heads and place them in a sack that would be delivered to the north bank of the river.[27]

In Washington, the director of the Bureau of Investigation, A. Bruce Bielaski, with the approval of Attorney General T. W. Gregory (a Texan), approved a reduced reward ($500 each for a total of $1,000) for the arrest and conviction of the two leaders. Bielaski, a competent Washington bureaucrat, did warn Bureau Special Agent in Charge Barnes that the reward could only be given for the two Plan of San Diego leaders "alive."[28]

However, copies of the two Bureau of Investigation agents' reports to Washington had been going to the United States Attorney for South Texas, J. E. Green, Jr., who was outraged at the proposal to kill de la Rosa and Pizaña. In a letter to Attorney General Gregory he stated that "we cannot afford to make government officers parties to a scheme to assassinate."[29] The attorney general, who was wise to the customs of the

Washington bureaucracy, responded that the rewards for the capture of the Plan leaders had his personal approval. But he noted that the Bureau agents had been advised "not to offer any reward for the defendants dead." Because of Green's letter, Gregory fired off another telegram covering his flank: "assume you understand must not be party . . . in any way plans involving assassination any individuals this country or Mexico. Should in fact discourage such attempts." The attorney general, however, did provide a loophole: "Killing defendant justifiable only self-defense if arrest resisted."[30] Finally, Gregory in a letter commended Green for his "promptness in taking action to correct the situation." But he slapped Green down for creating a flap in the first place, stating, "It is suggested . . . that the more effective and more simple way would have been to have called Agent Barnes on the telephone at Brownsville . . . and learned from him directly the situation."[31] The Bureau of Investigation agents were by no means off the reservation. Indeed the Southern Department was very much in favor of killing de la Rosa and Pizaña. The Chief of Staff of the Department, Major W. H. Hay, put it rather succinctly in a private letter to Captain McCoy at the border: "the Governor has offered a large reward for Pizano [*sic*] and de la Rosa, dead or alive. I hope . . . they are dead when delivered so much the better."[32]

Whether any of the secret agents who had been recruited to kill the Plan of San Diego leaders could have done so is impossible to say. Green's letter of outrage, however, effectively killed the operation.

The war crisis with Mexico abated by July 1916, by which time the Bureau had proven its competence in a counterintelligence role to both the War and State departments. Following the United States's entry into World War I, the Bureau quickly expanded to 425 agents. Its wartime counterintelligence activities were supplemented by the controversial 300,000-member American Protective League, the volunteer auxiliaries of the Department of Justice who investigated subversives.[33] Furthermore, between 1916 and 1918 the Bureau sent agents undercover to Mexico, Cuba, and Central America, where they collected intelligence and operated against the Germans.[34]

One reason for the overseas deployment was to follow up on leads provided by Charles Jones, who was arguably the best double agent that United State intelligence had during this period. Jones had been a newspaper reporter covering Mexican and Central American affairs. He was now an ammunition broker using a corporate shell titled the National

Arms Company. Operating out of an office in New Orleans, Jones met, apparently in 1914, Forrest Pendleton, the division superintendent of the BI based in New Orleans; the Bureau divided the country into divisions, each supervised by a senior agent. Since Jones sold guns and ammunition to foreign nationals, he was obviously a valuable source for the Bureau investigating neutrality violations.[35]

Under circumstances that are still unclear, Jones became an informant for the Bureau. Pendleton assigned him the cover name "Cresse." This was unusual, for it was standard practice for the BI to identify informants by name in its field reports. The use of a cover name for Jones was a security measure because he was such a valuable informant. Jones provided the Bureau with an enormous volume of information—more than three thousand reports encompassing tens of thousands of pages of documents.

Jones could supply intelligence on this scale because he was a highly successful munitions entrepreneur. He sent out mass mailings offering a wide range and large quantities of ammunition at attractive prices. Latin American revolutionists flocked to buy his wares. Because he dealt with dozens of insurgent factions from 1914 to 1919, Jones was able to supply the Bureau with timely and accurate intelligence on dissident groups throughout the Caribbean, Central America, and Mexico. In some instances he even provided their plans for the future. This kind of information constituted a window into an arena that both the Bureau and the State Department heretofore had seen only in dim outline. Jones, who was fluent in Spanish, was so successful in ingratiating himself with revolutionary factions that he became the de-facto archivist for several important exile groups. He thus obtained thousands of documents, and he and other Bureau agents were hard pressed to translate and process them in a timely fashion.[36]

Given the information provided the Bureau and thus the Department of State, the question can be posed whether or not Jones may have manipulated revolutionary factions under orders from Pendleton. Additionally, whether or not Director Bielaski received instructions from the Department of State either to support or to suppress certain Central American factions is a question that U.S. diplomatic historians specializing in Latin American-U.S. relations may wish to pursue. What is indisputable is that the quality of intelligence Jones was able to provide was unprecedented for a region of vital importance to the United States.

Ironically, Jones's reputation and his knowledge of Mexican revolutionary politics resulted in an unprecedented job offer: in 1918, the Carranza government asked him to become the head of the Mexican intelligence service in the United States. Jones declined the offer, apparently after conferring with Pendleton, who certainly would have consulted Director Bielaski.[37] Jones maintained his connection with the Bureau until 1919. Perhaps he tired of working under the strain of being a double agent, as he had been for the last six years. Or perhaps it was because his access to Director Bielaski ended when the latter resigned early in 1919. In any case, Jones severed his ties with the Bureau, leaving with a letter from his case officer, Division Superintendent Pendleton, lavishly praising his performance.[38]

Others were less fulsome. In 1919, Senator A. B. Fall led an infamous investigation of Mexican affairs. Judge Francis J. Kearful, one of the senator's closest advisors during the Fall Committee's investigation, stated that he knew Jones and his kind. Jones was nothing more than a blackmailer who dealt in stolen papers, including some that implicated [President Venustiano] Carranza and may have sold for $15,000. According to Kearful, Jones habitually played both sides, was extremely clever, and would stop at nothing, including murder; one should never be alone with Jones.[39]

Despite Kearful's caveat, the Fall Committee decided to use Jones's testimony because he was so knowledgeable about President Carranza's involvement in Central American politics. In April 1920, Jones testified publicly before the committee. His testimony, which was supposed to be a bombshell, proved to be a dud; President Carranza, the main target of the Fall Committee, was in the process of being overthrown and killed. Charles Jones died in 1920, less than three months after his appearance before the Fall Committee.[40]

The Bureau of Investigation, through operations such as running Charles Jones, had demonstrated its competence in the field of intelligence. Not surprisingly, when the United States entered World War I, Bureau agents were quickly recruited by other organizations. For example, the Bureau's supervising agent in San Antonio, Robert Barnes, was snapped up by Military Intelligence in 1917. He was commissioned as a major, was stationed at Fort Sam Houston in San Antonio, headquarters of the Southern Department, and was assigned as the Department Intelligence Officer, responsible for the Texas, New Mexico, and Arizona border.[41]

Military Intelligence (MI) was the third-oldest American intelligence organization, established in 1885. During the Spanish-American War the organization had performed creditably, infiltrating agents into Cuba and Puerto Rico to make contact with rebels and report back their findings. But it was in the years following the Spanish-American War that MI cut its eyeteeth in the craft of intelligence, in the Philippines, Cuba, and Mexico.[42]

The traditional history of MI propounds the view that for almost a decade, between 1908 and 1916, MI was consigned to oblivion by being assigned to a committee composed of a literal handful of officers in the Army War College. The rest of the legend is that MI was resurrected by Colonel Ralph H. Van Deman in 1917, following the American declaration of war.[43] Like most histories of intelligence, there are elements of both truth and fiction in this account. Van Deman, of course, is quite correctly identified as the father of army intelligence. However, traditional histories of MI suggest that almost nothing had been done after the merger of MI into the committee of the War College. This presentist point of view essentially propounds the thesis that only if there was a major Washington-based headquarters did MI really exist. The facts suggest otherwise.

Between 1899 and 1912, for example, a military intelligence bureau was set up in the Philippines and was decentralized to the district level, where dozens of native agents were recruited and run, often with considerable success. These agents penetrated the ranks of both Emilio Aguinaldo's rebels and the Muslim insurgents in the southern islands.[44] Thus MI was able to provide the intelligence that enabled Brigadier Generals John J. Pershing and Tasker Bliss, as commanders in the field, to disperse insurgent bands. In the Philippines, both Pershing and Bliss learned the value of good intelligence and how it could be obtained. Furthermore, the virtually autonomous Military Information Division of Army Headquarters based in Manila served as an advanced military-intelligence organization for the Far East. For example, Van Deman, then a captain, along with perhaps a dozen other army officers in the Philippines, was ordered to various parts of China and Formosa between 1906 and 1911, to prepare maps and collect intelligence.[45]

In addition, during the period 1906–1909 the United States Army was ordered to send troops to Cuba to keep the peace during a period of political upheaval over who would succeed to the presidency of the island. A network of paid informants was set up by MI to provide intelligence. This network proved to be effective in providing timely warnings of threatened guerrilla activity by various Cuban factions.[46]

But increasingly it was Mexico that provided a proving ground for MI. As early as the summer of 1907, Captain William S. Scott, who had served in MI during the Spanish-American War,[47] was dispatched on a confidential mission to report on conditions along the U.S.-Mexico border. Scott's intelligence report, which went to Secretary of War Elihu Root, dated August 26, 1907, stated prophetically that "there exists, particularly in the northern states of Mexico, much discontent with present conditions, and a strong leader would receive a strong following in case of a revolutionary outbreak."[48]

As noted earlier, a leader did emerge in the person of Francisco Madero, and by May 1911 a guerrilla insurgency centered in northern Mexico forced President Díaz to flee into exile. However, there were fears that Madero, who would be elected president later in the year, would be unable to keep the peace. As a result, MI (or the War College committee) dispatched a team of agents posing as American journalists to go to Mexico and report back on Madero's chances of remaining in power. Captains Charles D. Rhodes and Paul Y. Malone reported back to the Chief of Staff of the Army, in a report dated October 27, 1911, "it seems improbable that Madero can long continue peaceably as President." Further, the two captains also stated, accurately enough, "Intervention by the United States in from one to five years is a logical deduction."[49]

In addition, another agent, 1st Lieutenant William E. W. MacKinley, was sent undercover into Mexico in December 1911, to provide a second opinion on the prospects for stability. MacKinley, who unlike Rhodes and Malone spoke competent Spanish, was also given classic "Mission Impossible" instructions. The chief of the War College Division, Colonel John Biddle, informed MacKinley: "It is needless to remind you that the Department would have to disclaim all knowledge of your mission in case any question arose."[50] At the same time, a fourth officer, Major Augustus P. Blocksom, was sent down the west coast of Mexico to survey the region. Blocksom's report stated substantially the same thing as Rhodes and Malone and MacKinley: there was considerable instability in Mexico and whether Madero could survive was questionable.

All three intelligence reports proved to be accurate because two consecutive rebellions against Madero broke out in northern Mexico from the fall of 1911 through late summer 1912. During the Reyes rebellion, Major Charles B. Hagadorn, the post commander of Fort McIntosh, just outside Laredo, and who also served as the post intelligence officer, cooperated with the Bureau of Investigation in penetrating the conspiracy and smashing the abortive invasion of Mexico. Hagadorn was an experienced intelligence officer, having served as the intelligence chief for the Department of Mindanao in the Philippines, prior to his transfer to the U.S.-Mexico border.[51] The second uprising, the Orozco rebellion, was suppressed by September 1912. Much of the intelligence on this rebellion came from the able military attaché in Mexico City, Captain W. A. Burnside, whose reports from the field accompanying the federal army proved to be quite useful.[52] In addition, Madero intelligence operatives, working with the Bureau of Investigation in El Paso, supplied information to the army personnel handling intelligence at Fort Bliss, thus helping American authorities in suppressing gun-running operations.[53]

The overthrow of the Madero government in February 1913, by General Victoriano Huerta, and the subsequent Constitutionalist uprising in northern Mexico created enormous problems for the United States government generally and specifically for the army on the border. By April 1914, Huerta armies were in retreat throughout Mexico, when the arrest of a group of American sailors at the port of Tampico threatened to embroil the United States in war with Mexico. Although the sailors were quickly released, the demand for an apology by the American admiral commanding U.S. naval forces in Mexican waters was rejected by Huerta.[54]

As a result, the United States bombarded and occupied the principal Mexican port of Veracruz, mainly to prevent Huerta from receiving a shipload of arms from Germany. A division of U.S. troops remained in the city for some seven months. During this period a young captain named Douglas MacArthur was given an intelligence assignment to determine whether or not Mexican troops planned a major assault on Veracruz. MacArthur, using a railroad handcar, did not find the area outside the city populated with large numbers of Mexican troops, a classic case of collecting negative intelligence.[55] By the early fall of 1914, Huerta had fled to Spain and the winners of the Constitutionalist revolution were fighting among themselves.

As mentioned above, the Plan of San Diego plot in 1915 had a significant impact on the army in the lower Rio Grande Valley of Texas.

Initially the army's Southern Department at Fort Sam Houston responded slowly to Mexican raids near Brownsville. Beginning in August 1915, Captain Frank Ross McCoy was named intelligence chief along the river and veteran army intelligence officer Captain William E. W. MacKinley was sent to the valley under journalistic cover. By October 1915 the reports generated by McCoy and MacKinley had given army commanders in the field a handle on what they were dealing with in attempting to stop the raiders. The raids came to an end immediately after the United States gave de-facto diplomatic recognition to Venustiano Carranza's administration.[56]

However, this proved to be the proverbial lull before the storm. In March 1916, Pancho Villa raided Columbus, New Mexico. General Pershing and the Punitive Expedition crossed into Mexico after him. The army provided Pershing with some $20,000 to recruit spies and guides, and assigned several of the army's best intelligence officers to assist him. These included Captains MacKinley and Nicolas Campanole, one of only a handful of Japanese-speaking officers. Pershing also added a hotshot young cavalry officer, 1st Lieutenant George S. Patton, Jr., as a junior intelligence officer.[57]

During the period 1906–1909 Campanole had been in Japan learning Japanese. In 1913, he operated undercover in the Hawaiian Islands because of his Japanese language competence during the so-called war crisis in those islands. This little-known episode occurred when intelligence reports that the Japanese planned to attack Hawaii were circulated. Reinforcements and ammunition were secretly rushed to the islands.[58] In the event, the reports that the Japanese planned to attack the islands were correct, but only twenty-eight years premature.

Campanole's Japanese expertise proved invaluable, for Pershing's intelligence contingent recruited and ran more than twenty-five agents, including Mexican and Japanese operatives. It was the Japanese agents who were the most interesting. They were recruited in western Chihuahua in April by Campanole, who undoubtedly stunned them by interrogating them in Japanese. They had operated a mine in Chihuahua and the facility had been looted earlier by Villa and his men. They said that Villa personally knew them and they had gotten along with him and his men despite the ransacking of their property. However, they were understandably angry at being stripped of their belongings. When Campanole asked if they would be willing to work for the Punitive expedition for $5 gold per day, three of them signed up. They were initially instructed to locate Villa and join his ranks. By June they had succeeded in doing so.[59]

Campanole subsequently asked the Japanese if they would be willing to engage in an operation to kill Villa. They agreed to do so and were given an unidentified poison by a Punitive Expedition surgeon. After testing the poison on a dog, they rejoined Villa and apparently placed the poison in Villa's coffee. According to their account, Villa, who was most suspicious of any food or drink that he was given, handed the coffee to one of his officers, whereupon the Japanese agents prudently fled the Villa camp.[60]

The story of the attempted assassination was told by the U.S. Army's Japanese spies to the Bureau of Investigation's Japanese spies at a *sake* party in September 1916, in Ciudad Juárez, and was reported up the BI chain of command to the attorney general, who asked the secretary of war what was going on. However, a massive coverup was carried out both by the army and the Bureau of Investigation and the story never got out. But what is significant is that this operation was unquestionably carried out either at Pershing's initiative or with his full knowledge. Furthermore, even though the operation failed, it was a surprisingly sophisticated exercise in using third-country nationals, plausible deniability, and even a cover story planted in the Mexican press.[61]

Back in Washington, Major Ralph H. Van Deman was laying the groundwork for an augmented MI, operating out of the Army War College. Even before Van Deman arrived back at the War College, the War Department had begun to realize that it might be useful to assign intelligence officers to major commands. For example, in April 1916, the Acting Chief of Staff of the Army for the first time ordered intelligence officers assigned to each of the army's four continental commands and two overseas departments.[62] Since 1908, MI had been decentralized at the Department level, and commands such as the Punitive Expedition essentially ran their own intelligence operations. Historians of United States intelligence have focused on Van Deman's Washington operation of one officer and two clerks until May 1917, while totally ignoring Pershing's seven intelligence officers and twenty-five spies who operated for eleven months in a foreign country.[63]

An aspect of American intelligence in the decade before World War I that has been especially neglected is signal intelligence or "sigint." Only a few works, notably David Kahn's groundbreaking *The Codebreakers*, even treat this topic.[64] There are, of course, a number of explanations that account for the lack of research on early American signal intelligence. For one thing, the interception and cryptanalysis of foreign radio and message traffic was spasmodic at best and was diffused throughout the government. For example, one of the first U.S. government cryptanalysts was an amateur, the United States Commissioner for the Western District of Texas, one George Oliver, who in 1908, for his own amusement cracked the coded messages of the *Magonistas*, the Mexican revolutionary faction led by Ricardo Flores Magón that was attempting from exile in the United States to overthrow the Mexican government.[65]

Subsequently other Mexican revolutionary groups, such as the followers of Bernardo Reyes, who unsuccessfully attempted in 1911 to overthrow the Madero government, had their codes and ciphers seized.[66] Through a variety of methods including "black bag jobs," Bureau of Investigation agents, Customs officials, U.S. Army officers stationed along the border, and Justice Department officials obtained dozens of codes from various factions during the course of the Mexican Revolution, 1908–1929.

Since the Civil War the United States government had generally ignored the topic of code breaking. But beginning in 1913, the United States Army Signal Corps school had begun to teach courses on code breaking, and the army's first cryptanalyst, Captain Parker Hitt, wrote a manual on how to break codes and ciphers. By 1915, Signal Corps headquarters were actively seeking copies of coded Mexican revolutionary messages and turning them over to Hitt to decipher.[67]

In the same year, the Bureau of Investigation, the U.S. Army's Southern Department, and the Army Signal Corps began collecting codes and ciphers and exchanging them with the admonition to the receiving agency "please keep the matter entirely confidential." However, no U.S. government military or civilian agency was established to engage in code breaking. Even the Army Signal Corps handled both the acquisition of codes and code breaking as ad hoc operations for personnel to handle in their spare time. For instance, in 1916, Captain Hitt was commanding a company of the 19th Infantry at Del Rio, Texas, along the U.S.-Mexican border. Coded messages would be forwarded to him with requests to decode them as rapidly as possible. On one occasion, Hitt, responding to what amounted to an order to speed up his code-breaking activities, responded somewhat plaintively to Southern Department headquarters that he commanded his infantry company during the day and he could only handle his code-breaking activities late at night.[68]

But it was in the aftermath of the Columbus raid that the army began seriously to address the interception and decrypting of Mexican Army radio and telegraphic communications. Virtually the entire Signal Corps was assigned to Pershing's Punitive Expedition. Signal Corps units manned mobile intercept tractors that picked up Mexican Army radio traffic, and Signal Corps technicians succeeded in tapping key Mexican government telegraph lines along the border. Army intelligence officers, working with dozens of Signal Corps enlisted men, both in Mexico and along the border, were able to decrypt voluminous radio and telegraphic traffic. By the fall of 1916, it is quite likely that General Pershing was reading with his morning coffee more Mexican Army messages than Mexican Minister of War General Alvaro Obregón.[69]

Furthermore, by 1916 the Signal Corps had made contact with the most unusual research facility in the country—the Riverbank Laboratories at Geneva, Illinois. The Laboratories belonged to George Fabyan, a businessman who had made a fortune in textiles and had built the facility on his five-hundred-acre estate, Riverbank. Fabyan was wealthy enough to indulge his interests, so he maintained laboratories conducting research in chemistry, genetics, acoustics, and cryptology. He was obsessed with the notion that Francis Bacon had actually written Shakespeare's plays and that Bacon's authorship could be proved by cracking a cipher hidden in the writings. Among the staff working on this problem was a geneticist recently graduated from Cornell University, William F. Friedman, who began working at Riverbank in 1915. Friedman evolved into America's greatest cryptanalyst; he and his wife Elizabeth would form the most distinguished husband-and-wife team in the entire history of cryptology.[70]

Fabyan's Riverbank Laboratories had a much greater cryptographic capacity than anything the United States government possessed. Thus, when in 1916 Fabyan approached the Signal Corps and the State Department and patriotically offered them the services of his cryptanalysts without fee, his offer was gratefully accepted. Soon, coded and enciphered messages that Captain Hitt and others could not break were en route to Riverbank. Friedman and his colleagues were rather successful in the timely decoding of Mexican diplomatic and military traffic. Until at least 1922, the Riverbank Laboratories continued to work on a variety of coded messages for the army and the Office of Naval Intelligence.[71]

But the Riverbank Laboratories were not the only repository of outstanding cryptanalytic talent. The Bureau of Investigation had in its ranks an individual who would become one of the country's finest code breakers, Victor Weiskopf. As of 1916 he was stationed on the Rio Grande in one of the bleakest towns on the entire Mexican border—Presidio, Texas, in the isolated Big Bend region. The Director of the Bureau, Bruce Bielaski, had personally hired Weiskopf following the Columbus raid, when tension with Mexico was rapidly escalating. Weiskopf was able to acquire coded Mexican government messages. By the fall of 1916 he was decoding a respectable number of messages that were of value not only to the Bureau of Investigation but also to the army and the Department of State.[72]

Thus, by the spring of 1917 there existed a respectable cryptanalytic capability in the budding United States intelligence community. Both Weiskopf and Friedman, who helped train the first classes of Army cryptanalysts at the Riverbank Laboratories during World War I, joined Army Intelligence's code-breaking operation. Weiskopf was actually loaned by the Justice Department to MI-8 where he worked with the infamous Herbert Yardley. Friedman, in May 1918, was sent to France to head the code-breaking activities of General Pershing's American Expeditionary Force. Captain Parker Hitt also went to France as a Signal Corps officer, where he had some supervisory responsibility related to code breaking.[73] It is interesting to note that the United States Navy, which had pioneered the establishment of both shore-based and shipboard radio beginning in 1900, had no signal intelligence capability worth mentioning until the early 1920s.[74]

Whereas MI had been in existence for almost a third of a century, the still little-known Department of State's Bureau of Secret Intelligence (BSI) was not even informally established until 1914. But with private funding sources, apparently from Wall Street, the BSI quickly became an important player in the infant American intelligence community.[75]

The BSI reported directly to the Counselor of the State Department. Initially, the BSI concentrated on the U.S.-Mexico border, and in early 1914 the State Department recruited the United States Collector of Customs in El Paso, Texas, Zach Lamar Cobb, who was not only a political appointee but an employee of another government agency, the Department of the Treasury.[76] But Cobb was a natural as an intelligence agent, and in June 1915 he carried out a spectacular operation. He learned that the exiled General Victoriano Huerta was en route from New York to El Paso by train, where he planned to launch a rebellion against the Constitutionalists who had overthrown his government a year earlier. The Treasury Department had learned via the Secret Service that Huerta's conspiracy was being backed by German intelligence operatives in the United States. When Cobb learned from his sources, apparently railroad agents in El Paso, of Huerta's destination, he mobilized a squad of soldiers at Fort Bliss and roared off some twenty miles to the remote hamlet of Newman, New Mexico. Acting without orders from the Department of State, Cobb arrested Huerta when he got off the train, along with the exiled General Pascual Orozco, who was waiting to pick up Huerta and take him to the border. Although Huerta's arrest was unauthorized, since there had not been time to consult with Secretary of State Robert Lansing, the government heartily approved of Cobb's actions.[77]

In addition, Cobb put together a network of informants in a relatively brief period of time, concentrating on the state of Chihuahua. Utilizing his Customs District, which covered the New Mexico border and portions of southwest Texas, he collected intelligence on revolutionaries throughout northern Mexico. Cobb and his inspectors systematically interviewed both Americans and Mexicans entering the United States from Mexico, in what may well have been the first operation of its type. The same approach was used in 1941 by Dewitt Poole in New York City, interviewing principally Europeans arriving from overseas for the Coordinator of Information, the precursor to the Office of Strategic Service (OSS). After World War II, the Central Intelligence Agency established the so-called Domestic Contacts (DC) Division with offices in principal American cities. CIA agents would contact Americans who had been abroad visiting interesting places, such as the Soviet Union, and attempt to elicit useful intelligence.[78]

Since Customs passed all individuals entering the United States, Cobb used his personnel discreetly to interrogate those coming from Mexico, especially through El Paso. By comparing stories and learning, for example, which individuals had actually seen Pancho Villa and his troops, Cobb provided timely and accurate intelligence on the Mexican Revolution. Although there is limited evidence—the U.S. Customs files for El Paso were tragically destroyed decades ago—it seems that Cobb was able to obtain access to some Mexican telegraphic traffic particularly via telegraph operators for the Mexico Central and the Mexican Northwestern railway, the latter with its headquarters in El Paso.[79] Cobb also utilized a few agents, both in Chihuahua and individuals sent into Mexico from El Paso.[80]

Indeed, Cobb's reports prior to Villa's 1916 raid on Columbus were not only timely but substantially accurate. As directed by the State Department, Cobb had procedures in place promptly to notify the El Paso Patrol District, commanded by Brigadier General John J. Pershing and based at Fort Bliss, of any relevant intelligence from Mexico regarding the border. As a result of Cobb's intelligence reports, the commander of the 13th Cavalry based at Columbus, Colonel Herbert J. Slocum, was aware that Villa was headed north to the border and specifically in the direction of Columbus.[81] Unfortunately, Colonel Slocum did not place the Columbus garrison on alert, and the raid was a complete surprise. Although his superiors publicly refused to condemn Slocum, privately General Pershing and others were irate over his lack of preparedness given both the quality and quantity of Cobb's intelligence.[82]

If Cobb's network was the most successful BSI operation, the best-known operative recruited was easily the flamboyant soldier of fortune Lee Christmas, of whom more later. Other BSI secret agents who were recruited and sent to Latin America included Sprague Brooks, who spent eight months in Cuba; John Merrill, who had an eighteen-month tour in South America; and Randolph Robertson, a consular officer who became virtually a full-time intelligence officer covering northeastern Mexico during the first eight months of 1917. A few BSI operatives were sent to Europe and the Middle East, including one Zenophon Dmitrievich deBlumenthal Kalamatiano, a Greek-American who was personally recruited in 1915 by State Department Counselor and soon-to-be Secretary of State Robert Lansing. Kalamatiano was captured in September 1918, as a result of the failed Lettish Guards plot to kill Lenin and was sentenced to death by the Bolsheviks. He was finally freed with more than a dozen other Americans as a condition of the Hoover American Relief Organization, which fed millions of Russians during the great 1921–1922 famine.[83]

The BSI deployed less than fifteen agents abroad during World War I, most of them to Mexico and Central America.[84] But the agency served an important purpose by collecting information for the Counselor of the State Department. During World War I the Office of the Counselor developed into the clearing house for the American intelligence community.[85]

There was one United States intelligence organization, however, which during World War I and for the first time in American history dispatched dozens of spies worldwide—the Office of Naval Intelligence.

2. ONI and the Submarine Menace

The senior member of the American intelligence community, if one excludes the Secret Service, which spent its first decades chasing counterfeiters, was the venerable Office of Naval Intelligence (ONI), established in 1882. In a sense this was logical because it was the United States Navy that was most vulnerable to attack by a foreign foe during the post–Civil War era.

Initially, ONI's principal task was to compile information on new technology being used by foreign navies. For example, by the 1870s wooden warships were being replaced first by ironclads and by the 1880s by all-steel navies. And the change from sailing ships to steam-propelled vessels denoted the breathtaking technological change that was the hallmark of the era.[1] In the same year that ONI was established, the first U.S. naval attaché was dispatched to the Court of St. James's in London to report on the most advanced navy in the world, the great Royal Navy of Great Britain. Three years later the first attaché arrived in Paris and in 1888 an American naval attaché was posted to Rome. It should be noted, however, that the acquisition of intelligence by naval attachés via espionage was frowned on until the Spanish-American War began to loom on the horizon.[2]

On the night of February 15, 1898, the battleship USS *Maine* blew up and sank in Havana harbor. Although the Spanish were blamed for blowing up the *Maine*, the preponderance of evidence suggests that the explosion was an accident. Nevertheless, following an American ultimatum to the Spanish, which was not fully met, the McKinley administration reluctantly went to the Congress in April with a declaration of war that was resoundingly approved.

ONI responded quickly to the war. Lieutenant (later Admiral) William S. Sims, the naval attaché in Paris, put together an intelligence network to cover not only Spain but the Mediterranean. In addition, Sims and his ONI colleagues in Europe engaged in preemptive buying of ships and munitions either needed by the U.S. Navy or to keep them out of the hands of the Spanish Navy. In London the naval attaché suborned an employee of the Spanish Embassy and dispatched teams of agents to Spain. Closer to home, an intrepid young naval officer, Victor Blue, slipped into Cuba three times, where he successfully made contact with the Cuban rebels, who provided intelligence on Spanish forces. In addition, he provided crucial firsthand intelligence on the presence of a Spanish flotilla in Santiago harbor. By the time Spain surrendered in August, most observers agreed that ONI had performed very well.[3]

In the postwar period ONI continued to staff attaché posts both in European and Asian capitals. These officers reported on the naval race in Europe and watched Japanese-Russian rivalry in Asian waters, including observing the Russo-Japanese War that broke out in 1904.[4]

But events closer to home soon engaged ONI's attention. The outbreak of the Mexican Revolution in 1910 caused ONI to dust off the navy's war plans. In March 1911, a senior ONI officer, Lt. Commander Newton A. McCully, was ordered quietly to visit undercover Mexico's most important east-coast ports, including Veracruz and Tampico, to carry out a reconnaissance of potential landing sites. McCully was then ordered to prepare a plan for "attack on the city of Vera Cruz"; his plan was subsequently adopted by the Joint Board of the Army and Navy as a contingency plan for an invasion of Mexico and approved by President William Howard Taft in 1912. This was the plan utilized by the navy when bluejackets and marines captured Veracruz in April 1914.[5] In addition, ONI began to deploy secret agents to Mexico during periods of tension between the two countries. Although only a few agents were involved and the evidence is scanty at best, in one specific case in 1916 during the war crisis with Mexico, an ONI operative provided timely and accurate intelligence on forthcoming Mexican raids on the border under the banner of the Plan of San Diego.[6]

But it was the war in Europe on which ONI fixed its attention beginning in the fall of 1914. Unfortunately, the Wilson administration, with

Secretary of the Navy Josephus Daniels holding the admirals in check, refused to prepare for war even after the sinking of the British luxury liner *Lusitania* in 1915 in which 128 Americans died. Finally, in the late summer of 1916, the Congress appropriated a paltry $30,000 of the $50,000 requested by U.S. Navy Secretary Daniels, which authorized ONI to collect intelligence both overseas and in the United States. These meager funds were initially utilized to establish an undercover counter-intelligence operation in New York City and to dispatch a handful of agents abroad.[7]

While focusing on the war in Europe, the navy figuratively kept looking over its shoulder at the Pacific, where the Japanese lusted after the Philippines. At least by 1913, a number of prescient navy, marine, and army officers who had been stationed in the Pacific understood that Japan was America's number-one enemy—one that quite likely would attack suddenly and without warning.[8] In 1913, a war crisis caused the United States secretly to reinforce the army garrison in the Hawaiian Islands and to rush in additional supplies of ammunition. Although the attack did not occur, to naval officers it simply was a matter of time.[9] Given American possessions in the Philippines, Guam, American Samoa, islands like Wake and of course the Hawaiian Islands, a considerable percentage of United States military and naval resources were committed to defending American territory in the Pacific. For example, in 1916, approximately 25 percent of the U.S. Army was stationed in the Philippines and the Hawaiian Islands.[10]

Still, it was Germany that increasingly loomed as the immediate threat. Beginning in 1916, ONI began to prepare for United States entry into World War I. But Secretary of the Navy Daniels refused even as late as November 20, 1916, to allow ONI to hire spies with the funds appropriated by Congress. Daniels demanded that he and the Chief of Naval Operations be informed of every single expenditure.[11] As a result, ONI could only set up, in January 1917, a skeleton administrative structure for recruiting agents when and if approval and funds were granted.[12]

Finally, with the German government's announcement on February 1, 1917, that it would henceforth engage in unrestricted submarine warfare, ONI could begin recruiting agents.[13] The situation changed dramatically following the release of the Zimmermann Telegram on February 24 by the British government to President Wilson. The president ordered it leaked to the press on February 28. The telegram from the German foreign minister to the German Minister in Mexico ordered that diplomat to approach the government of Venustiano Carranza and offer, in case of war between the United States and Germany, arms and money to help Mexico retake the American Southwest, except for California, in return for an alliance with Germany. The German government hoped to precipitate a war between the United States and Mexico in order to tie down American troops and prevent them from being sent to Europe. The telegram created a sensation in the United States, driving public opinion firmly into the Allied camp.[14]

As a result, American entry into the war appeared inevitable by mid-March 1917. ONI was frantically trying to increase its personnel in order to meet the demands that were about to be placed on that organization. But the buildup was woefully inadequate: as of April 16—nine days after the declaration of war—ONI's personnel totaled a pathetic thirty-three.[15] ONI was not just understrength; its problems were of long standing and were deeply seated. For one thing, ONI had, since the Spanish-American War, become something of a professional backwater, a place where over-the-hill officers could be put out to pasture before retiring. Although there had passed through ONI a sprinkling of talented officers who had served as naval attachés, including the future admirals Chester Nimitz, William F. "Bull" Halsey, Jr., and William S. Sims, no Director of Naval Intelligence (DNI) had been a distinguished officer. Furthermore, Naval Intelligence, particularly in its espionage aspect, was viewed with some distaste by most naval officers who felt that spying was not an occupation suitable for gentlemen.[16]

In addition, the Department of the Navy had not undergone the same kind of administrative reform that the War Department had experienced in the first decade of the twentieth century. Instead, the Navy Department was frozen in the distant past, and most administrative units were ruled by bureaucrats whose ignorance concerning modern naval warfare was exceeded only by their lack of knowledge about modern organizational management. As a result, the navy was ruled, to a significant degree, by the "Bureaus"—the Bureau of Ships, the Bureau of Ordnance, the Bureau of Navigation, the Bureau of Supplies and Accounts, etc.—which operated much like autonomous feudal kingdoms.[17]

Furthermore, the civilian head of the navy, Secretary Josephus Daniels, was something out of Gilbert and Sullivan's *HMS Pinafore;* to paraphrase some lyrics from the operetta, he stayed close to his desk and never went to sea, and now he was the ruler of the Yanks' navy. When he assumed office Daniels knew absolutely nothing about the navy. For instance, "Naval men resented the new secretary's order to substitute 'right' and 'left' for 'starboard' and 'port'." Woodrow Wilson had appointed Daniels because he was one of five leaders at the Democratic National Convention who had led the fight for Wilson's nomination in 1912.[18] Although Daniels was not a fool, he was precisely what the United States Navy on the eve of World War I did not need—a pacifist and prohibitionist, who was ineffectual in preparing the navy for war. After World War I, Admiral William Sims testified before a congressional investigating committee and delivered a blistering indictment of Daniels's prewar performance.[19] To be fair, until March 1917, Daniels did precisely what President Woodrow Wilson wanted him to do, which was nothing. In this milieu ONI simply did not count. It was a pygmy among giant administrative units—small, unimportant, and ignored. Indeed, Daniels does not even mention the Office of Naval Intelligence in his multivolume autobiography of his years as navy secretary.[20]

But to the credit of the principals at ONI, they tried. They knew that the entry of the United States into World War I was coming and soon, and they did the best they could, with virtually no money, to prepare for the inevitable. ONI Assistant Director Lt. Commander Edward McCauley put it rather succinctly: "General plans had been drawn up for pre-war work, but before they could be put into effect it was of course essential to have money."[21]

Realizing that there would not be money available until war was declared, Director of Naval Intelligence Captain James Harrison Oliver and Assistant Director McCauley decided that the best they could do was to construct an organizational plan that could be quickly implemented when funds and manpower became available. Part of the mobilization plan had been formulated earlier, in 1915. Entitled the "War Information Service," it was to be implemented upon the declaration of war. There was also an overseas contingency version of the plan, entitled the "Navy Information Service," which called for sending thirty officers and thirty-six clerks (five officers and six clerks to each nation) to Germany or England or Japan or China or Argentina or Chile, in case of war by any of the major powers. The specific country where they would be sent would depend on who declared war on the United States. Essentially, ONI would station naval officers in neutral countries, from which they would send secret agents into the enemy homeland. The plan also provided for close liaison with the Departments of State, Treasury, Justice, Post Office, and Commerce, which would, of course, provide copious information in wartime to the Office of Naval Intelligence. Jeffrey Dorwart, a historian of naval intelligence, accurately described the plan as being long on secrecy and short on personnel.[22]

A more practical plan was implemented in 1916, when DNI Oliver directed Marine Corps Major John H. Russell to contact large American companies with overseas operations and request their cooperation in utilizing their personnel as intelligence agents for ONI. Unfortunately, the principal company selected to assist ONI, Vacuum Oil, with agents in 260 ports worldwide, after being given secret navy codes for communication, was found to have taken advantage of its connection with ONI for corporate profit. Furthermore, the company even traded with Germany after the United States declared war. They were quickly dropped. By January 1917, ONI had only six naval attachés and two assistant attachés stationed abroad. And in Washington there was a total of only eight civilians assigned to ONI's headquarters. There was also a small secret office in New York that had been established in early 1917, which had a staff of five.[23]

Against the backdrop of looming war, ONI put in place an internal reorganization. Under the director, deputy director, and chief clerk of ONI, there would be four sections: Section A, which recruited and ran secret agents; Section B, which coded and decoded messages to and from secret agents and attachés abroad; Section C, which organized intelligence received; and Section D, which sent intelligence to naval units and other government agencies. In 1917, Section E, responsible for translation, was added.[24]

A senior retired naval officer, Lieutenant Commander O. W. Fowler, was placed in charge of Section A, which by the summer of 1917 was subdivided into seven desks. Desk 1 was responsible for the Naval Districts in the United States and agents in the United States and Canada; Desk 2 was responsible for Latin America and the Caribbean. Commander Fowler assumed personal responsibility for this desk, which was considered in some respects the most sensitive area for ONI. Desk 3 handled Europe and Africa; Desk 4 was the Far Eastern desk responsible for Japan, China, and the Western Pacific; Desk 5 was responsible for all files, the War Information Service, and incoming and outgoing communications; Desk 6 handled translation; and Desk 7 was the financial office for the section.[25]

By midsummer 1917 the organizational charts continued to expand as additional personnel were brought on board. One undated organizational chart shows forty-seven personnel in ONI headquarters in Washington: officers, volunteers, and clerical staff. But it was in the Naval Districts that the most explosive growth in personnel occurred. At its height there were more than 3,190 ONI personnel assigned to individual Naval Districts, including the Panama Canal Zone and Hawaii. Almost all of these personnel were engaged in counterespionage activity. There were also eight branch ONI offices nationwide, which had more than five hundred staffers.[26]

At the same time, ONI in only a few months recruited and sent overseas undercover, more than eighty-five agents who were assigned to posts in the Canary and Madeira Islands, Canada, Alaska, Hawaii, China, Japan, Spain, Portugal, Denmark, Norway, Holland, Switzerland, France, Italy, Poland, Great Britain, the Azores, Argentina, Brazil, Uruguay, Peru, Chile, Venezuela, Colombia, Paraguay, Ecuador, Puerto Rico, Cuba, Haiti, and of course Mexico and Central America.[27] This was the largest group of American spies yet posted overseas in the history of United States intelligence; the number would not be surpassed until World War II.[28] While a number of these agents would subsequently be designated as "useless,"[29] hardly surprising given the haste with which they were selected and trained (initially there was absolutely no training other than how to code and decode messages), there proved to be many gifted individuals who were naturals in the great game of espionage. Agent rosters were among ONI's most closely guarded secrets, having notes attached that read "Not to leave your possession" or "This must always be locked in a safe."[30] In 1998, however, these lists were declassified, giving perhaps the only available picture of the spies working for a United States intelligence agency. The rosters, it should be noted, include some sixty naval attachés and several dozen special ONI agents who operated in the United States.[31] (See Appendix 4.)

There were of course enormous problems in administering more than 150 spies, naval attachés, and special agents of Naval Intelligence. For one thing, there were insufficient desk and payroll officers to handle so many agents. Secretary Daniels and ranking navy officials blindly refused to allow ONI headquarters to augment significantly the staff to administer what became a crushing workload. Whereas ONI had only run a handful of secret agents at any one time since the Spanish-American War, now virtually overnight the agency was faced with multiple problems of communicating with, paying, and efficiently directing the efforts of fifty times the personnel for which it had been previously responsible.

Furthermore, regarding ONI's secret agents, there was the enormous problem of communicating with them and paying them in such a way that their identities as spies would not be disclosed, since if this occurred their effectiveness would be limited and their lives could even be endangered. As an ONI memorandum noted:

> In April, 1917, this office was in a serious quandary to know how to be able to transfer necessary funds to its agents in the field . . . and . . . how to be able to pay salary allotments made by agents to their families, without divulging the name of the agent and showing his connection with this office, which facts if they should be discovered would have at once destroyed the agent's usefulness. When the matter was taken up with the National City Bank and the Riggs Bank, the [bankers] . . . instantly and generously agreed to handle all transfers of this office personally . . . [so] not even the employees in the two Banks could be able to learn the names of our agents and their connection with ONI. They not only performed this most confidential and indispensable service during the entire period of the war but have assured [us] . . . they will be glad to continue this service in the future.[32]

Joseph T. Crosby, vice-president of National City Bank of New York (today, Citibank) was the principal purveyor of funds to ONI secret agents overseas. Two other bankers who also assisted in the secret transmittal of funds within the United States were Avon M. Nevius and Robert V. Fleming, both assistant cashiers of the Riggs National Bank, whose offices were in Washington across the street from the White House. The three bankers received "certificates for service as volunteer aids" in January 1920.

Then there was the problem of directing the agents deployed abroad and processing the growing stream of intelligence they were providing. ONI had literally only a handful of desk officers to handle agent reports, and some of these desk officers were not really qualified to direct secret agents. Ideally, it would have been useful to have desk officers who had themselves been secret agents abroad and thus knew something about the care and feeding of spies. At the very least, desk officers should have had some knowledge of the countries where their secret agents were operating, but sometimes this was not the case. Indeed, the manpower situation in Section A was so critical that some reports in the early months of the war were apparently not read in a timely manner.[33] On occasion, agents were not even supervised. In one extreme case, an ONI operative in Latin America had his first communication from ONI/Washington *AFTER* the armistice in 1918.[34] Not surprisingly, some agents simply sat around and collected their pay and essentially quit reporting throughout the remainder of the war. Even the most enthusiastic agents, who had access and important targets, often went for weeks and sometimes months without receiving responses to their questions about where and against whom they should concentrate their intelligence-collecting activities.[35] But by the fall of 1917, ONI/Washington had begun to get its act together insofar as Mexico and Central America were concerned. There was good reason to do so. The German Navy planned to establish submarine bases on the Mexican coast. What made this threat even more serious was the policy of the Mexican president, Venustiano Carranza. To the dismay of Washington, when the United States entered World War I, Carranza adopted a policy of neutrality, but in practice it was very much a pro-German neutrality. German agents who had been operating in the United States were now based in Mexico.

On September 4, 1917, Admiral Sims warned from London (apparently based on information he had been given by British Naval Intelligence, but which he carefully camouflaged): "It is not at all inconceivable that German submarines may operate off the main harbors of America or the Panama Canal."[36] The following day Admiral Henry Mayo followed up with a cablegram to the Chief of Naval Operations, Admiral Benson, urging "increased vigilance be exercised to prevent establishment bases for submarine cruisers along coast of North and South America . . ."[37] Furthermore, by November 1917, Room 40, the famed code-breaking branch of the British Office of Naval Intelligence, had intercepted and cryptanalyzed a German intelligence telegram from Madrid that quoted the new head of German naval intelligence in Mexico, Kurt Jahnke, as stating that "it is proposed to make two bases on the coast of the Gulf."[38]

For a variety of reasons (including a classic bureaucratic battle between several competing German secret agents both in Mexico and Spain), the German Navy was unable to establish bases on the Mexican coast in the fall of 1917.[39] But the following summer the Germans were able to follow up on their earlier plan: on June 8 they ordered the German Legation in Mexico City to inform Jahnke to "prepare as rapidly as possible a naval supply base for submarines on the Mexican coast . . ." Evidently the plan was for sailing vessels to slip out from the secret base and resupply submarines at sea. In a sophisticated analysis of competing German military and diplomatic intelligence organizations in Mexico, historian Friedrich Katz, utilizing a number of German archives, covers in detail the subject of proposed submarine bases on the Mexican and Central American coasts.[40]

There were two areas of geographical concern associated with the submarine threat. One was the region in proximity to the Panama Canal, including the eastern coast of Central America, where German submarines could find an ample supply of ships transiting the Isthmus. The other was the area along the east coast of Mexico, where the great Tampico oil fields produced an estimated 60 percent of the oil consumed by the Royal Navy during World War I.[41] ONI defined the coastline from the mouth of the Rio Grande to the Mexican border with British Honduras as Area No. 1. This coastal region was divided into twelve districts: Tampico, Tuxpan, Veracruz, Alvarado, Puerto México, Frontera, Laguna de Términos (Carmen), Champotón, Campeche, Celestum, Progreso, and Puerto Morelos.[42]

It was to monitor Area No. 1 that ONI assigned one William R. Rosenkrans. He was a balding, jug-eared, forty-two-year-old Bureau of Indian Affairs administrator who had earlier directed public schools in the Philippines. A college graduate, Rosenkrans, who spoke fluent Spanish, signed on with ONI on July 2, 1917, as chief of Area 1. Designated as Agent No. 143, Rosenkrans was paid $150 per month plus another $120 per month per diem. He was issued a variety of codes (Number B-55, A-55, C-4, and E-100) with "Wallace" being his keyword for coding purposes. It should be noted that he was a resident of Wallace, New York; hence the keyword's origin. His mail drop in the United States was : Karl Hoffmeyer, P.O. Box 71, Penn Terminal Station, New York. Finally, his telegraphic cover address was "Gustav Koch," New York. Having been provided with essential information—how to code and decode telegrams from ONI—he was ordered to take the first ship available from New Orleans to Veracruz to take up his post.[43] In January 1918, Rosenkrans was appointed a vice-consul in the American consulate at Veracruz to strengthen his cover. In fact, by early 1918 the Department of State was, at ONI's request, appointing a number of navy spies as vice-consuls to provide them with diplomatic immunity.[44]

Although the airplane, the tank, poison gas, and radio were first used in World War I, it was the submarine that potentially was the war-winning weapon. Ironically, the military value of the submarine was judged by one British professional journal in 1914, just prior to the outbreak of World War I, as probably a waste of money.[45] This view began to change in the second month of the war when in approximately ninety minutes one German submarine sank three British cruisers. Still, in the first five months of the war, German submarines had only destroyed a total of seventeen ships.[46] But on May 7, 1915, a German submarine sank the British liner *Lusitania*, which was carrying munitions as well as passengers; 1,198 passengers died, 128 of them Americans. The Wilson administration was outraged and pressured the German government to have its submarines spare passenger ships. Furthermore, the rules of engagement for submarines under international law and convention were restrictive, and the German government through the remainder of 1915 and early 1916 generally adhered to these rules, in part to keep the United States neutral. However by the late summer of 1916 the Imperial German government began to change its stance, mainly because of the success of its submarines, which in February of that year sank 117,000 tons of shipping, and 167,000 tons in March. The torpedoing of a cross-channel ferry, the *Sussex*, in late March 1916, resulting in the deaths of twenty-five Americans, caused the United States to threaten a break in diplomatic relations if attacks on civilian vessels did not cease. The German government again backed down and restricted the targets that the U-boats could attack.[47]

The United States Navy, while on the sidelines watching naval operations in European waters, had submarine warfare brought to its front door in July 1916. The world's first cargo submarine, the German *Deutschland*, suddenly surfaced in the harbor of Baltimore, Maryland. At the beginning of World War I, most submarines in the world's navies were relatively small with a limited range at sea. The *Deutschland* however, was a monster, being 230 feet long and displacing 1,440 tons. It could easily sail from German ports to the United States and back. The cargo submarine made a second round trip in November 1916, and the Royal Navy was unable to locate and sink it.[48]

The two voyages of the *Deutschland* and a twenty-four-hour "courtesy" visit, in October 1916, of the German submarine U-53 to Newport, Rhode Island, brought home to the U.S. Navy, in a not-so-subtle way, the power of Germany's submarine fleet. It should be noted that immediately upon leaving Newport harbor the U-53 quickly sank five merchant ships, a vivid demonstration of the effectiveness of submarine warfare.[49]

By late 1916, the German Navy, which was sinking some 300,000 tons of shipping per month, felt that enough U-boats had been built or were under construction so that unrestricted submarine warfare could bring Britain to her knees in as few as six months, and that an American declaration of war would be immaterial. As a result, the Imperial German government informed President Wilson on January 31, 1917, that unrestricted submarine warfare would begin the following day (February 1). Three days later the president ordered German Ambassador von Bernstorff to be handed his passports, and diplomatic relations were severed.[50]

On February 24, 1917, the British government delivered to United States Ambassador Walter Hines Page the so-called Zimmermann Telegram for transmission to Washington. Both Secretary of State Robert Lansing and President Wilson were outraged at German perfidy. And following receipt of the intercepted and cryptanalyzed German diplomatic message, which was addressed to Mexican President Venustiano Carranza, the die was cast for the American entry into the war, although it would take another five weeks for the final decision to be taken.[51]

The first concern of the U.S. Navy was protection of the fleet and American merchant shipping in U.S. waters. But it was the submarine threat that overrode everything. Most ranking navy officers, like their British counterparts, were frankly frightened of German submarines. There were no easy answers to defeating the submarine—asdic (or sonar, as the Americans called it) was in its infancy, depth charges were generally ineffective, and mine barrages had not worked. The thought that the German Navy might be able to secure submarine bases on the east coast of Mexico or in Central America was a nightmare. The well-informed sentiment on the potential submarine menace in this time frame was expressed on March 13 in London by Ambassador Page, who wrote in his diary that "the practical certainty looms on the horizon of submarine bases somewhere in Central America."[52] Although the larger German U-boats could cross the Atlantic to operate on the lucrative shipping lanes off the East Coast of the United States, there were obvious limitations as to the endurance of U-boats before having to return to their bases on the German coast for refueling and resupply. However, the two "visits" of the *Deutschland* and the port call of U-53 had demonstrated that the German Navy had the capability of operating in American waters. If those operations could be extended by establishing refueling bases in Central American or Mexican waters, the threat was significantly magnified. Furthermore, beginning in 1916 there was a steady stream of reports, some of which seemed quite credible, identifying locations of U-boat bases.[53]

The army, too, was actively involved in searching for German submarine bases. In Venezuela the U.S. military attaché got into the act. In the spring of 1916, the United States Minister to Venezuela, Preston McGoodwin, authorized his military attaché, Major Cornelius C. Smith, to survey the Venezuelan coast for German submarine bases. After an exhaustive three-week survey of several hundred miles of Venezuelan coastline, Major Smith conceded, "Well, it had been a good idea. It simply hadn't paid off."[54] In a "Confidential" report dated December 8, 1916, Major General Frederick Funston, the commander of the U.S. Army's Southern Department, based at Fort Sam Houston, submitted a report styled "German submarine bases on the Gulf of Mexico" to the Navy Department, reporting that one of his secret agents had attended a banquet in Mexico City where President Venustiano Carranza was in attendance. A German was present and had arrived in the capital from Puerto México "with the object of obtaining from General [*sic*] Carranza a supply station on the coast of the Gulf of Mexico." But Funston's agent reported that Carranza had refused the proposition. According to Funston's spy, German agents had succeeded in obtaining a base on the Colombian coast. The same agent reported that his Mexican source, a Carranza officer, "knew positively that German submarines were seen at Tuxpan and also at Puerto Mexico."[55]

Even the Bureau of Investigation got into the act. Any scrap of information suggesting that German submarines were based on the Mexico coast was immediately forwarded to the Director of the Bureau, who sent it along to the Department of the Navy. While some of the reports in the summer of 1918 stated rather vaguely that there was a submarine base near Veracruz or Tampico, one former U.S. Customs inspector reported a conversation with a Mexican cowboy, who related how he had seen three submarines and had been allowed to board one of them and was then shown through the boat. The Bureau source was the U.S. Immigration inspector at Brownsville who had interviewed his former subordinate.[56]

If some of these reports seemed credible, there was at least one that was not. In June 1918, a Bureau special agent in San Antonio reported third hand that a Texan applying for a position with the Bureau of Investigation described a conversation he had with a Mexican national working in Oklahoma, who had provided the following story about how he had been working for the German government building submarines in Mexico. He said that "the Germans would dig a large underground cellar near the Gulf in which a sub would be built, then the sea would be let in by means of a flood gate, the boat passed out, and the gates closed again, water pumped out, and another boat put under construction."[57] Whether or not any of the parties involved had been drinking tequila at the time of the interview is uncertain.

What is certain is that bizarre stories kept coming, and in defense of ONI or anyone else in the American or British intelligence communities, the problem was that although German submarines had not yet been located, the very real possibility existed that they might yet be based at various sites on the Mexican or Central American coast. For example, another intelligence report dated November 10, 1916, stated: "I was informed today that recently two submarines were shipped, knocked down from Germany to Guatemala and from there were transported to Puerto Mexico [now Coatzacoalcos] where they are now being set up by Mexican mechanics and German foreman."[58] This was most improbable, if for no other reason than because of Guatemalan President Manuel Estrada Cabrera's intense hatred for the Carranza administration in Mexico. However, the Chief of Naval Operations, Admiral W. S. Benson, fired off a coded message to the captain of the USS *Illinois*, which was off the east coast of Mexico, ordering him to investigate. The captain of another American warship, USS *Wheeling*, which was in the vicinity of Puerto México, was ordered to that port to survey the scene of the alleged submarine construction. His response was dry and somewhat resigned. He noted that he knew nothing about such a project and did not believe it could take place without his knowledge since the *Wheeling* made frequent port calls at Puerto México. He also noted that there was a British-operated oil refinery at Minatitlán, some twenty-three miles from Puerto México, which supplied fuel oil to the Royal Navy, and politely suggested that if there were such a project the Englishmen at the oil refinery "are keenly interested in the subject of submarines."[59]

The following month, December 1916, a senior U.S. naval officer, onboard a warship operating in Mexican waters, was trying to squelch "Rumors of presence of submarines at Vera Cruz," and in a report dated December 10, 1916, stated positively that "there are no submarines at Vera Cruz." But before the ink was dry on this report, another sighting had surfaced that required a response from yet another U.S. Navy commander. This report elicited a response from the captain of the USS *Sacramento,* dated January 21, 1917, which debunked the submarine-sighting report and noted that he was operating from the port of Veracruz.[60]

By late March 1917, the captain of the USS *Wheeling*, operating off the Mexican port of Progreso, did report that the British consul in Mérida "several months ago" informed his superior, the British minister in Mexico City, that the "East Coast of Yucatán" offered "facilities . . . as a base for German submarines." He noted that the consul had suggested that the "Island of Mugeres" [*sic*] seemed to offer special advantages, and that Ascensión and Espíritu Santo bays seemed excellent possibilities. However, the captain of the *Wheeling* did point out in his radio dispatch "that inquiry and investigation shows that there are no submarine bases within the above mentioned limits."[61] But reports from British intelligence sources, who after providing the Zimmermann Telegram had considerable credibility, surfaced as the United States prepared to go to war. The American military attaché in Copenhagen, Denmark, reported on April 3, 1917: "British Legation receives report from their secret service German . . . submarines on the way to Mexico with army officers and also mine submarines are going too."[62]

It would have been a gross, and potentially catastrophic, dereliction of duty had the United States Navy not assumed a worst-case scenario and checked out these reports no matter how outlandish they might seem, much as American intelligence agencies, in light of September 11, 2001, have to check out every report of terrorist activity.[63] ONI got the assignment. The agency would deploy nearly thirty agents to Mexico and Central America.

3. Preparations

Deeply worried by rumors of secret German submarine bases in southern Mexico and in Central America, the Office of Naval Intelligence assigned a high priority to investigating these alarming reports. In the words of ONI's wartime director:

> When the United States entered the war there were all kinds of rumors afloat that the government of Germany had established submarine bases along the coast of Mexico, Central America, the Spanish Main and the West Indies. . . . It was no easy task to find in this country reliable men who could speak the languages required, to send to investigate the numerous reports reaching the Office of the location of supposed German bases in these countries. The pay which could be given them was frequently insufficient to cover all their expenses, but a few gentlemen volunteered their services and did not hesitate to spend their private means to be able to do their bit for the Government. These men, for their loyalty to the cause deserved the thanks of the Nation for their services that they so ungrudgingly gave.[1]

The key figure among these volunteers was Sylvanus Griswold Morley, "Vay" to his friends. He was arguably the best secret agent the United States produced during World War I. Morley hardly resembled the glamorous James Bond type of spy—he was short (5' 2"), slight (about 105 lbs.), and bespectacled. In short, "he was just a featherweight." In one respect, though, Morley reportedly resembled James Bond—he "did enjoy the ladies. And they enjoyed him. They never seemed to mind being taller than he was."[2] What characterized the diminutive and nearsighted Morley was his remarkable energy. As one of his friends put it: "No man literally lived more on his nervous system than did Vay Morley. Vay died as he had lived—at top speed. There was no changing gears in his life. He was always in 'high.'"[3] In 1917 Morley was a rising young archaeologist specializing in the study of the Maya, whose civilization had encompassed much of the area that now concerned ONI.

Morley was born on June 7, 1883, in Chester, Pennsylvania, the eldest of six children. His father taught chemistry and mathematics and served as vice-president of Pennsylvania Military Academy at Chester. His mother was the daughter of a Belgian language teacher at the academy. In 1894, Morley's father moved the family to Buena Vista, Colorado, because he'd become the operator and part owner of a nearby mine.[4] While in his teens Morley developed an interest in archaeology, much to the distress of his father, who envisioned a more practical career for his son. Accordingly, he sent Morley to the Pennsylvania Military Academy to study engineering. He graduated as a civil engineer in 1904, but promptly enrolled at Harvard to study archaeology. He intended to become an Egyptologist, but, inspired by his professor Alfred M. Tozzer, he became a Mayanist instead. By 1907 Morley had earned his B.A. and made his first trip to Mexico, visiting the magnificent Mayan ruins at Chichén Itzá in Yucatán. The year 1908 was a banner year for Morley. He received his M.A. from Harvard, got married—to Alice Gallinger Williams (whom he would divorce in 1915)—and got a job. That was fortunate, for he would never get a Ph.D. In 1909, Morley had inadvertently antagonized a wealthy patron of Mayan research at Harvard, Charles P. Bowditch, who had more wealth than talent. Bowditch was a prominent epigrapher, privately publishing his interpretation of Mayan material brought back by Peabody Museum expeditions, which he largely financed. In his innocence, Morley published his own commentary on some of this Mayan material without consulting Bowditch, expecting the paper to fulfill in part the requirements for a Ph.D. at Harvard. Bowditch allegedly took umbrage and used his considerable clout not only to ensure that Morley would never get the Ph.D. but also that the Peabody Museum would never underwrite Morley's archaeological endeavors.[5] So Morley was lucky that, while still a student, he had impressed the Southwest archaeologist Edgar Lee Hewett, prime mover in establishing the

Museum of New Mexico in Santa Fe. In 1908 Hewett selected Morley as one of the three professional staffers in the Museum-affiliated School of American Archaeology.[6] In this capacity, Morley assisted Hewett in conducting fieldwork in New Mexico.[7]

Morley's years in Santa Fe were not confined to archaeology, however. He had a significant impact on the development of Santa Fe itself. In 1912, Morley was appointed to the newly-formed City Planning Board, whose task was to reverse Santa Fe's economic decline. Morley quickly grasped that the city's main asset was its individuality, and he campaigned to combine architectural homogeneity with a style based on Santa Fe's Spanish colonial architecture. The result was the emergence of the "Santa Fe style," exemplified by 1913 in the restoration of the Palace of the Governors, a project on which Morley served as advisor. Morley himself rehabilitated an old adobe house as his residence.[8] Santa Fe's uniqueness would create a boom in the tourist industry of "The City Different," as the natives like to describe Santa Fe. But tourism was a double-edged sword, as Morley himself discovered. Years later he would complain that Santa Fe "is changed so unfortunately during the past ten years. It is now a cheap tourist center with all that objectionable hullabaloo and meretricious Westernism of the movies." Or again, referring to the local market, "which in these later years . . . has been greatly cheapened by a non-spending, slack-wearing, painted-hussy type of tourist from Texas and Oklahoma."[9] Morley thus expressed the elitism still manifested by many Santa Feans, who wish those tiresome tourists would just mail in their money and not clutter up the place with their grubby persons.

However much Morley loved Santa Fe, his real passion was the ancient Maya. He was fascinated by anything pertaining to the Maya, especially the study of their hieroglyphics; this quality helps to explain why Morley was such a fine scholar. In 1910 he conducted his first work on the Maya.[10] By 1912 the ambitious Morley approached the prestigious Carnegie Institution of Washington about funding his research. His proposal was competing with some for ethnological studies in the South Pacific, and Carnegie was inclined to fund the latter. To soften the blow, Carnegie's president, Dr. Robert S. Woodward, invited Morley to lunch at the exclusive Cosmos Club in Washington to explain why his proposal was being rejected. In the course of the meal Morley waxed eloquent about Mayan mathematics and astronomy. Woodward, who was a mathematician, became enthralled. The upshot was that Woodward persuaded the selection committee to fund Morley's research instead of the Polynesian projects.[11] On July 15, 1914, Carnegie appointed him as a Research Associate in archaeology at a salary of $200 a month.[12] Morley was now playing in the major leagues of his profession. The Carnegie Institution had excellent research facilities and spent nearly a million dollars a year on research. It did not burden its staff with additional duties, such as teaching, and the results of their research were routinely published. All this was possible because the Carnegie Institution had a whopping $22,000,000 endowment.[13] During the next two years Morley led expeditions to Central America, focusing on the ruins at Copán, a major Mayan site in western Honduras.[14] His good-natured enthusiasm was infectious. The locals generally found him to be *simpático*, despite his fractured but serviceable Spanish, which often produced malapropisms.[15] One of his companions recalled:

> As I reflect upon my several Maya explorations, and particularly upon my three or four trips in company with Morley, I find that my recollection of them becomes a kaleidoscopic montage—a patchwork of heavily laden mule-trains slogging through endless groves of *corozo* palm; of rivers winding interminably through lush forests of sapodilla and mahogany and fringed by thickets of sharp, spined bamboo and *escoba* palm; of one-night camps without adequate water but infested with fleas and *garrapatas* and swarms of mosquitoes; of overwhelming floods pouring unexpectedly down dry arroyos; of gunfire and sudden death; and of great pyramids and majestic temples rising high above the deep Peten bush in silhouette against the golden sunsets of Yucatan.[16]

The phrase "gunfire and sudden death" referred to the most traumatic event in Morley's life. It resulted from his 1916 expedition to Guatemala. In the fall of 1915, Morley, who was the Field Director of the Carnegie Institution Central American Expedition, met with Arthur Carpenter, the Field Director of the Peabody Museum Central American Expedition. The two men agreed to pool their resources in order to expand the scope of their expeditions. By the toss of a coin the joint enterprise was designated as a Carnegie Expedition, with Morley the Field Director and Carpenter the second in command.[17] The joint expedition assembled on April 17, 1916, at Belize, British Honduras, for a three-week trip into the

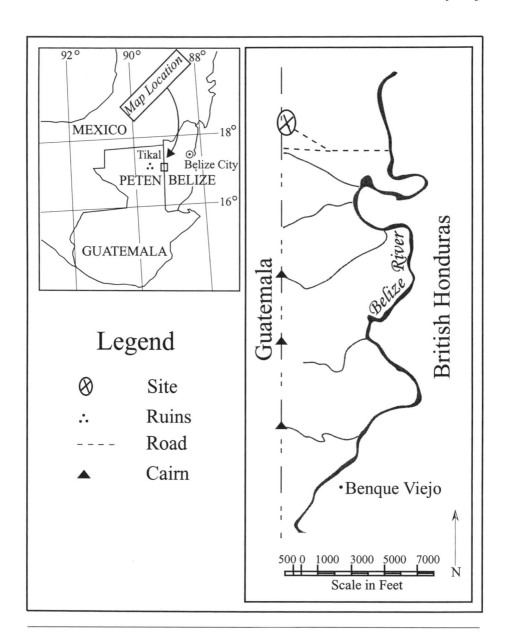

Map 1. Returning from the large Mayan ceremonial center at Uaxactun in the Peten region, Morley narrowly escaped death May 16, 1916 on the British Honduras/Guatemalan border when his expedition was ambushed by a squad of drunken Guatemalan soldiers. The inset map designates the site both of the ambush and the subsequent clash between British Honduras Territorial troops and the Guatemalans. At least five were killed and several wounded in the two skirmishes. Map by Risa Madoff.

sparsely populated Department of Petén across the border in Guatemala. The party consisted of Morley; Carpenter; Dr. Moise Lafleur, who was a young physician from Louisiana; and two camp servants from Belize.

A trip into the Petén was not without peril. For one thing, it was the preserve of *chicleros*, men who made their living by tapping sapodilla trees for the latex from which chewing gum was made. *Chicleros*, who lived under primitive conditions in the brush, were the dregs of society; every man was a law unto himself, and murders were common occurrences. But, in addition, a band of rebels fighting the government of Guatemala was currently operating in the Petén on the border with British Honduras, and Guatemalan troops were conducting counterinsurgency operations in the area. Nevertheless, the expedition plunged into the brush. Their efforts were rewarded in spectacular fashion. Morley and Carpenter discovered the ruins of a large Mayan ceremonial center, Uaxactún. Moreover, at the site Morley found the oldest Mayan monument yet known, Stela 9. Flushed with triumph, the party started back for British Honduras. En route they heard disquieting news about the revolutionists' activities. Morley, however, managed to engage a guide who possessed a safe conduct signed by the leader of the rebels. Since Morley and Carpenter already had letters of recommendation from the Guatemalan government, Morley was confident that the expedition could pass unmolested whether they encountered rebels or government forces. On the afternoon of May 17, they were within sight of the British Honduras border and everyone's mind was on a bath, a hot meal, and a comfortable bed.

The six members of the expedition were riding single file through the brush, the guide at the head of the column and Morley next, in his accustomed spot. A sudden shower made water collect on the lenses of Morley's glasses, and he took them off to put them in his pocket. But he dropped them, and dismounted to pick them up. Dr. Lafleur then rode by to talk with the guide. When Morley remounted he was now fourth in line.

As the column entered a clearing near the border, a volley of gunfire erupted from the brush ahead, followed by sustained firing. The guide was cut down immediately and fell mortally wounded. Dr. Lafleur dismounted and was trying to use his Winchester carbine when he too was hit. Morley was screaming for everyone to fall back, and they galloped back down the trail for some two hundred yards. In a great display of courage, Carpenter announced that he was returning to the site of the ambush to determine whether Lafleur were dead and to help him if he were still alive. Armed with a pistol, Carpenter did so, and nearly lost his own life, for he was sighted, shot at, and pursued by the ambushers.

Morley and the camp servants reached safety in British Honduras and informed the authorities that they'd been ambushed by bandits or revolutionists. Only gradually did Morley begin to realize that their attackers had been Guatemalan soldiers. Carpenter, meanwhile, had made his way on foot to the British Honduras border and had reported the ambush. A detachment of police and volunteers had set out to investigate. Not half a mile from the ambush site they encountered a small unit of Guatemalan troops. The British contingent informed them that they were on British soil and attempted to disarm the Guatemalans. The latter resisted, and in the resulting firefight two Guatemalans and Corporal Oziah Flowers, commanding the British, were killed and several more Guatemalan soldiers were wounded.[18]

In the aftermath of these events, Dr. Lafleur's body was recovered. The unfortunate doctor had had the top of his head blown off by a soft-nosed bullet, and his corpse had been mutilated, a blow from a machete nearly severing his head.[19] Lafleur was buried in British Honduras, but his body was later disinterred and shipped to the United States. It was further determined that the Guatemalan troops who had ambushed Morley's party were drunk and had fired thinking the expedition were revolutionists. Moreover, the Guatemalan government found itself involved in a diplomatic controversy not just with the United States but with Great Britain as well. Although the British were initially convinced that Corporal Flowers had been killed in British Honduras, a subsequent border survey determined that the affray had occurred in Guatemalan territory. The British dropped the demand for compensation they had been contemplating.[20] The American State Department, on the other hand, continued to seek satisfaction from Guatemala for Dr. Lafleur's death.

As for Morley, he was badly shaken by the affair. The realization that something as trivial as dropping his glasses had saved his life gave him pause for thought. And the very idea of going back into the brush on future expeditions was most unsettling. Yet he would steel himself to do so when the time came. But into the spring of 1917 he divided his time between the Carnegie Institution and the Peabody Museum at Harvard,

Figure 1. *Morley standing at a Mayan site, probably Chichen Itza, in the 1920s. Photo by J. Eric Thompson,* Maya Archaeologist *(Norman : University of Oklahoma Press, 1963).*

where he had been given desk space to carry on his research. At the Peabody he displayed that singleness of purpose that was such a salient feature of his personality. He was completely immersed in his study of Mayan hieroglyphs, even when he suffered recurrent bouts of the malaria he had contracted while in the field. While wracked by fever, Morley would simply don a large coonskin coat and, regardless of the temperature, continue to work at his desk.[21]

This, then, was the individual who approached ONI in March 1917 with an intriguing proposal. After sounding out some of his colleagues, Morley submitted to ONI a "list of available anthropologists."[22] These people, like Morley himself, were specialists in Mexico and Central America who were prepared to become intelligence agents using their professional activities as cover. While for ONI the use of civilian amateurs necessarily entailed a certain degree of risk, at least their cover would be much more credible than that of some newly minted Annapolis graduate dispatched to ferret out clandestine German activities in Central America. ONI gratefully accepted Morley's proposal. The archaeologists, anthropologists, and naturalists on the list were instructed to stand by until war was actually declared.

Morley passed his navy physical exam on March 27 in Washington, D.C., and was instructed to await further orders. On April 6, he took the oath and was commissioned the next day as an ensign in the Naval Coast Defense Reserve for a four-year tour of duty.[23] Technically he was under the Bureau of Navigation, but in reality he now worked for ONI.

Naval Intelligence assigned Morley to Central America. His mission was to search for rumored German submarine bases, to combat pro-German activities generally, and to organize an intelligence network to cover the coast. ONI designated him Agent No. 53. He was issued codes A-22 and B-22, his keyword being GRIS. Morley's written reports were to be sent to a letter drop. ONI coyly chose German and Japanese names for the addressees: "Taro Yamamoto," and "Adolph Schwarz," P.O. Box 139, Boston, Massachusetts. Morley's telegrams and cables were to go to "Gustav Koch," New York City. From these accommodation addresses Morley's communications would be forwarded to ONI headquarters in Washington.

The archaeologist's case officer would be Charles Alexander Sheldon, ONI Agent No. 246, the "Taro Yamamoto" to whom Morley would address his reports from the field. Sheldon was the prototype of the kind of man who would rush to join the Office of Strategic Services in 1942—a wealthy, well-connected sportsman and adventurer with an Ivy League background who was eager to serve his country. Sheldon was born on October 17, 1867, in Rutland, Vermont, into a well-to-do family whose affluence stemmed from Sheldon and Sons Marble Company, which Sheldon's grandfather had founded in 1850. Young Sheldon was raised in an atmosphere of privilege, attending an elite prep school—Phillips Academy in Andover, Massachusetts—then Yale University, where he was on the rowing team and where in 1890 he received his B.A. But his enviably carefree lifestyle came to an abrupt halt when financial disaster overtook the family business, which in 1891 ceased to exist. Sheldon now had to make his own way in the world.[24]

He did so with remarkable success. Through a friend he secured a junior management position with the Lake Shore and Michigan Southern Railway Company in 1890. Four years later he had moved up to being general manager and treasurer of Consolidated Car Heating Company in Albany, New York. Then in 1898, he began overseeing the investments in the Mexican state of Chihuahua of a group of American capitalists. He was general manager of the Chihuahua and Pacific Railway Company and the Chihuahua and Pacific Exploration Company, joint ventures with members of the Terrazas clan, the oligarchs who controlled Chihuahua. Not only did his years in Chihuahua provide Sheldon with ample opportunity to indulge his love of hunting, especially for bears and bighorn sheep, but they also made his fortune. He acquired an interest in a silver mine, El Potosí, and the income it produced made him financially independent. In 1902, Sheldon returned to the United States, settling in New York. In 1903 he was able to retire—at the age of thirty-five.[25]

Thereafter he devoted himself to collecting books, concentrating on hunting, exploration, and natural history, and working as a volunteer collector of specimens for the United States Bureau of Biological Survey. These expeditions took him to the Yukon and Alaska, where he became fascinated by the region around Mount McKinley, or Denali as the Indians called the mountain. Sheldon remained a hunter, but he was evolving into a fervent conservationist. He was elected to membership in the exclusive Boone and Crockett Club in New York, an organization of sportsmen-conservationists founded in 1887 by, among others, Teddy Roosevelt, who became a close friend of Sheldon's. As a conservation activist, Sheldon formulated a plan for a Denali National Park. He also managed to marry well—in 1909 he married Louisa Gulliver, daughter of a prominent attorney in New York City. For their honeymoon, he took her to Admiralty Island off the coast of Alaska to observe grizzlies. The Sheldons made their home in New York and, though they certainly had entrée, largely avoided the city's social whirl.[26] Sheldon found time to write two books about his adventures: *The Wilderness of the Upper Yukon* (1911) and *The Wilderness of the North Pacific Coast Islands* (1912). The books, especially the first, were quite well received.

Increasingly, Sheldon devoted himself to conservation causes, and in 1916 moved to Washington to lobby more effectively. His efforts culminated on February 26, 1917, when he personally took the bill creating Mount McKinley National Park to the White House for President Wilson to sign it into law.[27]

But with the United States heading for war, Sheldon found a more important cause to serve. He became an unpaid volunteer in the Office of Naval Intelligence in Washington. His service as a case officer perfectly suited his personality—"scholarly, reserved, and self-effacing, preferring to let others have the limelight." But once he made up his mind he was tenacious and strong willed.[28] For an outdoorsman like Sheldon it must have been a trial to work at a desk in Washington throughout the war. He did, however, manage to squeeze in at least one inspection trip to Latin America.[29]

Since 1906, Sheldon had belonged to the prestigious Cosmos Club in Washington. It was at the Cosmos Club, incidentally, that on January 13, 1888, thirty-three public-spirited citizens had organized the National Geographic Society. On occasion Sheldon did his recruiting for ONI in true gentlemanly fashion, over a leisurely luncheon at the club.[30] And it may be speculated that Morley, who was also a member of the Cosmos Club since 1915,[31] had presented his list of "available anthropologists" to Sheldon over a quiet drink on those elegant premises back in March.

As for Morley, armed with rudimentary instructions (for ONI's general instructions for agents, see Appendix 5) and having received virtually no training, he was ordered into the field to live by his wits. His initial base of operations would be Guatemala City.[32]

The Office of Naval Intelligence commissioned several other scholars besides Morley. One was Herbert Joseph Spinden. Born in Huron, South Dakota, on August 16, 1879, Joe Spinden had an adventurous streak. After graduating from high school in Tacoma, Washington, he worked with railroad survey parties in Washington, Montana, and Idaho. He also went to Alaska via the Yukon during the Gold Rush. By 1902, however, he enrolled at Harvard, receiving his B.A. in 1906, M.A. in 1908, and Ph.D. in anthropology in 1909. His doctoral dissertation, on Mayan art, would be favorably received when it was published in 1913. But as a fledgling anthropologist Spinden had gone to New Mexico to study the Pueblo Indians. He and Morley had become close friends, the result not only of their common Harvard background and interest in the Maya, but also because of their mutual professional respect. It was while Spinden was in Albuquerque, New Mexico, in 1909 that the American Museum of Natural History in New York City had hired him as an assistant curator of anthropology.[33] Spinden also continued to engage in fieldwork. In fact, his research in El Salvador and Honduras was so impressive that in 1915 the American Museum of Natural History began planning a five-year archaeological survey of those countries, to be directed by Spinden.[34]

On April 7, 1917, Spinden left the American Museum to become a sailor. He received a commission as an ensign in the Naval Coast Defense Reserve, for a four-year tour of duty. On April 16, he was ordered to report for duty with the Office of Naval Intelligence, which designated him as Agent No. 56. Spinden received codes A-24 and B-24; his keyword was PIND. In Spinden's case his written reports would be addressed to "Karl Hoffmeyer," P.O. Box 71, Pennsylvania Terminal Station, New York City. His cables, like Morley's, went to "Gustav Koch," in New York City. Spinden too would be quickly dispatched into the field, his assignment being the same as Morley's. Spinden's file, however, includes a command to destroy his orders after reading them.[35]

Spinden's cover as a scholar was, like Morley's, first rate. The American Museum of Natural History had just learned that the Carnegie Institution was sending their specialist, Sylvanus Morley, to Central America on an archaeological reconnaissance, and that Morley wanted Spinden to accompany him. The head of the Department of Anthropology at the American Museum, Clark Wissler, saw this as a great opportunity and requested approval to use $900 of his general North American fund to finance Spinden. He even gave this precedence over financing his own fieldwork. The museum's director, F. A. Lucas, approved, but he had some reservations about undertaking new field-work outside the United States because of recent difficulties experienced in Cuba, Nicaragua, and South America. The president of the American Museum, Henry Fairfield Osborn, objected, however. But he spoke with Spinden and learned that there were "especially good reasons" why Spinden should accompany Morley to Central America, and he withdrew his objections. The $900 appropriation was approved, and Spinden was provided with an official letter of introduction for use in Central America.[36]

The third anthropologist on ONI's roster was William Hubbs Mechling. He was a native of Germantown, Pennsylvania, born on December 10, 1889. Like the other new ensigns he was well educated: B.A., University of Pennsylvania, 1910; M.A., Harvard University, 1913; B.A., Oxford University, 1916; Ph.D., Harvard University, 1917.[37] In 1912 he had conducted research for the Canadian Geological Survey, which published his *Malecite Tales* in 1914. Mechling passed his navy physical on March 27, 1917, and was commissioned as an ensign in the Naval Coast Defense Reserve on April 6, for a four-year tour. Designated as Agent No. 52, he was issued codes A-17 and B-17, his codeword being MECH. His written reports were to go to "Jiro Kimura," P.O. Box 71, Pennsylvania Terminal Station, New York, and his cables to "Gustav Koch."[38] Mechling was initially assigned to duty in Central America.

The fourth scholar to be commissioned as an ONI operative was John Alden Mason, born on January 14, 1885, in Philadelphia. Unlike the others, he was not a Harvard man. But his academic credentials were certainly respectable: B.A., University of Pennsylvania, 1907, and Ph.D., University of California at Berkeley, 1911. Beginning in 1911, Mason had spent considerable time conducting anthropological research in Mexico. Moreover, in 1913 he had led an expedition to the Northwest Territories for the Canadian Geological Survey, in the course of which he had become a friend of Mechling. As of the spring of 1917, Mason was assistant curator of Mexican and South American archaeology at the Field Museum of Natural History in Chicago, now the Chicago Natural History Museum. On April 8, Mechling telegraphed Mason to come to Washington immediately and meet him at the University Club. By April 10 Mason was in Washington. On April 20, he took the oath and was commissioned as an ensign in the Naval Coast Defense Reserve. Like Mechling, his reports would go to "Jiro Kimura." Ensign Mason was designated as Agent No. 157.[39]

Mason, however, was evidently commissioned against the orders of Josephus Daniels, secretary of the navy. Concerned that Reserve commissions were being issued to undeserving and well-connected individuals, Daniels had ordered on April 10, 1917, that the issuance of Reserve commissions be suspended until further orders. The secretary intended that only men of demonstrated qualifications should become naval officers. He was, however, circumvented: some Commandants of Naval Districts continued to issue commissions anyway.[40] And the Director of Naval Intelligence strenuously protested against Daniels's policy, citing the rapid expansion of ONI and the consequent need for additional officers. Furthermore, ONI was losing many able men to Military Intelligence, which was continuing to commission officers.[41] The Director's plea was to no avail.

The freeze on naval commissions was a great disappointment for Morley, because he had personally introduced a promising recruit to ONI, in the person of John Held, Jr. Held was born in Salt Lake City on January 10, 1889. After graduating from high school he became sports cartoonist for a local newspaper. And he married the paper's society editor, Myrtle Jennings, who was the first of his four wives. In 1912, the restless Held decided to seek his fortune in New York City, arriving with four dollars in his pocket. There, he supported himself as a commercial artist while experimenting with various art forms. Held became interested in ancient art and the cultures that had produced it. This interest eventually led him to focus on the Maya, and he determined to visit their ruined cities.

His chance came because of Morley, whom he met through mutual friends. Held took a few art lessons—his only formal training—with Mahonri Young, who sculpted Southwestern Indian models at the American Museum of Natural History. As it happened, the anthropologist Herbert Spinden was an assistant curator at the museum. In 1916, Held and Young traveled to New Mexico, where they visited Spinden and met his friend Sylvanus Morley.[42]

When Morley was organizing his 1917 Carnegie Institution expedition to Central America, he offered Held the position of artist at a salary of $50 a month.[43] Although by this time Held was developing an impressive reputation as a cartoonist and illustrator, the opportunity was too good to pass up. Held accepted, leaving behind his wife and his home at 736 Riverside Drive in New York City.

Since Morley and Held would be working closely together in Central America, it was imperative that Held be recruited as an ONI agent too if Morley were to carry out his intelligence assignment effectively. Hence Morley's personal introduction of Held to ONI. Although that agency was unable to secure a commission for Held, he was hired on April 16, 1917, as a civilian employee at $100 a month plus $4 per diem for expenses. His function was as cartographer, whose maps would supplement Morley's reports. Held was designated as ONI Agent No. 154.[44]

As was the case with ONI's other hastily recruited agents, it remained to be seen whether the Central American contingent would be competent intelligence officers. Not surprisingly, the results varied. On April 24, 1917, ONI ordered William Mechling to proceed to New Orleans in company with J. Alden Mason and take the first available steamer for Tampico, Mexico. From there the two ensigns were to proceed on to Veracruz, making that port their headquarters. Their assignment was to search for secret German submarine bases, to frustrate pro-German activities, and to make a general survey of the coast. Mechling was instructed to "Destroy this order after you have fully informed yourself of its contents." Mason and Mechling accomplished very little. Precisely what occurred is still unclear. One writer states that Mechling was arrested; another version asserts that it was Mason who was arrested as a spy.[45] A third account is that on the way to begin their assignment Mechling had a fight, and when they reached Veracruz, he was detained at that port. Mason had to rush to Mexico City to appeal to Manuel Gamio, the prominent Mexican archaeologist, to use his influence with the authorities. Although the cautious Gamio must have been embarrassed at having to bail out his young colleagues, evidently he succeeded, for Mechling and Mason were able to continue with their mission.[46] They learned of a rumored German wireless station on a coffee plantation in the mountains of Chiapas state, and they began reconnoitering the coast of the Yucatán peninsula. But they were soon summarily recalled. On August 22, ONI requested that the State Department notify the American consul in Progreso, Yucatán, to inform the ensigns that they were to return to Washington by the first available vessel. They did so. Incidentally, by the time the feckless pair had paid their hotel bills and other expenses, they left Yucatán with exactly $1.00 between them. On September 27, the Director of Naval Intelligence, Captain (later Rear Admiral) Roger Welles, recommended to the Bureau of Navigation that

Mechling be "disenrolled" as an ensign. On October 15, Mechling was discharged from the navy.[47] Evidently he was cashiered.

Mason's ONI career was equally brief. The available records do not reflect any disciplinary action against Mason, but as of September 1917 his association with ONI ended.[48] Decades later, Mason stated that he was the last of the archaeologists to report for duty in Washington, coming from Chicago. And when he arrived he found that Secretary of the Navy Josephus Daniels had balked at so many non-Annapolis graduates being commissioned as ensigns. Thus, Mason claimed, he was never commissioned, although he understood that all the others were. Furthermore, when he was recalled from Mexico to Washington, he was "dismissed." He presumed that somehow the same thing happened to the ensigns. He said the whole affair was rather irregular in a number of ways.[49] In a more candid moment, however, he reportedly described himself as "the worst spy in the world. I spilled the beans and broke [our] cover." He referred to his wartime spying as "that nefarious business." As for Mechling, for the rest of his life he refused to discuss the affair.[50]

Whereas Mechling and Mason left something to be desired, ONI certainly got its money's worth from Morley, Spinden, and Held. During April 1917, Morley divided his time between becoming an ONI agent and preparing for his Carnegie Institution archaeological expedition, which of course was to be his cover in Central America. His headquarters in Washington were the stately premises of the Cosmos Club; among his fellow members were Robert S. Woodward, president of the Carnegie Institution, Walter M. Gilbert, assistant secretary of the Carnegie Institution, and, of course, Morley's ONI case officer, Charles Sheldon.[51] Though Morley spent much of his time in Washington, he made a quick trip to New York City to purchase supplies and equipment at the famed outfitters Abercrombie and Fitch, charging his purchases to the Carnegie Institution.[52] By April 20 he was back in Washington to make final arrangements with Carnegie.

First there was the matter of finances. The Carnegie Institution was fully aware of Morley's role as an agent for the navy. In fact, Carnegie benefited financially from that arrangement. On January 23, Carnegie's Board of Trustees had increased Morley's salary by 10 percent, to $2,640, or $220 a month, for calendar 1917. His salary as an ensign in the navy was $1,700.00 a year, or $141.66 a month. Carnegie's Board of Trustees voted to pay only the difference—$78.33 a month—with the checks to be deposited in Morley's bank account in Boston.[53]

Further, at its meeting on April 19, the executive committee formally authorized Morley, whose title was that of research associate, to proceed to Central America to conduct archaeological investigations. Because of the international situation, however, these would be limited to an "archaeological reconnaissance" of the area. An "archaeological reconnaissance" was a splendidly vague term calculated to provide abundant cover for Morley's intelligence activities. The executive committee stressed that Morley was to impress on Central American authorities that the Institution's interest was purely scientific—Carnegie had no intention of collecting artifacts. This was an important point, for the "collection of artifacts," even by reputable American cultural institutions, not infrequently amounted to little more than looting. The Latin American countries so despoiled were becoming increasingly annoyed by the practice. The executive committee issued Morley a letter of introduction on April 21, thereby establishing his Carnegie credentials.[54]

The next day Morley set forth from Washington by train for New Orleans. He had received exactly sixteen days' training; by May 1918, ONI was providing its agents with a whole three weeks' training before sending them into the field.[55] In New Orleans Morley stayed at the St. Charles Hotel, complaining about the heat and humidity and making a few last-minute purchases such as a toothbrush.[56] His final preparations also included writing a letter to Dr. Robert S. Woodward, president of the Carnegie Institution. Perhaps recalling the ambush of his 1916 expedition, Morley was realistic about the hazards of his Central American undertaking. He enclosed certain recommendations regarding the forthcoming publication of his report, "The Inscriptions of Copán, Honduras," in the event of his death. Morley hastened to add that he anticipated no such unfortunate occurrence, but was just trying to be prepared.[57]

Held and Spinden were also in New Orleans, but their stay received considerably more publicity. An enterprising reporter for the *Times-Picayune* spotted Held sketching in the French Quarter and descended on him for an interview, since Held was a minor celebrity. In the course of the interview, Held not only expounded on the history of caricature but introduced the reporter to his traveling companion, Dr. Herbert Spinden. The latter solemnly informed the journalist that they were going to Guatemala and elsewhere in Central America to study primitive developments of food values still in use among the natives. "They soak their grain and from a mash produce a white liquid that has a perfect food value, as well as acting as a refreshing drink, which will be of inestimable value to our soldiers," said the Doctor.

Spinden and Held managed to keep a straight face as the reporter duly jotted down this information. Held chimed in that he was going along "to make pictures." The *Times-Picayune* interview featured several photographs of Spinden and the boyish and bespectacled Held, as well as several of Held's cartoons.[58] Having publicized their imaginative cover story, the flamboyant pair sailed for Puerto Barrios, Guatemala. From there they would make their way to the capital, Guatemala City, where they would join Morley, who traveled alone.

For Morley, who was the team leader, and his associates, the whole intelligence enterprise would be an exercise in on-the-job training. As he would later inform his ONI control:

> When I first came down in April I was unfamiliar not only with the kind of information wanted–except in a very general way–but also with the nature of the German problem in this area and where it was most acute. It was therefore inevitable, I suppose, that we should lose much time before arriving at an understanding of these two points, or knowing what you wanted and where to get it.[59]

Nevertheless, Morley and his fellow amateur spies would perform remarkably well.

4. The "Archaeological Reconnaissance"

Sylvanus Morley sailed for Guatemala on April 26, 1917, aboard the United Fruit Company steamer *Suriname*. While the vessel was making its way down the Mississippi to the Gulf of Mexico, the archaeologist prepared his first report to ONI, writing it in longhand on the ship's stationery. The report was brief and informal. Eager to take up his assignment, Morley was miffed because the *Suriname* had departed five hours late; the crew had struck for higher wages. The only item of substance Morley mentioned was that a German friend of his had tried to land at Puerto Barrios, Guatemala, three weeks earlier. The Guatemalan port authorities had prohibited the German from leaving the ship, and he'd had to return to New Orleans, where the Immigration Service had promptly interned him as an enemy alien. Morley mentioned the incident approvingly as evidence that Germans could no longer enter Guatemala through regular channels. The archaeologist closed by observing that the Great White Fleet was white no more; the *Suriname*, like other vessels, had been repainted a dingy battleship gray as a precaution against U-boats, and he understood that additional antisubmarine precautions would be taken during the voyage. He sent his report ashore with the ship's pilot and promised that his next communication, from Guatemala City, would be properly typewritten.[1]

En route to Guatemala, Morley stopped over on April 29 in that sweltering backwater of empire, British Honduras.[2] The colony's population was predominantly of African descent. Belize, the seaport capital of British Honduras, had been founded in the seventeenth century by English buccaneers and logwood cutters. It was a small town of frame houses on the Belize river built on a reclaimed mudbank at the edge of a swamp. The town lacked modern streets, a water system, and sanitary facilities. Throughout Belize, mosquitoes bred in pools of stagnant water. One newly arrived British officer was simply appalled, comparing Belize to West Africa as it was twenty-five years earlier. But of course beauty was in the eye of the beholder. A longtime resident of British Honduras described Belize as one of the most delightful small towns along the entire Caribbean coast. He was especially proud of the market, held daily, which from 5 A.M. until breakfast was the hub of Belize, the long wharf fronting the market crowded with native dugouts bringing a variety of fish, fruits, and vegetables. He also mentioned that another prominent feature of the town was the multitude of black vultures scavenging everywhere. They thus performed a vital sanitary service, which unfortunately was offset by their droppings on the roofs, from where was collected the town's only water supply.[3]

Morley's purpose in Belize was to discuss local conditions with his friend Dr. Thomas Francis William Gann, the principal medical officer of the colony. Gann was a lean, six-foot tall, irascible Irishman. Born in Murrisk, County Mayo, in 1867, he became a surgeon and practiced in England. In 1894, he was appointed district medical officer in British Honduras. For the next twenty-two years he served in the Corozal district as assistant medical officer and sometime district commissioner. On April 25, 1916, he was promoted to the post of principal medical officer.[4] During his years at the hamlet of Corozal, near the Mexican border, he developed a passionate interest in the Maya. He got to know the Indians and their environment, learned their language, and began exploring the ruins of their ancestors' cities, such as the ceremonial center of Lubaantún, which he'd visited in 1903.[5] The doctor was establishing a reputation as an amateur but competent archaeologist.[6] He also became a close friend of Sylvanus Morley, accompanying the latter on several expeditions, the last being in March, 1916, to the ruins of Tulum, on the east coast of Yucatán; Gann made tracings of many mural paintings and took copious notes so the murals could be accurately reproduced. During the two days he entertained Morley at the Belize hospital, the doctor discussed with his friend the rumors of an invasion of British Honduras from Yucatán by Mexicans officered by German reservists. Gann reassured Morley that any German menace to British Honduras was problematical at best, but that precautions were nevertheless being taken; a recruiting officer had been sent over from Jamaica and a force was being raised for home defense. On a lighter note, Dr. Gann regaled Morley with John Held's misfortunes. Held and Spinden had stopped in Belize en route to Guatemala. But in wartime Belize, Held had gotten himself arrested for sketching in the marketplace, and Dr. Gann had to rescue him, after which he gave Held a tour of the city.[7]

Traveling on the *Suriname* again, on April 30 Morley landed at Puerto Barrios, which was teeming with colorful and unsavory characters of assorted nationalities. It has been described as "a typical O. Henry banana port . . . hot, dirty, and roadless . . ." with "innumerable *cantinas* and houses of ill-fame where sluts sat on dilapidated verandahs."[8] From Puerto Barrios he traveled by train to Guatemala City, making the Hotel Imperial his base. Morley was operating in a country where power resided in the hands of one man—President Manuel Estrada Cabrera, an iron-fisted dictator in the finest Central American tradition. Estrada Cabrera had seized power in 1898 and had periodically had himself not just "reelected" but reelected unanimously. A great believer in the cult of personality, he had had his birthday—and his mother's for good measure—declared national holidays. His regime, which would last until his overthrow in 1920, was characterized by tyranny, corruption, and the continued oppression of the Indian masses. Under Estrada Cabrera, Guatemala was a police state in which the military routinely stopped everyone, including foreigners, to examine their papers. Checkpoints, at which travelers had to register and show their identification, were a feature of the principal transportation routes. Because he had a paranoid fear of assassination, Estrada Cabrera maintained an efficient nationwide network of spies to crush any opposition.[9]

Although this situation was unfortunate for the Guatemalan people, events in Guatemala were developing favorably for the ONI mission. Relations between the United States and Estrada Cabrera had been strained by the 1916 ambush and murder of Dr. Lefleur. In fact the

---

Map 2. The famed cartoonist John Held, Jr. ONI Agent No. 154) was also a fine cartographer. This map traces Morley and Held's travels back and forth across Central America (British Honduras, Guatemala, El Salvador, Honduras, and Nicaragua) from late April, 1917 through February 1, 1918. Courtesy Office of Naval Intelligence, National Archives.

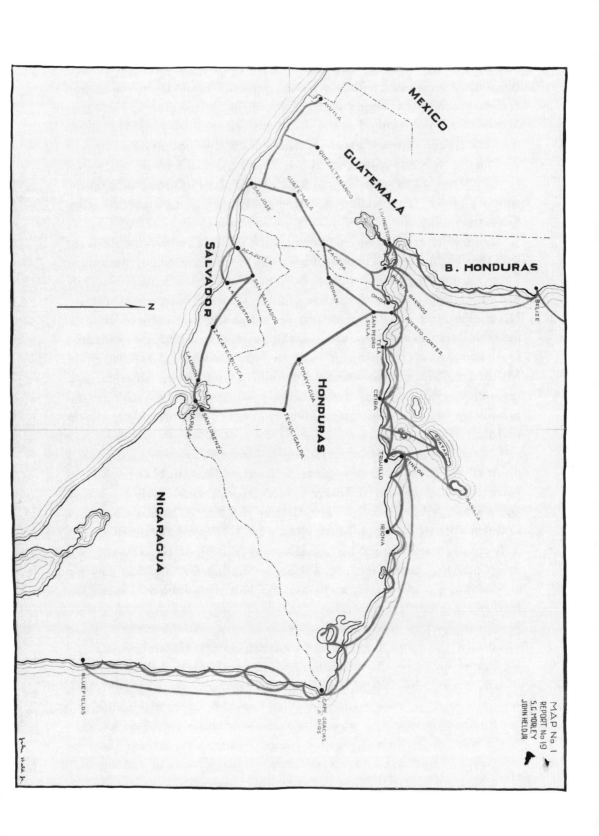

MAP No. 1
REPORT No 19
S. G. MORLEY
JOHN HELDJR

Carnegie Institution had been planning to postpone any further archaeological expeditions to that country until the State Department had resolved the matter.[10] But the exigencies of the United States's entry into World War I had resulted in the decision to send Morley and the others anyway. By the time they reached Guatemala, that country had broken diplomatic relations with Germany, on April 23, to the great satisfaction of the United States. Morley and his colleagues could now count on the support of the Guatemalan government as they sought to neutralize German activity.

Soon after arriving in Guatemala, Morley recruited a valuable agent for ONI. The individual in question was Morley's close friend, the archaeologist Samuel Kirkland Lothrop. Born in Milton, Massachusetts on July 6, 1892, Lothrop was a gentleman scholar, a man of independent means. His background was one of wealth and influence; his family owned, for example, extensive sugar plantations in Puerto Rico. Lothrop graduated from Harvard in 1915. From 1915 to 1917 he traveled extensively in Mexico, Cuba, the Dominican Republic, and Central America as a research associate of Harvard's Peabody Museum of Archaeology and Ethnology. In 1916, Lothrop had been a member of Morley's expedition to Tulum.[11]

Lothrop was excavating in Honduras for the Peabody Museum when on April 13, 1917, he received a telegram from his—and Morley's—old Harvard professor Alfred Tozzer: "Meet Morley Guatemala City May 3rd without fail." He did so. The meeting produced a radical change in Lothrop's plans, for when Morley made his ONI pitch, Lothrop agreed to become an agent, on May 4. He would be designated as Agent No. 173. Lothrop accepted terms of $100 per month salary and $4 a day for expenses, the same arrangement as ONI had with John Held. But, as Morley reported:

> Both of these men, however, are not satisfied with this arrangement not on any financial account but because they want the recognition of a commission for the hard and possibly dangerous work they are doing, and will have to do. If you could possibly secure ensignships for them it would greatly encourage them and would I believe increase their efficiency, since it is already apparent that there are very few of us to cover a vast territory and that we will have to separate from time to time and each of us take on temporary assistants.

> If Lothrop and Held can be commissioned it will give them more
> confidence, and as I say, materially increase their respective spheres
> of usefulness.[12]

Unfortunately, despite Morley's strong recommendation Lothrop and Held would remain civilian agents.

As for United States-Guatemalan relations, they had improved materially since relations with Germany had been broken; the Lefleur matter was now ancient history. And within Guatemala itself the level of tension had decreased noticeably. For example, passports were no longer required to ride on the trains, although no one could leave the country without special permission. One of the leading Germans in the capital had been imprisoned in the penitentiary for pro-German activities; the other Germans were now keeping a low profile. Morley added that

> I should not anticipate any further trouble here. This government is
> the strongest in Central America and exercises close control of every-
> thing. It should be remembered however that there are six thousand
> Germans in the republic, concentrated chiefly here in the city and in
> the highlands to the west where they control the coffee business and
> they constitute a potential source of trouble at any time. This lack
> of immediate danger here has determined our plan of action for the
> next month or six weeks at any rate, though some of us will return
> here later to keep the situation under observation.[13]

Morley was thus able to extend his "archaeological reconnaissance" into Honduras, El Salvador, and Nicaragua. He planned to deploy his augmented intelligence team as follows: he, Spinden and Held would proceed via Zacapa by mule to the Mayan ruins of Copán, Honduras. At Copán they would split into two parties. Morley and Held would go northwest to the village of La Florida, "mentioned by Lothrop as being a likely center for wireless activity, owing to its inaccessibility, prevalence of water power and its recent purchase by the largest German house in Honduras. The tract of land is not right in the village but several leagues out." After investigating this area Morley and Held would travel on to San Salvador, where they would meet Spinden. The latter would have gone from Copán southward by way of Esquipulas, Guatemala, to San Salvador. After investigating the region around San Salvador the three agents would proceed to the Pacific coast port of Amapala and from there to Tegucigalpa, the capital of Honduras. There they would link up with Lothrop, who would have gone directly to Tegucigalpa and been conducting his own investigations in that vicinity. Morley estimated that the four agents would be reunited by about June 1.

Having developed a plan of action, Morley addressed two issues that would continually concern the ONI agents: finances and—especially—communications with Washington. As team leader, Morley handled the finances and was solely accountable for expenditures, which he had to document in periodic expense accounts. For instance, before leaving Guatemala City he had to arrange finances for Lothrop, who would be operating independently for the next few weeks. Accordingly, Morley asked ONI to send Lothrop $600 for expenses, including his salary and per diem, to be cabled to Lothrop's account at the Banco Atlántida in Tegucigalpa.

But it was the problem of communications that was even more urgent. For one thing, diplomats then, as now, became extremely uncomfortable having on the premises "spooks," for whom they generally had disdain. State Department personnel in Central America were usually not anxious to facilitate the work of the ONI operatives. As Morley explained:

> There is one matter of great importance which if it is not attended to at once will largely decrease any usefulness we may have for the office [of Naval Intelligence]; I refer to the matter of sending off our reports in the legation pouches which are the only means of getting letters out of the country *unread*.
>
> I spoke about this matter when I was in Washington and I find that it is just as I had suspected; letters, especially those of foreigners are being opened and read. Indeed German activity is supposed to be behind this.
>
> No permission has been received by the American Minister here to allow us to send our reports via the legation pouch, and the only reason I am being allowed to do it this time is because I am addressing the whole enclosure to Mr. [Leland] Harrison [the Counselor of the State Department] and am obliged to leave it *unsealed* otherwise the minister will not accept it. Unsatisfactory as this method is it is by far the best which is now open to me and so I am taking

it. Will you be so kind my dear Taro to take this matter up with the State Department just as soon as possible and ask them to direct the Ministers at Guatemala City, Tegucigalpa, San Salvador, Managua, and San Jose to receive letters from us and also code cables. Indeed we cannot possibly send the latter unless we get this permission.

If possible this permission should be secured for all four of us as we may have to operate separately at any minute, namely, H. J. Spinden, S. K. Lothrop, J. Held, Jr., and S. G. Morley.[14]

In addition, Morley recommended that ONI accede to Lothrop's request for a code book, since Lothrop was working separately from his colleagues. With a code book Lothrop could communicate directly with Morley. Should ONI decide to send a code book, Morley stressed that the only safe method of doing so was by including it in the diplomatic pouch for the American legation in Tegucigalpa. Morley added a postscript to his report: "If you could send some Hondurense, Costa Rican, Salvadorenean [sic] and Nicaraguan maps to me at Tegucigalpa it might help."[15]

With the available communications channels slow and uncertain at best, time after time Morley would try to improve upon the arrangements in this vital area. It should be noted, however, that Morley's tradecraft—or rather lack of it—contributed to the problem of insecure communications. He habitually wrote his reports to ONI on Carnegie Institution stationery and signed his name, instead of using paper without a letterhead and identifying himself simply by his agent number—53. But then the security measures taken by ONI itself were not exactly watertight: both Morley and Spinden were listed as commissioned officers in the official Navy *Registers* for 1917 and 1918.[16]

Evidencing the difficulty in communications, it would be a month before Morley next reported to ONI. As it happened, his "archaeological reconnaissance" had not exactly unfolded according to plan. He, Spinden, and Held indeed left Guatemala City on May 13 and traveled to Zacapa as scheduled. In Zacapa, the fourth-largest city in Guatemala, Morley found no indication of German activity. Nor, in his opinion, could the few Germans in Zacapa engage in mischief because the French consul operated the leading cantina and thus had "unequaled opportunities for keeping abreast with the life of the town." The consul could be counted on to alert the authorities at the slightest hint of German machinations.

Part of the two days spent in Zacapa involved securing two trains of pack mules—one for Morley and Held, the other for Spinden and R. W. Hebard of the Hebard Construction Company of New York. Hebard was the railroad builder for Minor Cooper Keith, the American entrepreneur who linked San José, Costa Rica, by rail with the coast and who was the driving force in building United Fruit Company into a transnational powerhouse. Hebard had traveled on the same steamer to Guatemala as had Spinden and Held. The three became well acquainted on shipboard, and in Guatemala City Hebard stayed at the same hotel for three weeks as did Spinden, Held, and Morley. They had all traveled together to Zacapa.[17] When the group reached the ruined Maya city of Copán, some sixty miles east of Zacapa, they divided. Spinden, accompanied by Hebard, started out for El Salvador; Morley and Held remained at Copán for the next four days.

Their brief sojourn at Copán was frustrating in one respect. As Morley put it: "There is a world of archaeological work to be done here, but we took only a few nibbles at it, as it were." While maintaining their archaeological cover, the ONI agents received an unexpected piece of good news:

> It was at Copan that we first learned of the severance of diplomatic relations between Germany and Honduras. The manner in which this came to our ears is of sufficient interest to warrant a slight digression here in order to describe it.
>
> This region is now being devastated by a plague of grasshoppers, which during the days we were there literally darkened the sky at times. In the early mornings long before day break the men of the village to the number of more than three hundred assembled in the plaza and sallied forth to the fields to fight the common enemy. All day long these battles were waged and it was not until dark that they returned.
>
> One evening as we were sitting in front of our quarters in the cabildo (town-hall) we heard the music of this grass-hopper army returning from the fray. Presently they filed into the plaza, first the band, next the leaders mounted, and last the soldiers two by two dressed in dirty cotton shirts and pantaloons, straw hats, and sandals and armed with machetes and flails.
>
> By the way, Taro, has anyone ever suggested machetes for

use in the trenches? They are a wicked weapon at close range, and would bother the Boches in a trench raid. They are more effective than bayonets at close quarters. They balance easily in the hand and carry well at the side. In Latin America they are the universal implement; you can do anything from a major operation to opening a tin can with one. Why not?

Well to go on. The soldiers formed a hollow square and a few were told off to drag a cart into the center upon which the secretary of the municipality took his stand and commenced to read a telegram. His news was no less than a Presidential decree promulgated the day before severing diplomatic relations with Germany and placing the republic "en estado de sitio" which is the equivalent down here of our martial law.

The crowd received the news in apathetic silence. Such is the general ignorance where not one in twenty can either read or write, that the European war is more remote—less comprehended—than the life of the ancient races I am studying.

Not so with the two gringoes in the cabildo however. By good fortune we had an American flag with us in our outfit. We hurriedly got this out and raised it above the cabildo. Then we circulated among the leaders exchanging greetings and congratulations; "somos aliados, somos aliados ahora" we heard on all sides. The scene was not without a certain dramatic and patriotic interest: the little white plastered houses with their red tiled roofs, the waving palms, the mozo army in pyjamas drawn up around the plaza, the secretary in the middle reading the presidential decree, and their new allies represented by two dirty unkempt gringoes, and lastly the Stars and Stripes floating over the cabildo in the fast falling tropical twilight.

So far as I could judge however, the news left little real impression. The whole question of the war is too remote from the average Hondureno's life to interest him at all and save for a natural antipathy to America as a nation he does not take sides.[18]

On May 25, Morley and Held left Copán to reconnoiter the mountainous western border of Honduras. They were especially anxious to investigate rumors of a secret German radio station near the village of La Florida. The result was anticlimax. The handful of Germans, mainly merchants, proved inoffensive. Although the region abounded in streams that could furnish power for a radio station, the difficulty of transporting the necessary components seemed insuperable—the only form of transport was by mule train. More importantly, the Honduran authorities were keeping very close track of strangers. Held and Morley had not been in La Florida half an hour before the local military commandant summoned them to the town hall to examine their passports. And within an hour of their arrival in La Florida, the essential information from their passports had been telegraphed to Tegucigalpa, the capital.

From La Florida the Americans rode their mules another hundred miles, through a well-watered countryside devoted to cattle raising, to San Pedro Sula, the capital of the Department of Cortés. This town of some seven thousand inhabitants was in the center of a rich agricultural region and was located on the railroad that ran down to Puerto Cortés. Morley took pains to maintain his and Held's cover: "We presented our archaeological credentials to the governor of the province, and were cordially received." As for enemy activity, Morley reported that the ex-German consul had been engaging in propaganda, but to little effect. The archaeologist included in his report a list of the sixty-odd Germans in the region, most of them businessmen. The authorities in San Pedro Sula, as elsewhere in Honduras, were maintaining tight control over the movements of travelers, especially foreigners.

The most noteworthy feature of Morley's stay in San Pedro Sula was that he recruited an informant, the first in what would become a network covering much of Central America. "Before leaving San Pedro Sula I made arrangements with a Mr. J. T. Bennett a native born American citizen who operates the only American Hotel to keep his eyes open for me. I gave him my Carnegie Institution address and told him to call me direct there if anything breaks. He knows nothing of my other Wash. connections."[19]

At San Pedro Sula Morley learned of yet another Honduran control over travelers. He was told that in order to leave the country one had to secure permission from the minister of war. The archaeologist promptly telegraphed requesting such permission for himself and Held. Expecting a favorable reply, he and Held took the train for Puerto Cortés. On the way the passports of all the passengers were examined. And when the Americans reached Puerto Cortés they were informed that before being able to purchase a ticket on a United Fruit steamer they must present an exit permit issued by the local military authorities on telegraphic orders from the minister of war. Fortunately, Morley's and Held's requests had been approved.

Morley's conclusion about the area of Honduras he had reconnoitered was that German activity was limited to some ineffectual propaganda at San Pedro Sula. Nevertheless, there were enough Germans around to cause considerable trouble if a favorable opportunity arose, such as a revolution against the present government.

With this phase of his "archaeological reconnaissance" completed, Morley changed his plans. Instead of proceeding with Held to El Salvador as he had originally intended, he decided first to make a quick trip to Belize where the population still feared a Mexican invasion from Yucatán.

The United Fruit Company steamer on which the Americans sailed from Puerto Cortés made a stop at Puerto Barrios, Guatemala. There, a "New Orleans Jew one Rafael Conn" came aboard as a passenger. It happened that Conn had been on the same ship with Spinden and Held when they had first gone to Guatemala in April. Now the acquaintance was renewed, and on the voyage to Belize Held and Conn became quite friendly. Conn confided that President Estrada Cabrera of Guatemala had recently received twenty-nine machine guns and twenty carloads of ammunition. To convince Held that he was serious, Conn showed him telegrams from Estrada Cabrera indicating that indeed he had business dealings with Conn. Morley commented that other sources had subsequently confirmed that Conn had been selling munitions to Guatemala for several years. Conn, of course, was just one of the many arms dealers who found the turmoil of Central American politics such a lucrative market for their wares.

When Morley and Held arrived in Belize they immediately conferred with the archaeologist's old friend Dr. Gann about the invasion scare. *The New York Herald*, for instance, had announced: "British Honduras Invasion Included in German Plot." The article alleged that armed German reservists living in Mexico were being organized to invade British Honduras.[20] Back in February, the Colonial Office had become convinced that Mexican troops under German officers were to be shipped down the east coast of Yucatán to establish a base close to the border of British Honduras. From there the invaders would sweep south, seize the principal towns, and depict the whole affair for domestic consumption in Germany as a major blow to the British Empire.

Improbable as such a scenario was, the British had taken it seriously enough to initiate immediate defense measures. Brush was cut, search-lights were installed, and patrols were instituted to protect the govern-ment radio station in Belize. Security was also tightened around the city's electric-power plant. But the colony had no intelligence service, only two Maxim machine guns, and the British Honduras Territorial Force num-bered but 230 men.[21] In early April the British dispatched Lt.Colonel E. L. Cowie, followed by a small training cadre, from Jamaica to take charge of the situation. If necessary, the seven-hundred-man 1st Battalion of the 1st West India Regiment would be rushed from Jamaica to defend British Honduras. Cowie was an energetic professional officer who indeed strengthened the colony's defenses, quickly recruiting the home guard to over one thousand men. Besides arranging for additional arms and ammunition, he advocated the building of several armored launches to repel any invasion from Mexico. But Cowie and his methods antagonized the easy-going establishment in Belize, and when the invasion scare sub-sided he was recalled to Jamaica.[22]

Morley witnessed a review of about five hundred Territorials in Belize, and though they had been training only for about six weeks they made presentable soldiers. But, in Morley's opinion "the Belize creole so-called, really mixed black and tan, is an arrant coward, and I understand some doubt is felt as to their morale in a pinch." A garrison of 150 of these troops was now stationed at Corozal at the northern end of British Honduras. The entire home guard—six companies of infantry and half a troop of cavalry—was well equipped, boasting a recently delivered Maxim gun and six Hotchkiss guns. This military information that Dr. Gann gave Morley was presumably reliable, since Gann had been com-missioned a captain in the defense force and served on the five-man Committee of Military Defense for the colony.

As for the chances of invasion, Morley's analysis was that

Personally I think the possibility of any such an attempt extremely remote. I know the country through which such a force would have to pass, the difficulty of establishing a base on the east coast of Yucatan and the absolute impossibility of living off the region thereby necessitating the bringing in of all supplies from the outside—you may remember the article I sent you describing the region—the rains have broken and will grow worse for the next four months, and finally the inhabitants of the region, the Maya Indians, are bitterly hostile to anything Mexican. Such an invading force would be in hot water long before it ever reached the colony which I may add is also the opinion of the older residents of Belize.[23]

The three days spent in Belize reassured Morley that no threat was imminent, so he and Held sailed back to Puerto Barrios, Guatemala. There he found the government and United Fruit taking elaborate precautions to prevent people from leaving the country without authorization. Like Honduras, Guatemala now required both a passport and a permit issued by the local military on orders from the national government for anyone trying to leave the country. And as a precaution against sabotage, troops guarded railroad bridges and tunnels and patrolled Guatemala City. Thus as of June 13, 1917, Morley could reassure ONI not only about the situation in British Honduras but about that in Honduras and Guatemala as well:

> In conclusion it seems to me that so long as the two governments in question remain at odds with Germany and the two countries in a state of martial law, little or no trouble can start in either. In fact as matters now stand it would first be necessary to start a revolution against the two existing governments and overturn one or both of them before any anti-American movement could gain much headway.[24]

Morley and Held left Guatemala City the next day for El Salvador. They expected to join Spinden, who presumably awaited them in San Salvador, the capital. The communications situation for the agents was improving somewhat for they were now able to communicate with ONI by cables through the American legations in Guatemala, El Salvador, and Nicaragua.[25]

On the morning of their departure for El Salvador, Morley was up by 5 A.M. As soon as he had finished packing he went in to awaken Held, who was a notoriously heavy sleeper.[26] Held whined and pleaded for just a few more minutes of sleep, which the impatient Morley grudgingly granted. Having finally gotten Held awake, Morley noted with pleasure that an almost-unprecedented thing happened—their hotel, the Imperial, functioned efficiently. Breakfast was ready on time, their luggage was collected promptly and was loaded on the hackney coach waiting for them at the front door. Taking ceremonious leave of the hotel personnel, the Americans were in high spirits as their coach rattled through Guatemala City on its way to the railroad station.

Though they traveled in a first-class passenger car, the oppressive heat combined with the incessant squalling of several infants made the trip less than enjoyable. But they finally reached the port of San José on the Pacific coast of Guatemala. San José was a squalid little place, with ramshackle wooden buildings tilting at various angles, and a rickety pier stretching out into the pounding surf. Morley and Held joined the crowd jostling each other to secure the indispensable exit permits for leaving Guatemala legally. Having triumphed in this encounter with bureaucracy, the pair prepared to embark on the steamer *San Juan*. This proved to be a feat in itself. They had to climb from the pier into a lighter that was rising and falling some twenty feet in the turbulent swell. Many of their fellow passengers were busy vomiting over the side, but a tug finally came alongside, lashed herself to the pitching lighter, and conveyed the sufferers to the *San Juan* without major incident.

Held and Morley gratefully washed up in their stateroom and proceeded to celebrate with an excellent lunch. The steamer's overnight run southward to the small Salvadoran port of Acajutla was uneventful. But in the harbor early the next morning, they had to turn out hurriedly on deck for what proved to be a perfunctory quarantine inspection. Morley complained that he didn't even have time to wash, while Held cut quite a figure, for he sleepily appeared still wearing his lavender pajamas. After a frustrating encounter with the local Customs authorities regarding the disposition of their sixteen pieces of baggage, Morley and Held strolled along the beach to kill some time before their train left. They decided to stop for lemonade at one of the two nondescript hotels: the Miramar or the Hotel Inglés. Morley noted proudly that they chose the latter because its name was more pro-Ally.

As their train rolled inland toward San Salvador, Morley and Held began to see for themselves the enormous damage resulting from a devastating earthquake that had shattered the region on June 7. They eventually had to transfer from their passenger train to a construction train going a few miles farther, to repair a major bridge that had collapsed. From there they walked three kilometers to the next village, where, in company with a Scotsman representing the Singer Sewing Machine Company, they were able to secure mules and a guide. Their trip was about to become a harrowing experience.

Since it was now late afternoon, the guide was reluctant to set forth, emphasizing that the road was very dangerous. Faced with the prospect of having to spend the night in the guide's filthy hovel, Morley and Held would have none of it and demanded that they leave forthwith. By the time the mules were rounded up and loaded it was nearly dark. As they encountered huge rockslides across the road, large trees uprooted and smashed into kindling, and sections of hillside ready to collapse on them, the travelers began to feel that perhaps they'd been a bit foolhardy. The feeling intensified as they gingerly climbed over obstacles in the pitch darkness.

It was while negotiating a rockslide flanked on one side by a precipitous drop into a canyon and on the other by an overhanging mass of rock precariously balanced that disaster struck. The lead mule's pack slipped under its belly, and the terrified animal began to kick and plunge frantically, forcing the following mules to back into each other in panic and nearly knocking one member of the party over the cliff. All this while lightning and thunder announced that a violent storm was imminent. After a hurried discussion, it was decided to reload the lead mule and push on at all costs. With considerable difficulty, since the ropes had to be attached by feel in the dark, the load was secured and the shaken travelers reached the sanctuary of an abandoned house, where they spent the remainder of a miserable night. Morley was less miserable than his companions, however, for he had his air pillow with him. Nevertheless, they were all awakened during the night by a downpour and a sharp earth tremor.

By 4:30 the next morning they were on their way again. And again they witnessed a panorama of devastation: fissures in the ground, stretches of the road obliterated, and at one spot overhanging rocks so precariously balanced that the travelers spoke in whispers. They finally emerged onto the fertile plain in which was located the town of Santa Tecla. As Morley's group entered the devastated town, they saw piles of rubble alternating with primitive temporary shelters. Fortunately the railroad connecting Santa Tecla with nearby San Salvador was still operating, so Morley and Held were able to make the last leg of their journey in comparative comfort. Upon arriving in the capital, they checked into the Hotel Nuevo Mundo where their colleague Joe Spinden was already registered. There followed a jubilant reunion.

Morley, Held, and Spinden soon went to the American legation, which itself had experienced serious damage from the earthquake. The minister, Boaz Long, had been a friend of Morley's since the two had met in Mexico in 1907.[27] Long received them cordially, and they offered their services for earthquake relief, an offer that Minister Long gratefully accepted. Spinden had been in San Salvador, but had left on June 5 for Tegucigalpa en route to investigate German activity at Fonseca Bay. But by June 14 he was back at San Salvador to aid in relief work and because, as he cabled ONI, he was broke. ONI cabled back that funds had already been sent to Morley, and for Spinden to resume his original mission. He left on July 5 for Fonseca Bay.[28]

The earthquake and accompanying volcanic eruption were a national catastrophe for El Salvador. At 6:55 P.M. on June 7, a severe shock lasting several minutes caused little damage in San Salvador but destroyed two neighboring towns. But there followed an almost-continuous series of shocks, increasing in violence, which culminated at 9:05 P.M. in a cataclysmic upheaval that devastated the capital, a city of some sixty-five thousand inhabitants. At almost the same instant the volcano of San Salvador, eight miles to the west, erupted through a new crater, fortunately on the side away from the capital. The eruption relieved much of the subterranean pressure, but strong aftershocks were still occurring eighteen days later. The Salvadoran government estimated that up to 95 percent of the houses in the capital were either destroyed or rendered uninhabitable. Thousands of the citizens had fled to the countryside, and of the remainder many were living a wretched existence in makeshift shelters in the streets, plazas, and parks. Adding to their misery, it was the rainy season, and torrential downpours drenched San Salvador daily.

Morley's assessment was that the Salvadoran government had performed creditably in this crisis. Martial law had immediately been declared, "and after a few shootings, looting ceased." There was no shortage of food, sanitary measures were adequate, and there were no disorders. The most urgent need was for money and materials to build temporary housing for the homeless. The existing shelters were constructed of whatever was available—sheets of corrugated iron, odd pieces of lumber, old signboards, flour sacks sewn together, and even some old

U.S. mail sacks. With the daily drenching the occupants of these hovels were enduring, there was a real likelihood of epidemics unless adequate shelter were speedily provided.[29]

And that was where the United States could play a significant role. On June 16, two days after his arrival in San Salvador, Morley recommended to ONI that American aid be made available immediately. The cable, which was transmitted from the American minister Boaz Long to the secretary of state, read:

> Recommend five thousand dollars for immediate use be placed to the credit of the American Minister. We have arrived in Salvador. Spindel, Held, and I are working under the Minister. Emergency relief work imperative. Rains begun, nine tenths of houses uninhabitable, shelters necessary. Please forward to Gustav Vioch, New York, telegraph answer. Unequalled opportunity for creating favorable feeling towards United States Government.
>
> Morley[30]

What ensued was a comedy of errors. The State Department duly forwarded the cable to Gustav Vioch, New York City. The postal authorities there were unable to locate any such person and returned the letter to the State Department.[31] State also sent a letter and a copy of the cable to the Carnegie Institution, which knew nothing about any Gustav Vioch. Carnegie then sent copies of everything to Henry F. Osborn, president of the American Museum of Natural History in New York, in hopes that he might be able to shed some light on the matter. Osborn replied that his efforts to locate Vioch had been unsuccessful.[32]

The problem of course was that the original cable had been garbled in transmission. Spinden was spelled "Spindel"; more importantly, the name transmitted as "Gustav Vioch" should have been "Gustav Koch," the addressee for Morley's ONI accommodation address in New York City. So, even when Morley was able to use communications facilities provided by cooperative State Department functionaries such as his friend Minister Boaz Long, it was by no means certain that messages would reach ONI in a timely manner.

Assuming his cable of June 16 had been delivered, Morley followed up on June 25 with a written report to ONI in which he discussed the

Salvadoran situation at some length. He stressed that El Salvador was the most anti-American nation in Central America. This antipathy toward the United States had manifested itself in a variety of pro-German intrigues. Furthermore, Salvadorans bitterly resented efforts by the United States to acquire at the Gulf of Fonseca an anchorage for refueling the American fleet.[33] Fonseca Bay remained an "open sore," an issue which the government intentionally kept alive for anti-American purposes. And the two leading newspapers, *Diario de Salvador* and *La Prensa*, kept up a vigorous anti-American campaign.

Another important factor shaping public opinion was the long-standing enmity between El Salvador and Guatemala. The cordial relations currently existing between the United States and Guatemala produced a corresponding anti-American reflex in El Salvador. Conversely, El Salvador maintained very friendly relations with Mexico, which recently sent the former a German-built radio station and two airplanes. The radio equipment, which arrived in January 1917 and went on line in September, was able to tune in the German-built transmitter at Chapultepec in Mexico City, which put out pro-German or pro-Mexican or anti-American—depending on one's point of view—news items that the local newspapers then published. President Venustiano Carranza of Mexico had no use for President Manuel Estrada Cabrera of Guatemala, being convinced that Estrada Cabrera had given aid and comfort to Mexican exiles attempting to mount a rebellion against Carranza.[34] Morley reminded ONI that a month ago Joe Spinden had reported the hissing directed toward the Guatemalan and American flags at a theater performance he had attended in San Salvador. In short, Morley said, El Salvador habitually aligned herself "with our enemies and against our friends, which in the present international crisis means a pro-German attitude."

The archaeologist characterized the Salvadoran government as "distinctly pro-German." President Carlos Meléndez professed to be neutral in World War I, but was suspected of having German sympathies. His sister was married to a German merchant in Tegucigalpa. Of greater significance, however, was the clique of six presidential advisors, whom Morley named, who were anti-American in varying degrees. Their combined influence would probably prevent the president from breaking relations with Germany even if he were so inclined, which he was not.

Before the great earthquake, then, conditions in El Salvador were decidedly unfavorable for the United States. But all that had now changed dramatically for the better. The Salvadoran government was already in financial difficulties, and now with the coffee crop, the country's leading export, largely destroyed, and the enormous cost of rebuilding after the earthquake, the government was in crisis. According to Morley:

> This Government is too proud, too sensitive, too anti-American to humble itself to ask us for a loan outright, but they are in desperate need of money, and would probably accept a loan if one were proffered. Once such an arrangement had been effected, the danger of any active assistance being given to Germany by Salvador would practically be at an end. The establishment of a strong American banking institution here in the capital would, in Minister Long's opinion—almost certainly accomplish the same end.
>
> They need the money but are too proud to ask for it. If on the other hand we offered it to them, it would probably be accepted, and would do more to heal old wounds than anything else. A loan to Salvador heretofore might have looked like blackmail, "hush money" for acquiescence to our acquisition of the Fonseca Bay rights, but now in the face of this great national calamity, and with dire need staring them in the face it could be proffered and accepted as a humanitarian measure of the highest order without loss of face on either side. For once in Central American affairs, altruism and expediency would appear to coincide.[35]

Thus prompt and conspicuous American aid disbursed under the direct supervision of Minister Long would go far toward countering anti-American feeling.

The massive destruction that El Salvador had suffered would force her to adopt a much more circumspect foreign policy. Gone was any hope of helping Germany or attacking Guatemala. In fact, there was growing fear in El Salvador that Guatemala might take advantage of the situation to launch an invasion. Morley asserted that the Salvadoran army was superior to that of Guatemala in equipment and personnel; not only were the troops better clothed and equipped but—unlike the Guatemalans—they had shoes and raincoats. But the Salvadorans had only ten thousand to eleven thousand men as compared with Guatemala's "sixty-odd thousand."[36] This figure may have been technically correct, but it did not reflect the real combat capability of the Guatemalan army. The vast majority of the "sixty-odd thousand" were reservists, who had some training but virtually no equipment. The regular army was considerably smaller:

SOLDIERS	4,935
OFFICERS	649
MILITARY EMPLOYEES	167
MILITARY MUSICIANS	358
	6,209

This force was commanded by 21 generals on active duty (10 generals of division, 17 generals of brigade). Should this number of generals prove insufficient, there were 9 more in reserve (2 generals of division, 7 generals of brigade). Counting just the generals on active duty, the Guatemalan army thus boasted 1 general for every 365 other ranks.[37] In more conventional armies this ratio perhaps applied more to captains commanding companies. When Central American armies were involved, numbers tended to be rather unreliable. For example, in 1918 Honduras and Nicaragua were engaged in a boundary dispute. First reports had Honduras rushing 5,000 troops to the border. In later reports, the figure had fallen to only 2,000. When the troops were subsequently recalled to the capital, it turned out that the contingent sent to the border numbered exactly 270.[38]

Morley enclosed in his report a list of the principal German firms in El Salvador and estimated that there were probably not more than 150 Germans in the whole country. Joe Spinden had checked the island port of Amapala off the southern coast of Honduras and had found a strong German influence in business and politics. The ONI agents would investigate that situation further. Meanwhile, Spinden would operate in El Salvador and Lothrop in Nicaragua. Morley and Held left San Salvador on June 25 for Guatemala, where a new lead had developed. The ONI team planned to reunite in Tegucigalpa about the middle of July.

On reaching Guatemala City, Morley and Held again checked in to the Hotel Imperial. The archaeologist found a letter awaiting him from his ONI control, who mentioned that Dr. Woodward, president of the Carnegie Institution, had been to see him.[39] The ties between Carnegie and ONI remained close.

Morley was pleased to report that the situation in Guatemala continued to improve:

The Boche Bach who was arrested here some time ago for having electrical apparatus in his possession, and an alleged wireless outfit on his plantation was sentenced to 6 years and 8 months. A candy-maker one Weinberg was recently clapped into the penitentiary for no greater offense than too loudly "shooting off his face." These measures seem to have had a salutary effect and one hears little open German propaganda.

I am informed on reliable authority that when the war first broke out, the German minister Lehman was told by the President that any excessive pro-German activity would result in the wholesale confiscation of German property in the republic, and since the breaking off of relations in April, the principal Germans have been told that any demonstrations would lead to their prompt incarceration. The Bach and Weinberg imprisonments have added force to that warning.

That underground propaganda goes on however, I am inclined to believe. False Russian rumors, submarine news etc. crop up every so often undoubtedly emanating from German sources.[40]

On June 30 the Guatemalan army had conducted exercises outside the capital. "The President was there, and perhaps 3,000 troops. They were not as well equipped as the Salvadorenean [*sic*] soldiers we saw, nor as intelligent looking." This show of military strength was perhaps designed to intimidate the Salvadorans, whose relations with Guatemala were now much more cordial than before the earthquake.

With their "archaeological survey" of western Guatemala, El Salvador, and western Honduras fairly complete, and with little of intelligence interest transpiring in Guatemala City, Morley and Held could indulge themselves by looking at some collections of archaeological artifacts. By doing so they were, of course, burnishing their cover.

Held had been doing excellent work, according to Morley. His cartography was admirable, and in addition he had intercepted a couple of German letters from El Salvador; unfortunately, they contained nothing of importance. Moreover, Held had developed a relationship with a woman that might eventually prove useful. The woman was Adela Valenzuela, wife of the Guatemalan consul in Mobile. She was in

Guatemala City trying to use her contacts to advance her husband's career. She began confiding in Held, and soon "conceived a violent passion for Held and can only be worked through him. She knows nothing of his connections other than the ostensible one. I think he can find out anything she knows."[41] It is not known whether Held sacrificed himself for his country in order to get information.

It was the leakage of information that troubled Morley. He was particularly upset by an incident that occurred at the American legation:

> Minister Leavell in the presence of his Secretary, Mr. Walter Thurston, and the clerk of the Legation, a Cuban, told a third person, Mr. Lyman G. Sisley, a Special Agent of the State Department that Mr. Held and myself were connected with the Navy Department. The three Americans of course made no difference, though as a matter of fact we had been preserving our "incognito" intact before Mr. Sisley, until he told us he knew of our "connections" all the time; but the Cuban was another matter.
>
> This man has been in the Legation a number of years and is very efficient. It is rumored in Guatemala City—and rather generally—that he is in the pay of Estrada Cabrera.
> Minister Leavell, I understand, does not believe in this alleged secret connection, but in view only of the suspicion thereof it appeared to me incautious on his part to have mentioned our connection before the man at all.
>
> We were in Guatemala City too short a time after the incident took place to be able to judge how it would affect our freedom of movement about that country. We will doubtless have future opportunities however for finding this out.[42]

As the above quotation illustrates, Morley had a simplistic view of national loyalty: if a man were an American it was automatically assumed he was loyal to the United States. It was the same mentality as upper-class Englishmen manifested into the Cold War era: "He can't possibly be a spy; I was at school with his father." Sadly, Kim Philby and other upper-class English traitors proved otherwise.

Although justifiably upset by the sloppy security at the legation, Morley soldiered on. While in the Guatemalan capital Morley recruited an informant, an American businessman named James Roach. He was the second—James Bennett at San Pedro Sula, Honduras, being the first—in Morley's growing network of subagents:

> Neither of these knows the exact nature of my connection and should be communicated with under my name, if you get in touch with them directly.
>
>   I have a good man in mind for San Salvador, and will look up your friend in Tegucigalpa. I will send complete expense accounts for all when we get together in Tegucigalpa. In the meantime if you wish to reach me by cable, address me care of the Legation here.[43]

On July 13, Morley and Held again left Guatemala City for San Salvador accompanied by Lyman G. Sisley, the State Department agent. Sisley had been ordered by Leland Harrison, the Counselor of the State Department, to undertake a confidential mission at San Salvador. They traveled to the Pacific coast port of San José de Guatemala. The port was small and primitive—an open roadstead with a single wharf at which ships could not dock because of the surf. A half-dozen lighters transported goods and passengers between ship and shore. The surf ran so high that frequently Pacific Mail steamers had to lie offshore for days before they could land their cargo. After braving the surf, Morley and Held sailed on July 15 aboard the Pacific Mail steamer *City of Pará*. The ship, incidentally, carried eleven hundred tons of Red Cross supplies, chiefly lumber for shelters, designated for Salvadoran earthquake victims. The ONI operatives landed at Acajutla, El Salvador on the sixteenth and reached San Salvador that night.[44]

      They would soon be driven to distraction by a ridiculous security blunder on the part of ONI. Morley had received only two letters from his case officer: one dated June 25, which he had received in Guatemala about ten days later; and another written June 16, but not received by Morley until he arrived in San Salvador. The June 16 communication ordered the agents to proceed directly to the north coast of Honduras, while the June 25 missive instructed them to gather political intelligence. Morley and Held consulted with Spinden, who had joined them in San Salvador, as to which set of instructions they should follow. The trio decided that Morley should cable ONI for clarification. He did so on July 18 and received an answer two days later directing them to the north coast. Morley cabled his acknowledgment and prepared to carry out his instructions. But, he said,

I am enclosing your cable as it was delivered to me by the Salvador government telegraph office. It speaks for itself. It indicates a fairly intimate connection, hardly archaeological, between the Department and myself, and it first passed through the government censor in San Salvador before being delivered to me. I take it therefore, that so far as Salvador is concerned, my alibi [that is, cover] and that of Held and probably that of Spinden as well, is gone. These people are past masters at intrigue and it does not require a house falling in on them to let in the light.

Fortunately the tension there has lessened very materially since the earthquake; and although still anti-"gringo," the Salvadorenos are too busy rebuilding their city to make any trouble for us. Even the Huns are quiet.[45]

The nature of ONI's blunder was underlined by Boaz Long, the American minister to El Salvador. On July 22, Morley was preparing to leave San Salvador and, through Minister Long, sent a cable to ONI: "Leaving for Tegucigalpa, thence to Truxillo." Long not only sent the cable, but added acidly: "Since all cables in these countries pass under Government inspection, I respectfully suggest that future messages not be signed DANIELS, Secretary of the Navy, as they are liable to arouse suspicion."[46] Minister Long did not suffer fools gladly.

He was also an able diplomat. Morley, whose good friend he was, had nothing but admiration for Long's abilities, declaring him to be the best American diplomat in Central America. Since El Salvador was a hotbed of anti-American sentiment, Long's job of protecting American interests was an arduous one. Morley was thus quite pleased that the State Department agent, Lyman Sisley, had arrived to assist the minister. In fact, Morley was quite taken with Sisley, whom he described as a "live wire," wistfully expressing the hope that Leland Harrison and the State Department might be induced to part with Sisley, whom Morley badly wanted to recruit for his forthcoming reconnaissance of the north coast of Honduras. Sisley was an experienced Bureau of Secret Intelligence operative, having previously done undercover work in Panama for the State Department. Minister Long currently had Sisley nosing around the ports and villages along Fonseca Bay in order to make a comprehensive report on conditions there.[47] To Morley's disappointment, Sisley remained a State Department agent.

Their cover in El Salvador blown, Morley, Held, and Spinden left the capital of that country on July 22 and by the next afternoon reached La Unión on Fonseca Bay. A waiting motor launch took the trio on the two-hour trip to the Isla del Tigre, Honduras, out in the bay. The port of Amapala was of particular interest to the ONI team. Spinden had previously been there and had reported that trade, the waterfront, and all lighterage facilities were controlled by the German firms of J. Rossner and Theodore Kohneke. Morley commented indignantly that during his previous stay in Tegucigalpa when he had needed to send money to Spinden he had to do it through a German bank, the Bank of Honduras, to a German house in Amapala, J. Rossner. Morley complained that "the situation is unfortunate, to say the least, and it might very easily become dangerous. Will we never go out effectively and efficiently for this Latin American trade?"

Germans might dominate trade at Amapala, but they were being closely monitored by the Allies. The British, however, were monitoring not just the Germans but the Americans as well, being suspicious of American designs on Fonseca Bay and apprehensive that the latter sought a postwar monopoly on trade.[48] The British vice-consul, Percy Hope Stormont, was quite capable and had special instructions to tour the island frequently to keep abreast of local developments. Stormont indeed had "special instructions"; he was an agent of British naval intelligence.[49] Morley suggested that ONI cooperate with "whomever he sends his information to," since if any German activity occurred Stormont would probably be the first to hear of it. Stormont reported to Alban Young, the British minister in Guatemala. Young, however, had a rather low opinion of Stormont, stating that news from him was always to be mistrusted; although Stormont was energetic and industrious, he was naive and lacked a sense of proportion.[50] Reinforcing Stormont at Amapala was the American consular agent, George A. Makinson, who spoke German fluently, had lived in Germany, and even ate at the German mess. Despite the recurrent rumors, Makinson did not believe there was a German submarine base in Fonseca Bay. Neither, for that matter, did Stormont, Morley, Spinden, or Held. The water in many places was very shallow, there were numerous bars, and many of its estuaries were mere culs-de-sac.[51]

Since Fonseca Bay was being watched so closely, Morley decided not to waste any more time there and pressed on to Tegucigalpa. Compared with many of Morley's journeys, the trip was sheer luxury. From the town of San Lorenzo on the mainland the party traveled by auto the eighty miles to the capital on the best highway in Central America, one comparable to American roads.

But when they presented themselves at the American legation in Tegucigalpa Morley was distressed by what he found. As Spinden had reported to ONI months earlier, an extraordinary situation obtained at the legation. Morley now reiterated Spinden's concern. The problem was Minister Ewing. An elderly alcoholic, his health was failing. The year before he had been hospitalized in what everyone thought was a terminal condition. But he had rallied and had resumed his post the previous November. Although his health was much improved, his memory—and his mind—were rapidly failing. Morley cited as an example the minister having received a caller in Morley's presence in the morning and having absolutely no recollection of the event in the afternoon. With Ewing suffering from some form of dementia, he had for some time been incapable of performing his duties, even routine ones. He had turned the work of the legation over to the clerk and since June 1 to the new secretary, John W. Belt.

What especially concerned Spinden and Morley was that the minister's condition left him vulnerable to manipulation and betrayal by his son-in-law, M. H. von Liebe. The latter was an Austrian in his mid-thirties. Although he had served in the U.S. cavalry at Fort Meyer, Morley did not think he was a U.S. citizen. Worse still, his brother commanded an Austrian submarine, and his father was a field marshal in the Austrian Army. Von Liebe himself was said to have served in the German Army. He had married Minister Ewing's second daughter several years earlier. According to the State Department agent, Sisley, who had worked on the case himself, von Liebe had been kept under surveillance in Panama as a suspected German spy, but he was extremely clever and nothing could be proved against him. The Austrian now worked for a paint company in San Francisco and was currently living in Valparaiso, Chile, with his wife. Morley understood that "they have been entertained at our Legations all the way South, as would be perfectly natural under the circumstances, his father-in-law being American Minister here; and indeed they appear everywhere under the American aegis, so to speak."

While the von Liebes were in Tegucigalpa, about three months earlier, they had lived at the legation. The legation clerk claimed to have concrete proof that von Liebe had access to the safe where the codebooks were kept. Further, he asserted that on at least one occasion von Liebe had opened the ONI pouch. Morley stressed that these allegations might not be true, but there was certainly enough circumstantial evidence concerning von Liebe that even if no security breach had occurred, the situation was dangerous and could be disastrous for Morley and his colleagues. It was urgent that something be done to prevent von Liebe's return to Tegucigalpa and to ensure competent operation of the legation.[52] Morley's concern was reiterated by the new legation secretary, John W. Belt, who had been assigned to the legation "for confidential work in Honduras." Belt sent through State Department channels his own reports concerning lax security. He, in fact, reported that von Liebe had secured the keys to the diplomatic pouch and had opened it. As an indication of just how alarming the security situation was, Mrs. Ewing and her daughter communicated in a code that von Liebe had given them, and Mrs. Ewing warned her daughter to beware of Dr. S[pinden] and Sam L[othrop], adding that everybody and everything is a spy.[53]

The solution to this outrageous state of affairs was of course the immediate removal of Ewing as United States minister to Honduras. But there was a serious complication, of a political nature. Ewing's brother, Robert Ewing, was a powerful Democratic political boss in Louisiana, which was why his dipsomaniacal brother had been appointed as minister in the first place.[54] Belt's and Morley's reports went up the chain of command to Secretary of State Robert Lansing, who considered the matter so sensitive that he brought it to the personal attention of President Woodrow Wilson.[55] Finally, in January 1918, Ewing was recalled to Washington. His permanent replacement arrived in the person of one Sambola Jones, who was from Baton Rouge, had been a journalist and a judge, was a staunch Democrat, and had no previous diplomatic experience.[56] It seems that the position of United States minister to Honduras was still a political plum for Robert Ewing of Louisiana.

Besides trying to get the situation at the American legation rectified, Morley carried out a recruitment assignment. His ONI case officer had instructed him when he got to Tegucigalpa to approach one Edwin E. Huber as a possible ONI agent. Morley reported that Huber was about twenty-seven years old, born in Ohio. He appeared to be of German or Swedish extraction, with blue eyes and curly blonde hair cut in a pompadour. One of his brothers was in mining in El Salvador, and another was in the U.S. Army. Huber had been a journalist in Marquette, Michigan, and at present sold Royal typewriters in Central America. He spoke Spanish fluently and knew Central America well, especially El Salvador, Honduras, and Costa Rica. His occupation provided good cover and he was fairly well known. Huber, however, was not familiar with the north coast of Honduras, which was Morley's current interest. If Huber's loyalty was unquestioned Morley thought he would be a good man. But the archaeologist wanted to watch Huber for a few more days and learn what Consular Agent Makinson at Amapala, who knew him well, had to say. Morley's preliminary evaluation was "I personally believe he is all right." But after he and Held had had several more conversations with Huber, Morley changed his mind: "his apparent and not too far remote Swedish or German ancestry together with a rather heavy type of mind appears to disqualify him. So we divulged nothing to him."[57]

Regarding the ONI team's future plans, both Spinden and Lothrop were again operating independently. Both of these men had come under suspicion in Tegucigalpa, Spinden because he was too interested in Germans and Lothrop because he had lived at the American legation. Spinden had left for the port of Bluefields, Nicaragua, via Costa Rica, which appeared to be the most direct route. Lothrop had gone to Panama three weeks before Morley's arrival in Tegucigalpa. Beyond knowing that Lothrop was now in Panama, Morley knew neither his whereabouts nor why he had left. Morley had written him to remain in Tegucigalpa until Morley's arrival, but the letter had not gotten there in time. Spinden would now try to make contact with Lothrop.

Because of the suspicion that Spinden and Lothrop had aroused in Tegucigalpa, Morley went to great pains to stress the archaeological nature of his—and, by extension, their—activities. He therefore secured an appointment with the minister of foreign relations, Doctor Mariano Vázquez, to whom he ceremoniously presented his Carnegie credentials. Morley quickly ingratiated himself with the foreign minister, who granted him a number of interviews. Vázquez even asked Morley to write an article on the ruins at Copán for publication in the government newspaper, *El Nuevo Tiempo*. Morley of course did so with alacrity, sending a copy to his ONI control and hoping that "it may help bolster up our staggering alibi [cover], which received such a solar plexus across the line in Salvador." He ended the article by stressing the alliance between Honduras and the United States in the present righteous war against the

Central Powers.⁵⁸ This precisely reflected the views of his friend, Dr. Vázquez, who was strongly pro-American. The other side of that coin, of course, was that Vázquez "dislikes Salvador and its people." The foreign minister quite freely expressed the hope that "we would soon put the screws on them for their failure to fall in line with his country and Guatemala in the present world crisis." Vázquez suggested a simple way virtually to paralyze El Salvador—to prohibit Pacific Mail steamers, the only line still serving El Salvador, from touching at any of her ports.

Morley heartily agreed with this sentiment. Supporting the United States and breaking relations with Germany had made the Honduran government feel important, and Honduras expected some recognition for her stand. Morley stressed the point that the United States should treat friendly neutrals such as Honduras and Guatemala better than countries such as El Salvador, whose neutrality barely concealed its hostility toward the United States. He worried that without some gesture of appreciation, financial or otherwise, the United States might lose the goodwill she currently enjoyed in Honduras, and the Germans in that country would capitalize on the resulting disenchantment.⁵⁹

An important result of Morley's friendship with the Honduran foreign minister was that the latter introduced him to the president. Twice Vázquez took the archaeologist to meet with President Francisco Bertrand, and Morley made the most of these occasions. Vázquez and Bertrand informed Morley about several large deposits of saltpeter, mainly in western Honduras, and said it could be exported through Amapala. Since saltpeter was used in the manufacture of gunpowder, Morley was interested in this potential new source of supply for the war effort. While in Guatemala he had met with members of a War Department commission investigating the nitrate deposits in that country, and they had asked him to notify them of any saltpeter deposits he might learn of in other Central American countries. He was now duly passing the information to his case officer, who should notify the War Department.

The meetings with President Bertrand also produced something of more immediate and personal benefit for Morley. He explained at length his proposed archaeological reconnaissance of the north coast, and he charmed the president into issuing him a letter of introduction, to be shown to the military commandants in the towns he and Held intended to visit.⁶⁰ Given the infinite capacity of petty officialdom for being obstinate and insufferable, Morley could now counter with this presidential magic wand. And his and Held's archaeological cover was now secure.

Whatever elation Morley might have felt at obtaining such an invaluable document was tempered by the realization that it was no longer feasible for him to act as supervisor and paymaster for the other ONI operatives. He could continue to keep track of his and Held's finances—on July 31 he sent his case officer his expense account "from the time I first saw you in Washington" to date. He also enclosed Held's account from May 8 to date. Of the $1,800 Morley had received from ONI $400 was left. But after paying their bills in Tegucigalpa and hiring a mule train for the journey to the north coast there would be only about $200 left. Therefore, on August 6 Morley cabled for an immediate allotment of $1,500 so that financial arrangements could be completed before he started for the coast. Since it would be difficult to get funds while on the coast, Morley wanted to be able to draw on his account in Tegucigalpa.[61]

ONI had given Morley the assignment of making a comprehensive examination of the north coast. To accomplish this task Morley planned to travel together with Held to the port of Trujillo, making it his base of operations. He would then investigate along the coast eastward as far as Cape Gracias a Dios and then westward to Livingston, Guatemala. Spinden had gone to the Nicaraguan port of Bluefields and would work northward along the coast to Cape Gracias a Dios.

But Morley urged that "Spinden and Lothrop be sent their funds direct at Bluefields, since Bluefields and Trujillo are literally further apart as far as any communications are concerned, than Vladivostock and Palm Beach." Though the ports of Bluefields, Nicaragua, and Trujillo, Honduras, were only some three hundred miles apart as the crow flies, Morley's statement was not mere hyperbole. His suggestion underlined the continuing problem of communications.

ONI's original plan of having Morley control all the finances for agents in Central America was breaking down. Spinden and Lothrop were now operating in Nicaragua and Costa Rica; funneling their salaries and expense money through Morley was increasingly impractical. In fact, in July Lothrop had already notified ONI directly that he had only enough money to reach San José, the Costa Rican capital, and that until more funds were forthcoming there was little he could do. ONI had instructed Lothrop to ask Morley for money.

But soon ONI had Lothrop investigating several banks in San José so that funds could be transferred there directly from Washington. To an increasing degree, then, Spinden and Lothrop were operating independently of Morley and Held. By November, ONI was giving serious consideration to putting Lothrop solely in charge in Costa Rica. His reports to Washington would be transmitted through the naval authorities in the Panama Canal Zone.[62]

Morley's frustrations with finances delayed his departure from Tegucigalpa for a week. As he explained to ONI, when he cabled on August 6 for an additional $1,500, he was unaware that on August 2 an ONI draft for $1,000 had arrived at the Bank of Honduras for Morley. The archaeologist only learned of this when, not hearing from ONI, by August 13 he became desperate and went to the bank to inquire if any money had arrived for him. When informed that funds had been there since the second, Morley "hauled them over the coals for this unbusinesslike and most inconvenient negligence." The bank personnel indignantly informed him that they had notified the American legation the very day the funds had arrived. "At the Legation no one remembers receiving this message and there the matter rests, like Mohamet's coffin suspended in midair between Cental American inefficiency and the more or less chaotic conditions prevailing at the Legation, where everybody uses the one phone which is located in the Chancellery and anybody could have received the message."[63]

The American legation in Tegucigalpa was currently being managed by the secretary, John W. Belt, who, to Morley's infinite relief, was quite cooperative, especially regarding that perennial problem area—communications. Morley was not at all optimistic about facilities on the north coast, but he was certain that it would be impossible to transmit cipher cables except by radio. Cables went through without delay, whereas a letter from Washington took three weeks to reach Tegucigalpa. The government telegraph office in the capital would not accept cipher messages, and there existed no direct cable links on the coast to the United States. The only possibility for direct communication would be to transmit radio messages on the two United Fruit steamers *Coppename* and *Suriname*, which touched at the port of Tela, or alternatively, on the Vaccaro Brothers steamships that left from La Ceiba. As Morley explained, "If the captains of these vessels were severally instructed to receive cipher messages from us it would greatly expedite my getting information into your hands. Indeed without it we could not reach you in haste with confidential matter except through Secretary Belt in Tegucigalpa." In anticipation of such an eventuality, Belt and Morley were working out a crude code in the form of apparently innocent messages in Spanish relating to his archaeological work. Certain words and phrases would have prearranged meanings, and they should cover every ordinary emergency. Should, for example, Morley discover a German submarine base thirty miles east of Trujillo, he would use the government telegraph to inform Belt that he'd discovered important archaeological remains thirty miles east of Trujillo at a specific location. Belt would then notify the State Department by a priority cable in his own code.[64]

There was no lack of rumors about German activities. The American consul at Puerto Cortés, Walter F. Boyle, had been in frequent communication with the legation in Tegucigalpa, forwarding reports of an alleged German submarine base somewhere on the north coast east of Trujillo. The consul was also concerned that some employees of the American Chicle Company were implicated. Morley of course planned to investigate, but he believed the submarine base story to be only idle rumor. As for American Chicle's involvement, the archaeologist was equally skeptical. He had known the company's manager, C. C. Jones, for ten years and was convinced he was a loyal American. In Morley's opinion, these rumors centered around the Caratasca Lagoon, where American Chicle's camp was located. The lagoon was the heart of and least-known area of the Mosquito Coast. Because of the Caratasca Lagoon's mysterious reputation, it furnished unending fodder for rumormongering.[65]

Among Morley's preparations for the trip was to ask his control to have Dr. Woodward, president of the Carnegie Institution, forward Morley's and Held's mail to the archaeologist care of the United States consulate at the northern port of Ceiba, Honduras. Morley also informed his ONI handler that this latest report of his from Tegucigalpa was the last time he would be able to express himself freely since it would be some time before he would again have access to a legation diplomatic pouch. His next report, number 10, should be read in light of this. On his way to the coast, Morley planned to stop at San Pedro Sula for a few days to investigate a rumor and check on the enemy, since there were some fifty Germans in that vicinity. He and Held would then continue on to Puerto Cortés, Tela, La Ceiba, and Trujillo. At Trujillo he intended to have his friend Jones, the American Chicle Company's manager, furnish him with letters of introduction to Jones's chicle camps, especially those around the Caratasca Lagoon.[66]

But after nearly four months in the field, Morley's morale was sagging, and he was becoming unsure of his role. As he informed his case officer:

> I do not know, my friend, whether we are giving you the information you want—indeed latterly all our material has been more suited to the State Department than to you—but we are always yours to command, and we are only actuated by the desire to serve where we best can. If others could be more useful down here, we are ready to return and go into something else.[67]

On August 18, 1917, Morley and Held set out for the north coast. Just getting there was going to take some doing, for it was the rainy season, and the rivers were raging torrents. Many of Morley's trips were arduous, but the north coast expedition would be in a class by itself.

5. The Mosquito Coast

Morley and Held set forth from Tegucigalpa for the north coast in style.[1] They traveled comfortably by automobile—for all of twenty miles. Then they reached a washed-out bridge and had to continue on by muleback. Morley was dismayed not only by the appearance of his little black mule (Morley hated mules), but also by the wretchedness of his saddle; one of the stirrups had been fashioned from a barrel hoop. His disposition was not improved when, as the party entered a narrow pass, one of the muleteers drew his revolver, explaining that the pass had been the scene of recent holdups and murders. They made it through without incident, however. Thereafter they had to concentrate on picking their way along a precipitous and treacherous trail. Held conceived the happy idea of using his air pillow on his saddle as a kind of shock absorber, an idea that Morley soon copied to good effect—until he managed to lose his pillow. The only break came when they stopped for a lunch of tortillas, beans, chicken, local cheese, and coffee. They finally reached Comayagua, Honduras's second-largest city and until 1880 the country's capital.[2] Morley and Held checked into the Hotel Central, on the plaza. Although they were exhausted, Morley dragged a reluctant Held off to inspect the imposing cathedral, which dated back to the colonial period. This first day on the road ended back at their hotel with Morley trying various remedies to alleviate the maddening itching from his numerous flea bites.

Succeeding days became a routine of rising early, coping with problems involving their mules, traversing mountain ranges, gingerly crossing swollen rivers, administering medicine to the muleteers when they became ill, and eating meals and spending the night in private homes along the way. Morley and Held slept on folding cots that were part of their considerable baggage. From time to time their journey was enlivened by drenching downpours. In addition to his other discomforts, Morley was covered from head to toe with prickly heat, while Held, who was not an accomplished equestrian, was extremely saddle sore.

Finally, after five days on muleback, they reached the railhead, Potrerillos. The weary travelers promptly drowned their troubles in an iced orangeade. Morley was not impressed with Potrerillos, observing that the town's only claim to fame was its location at the end of the railroad. When the line was extended Potrerillos would fade into richly deserved obscurity. The archaeologist's distaste for Potrerillos was heightened by the incredible swarms of mosquitos that added to his misery. He was already suffering so badly from heat rash and flea bites that he could not sleep. In desperation he bathed himself in whiskey. It stung like hell, but it did provide some relief.

While riding the train from Potrerillos to San Pedro Sula the miserable archaeologist and his equally flea-bitten colleague John Held could take considerable satisfaction in having completed a monumental reconnaissance that encompassed much of Guatemala, almost all of El Salvador, and the western third of Honduras. And in this vast territory they had found no indications of significant German activity.

Nor was there much German activity at San Pedro Sula, which they reached on July 23. The only potential threat was in the person of one Boem, manager of the local branch of the powerful commercial house of P. Rossner & Co., one of the two German firms that controlled shipping at the port of Amapala. Morley was told that Boem had been arrested in England at the beginning of World War I, but had secured his release because he was an honorary Honduran consul.[3] But the authorities were keeping an eye on him. Morley presented his letter from President Bertrand to the governor of the Department of Cortés, who extended him every consideration. A delighted Morley now compared his cherished presidential letter to Aladdin's lamp, for it was instantly smoothing his path wherever he presented it.

In San Pedro Sula, Morley was finally able to secure some talcum powder, which greatly relieved his skin condition. He spent much of the next few days continuing the treatments and writing in his diary, which he kept in a series of ledgers. Anticipating that he would soon finish filling up the current ledger, Morley went shopping for a stock of blank ones.

To his utter amazement he found a store carrying the same one he was using, and he quickly bought three more. Morley commented on what a unique experience it was in Central America to find exactly the item one was looking for.

Morley also confided in his diary his political views regarding Mexico and Central America. To him the issue was clear cut. Did these countries have the right to settle their domestic disturbances, which often involved the destruction or confiscation of foreign property, by themselves, or did foreign nations have the right to intervene, militarily if necessary, to prevent such disturbances? The answer was obvious: if they were unwilling or unable to maintain order, the United States and other nations would have to do it for them, by force if necessary. But Morley favored this approach not just for Latin America. He felt that this was what World War I was all about—Germany as an outlaw nation running amok and having to be subdued by an alliance of decent countries.

Having unburdened himself, Morley could now concentrate on preparations for the next phase of his assignment—investigating the north coast. While in San Pedro Sula, he made good use of his letter from President Bertrand, employing it to secure letters of introduction to the military commanders at the ports of La Ceiba, Trujillo, and Iriona. Morley and Held took the train to Puerto Cortés, where Morley conferred with Consul Boyle, who had been forwarding to Tegucigalpa rumors of a German submarine base on the Mosquito Coast and of American Chicle Company employees being involved with Germans. The consul was now of the opinion that the rumors amounted to nothing more than a proverbial tempest in a teapot. Morley concurred, referring to "the inevitable spy scare which has swept all over our country, and which down here immediately takes form as a submarine base on the Mosquito coast—chiefly because that region is so inaccessible and so little known." The American Chicle Company was above suspicion, even though there were a few German surnames among its officers. At present the company had 130 men, brought over from Belize, cutting chicle in the brush around the Caratasca Lagoon.[4]

At Puerto Cortés, Morley and Held had a bit of luck—the steamer *Coppename* was in port. The American consul took them out to the vessel, and Morley was able to mail letters directly on board, thus circumventing the Honduran authorities. He also bought a supply of cigarettes and caught up on world events through the ship's radio. Morley also prevailed on a passenger in a sailing vessel leaving for Belize to carry a letter to Dr. Gann, one which hopefully contained nothing compromising.

As for Morley himself, he and Held took passage on a sailing vessel traveling eastward along the coast to Tela. Morley noted that there existed two Telas, one on either side of a small stream: Old Tela was filthy, squalid, native; New Tela was clean, orderly, American. In Morley's view, the contrast was complete. Morley's letter from President Bertrand overawed the local authorities who were now eager to extend every assistance. So were the United Fruit Company's local managers, provided they received the necessary instructions. As Morley explained to his ONI case officer:

> The United Fruit Co. has wireless stations both at Tela and Trujillo, either of which is by far the quickest way we can get information out to you. As matters stand now, of course, they would refuse to accept a straight message from me, much less a cipher one. If you desire me to use that method of communication, Mr. Goodell the manager at Tela and Mr. Scott the manager at Trujillo should be notified to that effect. If any such step is taken will you kindly let me know in your letter to me at Bluefields.[5]

Pending access to United Fruit's radio facilities, Morley and Held were soon comfortably ensconced in the company's installations at New Tela. They dined at the mess and lodged with the Tela manager, but they soon transferred to the company hospital—Held was suffering from dysentery and Morley had come down with a serious attack of malaria. Yet Morley considered himself most fortunate that it occurred where it did. He commented that he didn't know what the archaeologist in the field in Central America would do without United Fruit. Its installations were the only places where one could live as in the United States, and its employees were almost the only congenial people to be found along the coast.

Even while battling malaria with heroic doses of quinine, Morley remained surprisingly active. For example, he devoted long hours to writing in his diary, which at this point was up to Volume IX, Part 1 (merely for the period covered in the present study, *i.e.*, April 1917–March 1919, the diary runs to approximately 1,050 typewritten pages). Evidently, the ultimate objective was to polish the diary for publication by the Carnegie

Institution. From time to time Morley used the phrase "gentle reader," hardly the kind of language to be found in a diary written just for Morley's personal consumption. While in the hospital, he also spent considerable time conversing with and questioning a local American, one "Red" Henry, who had recently returned from a month-long trip to the Mosquito Coast of Nicaragua as far as the Caratasca Lagoon. He had used a small United Fruit motorboat to search for German submarine bases. None was found.[6]

Morley continued making preparations for his coastal reconnaissance. He paid bills, cashed drafts, retrieved his and Held's passports from the local military, and laid in some supplies from the United Fruit commissary. On August 31, the Americans went aboard an eighty-foot sailing vessel, the *Kate Esau*, for the forty-four-mile run down the coast to La Ceiba. The boat was loaded to the gunwales with baggage and with fellow passengers who did not impress Morley; he found them to be malodorous, grubby, and obviously disreputable. Nor was the *Kate Esau* impressive; her engine broke down shortly after leaving port. Repairs were eventually made, and the *Kate Esau* managed to reach La Ceiba late in the day without further mishap.

Morley decided to make La Cieba, rather than Trujillo, his base of operations because it had better communications with the outside world—two direct sailings a week to New Orleans on the Vaccaro Brothers steamers, whereas Trujillo had none. Checking into the optimistically named Gran Hotel Paris in La Ceiba, Morley and Held found several telegrams awaiting them at the local telegraph office. For Morley, the most important of these messages was a cable from Dr. Woodward stating that the Carnegie Institution had allocated an additional $1,500 to support Morley's archaeological work. This sum, combined with the drafts from ONI, relieved much of the financial pressure. There was, however, no letter from ONI. Upon investigation several days later, the letter Morley was expecting turned up—dated August 9, it had been forgotten in a desk drawer at the American consulate in La Ceiba. Communications were still a problem. In his next report Morley mentioned to his control that he had received only four letters from him, dated May 28, June 18, June 25, and August 9. If ONI had sent him any others they had gone astray. And on the subject of communications:

About Sam Lothrop's work in Costa Rica. I have been out of touch with him for nearly four months now, in fact since the middle of May; letter communication between these countries is practically impossible, and telegraphic communications are scarcely better. I tried to reach him twice from Tegucigalpa but was unable to do so; and where we are now headed for, will be even worse.

I believe you will be able to reach him much more easily yourself, if you write to him directly from Boston, as I have not heard from him for a long time and do not even know where he now is.[7]

Morley left Held at La Ceiba, while he made a hurried trip to the Bay Islands to charter a vessel for their forthcoming expedition to the Caratasca Lagoon. The Bay Islands—Utila, Roatán, and Guanaja—lay some thirty miles off the north coast and were a part of Honduras. Their principal export was coconuts. A government boat was about to leave for Roatán, but was taking no passengers. The enterprising Morley promptly went to the governor's office and produced his presidential letter. He secured passage.

Morley was charmed by the Bay Islands and their inhabitants. The islanders were simple, kindly folk, predominantly of mixed English and African descent who spoke English and had a fierce hated for their Honduran fellow citizens. They were staunchly pro-British and could be counted on to report any German intrigues immediately. This was significant, for the islanders were born sailors and dominated the coastwise traffic, which they carried on in small craft of ten to fifty tons.[8] Most of these boats were built on Roatán, whose single town was a straggling village of houses with corrugated iron roofs, which Morley characterized as a kind of poor man's Belize, which was saying something indeed.

His trip was successful. He chartered the *Lilly Elena*, an unprepossessing sailing vessel, yawl rigged. She had a twenty-eight-foot keel, an eleven-foot beam, five-foot hold, and an eighteen-horsepower Monarch engine that ran on either gasoline or kerosene. The *Lilly Elena* had a draft of just three feet six inches, and her captain claimed that she would clear any bar along the Mosquito Coast, with which he was intimately familiar. The vessel had a crew of three—captain, engineer, and a deckhand. In addition, Morley hired a cook—a Jamaican who had served for fifteen years in the 1st West India Regiment. It cost $275 a month for the boat and four-man crew, and Morley also paid all port charges and fuel. He bought four hundred gallons of gasoline and kerosene, enough to reach Bluefields. The archaeologist was anxious to get under way from La Ceiba because there was only about a month of fair weather before the season of northers set in, making the north coast extremely hazardous for small craft.[9]

Upon returning from the Bay Islands to the hotel in La Ceiba, he was surprised to find his colleague John Held recovering from a serious bout of "distemper" that had kept him bedridden during Morley's absence. However, Held was on the road to recovery, and Morley's spirits were further raised by the mailbag of letters and newspapers awaiting him. He spent a whole morning happily reading all this material, and in the afternoon he celebrated with a leisurely bath, some more reading, an ice cream treat, and generally reveled in an interlude of unaccustomed idleness. But by the following day he was back at work. He spent hours writing his archaeological report for the Carnegie Institution *Year Book* and arranging for it to be typed. And he finished his report for ONI.

On the night of September 8, 1917, Morley and Held went aboard the *Lilly Elena*. The sea was rough even in the harbor of La Ceiba, and the pair were rowed out to their boat in a dory that they were terrified would capsize. Morley made no bones about the fact that both he and Held were thoroughgoing landlubbers who cut a pathetic figure at sea.

The next day the *Lilly Elena* arrived at the port of Trujillo, built along a bluff above the harbor. Dating back to the colonial period, Trujillo's location had given the Spaniards a panoramic view of any approaching buccaneers, the English in particular. A crumbling Spanish fort dominated the harbor, while along the beach were a few warehouses and commercial establishments, as well as United Fruit Company's railroad station. Trujillo's most recent claim to fame was that the American filibuster William Walker had been executed there on September 12, 1860.

Morley, curious as ever to explore his surroundings, took Held on a sightseeing tour of Trujillo that produced unforseen results. As Morley was preparing to take a snapshot of the charming old gate that was the main entrance to the fort, several soldiers rushed out and sternly announced that taking pictures was prohibited. When Morley protested, he was escorted to the commanding officer's quarters. That worthy sent word that he was too ill to talk with the likes of Morley. Outraged, Morley sent in his letter from President Bertrand, which heretofore had acted as a kind of magic wand when dealing with officialdom. The commander was not impressed, however. He sent back word that the matter was out of his jurisdiction and that Morley must secure permission from the mayor of Trujillo.

Morley's dander was now up. Fuming, he was escorted to the mayor, explained the problem, and was informed that the mayor had no objection to photography but that it was up to the commanding officer, whose fort after all it was. Back to the fort went Morley, to be told this time that he could not take photographs without a written order from the commanding officer. Despite protesting and brandishing the presidential letter, Morley had to make another trip to the commandant's quarters. The latter, perhaps realizing that the pesky gringo intended to persist over what the officer considered an inconsequential matter, grudgingly issued an order by telephone authorizing Morley to take photographs. Not only did Morley get to take his pictures, but he was permitted to roam all over the ancient fortification. The episode was an unpleasant reminder of the frustrations often involved in dealing with government officials, and it illustrated the dogged determination that figured so prominently in Morley's character.

He and Held enjoyed a brief taste of the good life, at Rincón, across the bay from Trujillo. The United Fruit Company had an installation at Rincón, and the travelers were hospitably received upon presenting their letter of introduction from the company. They enjoyed a delicious turkey dinner, had a checkup from the company doctor, and reveled in the house assigned to them—a dwelling that boasted a shower, indoor plumbing, beds with real springs and mattresses, and a screened veranda. The only drawback to this idyllic existence were the ubiquitous sandflies; even at social gatherings in the evenings, everybody scratched.

While at Rincón, Morley availed himself of United Fruit's resources for his coastal reconnaissance. He conversed at length with the manager about conditions along the coast, inspected company maps and charts, and arranged for Held to copy a navy chart that detailed the coast to a point about one hundred miles north of Bluefields. The United Fruit personnel even offered to assist Morley and Held in making a map of the entire coast, and the ONI operatives were given access to all the relevant data on file. In addition, Morley was allowed to buy whatever supplies he wanted at the commissary. The archaeologist hoped to take full advantage of these facilities on the return trip. At the moment he was concentrating on combating a major recurrence of heat rash that, among other things, made trying to sleep sheer agony.

After three days at the United Fruit complex at Rincón, Morley and Held were back in Trujillo making preparations to depart. To Morley's dismay, he learned that a special exit permit to clear the port was needed, and that it had to come from the same commanding officer who had given him the runaround over taking pictures at the fort. That obnoxious officer now adamantly asserted that no permit would be forthcoming because Honduras was under martial law. After heated discussion, Morley again produced his presidential letter, which of course the officer had already seen. Finally, he condescended to sign the necessary documents. Morley's blood pressure presumably then returned to normal.

The *Lilly Elena* sailed from Trujillo to Rincón, putting in there overnight to escape a norther that made sailing hazardous. Venturing out the next day, the vessel encountered heavy weather and soon ran aground on a bar. Morley later recalled that the sea pounded the boat for what seemed an eternity, and both he and Held were petrified with fear. Their terror actually lasted only some five minutes, though, for the captain worked the craft off the bar, and they soon entered a channel between two coastal villages. At one of these hamlets, Santa Rosa, the travelers celebrated to such an extent that they brought their gramophone ashore and proceeded to have a dance.

Resuming their journey, they dropped anchor off the port of Iriona, located on an exposed beach. Once again a reluctant Morley had to climb into a dory, this time to go ashore. At Iriona, Morley telegraphed to his colleague Joe Spinden, informing the latter that they hoped to meet him in Bluefields around October 15. Also, at Iriona they hired a pilot to navigate the *Lilly Elena* over the bar of the Black River, which led into a series of lagoons Morley wanted to investigate for any sign of German activity.

A painstaking examination of the area uncovered no Teutonic traces. What Morley and Held did find was a sprinkling of settlers living a marginal existence. A few of these forgotten souls were expatriate Americans, prompting Morley to comment disapprovingly on how the morals of whites in the tropics collapsed because of easy living and easy women. Still, Morley was certainly not averse to enjoying the hospitality of the locals, for whenever possible he and Held preferred to sleep ashore. Occasionally the Americans' constant inquiries about conditions produced suspicion and hostility, as in the case of one settler who initially refused to talk with them, being convinced that Morley and Held were detectives of some kind. As a welcome break from the detailed intelligence data they were amassing by taking soundings of the rivers, bays, and lagoons, Held amused himself by painting in water colors, including one of the *Lilly Elena*. Morley relaxed by writing in his diary.

By September 17 the intrepid explorers had worked their way along the northeastern coast of Honduras into the region known as Misquitia. Hiring a succession of native pilots, they had been systematically investigating the complex of godforsaken rivers and lagoons. But when they reached the Patuca River they came to grief. The Patuca was a sizeable river, and its bar had a fearsome reputation among captains plying the coast. But it was not this natural feature that caused the trouble; once again it was petty officialdom that aroused Morley's ire. The *Lilly Elena* crossed the Patuca bar and anchored near a village of Misquito Indians. The local military commander soon came aboard to examine the vessel's papers. He informed an incredulous Morley that the papers were not in order and therefore he could not clear the *Lilly Elena* to proceed on to the extensive Caratasca Lagoon—Morley's principal intelligence objective. In fact, the officer asserted that he would only clear the boat for the port of Iriona, which Morley had left fifty-five miles behind him. Despite Morley's protestations, the commandant was adamant.

The dilemma now confronting Morley was whether to proceed on to Caratasca without official permission, and run the risk of having the *Lilly Elena* seized, or somehow dispatch a letter to the authorities back in Iriona asking for guidance. Morley learned that the commandant was sending a soldier to Iriona with his report of the incident. The resourceful archaeologist dashed off a letter of his own, explaining to the authorities at Iriona what had happened and requesting that the *Lilly Elena* be cleared straight through to the Nicaraguan border. Morley then had a confidential chat with the soldier, offering him an honorarium if he returned with an answer by the following night. All Morley could do now was to wait and fume. His sense of outrage was intensified because he had sincerely tried to observe the letter of the law and was now being thwarted by an ignorant official so petty that he didn't even draw a salary. Morley and his companions roundly cursed him in several languages.

While awaiting developments, Morley worked on his diary and Held passed the time by reading. Periodically they would take time out to curse the commandant. Becoming bored, Held went hunting, for both doves and deer. Morley amused himself by playing gramophone records. To his amazement, the commandant had the gall to come aboard in order to enjoy the music. Morley cut him dead and the discomfited official soon left.

Besides coping with the usual irritants of sandflies and mosquitos, Morley and Held passed some of the time by sailing about twenty miles up the Patuca. In the course of this excursion, they shot at a large alligator, Held continued sketching, and Morley wrote in his diary. After forty-eight hours of anxious waiting, Morley and his companions spotted the returning messenger and hurried ashore to learn their fate. Morley was ecstatic to learn that among the documents the soldier had brought back from headquarters in Iriona were papers clearing the *Lilly Elena* through to Nicaragua, with stopover privileges anywhere along the way. Morley was so overjoyed that he even presented the intransigent commandant with tins of meat and some fruit as a parting gift.

They weighed anchor for Caratasca in high spirits, which were somewhat dampened when the *Lilly Elena* encountered frequent squalls. Nevertheless, on September 20 the yawl entered the forbidding Caratasca Lagoon, which was really a huge maze of interconnecting lagoons. To Morley's great relief, when the local military commander examined their papers he pronounced everything in order. Held promptly went ashore to hunt for birds in the vast savanna along the southern shore of the lagoon, while Morley busied himself taking photographs and gathering information. For days the *Lilly Elena* gingerly probed the labyrinth of waterways; not infrequently her propellor became fouled in grass and weeds, or the craft ran aground in shallow water, or progress was impeded by intermittent squalls. And at the end of each day's labors, her weary crew had to be in bed under mosquito netting by 7 P.M. to escape the swarms of voracious insects. As Morley had expected, their detailed reconnaissance of the Caratasca Lagoon turned up no sign of Germans.

By September 24, they emerged from the Caratasca Lagoon and sailed southeastward to Cape Gracias a Dios, the boundary between Honduras and Nicaragua. It was Christopher Columbus who had named the cape. During his fourth voyage to the New World, after battling foul weather along the Honduran coast for twenty-eight days, on September 14, 1502, he rounded a cape and enjoyed favorable currents and winds. In gratitude for his good fortune, he named the cape "Gracias a Dios"— "Thanks be to God."[10]

The Nicaraguan town of Cabo Gracias a Dios was an unimpressive collection of shabby wooden houses, but it contained a bit of good news for Morley. He learned that his colleague Joe Spinden had been there only a week earlier. Morley was frankly surprised that Spinden, with whom he had had no contact since they parted on July 25 at Amapala in the Gulf of Fonseca on the southwestern coast of Honduras, had turned up on the Atlantic coast of Nicaragua. The next day Morley received a letter Spinden had written him from Bluefields on September 18, upon returning from his trip to Cabo Gracias a Dios. Spinden was circumspect in what he wrote, but he indicated that Morley would find little of intelligence interest at Bluefields.

As the *Lilly Elena* worked her way down the Nicaraguan coast toward Bluefields, Morley adhered to his plan of systematically exploring the rivers, bays, lagoons, and mangrove swamps along the way. Despite the practice of taking soundings as they went, the *Lilly Elena* repeatedly grounded and had to be refloated with difficulty by her weary and exasperated crew.

A memorable incident of the journey occurred when they spotted a group of some fifteen treasure hunters on a beach. Given the level of pirate activity along this coast, especially during the seventeenth century, it was a wonder that many more people were not engaged in digging for buried treasure. Morley decided to investigate. Prudently strapping on his revolver, he went ashore. The treasure hunters proved to be harmless; Morley wished them luck and started back to the *Lilly Elena*. A short distance offshore, however, he was frightened out of his wits when the treasure hunters set off a dynamite charge near the water's edge, a procedure they repeated several more times before the *Lilly Elena* got under way.

Farther down the coast, in the Karata Lagoon, Morley finally got a whiff of Germanic machinations. There was a brisk trade in mahogany logs along the Wawa River, which emptied into the Karata Lagoon. The Wawa Commercial Company figured prominently in this traffic, and its head, Richard Lehmann, was a German. Although Lehmann claimed to be an American citizen and vehemently expressed his pro-Ally sentiments, Morley didn't trust him. He felt that Lehman was clever, much more so than his cousin Otto, who had given Morley the letter from Spinden. Otto was merely a "fat ordinary type of German Jew," whereas Lehman was quite obviously a man to be reckoned with. In Morley's considered opinion, Lehmann could be counted upon to be for the Fatherland and against the United States in any situation where Germans had at least an even chance of winning. But then this assessment could also apply to virtually every other German Morley encountered in Central America.

The next stop for the expedition was the port of Prinzapolka, which Morley described as being both larger and better looking than Cabo Gracias a Dios. Prinzapolka was surrounded by water on three sides, and its structures were built of sawed lumber, were painted, and had corrugated iron roofs. Prinzapolka even boasted boardwalks. Morley was of course anxious to get in touch with Spinden. He tried to telephone him, but the line was down. The best Morley could do was to send Spinden a telegram announcing that he would be in Bluefields in two or three days.

Discovering that a circus was in town, Morley and company excitedly planned to attend. They learned, however, that no performance was scheduled that night, and the *Lilly Elena* was to depart from Prinzapolka the next morning. Morley rose to the occasion. Feeling that he and his companions were overdue for something enjoyable, he proposed that the circus give them a private performance. After lengthy negotiations, a price of $10 was agreed on. As one can imagine, this circus was hardly Ringling Brothers, but to its appreciative audience it might as well have been. Morley was quite satisfied that they had gotten their money's worth.

The *Lilly Elena* finally reached Bluefields at 6 P.M. on September 30, anchoring off the customshouse wharf. Morley found Bluefields comparatively impressive. The town stretched for about a mile along a small bluff. The houses were more presentable than those of most coastal towns, being made of sawed lumber with roofs of corrugated iron and, for the most part, painted white. What also struck Morley was the number of Chinese-owned stores. But these thirty-odd establishments were really only glorified trading posts. Bluefields also had, of all things, a Moravian church. The town's main street, moreover, boasted cement sidewalks. The town lacked electric street lights, but it did have an ice plant.

While waiting to clear Customs, Morley was introduced to a young Frenchman named Craput, who had an import-export business in Bluefields. His partner, a young German named Kooper, had just lost his position because of his Teutonic origin. Whatever satisfaction Morley felt from learning that yet another German had been removed from a position of influence was more than offset by what he learned from Craput. The Frenchman and the archaeologist became involved in a conversation about American involvement in Nicaragua. According to Craput, the only explanation for the way the United States had permitted Brown Brothers of New York to exploit Nicaragua on a wholesale basis was as a preliminary to preparing the Nicaraguan public for the annexation of the country! Craput seemed to have the facts at his fingertips, and his denunciation of American imperialism shook Morley. The latter had naively believed that for the last few years the United States had been lending a helping hand to its "little brother," but it turned out that this lending was at compound and extortionate rates of interest. American policy had left the Nicaraguan government with little credit, either financially or in the public mind. The government was in such straits that it had trouble even meeting its payroll. Morley was chagrined to admit that he could offer only a feeble defense of his country's actions. For Morley, who tended to see things in black-and-white terms, Craput's interpretation of U.S. relations with Nicaragua was a revelation. Like it or not, Morley's mission in Central America was broadening his political vision.

But his main focus remained his ONI assignment. At his hotel, Morley spent the entire day preparing his reports. His progress was impeded by a malfunctioning typewriter, but fortunately he had a spare aboard the *Lilly Elena*. In his report, Morley gave his general conclusions. Based on his painstaking investigation, he cited three elements that characterized the Mosquito Coast. First, the water at the bars at the mouths of the rivers was shallow, with an average depth of five to nine feet. Generally speaking, the water was deepest in September and October and shallowest from March through May. Second, the bars were constantly shifting, and these changes were often abrupt. Thus, charts of the coastal waterways were quickly made obsolete. Third, from October to March was the season for northers, which churned up such heavy seas that crossing the bars was usually impossible, even for small craft. Steamers hauling mahogany sometimes had to stand out to sea for a month before the water subsided enough for tugs to tow the rafts of logs out to the ships. During a norther even the intrepid Bay Island captains raced for shelter, either back to their home ports or to Cape Gracias a Dios. Morley stated that "all things considered, therefore, it would seem that the physical conditions of this littoral are such as to practically preclude its use by the Germans for submarine bases." Another fact of equal importance was the small number of Germans on the Mosquito Coast. From Trujillo to Bluefields there were not more than fifty, while Americans outnumbered them three to one. Morley concluded: "I believe danger from submarine bases on this coast to be remote, and with any reasonable sort of surveillance little short of impossible."[11]

He strongly recommended that such surveillance be conducted by American or English residents of the region who were already thoroughly familiar with local conditions, rather than by secret agents such as himself. The locals could be instructed to report any suspicious circumstances by letter or, if urgent, by radio to the State, Navy, or War departments in Washington. Morley was already constructing such a network. On his way down to Bluefields he had evaluated potential subagents, and on the return journey to Trujillo he would recruit them. But the archaeologist was cautious; he was not going to give them ONI's accommodation addresses, feeling that these should be kept in as few hands as possible. Besides, if the subagents should have anything to report it would in all probability be of an urgent nature, and would be sent by radio.[12]

Attached to his letter was a more detailed report containing information on every place they had visited, and they had visited a lot of places: "During the trip we crossed every bar on the Mosquito Coast between Trujillo and Bluefields, which a boat drawing 4 feet could get over, and explored the rivers, bays and lagoons to which they bar entrance."[13] This fifteen-page, single-spaced typed supplement was not limited to describing rivers and lagoons, however. It included lists of Americans, Britons, and Germans living on the Mosquito Coast, their ages, and brief comments about each one. In addition, Morley listed and described every powerboat and riverboat in the region. (See Appendix 1.)

The next day, October 12, he wrote another report to ONI outlining his future plans. By the end of the month he hoped to be back in La Ceiba. But on the way he wanted to check out a few things on the Bay Islands. He also intended to tie up some loose ends in Guatemala and northern Honduras. First on the agenda, though, was a quick trip to Belize—twenty-four hours from La Ceiba—to see a dentist. Morley had broken a tooth on a piece of candy; a local dentist had put in a temporary filling, but the archaeologist wanted to get the tooth crowned before he lost it. From Belize he could investigate how to organize a reconnaissance of the Yucatán coast. If such an enterprise met with ONI approval his case officer could notify him in his next letter.

Morley asked that he and Held be permitted to return to Washington around the first of the year

so that I can lay before you personally the nature of the problem
here, and its special needs and requirements. A great deal of this,
particularly the organization of our field-parties, methods of communication, spheres of operation etc. can best be worked out there
in Washington through personal conferences. The past six months
has given us a great deal of practical experience in the work and if
this can be effectively utilized, I believe the general efficiency of the
whole project would be promoted.[14]

In addition, Morley had some matters to attend to at the Carnegie
Institution. And a month or so of Washington winter weather would do
him and Held a world of good. They were both rather run down after
six months of almost-continuous movement in the tropics under all sorts
of conditions. But the archaeologist was most anxious that ONI not mis-
understand his motives in requesting leave:

If we are doing any real and useful service for the good of the cause,
we both want to continue to serve wherever and whenever you think
best. As I wrote you in an earlier letter, we want to serve where we
can be of the most use. On the other hand if this work is to continue down here, I believe the above suggestion will result in its
improvement if followed out.[15]

The archaeologist did not of course spend all his time working on
reports. There was a joyful reunion with Joe Spinden, who got Morley
and Held rooms in the hotel where he was lodging. This establishment—
Petersen's Hotel—was owned by a Prussian, but Morley was able to
overlook that fact, perhaps because Petersen gave them two rooms—
with a bath. The private bath was a wholly unexpected luxury on the
Mosquito Coast.

Morley thoroughly enjoyed seeing his good friend Joe Spinden again,
for he had sorely missed Spinden's contentious ways and his always
insightful comments. A whole afternoon was given over to catching up.
In what was a most rational arrangement dictated by circumstances,
Spinden was now being run by the ONI station in Ancón, Panama Canal
Zone. Morley helped him decode a letter that arrived from that head-
quarters. It was from J. J. Perdomo—ONI Agent No. 93—informing
Spinden that all United Fruit radio stations except the one at Santa Marta,

Colombia, had been instructed to accept all messages whether encoded or not, for a certain address in Panama, to which Morley was now privy.[16]

Just prior to the arrival of Morley and Held, Spinden had been going through newspaper files in Bluefields, taking copious notes on articles dealing with Nicaragua's financial crises. Earlier, he had seen the archaeologist Samuel Lothrop, who was currently operating in Costa Rica. Lothrop had been joined by his wife, Rachel, who would prove to be no mean intelligence agent in her own right. At another level, Morley and Spinden indulged in prolonged archaeological gossip. Spinden also brought out a copy of a handbook he had written. Morley was impressed. Having brought each other up to date, they took a leisurely stroll through Bluefields and topped it off with oyster cocktails at Borden's ice cream parlor.

Unbeknownst to Morley, he, Held, and Spinden weren't the only secret agents in Bluefields. On October 5, Morley ruefully recorded in his diary that he and Held had been summarily evicted from their comfortable hotel room to make way for some American who had arrived the day before on a sailing vessel from down the coast and who was going to be in Bluefields for some time. That evening Morley met the individual who had so abruptly dispossessed him and Held—one Cyrus F. Wicker of New York. Though Wicker was only thirty-four years old, he looked much older because, going bald, he had shaved his head. Morley and Spinden soon found themselves playing cards with Wicker, whom they came to view as a very decent sort of chap. Their opinion of Wicker soared when the latter casually mentioned that he was interested in the Maya and had even read John Lloyd Stephens's classic travel accounts on the subject.[17] Spinden and Morley immediately bombarded Wicker with Mayan lore and, as scholars are prone to do, recommended a long list of books he must read.

Spinden pursued their ripening acquaintance with Wicker, conversing with him for an entire afternoon. He learned that Wicker had been secretary in the American legation in Managua, Nicaragua, two years earlier, but had in effect been fired because of his outspoken criticism of what the United States was permitting Brown Brothers to do. Wicker was an attorney specializing in international law. He was currently considering writing an exposé of American involvement in Nicaragua. And it turned out that Wicker was a member of the Cosmos Club, as were Morley and Joe Spinden.[18] The three men held their improbable Cosmos Club reunion in a sweltering Nicaraguan seaport.

Wicker, who was ostensibly in Nicaragua representing some American sugar interests, eventually revealed that he too worked for the Office of Naval Intelligence. He was in fact ONI Agent No. 165.[19] Wicker had been reconnoitering the coast from Limón, Costa Rica, up to Bluefields. He planned to return to Limón in a few days. For Morley and Spinden, this was a splendid turn of events—encountering a convivial fellow ONI agent who seemed passionately interested in the Maya and belonged to the right club to boot. The three were now not just colleagues but boon companions as well.

Unfortunately, at the very time that Morley, Spinden, and Wicker were becoming such friends, Morley's relations with John Held, his loyal associate throughout his Central American adventures, reached a crisis. While Morley worked on his next ONI report, he had assigned to Held the task of preparing a detailed map of the coast to accompany it. Held dashed the map off in the short space of three hours. Morley considered the map wholly unsatisfactory. For one thing, the paper didn't take ink well; for another, Held had hurried. Morley was reluctant to send ONI such a shoddy product. Held maintained that it was good enough for government work. An irate Morley informed him that "good enough" was his worst fault, that he should make "best possible" his motto. Held became furious, snatched the map and tore it up. Morley ruefully ascribed Held's tantrum to an outburst of "the artistic temperament."

Although this was only the second quarrel the two men had had during six months of living together under often trying circumstances, it was nevertheless serious enough to produce sober reflection on each one's part. By the end of the day they had made up. Yet, even though mapmaking was Held's principal intelligence duty, Morley had decided to find another cartographer for the wretched map in question. Held did not object. Morley managed to locate an old Frenchman who knew how to draw maps, and engaged his services. With Morley stressing that time was of the essence, the Frenchman took Held's torn map as a basis for his work and promised to do his best. Most improbably, he delivered. Within forty-eight hours he returned with a map that even the demanding Morley considered "a really good job." Morley was delighted to pay him his fee of twenty dollars. The archaeologist proudly enclosed the map with the report to ONI that he mailed from Bluefields in a local merchant's private pouch. But sending sensitive material through an insecure channel was probably not what a professional spy would have done.

Though Morley had failed to find any German submarine bases on the Mosquito Coast, he did strike a blow for the Allied cause while in Bluefields—in a manner of speaking. The archaeologist entered into a heated discussion about World War I with Nicolay Petersen, the Prussian from Konigsberg who owned the Hotel Petersen. It may be speculated that Morley's antagonism toward Petersen stemmed not only from the latter's spirited defense of Germany's conduct, but also from the fact that Petersen had evicted Held and Morley from their pleasant hotel room in favor of Wicker. In any case, the thrust of Morley's argument was that the Allies were having to fight the whole German nation, not just the German government. He confided in his diary that it might be necessary to kill all the older Germans—like Petersen—who belonged to the generation of 1870, which had been brought up believing in German invincibility. Morley just didn't like Germans—at least not adult male Germans. But he did get along quite well with Mrs. Petersen, who prepared their meals, referring to her as "a good German lady."

A much more pleasant aspect of his stay in Bluefields had to do with his health. Morley was finally able to get relief from the prickly heat that had been torturing him for the past three months. He consulted an American doctor, who quickly diagnosed the trouble as not being prickly heat at all, but rather a type of fungus transmitted by bacteria in the water. The doctor and his wife had even suffered from the same skin condition when they first came to Bluefields. In the doctor's opinion, Morley had become infected when his clothes had been washed by native washerwomen. As a cure he prescribed a strong sulphur ointment, and urged Morley to have his clothes boiled after every washing to prevent reinfection. Although greasy and smelly, the salve worked.

On Morley's last afternoon in Bluefields, Wicker arranged for him to meet a Mr. Easton, who was superintendent of the United Fruit radio stations at Limón, Costa Rica, and at Swan Island.[20] Back at Morley's hotel, the archaeologist asked if Easton could arrange for the ONI agents' messages to be accepted at Tela and Rincón by United Fruit's radio stations. Morley reminded Easton that other United Fruit stations had been instructed to accept ONI messages. Disappointingly, Easton pointed out that the concessions under which United Fruit operated in Honduras were very strictly worded, and only regular company traffic was permitted to go through those stations. Easton did speculate that since Honduras was a quasi-ally, if the State Department requested a general permission to use those radio stations for official business it would be readily granted. But, unless the Honduran government granted formal permission for the United States government to use those facilities in emergencies, the only way Morley could make use of those stations was clumsy at best: Morley would have to give his message to the local United Fruit manager and request that he send it under the manager's name to the company's head office in Boston with a request that it be forwarded to Washington. To make the best of an unsatisfactory situation, Morley recommended that some arrangement be made so that the United Fruit stations at Tela and Rincón, as well as the Vaccaro Brothers station at La Cieba, could be so utilized.[21] The problem of communications thus remained perhaps Morley's greatest worry.

This last bit of business having been concluded, there followed a round of festivities highlighted by the drinking of much beer and the playing of gramophone records. The travelers were then escorted to the wharf by a group of boisterous well wishers that included Wicker and Joe Spinden. Morley was moved, especially by having to leave Spinden. Why, Morley later mused, was he always having to say goodbye to Spinden, whose mind he admired more than anyone else's and whose friendship he cherished above anyone else's.

The American Museum of Natural History was quite pleased with Spinden's anthropological endeavors and, in March 1918, asked him to continue his fieldwork in Central America, at his present salary of $2,200 a year. Spinden, of course, did so, but he also continued his undercover work for ONI. In Nicaragua, he kept an eye on the local Germans and also stimulated the output of mahogany, for airplane propellers. In August 1918, he would send a detailed report on these matters to Charles Sheldon, a.k.a. "Taro," at the Cosmos Club. Spinden had been on leave and sailed from New Orleans, via Havana and Panama, to Colombia to report on that country's platinum deposits, an assignment on which he cooperated closely with the British minister. He operated under anthropological cover, returning to the United States in December 1918.[22]

Leaving Spinden behind, the *Lilly Elena* sailed majestically out of Bluefields with Morley's gramophone on deck blaring out a jazz tune. The voyage was unpleasant from the start. The first day out, Morley was prostrated by seasickness, spending the whole day sprawled miserably on deck. The next day, the *Lilly Elena* ran aground on the bar as she sailed into Cabo Gracias a Dios. When it became evident that the yawl was stuck fast, Morley joined the captain in what proved to be a terrifying ride in the dory to secure assistance ashore. A tug eventually went out and freed the *Lilly Elena*. This matter of the *Lilly Elena* running aground at bars had become an unpleasant routine. For example, Morley reported that when both entering and leaving the mouth of the Wanks River they grounded on the bar. The water had been five feet deep when they had been there only a fortnight earlier on their way down to Bluefields. Now it was less than three feet deep. And, Morley reminded his case officer, the Wanks was the largest river on the Atlantic coast of Central America. Tough going for any German submarine.

At Cabo Gracias a Dios, Morley met the British consul, a Mr. Blakesley, and they hit it off from the start. Blakesley had been keeping the Lehmann cousins, Otto and Richard, under surveillance, because he didn't trust that pair of Germans. Neither, of course, did Morley. And Morley expressed his satisfaction at knowing that a person of Blakesley's intelligence was looking after Allied interests on this part of the coast. But just to be sure, Morley recruited a subagent at Cabo Gracias a Dios, one P. A. Bischoff, acting manager of the C. C. Mengel Brothers Mahogany Company.[23]

Morley's career nearly ended prematurely while he was in Cabo Gracias a Dios. He amused himself not only by dining at a Chinese restaurant and by exploring the town, but also by attending a performance of a circus that happened to be in town. But just before the performance Morley was accosted by a drunk who drew a revolver and announced his intention of shooting the archaeologist. Since he was only some eight feet away, he could hardly have missed. Morley, who was unarmed, kept his head, explaining to the man why shooting him was not a good idea. He gradually moved near the man, finally being able to put his arm around the drunk's shoulder, guide him gently back into the crowd, and suggest that he put the gun away. The drunk moved on, but he defiantly fired a shot in the air; the ensuing panic delayed the circus performance by half an hour. Nearly being shot by a drunk was not the only peril Morley faced that night. During the performance, Morley began lusting after the lovely bareback rider. He went backstage and propositioned her. Unfortunately for the archaeologist, she was married to the circus strongman, who took violent exception, grabbed Morley by the nape of the neck, and started with him for the end of the pier, explaining to the struggling American that he was going to shoot him and throw his body to the sharks. Yet by the time they reached the end of the pier, not only had Morley dissuaded him, but he had established an instant rapport with the outraged husband. They returned arm in arm and proceeded to visit every cantina in the vicinity. In recounting this incident, a friend commented admiringly: "That was Morley. He could charm a bird out of a bush."[24]

Even the *Lilly Elena*'s departure from Cabo Gracias a Dios was not without excitement. The boat quickly ran aground in the channel. The crew hoisted her flag upside down in hopes that someone would see the distress signal. No one did, but with great effort the crew succeeded in backing the *Lilly Elena* into deeper water and returning to port. To prevent a recurrence when the yawl tried again to leave the next day, the tug towed the *Lilly Elena* over the bar. The vessel made it this time, although she scraped her bottom for some fifty yards before being towed into deep water.

This rough treatment had repercussions. Sailing along with a favorable wind and current, the *Lilly Elena* was passing the entrance to the Caratasca Lagoon when it became apparent that she had sprung a leak. The crew pumped furiously, but water continued to rise in the hold. After a while, the level reached the engine flywheel, which sprayed water on the magneto, which short circuited. The *Lilly Elena* was dead in the water.

The crew redoubled their efforts and pumped out the hold, at least temporarily. When the sodden baggage was checked, Held found his best pair of trousers ruined, while Morley lamented the soaking of a brand new pair of pajamas. More importantly, the vessel still leaked and had to be pumped out every half hour to keep from foundering. She got under way again, her engine now powered by batteries. But by evening the batteries were running down, and the engine started missing. The captain decided to stop the engine in order to conserve the batteries; the *Lilly Elena* was now propelled only by whatever slight breeze her sails could catch. The situation was more inconvenient than dangerous, except of course in the event of a sudden norther. Fortunately, the weather held.

One of the crewmen had been trying to rebuild the magneto, but couldn't for lack of a hacksaw. Morley to the rescue! For the past three years he had been carrying around a repair kit that an enterprising Abercrombie & Fitch salesman had convinced him was indispensable. The heretofore-unused kit contained a hacksaw. The magneto was repaired and, to the general jubilation, actually functioned—for all of twenty minutes before it burned out. The last battery was then connected and the engine ran—for another five miles before the battery ran down. To the crew's infinite relief, however, a strong breeze sprang up. The *Lilly Elena* limped into the harbor of Trujillo on October 17.

At Trujillo, Morley and Held temporarily parted company. Held remained aboard the *Lilly Elena*. The vessel was bound for the Bay Islands, specifically for Guanaja, where she would be repaired. The yawl had suffered significant damage. Not only was there a major leak where the propellor shaft entered the stern, but the keel was badly wrenched and had even come loose in one place. The vessel would need repairs in a dry-dock. While Morley was on the wharf examining the *Lilly Elena*, to his amazement he saw a familiar figure approaching. It was Arthur Carpenter, who had been Morley's associate on the ill-fated 1916 expedition.[25] The last Morley had heard of Carpenter, the assistant secretary of the Carnegie Institution, Walter M. Gilbert, had taken him to lunch at the Cosmos Club. Gilbert had told Carpenter that Morley was traveling in Central America. Carpenter was currently working for a New York dyewood firm that had contracts with the Quartermaster Department. He was passing through Trujillo en route to inspecting a tract of timber in the interior. Always starved for news, Morley listened avidly to Carpenter's account of the latest doings in Washington, where confusion reigned as usual. Morley was amused, but he also attributed the confusion to a great, complacent democracy gearing up for the serious business of fighting a war. After their brief and unexpected reunion, Morley and Carpenter went their separate ways, hoping to meet again in La Ceiba in about ten days.

Morley took the United Fruit Company's train to Rincón and again was hospitably received by the company's manager, who put the archaeologist up in his own home. Waiting for Morley at the company office was a letter from J. J. Perdomo, the ONI agent stationed in Panama. When Morley read the letter, he found that it covered the same ground as Perdomo's letter to Spinden that Morley had helped the latter decipher in Bluefields.

While in Rincón, Morley did accomplish several pieces of intelligence work. He made his pitch to the Rincón manager, Harry D. Scott, who enthusiastically agreed to become a subagent. Scott obligingly had his staff prepare a better map of the Mosquito Coast than the one Morley had sent ONI from Bluefields. This involved considerable frustration because the paper was humid and absorbed the ink, which was too watery; the

pen points rusted; and the erasers dried out. Morley observed philosophically that like everything else in the tropics, such as men, morals,
and money, even drafting supplies deteriorated. Morley dispatched the
improved version by the next mail. He had such confidence in Scott that,
with his consent, the archaeologist sent John Belt in Tegucigalpa Scott's
name and address as a trustworthy person with whom Belt should
communicate.[26]

Except for the maddening sandflies, Morley's stay at Rincón was
quite pleasant. He spent several mornings bringing his diary up to date.
His problem here was his verbosity; even he recognized that the diary
entries were much too long. Although he recognized the problem, he
seemed unable to adopt a briefer style. Morley also caught up on his reading, and he visited a nearby Maya archaeological site. Moreover, he began
writing a review of his friend Joe Spinden's *Ancient Civilizations of
Mexico and Central America*, which was No. 3 in the American Museum
of Natural History's Handbook Series. Ever the tourist, Morley secured
new permission to photograph the old fort at Trujillo; his earlier photos
had been ruined while being developed. What made this excursion delicious was that the individual assigned to escort Morley around was the
same churlish officer who had given him so much trouble earlier. The
archaeologist took a perverse delight in leading him all over the plaza in
the blinding sunlight. Morley even managed to do a bit of shopping. He
bought a selection of gramophone records including, thoughtfully
enough, one that had John Held's favorite piece—*Swing Low Sweet
Chariot*, as performed by a double quartet from the Tuskegee Institute.

The interlude of relaxation ended on October 23, when the refur-
bished *Lilly Elena* sailed into Trujillo harbor. The next day Morley sailed
to the Bay Island of Roatán, for it developed that the *Lilly Elena* required
still further repair. He thoroughly enjoyed the hospitality of the islanders,
dancing enthusiastically with a succession of comely young ladies, playing cards, and feasting. He also had a pleasant reunion with John Held.
When the two Americans separated at Trujillo on October 17, Held had
sailed on the *Lily Elena* to the island of Guanaja. While awaiting the
repair of the vessel, Held had thoroughly inspected the island, conclud-
ing what everyone already knew—that there was no sign of German activity and that the population was staunchly pro-Ally. But soon it was time
to get back to work. The voyage from Roatán, however, turned out quite
differently from what Morley had anticipated.

6. Banana Country

Morley and Held sailed from the small port of Oak Ridge on Roatán in the early morning of November 2, 1917. Their destination was La Ceiba, only thirty miles away. They were halfway there when, to their growing dismay, they were caught in the first norther of the season, and not just any norther but the worst storm in twenty years. For this pair of land-lubbers, it must have been an absolutely terrifying experience. As the force of the gale increased, the twenty-seven-foot *Lilly Elena* was soon in trouble. The captain faced a grim dilemma—they couldn't make it to La Ceiba, and even if by some miracle they reached that port, there was no safety. La Ceiba was an exposed roadstead with no protection of any sort. Whatever shipping was there had already fled for shelter in the Bay Islands. In desperation, the captain steered for Los Cochinos—the Hog Islands—twenty miles east of La Ceiba, which proved the truth of the saying, "Any port in a storm," for there was no harbor at Los Cochinos, a five-hundred-foot rock with a fringe of coral and sand, some three-fourths of a mile in diameter and surrounded by dangerous shoals and reefs. The Americans' boat and two other small craft that also took refuge at Los Cochinos had to keep moving from the east to the west side of the island and back again as the norther shifted direction.

The ONI agents had a frightening experience, but they could count themselves fortunate. A schooner of about forty tons, the *Brilliant*, had fled from La Ceiba at noon on November 2, seeking the safety of Roatán. But throughout the afternoon and evening the gale increased in force and the vessel finally went out of control. At 10 P.M. she smashed into the reef just off the western end of Los Cochinos. As the *Brilliant* began breaking up the crew abandoned ship in their lifeboat. They came very close to drowning in the surf along the reef; according to the captain it was breaking fifty feet high. The *Brilliant's* crew finally managed to reach Sandy Key a half mile offshore, and happily they were rescued the next morning.[1]

The Americans were spared that kind of ordeal, but their situation still left something to be desired. They immediately went ashore on Los Cochinos to wait for the weather to clear sufficiently for them to resume their voyage to La Ceiba. They couldn't continue on the *Lilly Elena* because she had sailed off for repairs. So they settled down to await developments. And developments were slow in coming—they were to be stranded on Hog Island for the next eighteen days.

Although in his next report Morley said of his and Held's involuntary stay that they had been "living in a little driftwood shack in a grove of cocoanut . . . [in] the most approved Robinson Crusoe fashion . . ." this was not exactly the case.[2] They had been taken in by a local family who extended cheerful hospitality to their unexpected guests.[3] During his enforced stay on Los Cochinos, Morley spent most of his time writing, on one day from 7 A.M. until 10 P.M., with time off for meals and a brief swim. He wrote in his diary, finished his glowing review of Spinden's book, worked on a forthcoming Carnegie Institution publication, and typed his next ONI report.

Quite reluctantly, he also tackled his ONI expense account from August 1 on—a most distasteful task, for Morley was certainly no accountant. As he himself admitted, he tended to spend money but often forgot to record or document the expenditures, and then had to make it up out of his own pocket. This comment was no exaggeration—the last time Morley had prepared his expense account he had had to contribute $200 of his own money to make it balance. This was no inconsiderable expenditure for a man earning $2,640 a year. Now he was faced with accounting for expenditures at Tegucigalpa and the trip to San Pedro Sula, to Puerto Cortés, to Tela and La Ceiba, then to the Bay Islands, to Trujillo, down the Mosquito Coast to Bluefields, and back to Trujillo and the Bay Islands, plus the *Lilly Elena's* charter. Understandably, he had procrastinated about tackling the job, which he compared to cleaning the Augean stables. When he finished wading through the mass of bills and receipts he discovered to his horror that he was $250 short. But he found some additional vouchers, so this time the hapless archaeologist only had to contribute $100 of his own money to make the account balance.

While Morley toiled with the expense account, his companion passed the time by plunging into "a frenzy of work." Held not only sketched furiously, but painted three or four watercolors a day; in Morley's opinion, Held's sketches were usually better than his watercolors. Besides, Held was happier and less restless when painting instead of sitting around cursing the bugs, the food, the heat, the people, and the country. Held also worked off some energy by volunteering to do odd jobs for their hostess, such as building a new kitchen floor and repairing the kitchen stove. A possible reason for Held's frenetic activity was that he had run out of tobacco; Morley, on the other hand, could feel morally superior because he had stopped smoking on September 1.

Though not suffering from nicotine deprivation, Morley too was restless. This period of enforced inaction on Hog Island was making him increasingly impatient, for his temperament was one of continual activity fueled by nervous energy.[4] Although Hog Island was only a tantalizing eight miles from the mainland, it seemed impossible to get transportation there. Once again Morley displayed his letter from President Bertrand, but even so the captain of a government boat refused to give them a lift. Several sailboats touched at Hog Island, but Morley couldn't persuade any of their captains to take him and Held to La Ceiba, partly because of adverse weather—a series of northers. Morley was beginning to think they were jinxed.

The oddest aspect of their sojourn had to do with their diet. In his report, Morley made a point of stating that he and Held had subsisted on beans, bread, and tea three times a day for the first ten of their eighteen days on Hog Island, and he implied that beans were their staple diet for the remainder of their enforced stay.[5] And indeed they consumed more than their share of beans. Morley had indigestion every night and wondered which would last the longer—the beans or Eno's Fruit Salts, the only antidote at hand. But in his diary Morley also noted that there were many chickens and pigs running around, and mentioned that local fishermen had caught five lobsters. One can only wonder why the Americans didn't try some of this more appetizing fare. Perhaps Morley was embroidering the "Robinson Crusoe" aspect of their Hog Island interlude.

After weeks of eagerly scanning the horizon for vessels, on November 17 deliverance arrived in the shape of the *Sybilla*, a shabby tramp steamer that plied between the north coast of Honduras and New Orleans carrying bananas. The *Sybilla* was a study in downward mobility. The thirty-three-year-old vessel, 110 feet long, had been built as a yacht for a member of the Busch brewing family for use on the Great Lakes. Then she was converted into a fancy floating gambling den, and now she had sunk to being a tramp steamer. The *Sybilla* was in such a rundown condition that she couldn't carry freight; she had been condemned by the underwriters as uninsurable. But to Held and Morley she must have looked like a luxury liner.

The *Sybilla* had stopped at Hog Island to blow her boilers. Somehow Morley learned that the captain was a Mason, at which point the archaeologist knew they were home free. Presumably, Morley gave the captain the Masonic grip, for the latter readily agreed to take them to La Ceiba. Moreover, he fed them wonderful things, things that made beans seem like just a bad dream. Captain Sánchez invited Morley and Held aboard for a lunch of lobster, potatoes, fried onions, and even an apple. For dinner the menu was corned beef and cabbage, spaghetti, pickles, bread, and tea. Best of all, the captain took them off Hog Island, on November 20. The voyage to the mainland took less than an hour.

The ship stood off the port of Nueva Armenia to load bananas, and Morley went ashore to have his and Held's names added to the *Sybilla's* manifest. While in town, the archaeologist encountered a pair of Germans, one of whom he described as a little rat-eyed specimen. Although both Germans professed pro-Allied sentiments, Morley was not unhappy to leave the company of "these alien enemies."

The *Sybilla* finished loading and wheezed down the coast to La Ceiba, reaching that port before the weather again became dangerous. The two Americans checked into the Hotel Paris, Morley having collected their mail on the way. And what a collection of mail it was: there were nearly a hundred letters, some of which had been written as far back as June and had been following them from Guatemala City to San Salvador to Tegucigalpa to San Pedro Sula and had finally caught up with them in La Ceiba. But there was one letter in particular that sent Morley's morale soaring:

November 3rd, 1917.

My Dear Morley,

I was very glad to receive your letter dated October 12th giving me an account of your interesting trip to Bluefields. I think that you have done splendidly and send you hearty congratulations and assure you of my appreciation of the work that you have accomplished. I realize that the trip must have been a strenuous one but am certain that the results obtained justify it. Your scheme to take a similar trip along the coast of Yucatan is an excellent one and I hope that the weather conditions will permit of this being done. I know that the coast is a bad one with few sheltered anchorages into which you might put in case of bad weather, so I trust that you will use every precaution to avoid an accident of any character.

By all means go over to Belize to have your teeth attended to and to get a little change.

In regard to your proposed return to Washington at the first of the year, I shall try to arrange that for you but I do not think that it will be possible to have Held come back at our expense. If he will pay his own expenses I believe that it can be arranged in case you can find some reliable man to look after the outfits, etc. during your absence.

I have taken up with the United Fruit Company the matter of your using their radio at Ceiba and Trujillo and they have given the necessary instructions to their operators at both places. It might be well to use this means of informing me of your arrival at Ceiba. Send thru Colon just to see if this means of communication is quicker than the regular cables.

Your letters are always interesting and I hope that you will write to me, not only upon the results of your work for Carnegie, but also upon matters of political interest and upon conditions in general in that section.

In conclusion I wish to assure you that you are doing work of real value for us and to inform you that it is appreciated by all members of the Board. You will understand that with so many of our men called to the colors, we are very busy in the Office and have been unable to communicate with you as often as we should have liked.

Hoping soon to learn of your safe arrival at Ceiba, and with kind regards to you and Held, I am

Very sincerely yours,

["Taro Yamamoto"][6]

This letter from his ONI case officer restored Morley's spirits:

On reaching Ceiba I found a big accumulation of mail including your letter of November 3 which heartened me considerably. I could not tell heretofore whether you had approved of the different things I had been doing; whether in fact, I had been doing any of the things you wanted done, but most of all whether I was really being useful down here. I do so want to do my part whatever that may be. In a word I was feeling pretty blue. You are so devilishly out of everything down here. Your letter therefore came at the psychological moment for me and has encouraged me and bucked me up tremendously.

I am much more contented now that I know I have been turning in the kind of stuff you want to know about. I only wanted your assurance thereof. Of course we want to stick until the cows come home, if we are wanted.[7]

In addition Morley was delighted to learn that there was also money waiting for him. There was a $1,000 draft at the Banco Atlántida from the Carnegie Institution and there were also two drafts, for $1,000 and $500, sent by ONI from Costa Rica through the Banco Hondureño in Tegucigalpa. This monetary infusion was particularly welcome since Morley and Held were down to $12 between them.

His spirits and bank account buoyed, Morley returned to his hotel room to write his reports to ONI. The hotel room was a bit depressing, however. A large puddle of water collected in the middle of the floor whenever it rained, and it rained constantly. Nevertheless, Morley conscientiously sat at his typewriter and pounded out his reports. Besides his regular periodic account of his activities, he also prepared one devoted to shipping on the north coast and Bay Islands. There existed a serious shortage of shipping in these waters because of the war, and commerce between New Orleans and Mobile and the Bay Islands and north coast of Honduras had suffered considerably. An effort was being made in the Bay Islands to alleviate this situation by building wooden vessels. Morley had spent a week on Roatán investigating. His interest in the building of wooden vessels stemmed from the United States government's plan to build one thousand such craft as a wartime emergency measure.[8] Morley now reported that a three-masted schooner of 260 tons, the *Rubicon*, had been built at Oak Ridge and was launched on May 27, 1916. Morley gave the specifications of this vessel as published in *El Nuevo Tiempo*, the Honduran government's official organ. The *Rubicon* was said to be able to carry 500,000 coconuts. But this schooner was the exception. Four much smaller craft, of thirty tons each, were currently under construction, and the Bay Islanders planned to produce a number of small freight and passenger sailing vessels, including one for postal service between the Islands and the Honduran coast. The ships would be built from Honduran materials as much as possible, supplemented by whatever components could be imported from the United States.[9]

Having done his ONI duty, Morley could in good conscience join Held in living a little. They were in a jubilant mood, and one way in which they expressed this was by continuing to eat well. Their late diet of beans was now but a fading memory. Held, by the way, not only ate well, but he would eat anything. As Morley delicately put it, Held's stomach would put an ostrich to shame. Held's appetite perhaps stimulated his creativity, for he was full of ideas for cartoons with a patriotic wartime theme. Morley greatly admired Held's artistic talent, commenting on his friend's ability to infuse his work with a sophisticated humor that undoubtedly appealed to a smart, worldly New York audience.

Just when things seemed to be going so well, something most disquieting occurred. Morley discovered that he and Held were suspected of being spies. The very idea! Upon making discreet inquiries, he learned to his dismay that this rumor stemmed from two sources. First, the captain of the *Lilly Elena* had carelessly listed the two Americans on the manifest as crew instead of as passengers, as they obviously were. Second, it was known that Morley and Held had money. Taken together, these facts had raised serious suspicions about the Americans. In fact, an official in Trujillo had been so alarmed that he'd wired the minister of war about the pair and had asked for instructions. The ministry of war had contacted Governor Inestrosa at La Ceiba to watch them closely. Morley decided to take the bold course and confront these ugly rumors head on.

He called on the governor and presented both his credentials from the Carnegie Institution and his letter from President Bertrand. The governor was suitably impressed with Morley's bona fides, and he was soon scoffing at the very suggestion that Held and Morley could possibly be spies. Morley couldn't have agreed more. The archaeologist and the governor parted on terms of great cordiality. Morley and Held went to a cantina for a drink that was part celebration and part relief.

While still in La Ceiba, Morley, on November 27, wrote a lengthy report to ONI covering the local situation, his and Held's plans for the next three weeks, requests for funds, and recommendations about the projected Yucatán trip. He also enclosed their expense account for the period August 1 to November 30, pointing out that since he had done practically all the disbursing, the items in his account for hotel bills, food supplies, railroad fares, and boat charters were in almost all cases for both himself and Held.[10]

Honduras being the original banana republic, it was perhaps appropriate that Morley began his report with a detailed account of "the big outstanding feature of north coast history since we left Ceiba three months ago"—the strike at the three banana companies operating on the Atlantic coast of Honduras: the Cuyamel Fruit Co. at Cuyamel, the United Fruit Co. at Tela, and the Vaccaro Brothers Co. at La Ceiba. The strike had begun at Cuyamel on October 1, spread to Tela, and reached La Ceiba on October 10. The walkout had lasted approximately a month.

The causes of the confrontation were twofold. First, there had occurred a spectacular rise in the price of silver bullion in the United States during the summer and early fall of 1917. This, in turn, had caused the *sol*, the Honduran silver dollar, to rise above the government exchange rate. Second, the Honduran government had stubbornly attempted to maintain the old rate of exchange despite the silver *sol's* increased marketable value elsewhere: great quantities of *soles* were smuggled out of Honduras to Belize and New Orleans during the summer and early fall for their silver content, in spite of the most stringent prohibitions by the Honduran government. The attractive prices offered in Belize—as much as 20 percent higher than the official rate of exchange—proved too tempting for many enterprising Hondurans, including some government officials, and *soles* "flowed out of the country like water." The government found itself powerless to halt this movement in which everyone who could was engaged. The wholesale traffic in *soles* produced

an economic crisis and profiteering by merchants, which caused the purchasing power of a worker's wages to shrink by some 25 percent. The
workers were unhappy, and they went on strike.

By October 10 the strike had spread to Vaccaro banana plantations.
Some five hundred laborers marched on La Ceiba. Governor Inestrosa
himself went out to reason with them, but failed to halt the march. The
next day he sent out troops with a machine gun. The officer in command
demanded to know who was leading the strikers. That worthy not only
stepped forward, but took a shot at the officer. The latter had his men
open fire, killing two strikers and wounding eight. This show of force
cowed the strikers, and although they still seethed with discontent, negotiations ensued and they eventually agreed to return to work.

The question that immediately came to mind of course was whether
the fine hand of Germany was behind the labor disturbance. Although it
had been suggested at the time, Morley's investigation led him to conclude that economic conditions, not German agitation, caused the strike.
"As anxious as the Hun undoubtedly is, to cause just such disturbances
as this, I think that for this once at least, we may probably exonerate him
from all complicity."[11]

But Morley was not going to give the Germans an inch. He reported
that at La Ceiba there was a German named George Luttick who had
been a bookkeeper and customs broker for several years. He had just
opened a wholesale import firm that was to distribute American manufactured goods. Morley had it on good authority that Luttick had two
silent partners—Joaquín Alvarado, the administrator of Customs "and
the most bitter anti-American pro-German in Ceiba, openly Hunnish in
his sympathies," and a Prussian named Weinstock who was currently in
the commission business in San Pedro Sula.

> Alvarado hates the gringo, and the other two are of course alien
> enemies both by birth and citizenship. It appears to me, that any
> American firm opening an account with this house would be vio-
> lating "The Trading with the Enemy Act," or at least aiding and
> comforting the enemy. I am passing this information along to you,
> so that you can notify the proper people, if you see fit, and thus
> scotch this promising little viper's nest in the embryo stage.[12]

To keep an eye on the vipers Morley approached D. H. McCollough, the acting United States consul in La Ceiba. McCollough, who was only temporarily acting as consul until the incumbent arrived, was the leading American importer in town. His business brought him into daily contact with both officials and merchants; he was abreast of shipping news; and he occasionally visited clients both east and west along the coast. Morley considered McCollough to be able, discreet, and loyal, just the man to look after ONI's interests. McCollough enthusiastically agreed when Morley made his pitch, and the archaeologist could report that "I have no doubt he will make an effective link in the chain we are trying to leave behind us."

Having recruited yet another subagent, Morley turned his attention to draft dodgers. A young American from Milwaukee named J. J. Shock had been in town recently. He was openly pro-German and announced to the world that he had come to Honduras to escape the draft. Shock had gone to Tela, where he was currently employed by United Fruit. As Morley put it, "If I find out that he really is a draft-dodger, I will try to have him fired just to show him that there are no hard feelings."[13] An equally undesirable character was a Canadian, one Charles Lock. He had taken out his first citizenship papers in California, and although he had resided in the United States until eight months previously he had never troubled to complete the citizenship process. Lock worked in the Vaccaro Brothers offices, was pro-German, consorted with Germans, and continually denounced the United States. He had recently been denied an American passport.

Then there was the matter of Germans still employed by American firms. Morley understood that American companies were supposed to have discharged all enemy alien employees. But the Vaccaro Brothers still had about a dozen Germans, some of whom had already been fired by United Fruit, on their payroll. Morley enclosed a list of these Germans.

The general situation at La Ceiba was satisfactory. True, most of the government officials were anti-American, some, as in the case of the aforementioned Joaquín Alvarado, being pro-German. But, said Morley, this feeling was so prevalent throughout Central America as to cause no particular uneasiness as far as La Ceiba was concerned.

The largest local business enterprise was American—the Vaccaro Brothers Company with headquarters in New Orleans. This firm represented a remarkable success story. In 1899 frost wiped out the orange

groves in the Mississippi delta belonging to three Sicilian brothers in New
Orleans—Luca, Felix, and Joseph Vaccaro. They, together with Joseph's
son-in-law, Salvator D'Antoni, subsequently established themselves on
the coast of Honduras, forming the Vaccaro Brothers Company, and
within a few years were opening banana plantations in the interior. In
1905, they began constructing a narrow-gauge railroad, which by 1908
had reached La Ceiba, which town became the company's Honduran
headquarters. There they prospered, in part because the Honduran government permitted them to import duty free the materials needed for their
operations. And in 1912, the Honduran government allowed them to
open the Banco Atlántico in La Ceiba. This enterprising family transformed La Ceiba into an important port boasting a wharf designed to
withstand hurricanes. The town was also the terminus of the 120-mile
narrow-gauge line linking the company's 160,000 acres of banana plantations.[14] Morley reported that the only steamships currently calling at
La Ceiba were the Vaccaro vessels *Tegucigalpa*, *Ceiba*, and *Yoro*, which
carried bananas to New Orleans. In addition, the local radio station was
owned by the Vaccaro Brothers. In short, La Ceiba's contacts with the
outside world were in American hands. This was fortunate since the
strategic importance of La Ceiba was much greater than that of, say, San
Pedro Sula, where German influence predominated.

To Morley the key difference between the two places was the presence at San Pedro Sula of important German mercantile houses such as
P. Rossner & Co., and Bennaton & Co. Rossner and Maier had their
headquarters in Tegucigalpa, but had branches in most of the large cities
in Honduras except on the north coast. There, German firms had been
unable to secure a foothold because the American fruit companies operating in the region had so completely preempted the territory. It was for
this reason that Morley recommended so urgently that the nascent import
firm of the German George Luttick in La Ceiba be crushed forthwith. If
Luttick were denied American goods, his promising enterprise would die
aborning. Morley stressed that in La Ceiba, as everywhere else, German
propaganda followed German trade.[15]

Having covered the local situation, Morley turned to outlining his
proposed itinerary. He and Held would depart from La Ceiba on
November 29 and sail to Tela, where they would turn in their trusty yawl,
the *Lilly Elena*. At Tela, Morley also planned to confer with the United
Fruit Company manager, R. H. Goodell, regarding use of the company's

radio station, the most powerful facility on the entire north coast. From Tela they would take a United Fruit steamer to Puerto Barrios, Guatemala, proceeding on to the capital. From Guatemala City they would go back down to Puerto Barrios, where they would take a small motorboat to Livingston and up the Dulce River. Having finished their Guatemalan investigations, the pair would proceed to Belize, hopefully by Christmas. Belize would be their base for the reconnaissance of the eastern and northern coastline of Yucatán, their investigation extending as far as the port of Progreso and ending in February or early March 1918.[16]

Obviously this would be an expensive undertaking. ONI was currently sending Morley $500 for expenses on or about the twentieth of each month. Morley requested that the installment for January be advanced, so that $1,000 would be available in Belize by December 20 at the only bank in town, a branch of the Royal Bank of Canada. He explained that there would be heavy initial expenses in Belize—chartering a boat, paying for food and fuel for the trip, etc., and there was nowhere between Belize and Progreso where he could receive funds.

He also requested that ONI obtain from the Navy Hydrographic Office and send to him six charts, "which we will need on the coming trip to navigate those bays, lagoons and key-infested waters." The charts should be at Belize before the end of December. Moreover, there was at Belize a British government radio station, and Morley inquired whether ONI could arrange with the British embassy in Washington for him to use it to communicate with ONI in Washington and with the ONI station in the Panama Canal Zone. If this could be arranged, Morley would report in from Belize in about a month.

Turning to more personal matters, Morley stated that he and Held were anxious to take the leave that ONI had said was feasible after January 1. Held was agreeable to ONI's condition—that he pay his own way home—although one suspects that he wasn't too happy about this latest manifestation of governmental niggardliness. Morley reassured his case officer:

> The work will hardly suffer in our absence, I believe; the links in our chain are all good men, held by the necessities of their several businesses to the regions for which we picked them, and thus always on their jobs. Judging from present indications, as well as from the experience of the past six months, they should have no difficulties

in holding down the lids of their respective regions while we are away, and in case of unforseen emergencies arising, each knows what to do.[17]

When they finished at Progreso, Morley wanted—if ONI approved—to go directly from there to the United States. Both his and Held's passports were valid for Mexico. The archaeologist was anxious for his control to write to him in Belize, informing him whether or not these plans were approved.

Morley was in a particularly loquacious mood, for in addition to the above lengthy report on November 27 from La Ceiba, the archaeologist churned out a lengthy continuation, from Tela, on December 3. He and Held had traveled overland from La Ceiba to see the country. The Vaccaro Brothers' plantations lay west of La Ceiba, and their railroad ran westward along the coastal plain for forty-one miles. Then there was a gap of some twelve miles of brush and banana lands before the travelers could board United Fruit's Tela Railroad for the last sixteen miles into Tela. Held prepared maps of this region that Morley enclosed in the report.

Conditions at Tela were satisfactory. The strike had been over for nearly a month and all was quiet. The archaeologist was particularly interested in getting access to the Tela radio station, the most important facility on the whole coast. Accordingly, Morley spoke at length with R. H. Goodell, manager of United Fruit's Tela Railroad Co. and Trujillo Railroad Co. According to Morley, Goodell was "easily the foremost American in this general region"; Harry Scott at Rincón was assistant manager under Goodell. The latter was an old Central American hand who had lived for eighteen years on the Mosquito Coast in Nicaragua before coming to Tela. Goodell had traveled frequently along the coast between Bluefields and Cape Gracias a Dios and occasionally up to the Caratasca Lagoon. Morley asked Goodell's opinion about the possibility of German submarine bases or secret radio stations in that region, and the archaeologist was gratified when this experienced individual agreed completely with Morley's own conclusions. The same was true for the north coast. Goodell was certain that from Trujillo west to Livingston, Guatemala, nothing could be started by Germans without it being immediately known. There were no strange vessels along the north coast. The steamers of the various fruit companies were all well known, as were the small craft from the Bay Islands. No unknown vessel could touch any-

where on the coast without news of it spreading like wildfire.
Furthermore,

> the chain of fruit companies operating all along this coast from
> Trujillo to Livingston: at Rincón, New Armenia, Ceiba, Colorado,
> Tela, Puerto Cortez, Omoa, Puerto Barrios and Livingston make
> an excellent "first line of defense" for securing and forwarding
> information of hostile activities.[18]

What really pleased Morley about his talk with Goodell was when the
latter told him he had been instructed to receive and transmit messages
for J. J. Perdomo, the ONI agent stationed in the Canal Zone. A jubilant Morley immediately sent Perdomo a radio message to mark the
occasion, and the relieved archaeologist later commented to his control:

> This satisfactorily and adequately settles the whole matter of the
> transmission of information of an urgent nature along this coast.
> I gave Scott at Rincon the address of your Panama friend, and also
> McCollough at Ceiba, and of course they now have it here. Thus,
> men are on the lookout in these three places, and will promptly
> report to Panama any suspicious circumstances that may arise in
> their respective districts.[19]

Commenting further on the now vastly improved communications situation, Morley stressed that the Tela radio station was the key, for the
stations in Belize, La Ceiba, and Rincón all transmitted through Tela to
the United Fruit station on Swan Island. For this reason, and because of
his responsible position, Morley had recruited Goodell as a subagent. In
the event of an emergency Goodell would immediately get in touch with
Panama. Morley went on to suggest that if ONI should urgently require
any information about the north coast it should communicate directly
with Goodell by United Fruit radio; Goodell was in daily contact with
Belize, La Ceiba, and Rincón, and, further, he could dispatch trusted
employees at any time to secure needed information.

Not content with the worrisome problem of radio communication
being substantially solved, Morley was also interested in intercepting any
German transmissions. He conferred with the radio operator at Tela,
one Renard, as to whether the latter had intercepted any suspicious

transmissions that might possibly be from German "or other unfriendly operators"—read "Mexican"—in his region. Renard had not, but he pointed out that his station was not equipped to intercept such transmissions, especially if they were sent by an arc instrument. Renard therefore suggested that a Deforest Audion Detector and circuits to connect with a wireless Specialty Apparatus Co. Receiver would enable him not only to intercept such messages, but possibly to determine their direction. Morley strongly urged that such equipment be sent to Tela, pointing out that Renard and his assistant could install it. Should ONI be interested, the man to see was G. S. Davis, general superintendent, Wireless Department, United Fruit Co., 17 Bellview Place, New York City. Morley recognized that installing detection equipment was only a precautionary measure, but it might pay huge dividends at any time.

The archaeologist related that on the trip over from La Ceiba he had had the opportunity to chat with an American named Hill, who was the chief engineer on the Vaccaro Brothers railroad. According to Hill, there were probably two dozen Germans in the various departments of the company, some of them in responsible positions in La Ceiba—the head of the brewery there, the master mechanic of the railroad, the head carpenter, and others in the Banco Atlántico and in the company's main offices. Many of them had been hired after United Fruit had dismissed them. An outraged Morley asked, "How about this for 'aiding and abetting the enemy?'" Three of these Germans in particular bore watching: J. J. Shock and Charles Lock, whom Morley had already mentioned as being draft dodgers, and a German-American electrician named C. C. Toussant. The trio had arrived in La Ceiba several months earlier, claiming to have no previous knowledge of each other. But it later turned out that they had all participated in a failed colonization scheme on the Patuca River, had become discouraged, and turned up in La Ceiba looking for work. These young men were probably not actively plotting, but in case of trouble Hill thought they would certainly be among the ringleaders. On the bright side, Morley had met the manager of the Vaccaro Co. in La Ceiba, C. D'Antoni, who was "an Italian of unquestioned loyalty and would, I am confident, suppress any German activity that may arise among his subordinates."

Morley apologized for writing the latter part of his report in pencil, explaining that his typewriter had "definitely collapsed." For his case officer's sake, he would try to have the typewriter repaired in Guatemala

City.[20] As it developed, Guatemala City would provide Morley with all the excitement he could handle.

7. Guatemala Again

On December 4, Morley and Held sailed from Tela on the steamer *Sixiola*.[1] Morley was quite miffed because, due to a stupid blunder, their suitcases had been put in the hold, and they had to sleep without pajamas.

The following day they arrived at Puerto Cortés, and during the ship's layover Morley went ashore to confer with American Consul Boyle. On the way to the consulate, the archaeologist stopped at the Hotel Palm to inquire whether the puttees that Held had left were still there. Then there occurred something truly remarkable. As Morley recounted the incident in his Diary, he was talking with the proprietress when a short, odd, rather Semitic-looking old man wearing a plaid suit and a crush linen hat came in and asked her if she happened to know a Mr. Morley. The flabbergasted archaeologist identified himself and asked who the stranger might be. To Morley's utter amazement, he replied—J. J. Perdomo. J. J. Perdomo—the ONI agent whom Morley imagined was at his post in Panama, a thousand miles to the south. It took Morley a few minutes to regain his composure, whereupon he invited Perdomo outside. The archaeologist quizzed Perdomo until he had assured himself of the man's identity. Perdomo then proceeded to pour out a tale of woe.

Practically quivering with indignation, Perdomo blurted out that the United States had been grossly insulted in his person—his luggage had not only been opened, but had been kept overnight. Even more insulting, his personal correspondence had been read. Morley dryly observed that it seemed as if Perdomo were suspected of being a spy. He and Perdomo promptly went to the consulate to discuss the matter in private with Consul Boyle. Held later joined them, and after recovering from his amazement at the story of the meeting he was treated to another recitation of Perdomo's troubles. Not the least of these was the local military commandant's refusal to issue an exit permit for Perdomo. The upshot of the Americans' strategy session was that Perdomo should get out of Puerto Cortés immediately, preferably on the same steamer as Morley and Held. It was decided that Perdomo should make one more attempt to secure the indispensable exit permit. If the commandant still refused to issue the document, Morley would try his luck by showing the officer his magic letter from President Bertrand. Perdomo left to confront the commandant. The others discussed the situation for about an hour, and when Perdomo failed to return Morley went out to look for him. To the archaeologist's enormous relief, he found that Perdomo had succeeded not only in obtaining the permit but also in having his trunks released; they were undergoing the mandatory inspection. Morley hurried back to the consulate with Perdomo's passport so that Consul Boyle could issue a visa. He found the purser of the *Sixiola* in a state of considerable agitation because Boyle was holding up the ship's clearance papers until Perdomo could be hustled aboard. This was successfully accomplished with Boyle shepherding the operation. The travelers then took their leave of the consul, who went ashore. Morley commented that this was his first experience at holding up the sailing of a steamship.

It might be thought that Morley had invented, or at least embroidered, the whole incident to add interest to his Diary. But evidently such was not the case. In his next ONI report, he gave the unexpurgated version of the affair. On December 5, while he and Held were en route to Puerto Barrios, their steamer put in to Puerto Cortés for a couple of hours. Morley went ashore to confer with Consul Boyle, to learn if anything of importance had occurred since his and Held's last visit.

> While in the lobby of the hotel a short foreign-looking individual came up and asked the proprietor if she knew a Mr. Morley. I admitted my identity as such, and asked him what he wanted of me. To my amazement—not to say utter dumfoundment—he announced himself as J. J. Perdomo. I could scarcely believe my ears.
>
> My last advises—to be sure, then at least three months old—had indicated him as being in Panama, nor had I received subsequent contrary information, least of all, any intimation of a projected journey northward. And as I say, I could believe it was he only with difficulty.

When we passed out of earshot of the proprietor he began to talk freely but I did not dare to loosen up until I had more convincing proofs of his identity; that he was, as he claimed to be. Finally I came out bluntly and asked him for such proofs and I must say he came across strong. He knew such a mass of information about me, Held, Spinden, Lothrop etc. that I was convinced.

As soon as he found that I was on my way to Puerto Barrios he decided to go back with me on the same steamer, and although he was then under strong suspicion of being a German spy, and had his baggage seized and searched, he finally got off with us.[2]

On his next visit to Puerto Cortés, Morley learned additional details about Perdomo from Consul Boyle. It seems that Perdomo had come under suspicion as a spy in San Pedro Sula. Ironically, he was suspected of being a *German* spy. He was so obvious and so inept in trying to gather information that the Americans in San Pedro Sula became alarmed and reported him to Consul Boyle. Perdomo had

set the town by the ears all right and incidentally acquired some information from a Mexican named Echegaray implicating Salvador, Honduras and Mexico in a plot against Guatemala, which he believed to be of extreme importance, with which Consul Boyle agreed.

Several days later, from Guatemala City, Perdomo cabled you this situation. For my own part I could not believe conditions were as acute as he did, and three weeks later on my return to Puerto Cortez, Omoa and Cuyamel I found the whole story had been greatly exaggerated to him—in fact entirely so, insofar as the international phase of it were [sic] concerned.[3]

It was Perdomo's actions at San Pedro Sula that had aroused the suspicion of the Honduran authorities. Perdomo was a loose cannon. It must have worried Morley that Perdomo knew so much about himself, Held, Spinden, and Lothrop. The reason Perdomo was so knowledgeable was because he had been dispatched by the 15th Naval District in the Canal Zone to coordinate the activities of Morley and the other agents in Central America.

Perdomo conferred at length with his fellow ONI agents during the voyage to Puerto Barrios, Guatemala. But upon reaching that port, trouble continued to dog him. As was customary with arriving passengers, their luggage was inspected upon landing. But what complicated this tiresome ritual was that their trunks were checked through to the customshouse in Guatemala City, and off they went. Worse still, the Customs inspector also inspected Held and Perdomo, confiscating two revolvers from Held and one from Perdomo, thus seizing their total armament. Morley, however, was more astute than his companions; he quickly shoved his pistol into the pocket of his raincoat, which he carried through Customs draped casually over his arm. Perdomo continued to arouse suspicion. Customs officials inspected his papers minutely and were on the verge of seizing them, but after a lengthy and heated argument in Spanish Perdomo was finally permitted to keep the documents.

Following their ordeal with Customs, the trio turned to finding overnight accommodations. Morley and Two-Gun Held were soon comfortably ensconced at the United Fruit Company offices, while Perdomo, with considerable difficulty, finally got a room at the Occidental Hotel. After dinner, Morley and Held brought Perdomo to their quarters for further talks. Morley was quite pleased with the result of their conversation. He drafted a coded report of these proceedings to be transmitted to ONI via the *Sixiola's* radio. He and Held then walked Perdomo back to his hotel, only to discover that he was locked out. Perdomo finally managed to rouse a female guest, who was kind enough to open the front door for him. As Morley observed, Perdomo seemed to be one of those people who was always pursued by bad luck.

The next day the trio of American operatives rode the train together up to Guatemala City, with Morley and Perdomo deep in conversation the entire way. The travelers were met at the station by Walter Thurston, secretary of the American legation, and by a friend of Perdomo named Watts. Perdomo introduced Morley and Held to Watts, who had a prior engagement that prevented him from accepting their dinner invitation. But they arranged to meet later with Watts. Such a conference was in order because, as it happened, Joseph H. Watts was also an ONI agent— No. 84 to be precise. Morley described him as an interesting man who was a navy veteran, and who now ran the Guatemalan government's radio station in the capital. The station operated under the personal direction of President Estrada Cabrera.[4] In Morley's opinion, Watts was not only a good man but a loyal American; his patriotism was beyond question.

The forty-year-old Watts had been a career sailor, serving during the Spanish-American War and then continuously from July 31, 1900, until January 9, 1917. He was a chief electrician who had specialized in radio communications. According to Watts's own account, in 1907 he set up a radio station at the navy's Guantanamo Bay installation in Cuba; in 1913 he was loaned to the Guatemalan government as chief electrician; and in 1914, upon the outbreak of World War I, he was ordered to build a large radio station in Guatemala City and smaller stations throughout the country, for the purpose of detecting German stations and locating German submarine bases. Watts allegedly had five Immigration inspectors assigned to him to investigate rumors involving Germans. Further, he stated that he was in constant communication with the American diplomat Walter Thurston.[5]

What ONI's archives reveal is that on February 19, 1917, Watts took the oath as a special agent for ONI. On February 19, he was formally enrolled as a civilian employee of that organization at a salary of $100 a month plus expenses from February 5, the same pay scale as for John Held and Samuel Lothrop. Watts was issued codes A-7 and B-7, his keyword being "Watts." His cables were to go to "Gustav Koch" in New York City. For his mail accommodation address, ONI came up with a rather outlandish name, "Gitaro Ando," P.O. Box 91, Philadelphia. Mail sent to Watts was to go in care of the American legation in Guatemala City. In June 1917, Watts, accompanied by his wife and daughter, took up residence in Guatemala, his assignment being to investigate conditions in that country. He was in business for himself and used this as cover for his ONI activities.[6]

Exactly what Watts did in Guatemala remains somewhat murky. As Morley noted, Watts operated the government radio station in Guatemala City. That installation was located on the outskirts of the capital near old Fort San José; a barbed-wire stockade surrounded the base of the tallest tower, which was 350 feet high. Security was rather whimsical; the station was heavily guarded by Guatemalan soldiers during the day, but it was virtually deserted at night. This situation caused Morley to fret about how easy it would be for the Germans to dynamite the facility at night, putting it out of action indefinitely. From ONI's point of view Watts was a valuable agent not only because he was in a position to monitor government traffic, but also because he had developed close ties to the dictator Estrada Cabrera himself. In fact, the latter was now paying his salary. As of June 1, 1917, the Office of Naval Intelligence took Watts off salary but continued to pay his expenses, the conduit being a Mr. Udell, secretary to a vice-president of United Fruit.[7] Watts began building a network of subagents.[8]

Watts may have been a strange character, but Morley took a real liking to him. The two spent many pleasant hours chatting over drinks at the American Club. In Morley's view, Watts was not only a congenial comrade in arms, but he was also very capable professionally. The archaeologist would report to ONI that "Guatemala City . . . is being extremely well covered by No. 84 [J.H. Watts], than whom I have met no one in the work more able, alert and efficient."[9]

Morley spent an entire morning getting a briefing on local conditions from Watts. The radio expert was of the opinion that any threat to Guatemala from Mexico, El Salvador, or Honduras was greatly exaggerated. Watts also gave Morley a card of introduction to Jack P. Armstrong, the British consul general, who was acting for the British minister during the latter's absence.[10] Decades later Armstrong recalled their meeting, albeit somewhat inaccurately:

> I first met Dr. Sylvanus Griswold Morley, "Vay" as I eventually knew him, either at the end of 1914 or early in 1915 [sic]. At the time I was British Consul attached to the British Legation, at Guatemala City, on special duty. He called at the Legation to introduce himself and to tell me that he had a "war assignment" in the Gulf of Fonseca, and that his job was to investigate and report upon enemy naval activities in that area and to suggest cooperation between British Consular Officers in that district and himself.[11]

Morley and Armstrong agreed to have further meetings. But as we shall see, Morley's dealings with Armstrong would not be the archaeologist's last exercise in Anglo-American intelligence cooperation.

Morley missed no opportunity to gather useful data. For instance, he sounded out influential Guatemalan friends as to what they thought of their army and its ability to repel an invasion, or of the American Black List of German businesses and the ramifications of its enforcement in

Guatemala. And Morley habitually discussed his findings in sessions with Watts and Perdomo.

Among the many contacts Morley developed while in Guatemala City was a young American named Wilson Popenoe. Born in Topeka, Kansas, in 1892, Popenoe moved to Pasadena, California, while in high school; he attended Pomona College for a year. Ever since 1913 he had worked for the Department of Agriculture, searching for new plants in the Orient and in the tropics of the Western Hemisphere. Besides being widely traveled, he spoke Spanish fluently and French and Portuguese less so. Among his references was Alexander Graham Bell. Popenoe had been in Guatemala since August 1916, under the auspices of the U.S. Department of Agriculture's Bureau of Plant Industry. His official title was rather grandiloquent: "Agricultural Explorer." Popenoe, who struck Morley as being pleasantly efficient, helped operate an agricultural station outside Guatemala City. He was investigating avocado growing in order to obtain varieties suitable for conditions in Florida and California. Popenoe was about to leave for the United States, to recuperate from a serious bout of malaria. But he would soon be returning to the region. In February 1918, Popenoe was dispatched to Puerto México on the Gulf coast as ONI Agent No. 219. His cover was that of an "agricultural explorer" for the University of California. Popenoe's ONI salary was $4 a day plus another $4 per diem for expenses.[12] Besides being an ONI agent, the other thing Popenoe had in common with Morley was that he became a member of the Cosmos Club, in 1919.[13]

Despite his full schedule, Morley managed to find time for cultural enrichment while burnishing his cover. He made visits to the national archives to examine some of the country's historical manuscripts, things such as Bernal Díaz del Castillo's eyewitness account of the conquest of Mexico. Located in the city hall, on the main plaza, the treasure trove of material for the history of Guatemala contained in that little twelve-foot-square room was mind-boggling.

In the meantime, Morley's colleague J. J. Perdomo had been engaged in less scholarly pursuits. The archaeologist looked him up back at their hotel, and found Perdomo in a jubilant mood. He had just returned from an interview with President Estrada Cabrera, and he felt that it had gone splendidly.[14] Morley subsequently had a more sober assessment:

Perdomo saw President Estrada Cabrera several times while we were in the city. Sometimes he would believe that the wily old Indian was with us heart and soul, and then again he would become convinced that he was double crossing us right and left. Truth is Manuel Estrada Cabrera serves himself, first, last and all the time, and his every act, word and promise should be interpreted with this fact constantly in mind. He is with us, not because of any altruistic feeling about the rape of Belgium, and the violation of Serbia, but because his own selfish interests are best to be served by such a course of action. I believe therefore self-interest—for Mexico and Salvador both hate him—will keep him in line, and now more than ever since he entertains a very lively fear that these two neighbors may fall upon him in his present extremity.

He clearly realizes we are his best assurance against such a catastrophe, just as he is ours, against a Central American-Mexican upheaval made in Germany, and he will, I believe, act accordingly.[15]

Perdomo's high spirits had resulted not just from the outcome of his meeting with Estrada Cabrera, but from the president having sent for him in his personal carriage and having received him alone in a hall of state in the palace. This was heady stuff for someone who had been an Immigration inspector in Buffalo before the war.[16] Estrada Cabrera may have conferred these signal marks of honor on Perdomo as a representative of the United States government, but the conspicuous attention did little for Perdomo's cover as an intelligence agent.

There seems to have been no lack of intelligence agents in Guatemala City at this time. Rumor had it that there were fourteen American agents alone.[17] However many there may have been, their activities were quite irritating to the British minister, Alban Young. He would complain bitterly to the Foreign Secretary about the "raw" American secret agents who were prone to take too literally their instructions to report whether individuals or firms were pro-German or anti-American. This simplistic standard all too often resulted in the American Black List being applied unfairly and without any right of appeal.[18] The reported number of American agents was probably exaggerated, but it can be established that the ONI contingent consisted of Morley, Held, Watts, and Perdomo.

Whatever the actual number, Perdomo was eager to increase it by one—he was anxious to recruit Arthur Carpenter. It will be recalled that

Carpenter had been Morley's associate on the 1916 expedition and in October 1917 had encountered the archaeologist on the dock at Trujillo. Perdomo had met Carpenter while passing through San Pedro Sula in November and had been quite impressed with him, thinking he would make a fine agent. Morley had serious reservations, and the archaeologist was especially irritated because Perdomo insisted that he go see Carpenter, who was playing hard to get, at Puerto Cortés and persuade the latter to sign on.

But before setting forth, Morley had further meetings with the British consul Jack Armstrong, and additional strategy sessions with Watts and Perdomo. He also expanded his network of subagents by securing the cooperation of a local American businessman, one Arthur Clark. In addition to everything else, Morley maintained a full social schedule, a constant round of parties, balls, trips to the theater, and dinner engagements with his numerous friends, both Guatemalans and foreigners. On one occasion Morley, Held, and a Guatemalan friend were having drinks in a local cantina when a party of Germans came in. To Morley, they were arrogantly swaggering square-headed Huns with faces like pigs. He hated their guts. He and his friends immediately left in disgust. Morley's Belgian mother would have approved.

As they were driving back to their hotel, Morley had an opportunity for a bit of acerbic social commentary. They passed one of President Estrada Cabrera's sixteen-odd mistresses, an overweight, plain-looking, middle-aged woman. Why, wondered the archaeologist, if Estrada Cabrera were determined to emulate King Solomon, didn't he exhibit some of that monarch's good taste in women?

Morley and Held left Guatemala City by train on December 17, bound for Puerto Cortés, Honduras. The object of this exercise was to carry out Perdomo's desire to recruit Arthur Carpenter as an ONI agent and to investigate further Perdomo's lurid tale of a Mexican-Honduran-Salvadoran plot to invade Guatemala, which Perdomo had already reported to ONI. What gave Perdomo's story some credibility was the fact that there existed a long-standing boundary dispute between Guatemala and Honduras that was currently heading toward a crisis. Neither Morley nor Held put much stock in Perdomo's story, but it still had to be checked out. Held traveled to Puerto Barrios, Guatemala, where United Fruit had agreed to loan the agents the company launch *Florencio* for the trip over to Puerto Cortés. Morley stopped off at Quiriguá to consult a company doctor about a recurrence of his painful skin condition. While there, he also visited the Mayan ruins and examined recently discovered artifacts, as any inoffensive archaeologist would do.

But when Morley arrived in Puerto Barrios the next day, Held informed him that the *Florencio* wasn't available after all. It seems the launch was not registered under any flag, and if the vessel ventured out of Guatemalan territorial waters she was subject to seizure. Not only was Morley irked by this development but so was General Lee Christmas, the legendary American mercenary of whom more later. Christmas had been hanging around the hotel in Puerto Barrios in hopes of hitching a ride with Held and Morley on the *Florencio*. While awaiting the next vessel bound for Puerto Cortés, the energetic Morley employed his time usefully. He and Held made a side trip to the little port of Livingston, Guatemala, where Morley enlisted the U.S. consul, E. Reed, as a subagent. The two ONI operatives then made a quick trip by launch up the Dulce River to Lake Izábal, with Morley taking his usual careful notes, which he enclosed in his next report. They returned to Puerto Barrios, where they decided to separate temporarily. Held went to Quiriguá to sketch the ruins, while Morley proceeded alone to Puerto Cortés. He sailed aboard the coastal vessel *Harriman*, in company with Lee Christmas. During the overnight run the passengers had to sleep on deck, as there were no accommodations.

In Puerto Cortés, Morley immediately looked up American Consul Boyle. The latter conveyed some interesting news. Not only had Perdomo acted so suspiciously in San Pedro Sula that the Americans there became convinced he was a German spy, but because Arthur Carpenter had had a long conversation with Perdomo, they took Carpenter for a German spy as well. No American would extend credit to Carpenter, who was destitute because he couldn't get a check cashed. Presumably Morley found all this at least mildly amusing, given his reservations about Carpenter. The archaeologist conferred with Carpenter at the American consulate in Puerto Cortés. He loaned Carpenter $15 in cash and advised him to return to Washington at once and clear his name. To that end, Morley had Consul Boyle give Carpenter a letter stating that the suspicions against him were unfounded. Carpenter hoped that with this letter he would be able to cash a check and get a ticket home.[19]

Moreover, Morley made his recruitment pitch. But he stressed to his case officer that he did so only at Perdomo's express insistence. As Morley

explained, he had known Carpenter for four years; in 1916 he had taken
Carpenter along as his photographer on his Central American expedition. "During the first three years of the war, that is before we got into
it, he was pro-German in sympathy and for that very reason I did not
include his name in the list of available anthropologists which I laid
before you in March last. In other words the omission was deliberate."[20]

Before offering Carpenter a position with ONI, Morley sounded him
out on this point. Carpenter stated that he had been not so much pro-
German as anti-English. "The hair appeared too finely split, I thought,"
commented Morley. The archaeologist stressed that he wanted to maintain a position of "benevolent neutrality" regarding Carpenter:

> There is no denying the man's unusual ability, and now that we are
> actually in the war it is a different matter, and I believe his loyalty
> will be above reproach. For this latter reason alone, I was willing
> to approach him with the matter at all, and since he was returning
> to the states immediately, to provide him with a letter to you.
>
> He has an expert knowledge of photography, electricity and
> radiography, and in addition is a capable field man. He loves mys-
> tery, adventure and his own importance, and this whole business
> should appeal to him tremendously: a happy union of efficiency and
> inclination.
>
> Moreover in the region where he can be of most use to us just
> now, i.e., the north coast of Honduras with headquarters at San
> Pedro Sula, the hottest German center on the Atlantic coast-plain
> of Central America from here to Bluefields as I have reported sev-
> eral times before, and where we badly need a man all of the time—
> he is already suspected of being a German spy because of his
> intercourse and relations with Perdomo there, in consequence of
> which he is thoroughly distrusted by the resident Americans.
>
> If his loyalty can be depended upon, and I believe it now can,
> he ought to be a valuable addition to our ranks.[21]

There is, however, no evidence that Carpenter ever became an ONI
agent.[22]

Having concluded his business with Carpenter, Morley could discuss
other matters with Consul Boyle. First and foremost was Perdomo's story
of an invasion plot against Guatemala. It developed that while Perdomo

had been in San Pedro Sula between December 2 and 4 he fell in with some Germans and a Mexican named José N. Echegaray. By passing himself off as a Colombian who hated the United States, Perdomo ingratiated himself with these people. The following morning Echegaray showed Perdomo some envelopes—but not the contents—addressed to Echegaray in San Salvador. The Mexican claimed they were letters from important government officials in his native country, including President Venustiano Carranza. He intimated that this correspondence was linked to a conspiracy brewing between Mexico, El Salvador, and Honduras to invade Guatemala from three directions. And at the same time Mexico would declare war on the United States. Moreover, Salvadoran laborers "by the hundreds" were entering Honduras from El Salvador for the plantations of the Cuyamel Fruit Company, and at the appointed time they would be supplied with arms and would attack Guatemala from this northwestern corner of Honduras.

Perdomo, never having seen any of Echegaray's alleged conspiratorial correspondence, had inexplicably and naively accepted the Mexican's story at face value. Consul Boyle too had become excited—he heard a rumor that eighteen hundred Salvadoran laborers had recently arrived in Cuyamel. When Morley had first met Perdomo, in Puerto Cortés on December 5, Perdomo was greatly upset over the alleged impending invasion. Not content with reporting his anxieties to ONI, Perdomo had even cabled for an American gunboat to be sent to the region.

Morley, who together with Held discounted the whole invasion story, put the matter in perspective when he observed philosophically: "If you stay on the north coast of Honduras long enough you can hear, and you will believe, anything." Still, before leaving for Belize and Yucatán, he felt it his duty to investigate the matter personally. "If only the half of what Echegaray said was true the situation demanded immediate action."[23] Hence his return trip to Puerto Cortés.

While he was still discussing with Consul Boyle the Echegaray-Cuyamel-Honduras-Salvador-Mexico imbroglio, the consul received an urgent message that Guatemalan troops had invaded Honduras south of Cuyamel. Morley and the consul rushed off to investigate. It happened that the local manager of the Cuyamel Fruit Company, an American named A. G. Greeley whom Morley was considering recruiting as a subagent, was returning to Omoa in his motorboat, and they went with him.

As usual, Morley was a less than adequate sailor. Although the run over to Omoa was a mere eight miles, the motorboat rolled and pitched, and by the time they reached Omoa, Morley was indisposed. Back on dry land he brightened up considerably and took an interest in his new surroundings. Omoa was a small but typical banana port. The Cuyamel company's installations consisted of a wharf, offices, living quarters, and a railroad terminal. Presiding over the whole complex was an old Spanish fort whose semicircular wall faced the sea.

No sooner had the Americans reached Omoa than they learned that the invasion was a myth. Morley thus had the opportunity to explore to his heart's content the old fort that the Honduran army was using to house a garrison of about one hundred men. Morley and Consul Boyle got an escorted tour of the place. Consul Boyle decided to return to his post in Puerto Cortés. Morley, however, accepted Greeley's offer of hospitality. They traveled on the company's railroad the fifteen miles from Omoa to the firm's headquarters at Cuyamel, another typical but larger banana port, where Morley spent the night at Greeley's house.

It was a productive visit. First, Morley recruited Greeley to be the ONI subagent in Omoa and Cuyamel. Second, from Greeley and his private secretary, a man named Bradley, Morley learned the real story of Echegaray and the eighteen hundred Salvadoran laborers. Bradley had known Echegarary in Mexico several years earlier; the Mexican was in his early thirties and came from a good family. He was a graduate of the Mexican national military academy and for six years was in the reinforced-concrete business in Mexico City. During the Mexican Revolution he served with Pancho Villa against Venustiano Carranza. When the latter's faction triumphed, Echegaray had to flee the country. He went to San Salvador, where he worked on railroad construction. According to Bradley, Echegaray soon gained a bad reputation in San Salvador as a hell-raiser, womanizer, and drunk who was always talking about himself and who was full of cock-and-bull stories. Morley commented that this description certainly agreed with what Perdomo had said about Echegaray, which makes Perdomo's actions even more puzzling.

Echegaray had turned up in Cuyamel in September 1917, and Greeley had hired him as assistant railroad engineer. The Cuyamel Fruit Co. was very short of engineers, several having returned to the United States to enlist. The Cuyamel company was also short of laborers, partly because of the strike in September, and partly because the military commandant in Omoa, who hated gringos, was conscripting the company's best workers into the army "for the national defense."

Greeley thus had to secure laborers where he could find them. Ever since the Cuyamel company began operations it had employed some Salvadoran laborers. When Greeley learned that Echegaray was conversant with the Salvadoran labor market, he dispatched him together with a trusted American named Hal Miles to El Salvador to recruit workers. The Cuyamel company secured permission from the Honduran government for these workers to enter the country. Echegaray brought back 250 and Miles 95. They were assigned to work in the plantations and as section hands on the company railroad. Greeley stressed that these workers had never caused any trouble and they certainly were not armed. As for Echegaray, both Greeley and Bradley were convinced that his whole story to Perdomo was a hoax, just the kind of thing he had done many times before. "He will talk to anyone who will listen to him."

Morley's conclusions were that the movement of Salvadoran laborers to Cuyamel was a purely commercial transaction and was in no way sinister. And the numbers involved were greatly exaggerated—345 workers as against the 1,800 reported. Moreover, there was absolutely no evidence of a Mexican-Salvadoran plot to attack Guatemala, nor of any German involvement in the whole affair. Finally, Echegaray was certainly not an agent of the Mexican government, but was only "a common or garden variety of Mexican braggart, a well known species in this vicinity."[24]

Morley emphasized, however, that although this particular rumor had proved groundless—Perdomo notwithstanding—there was still cause for concern. The long-standing boundary dispute, dating back to the Spanish colonial period, between Guatemala and Honduras threatened to explode into armed conflict. The dispute had only become dangerous very recently, and as a direct result of the Cuyamel Fruit Company's aggressive expansion. This drive to expand reflected the hard-driving character of the company's owner, Samuel Zemurray. His life was the American Dream. Zemurray began as a penniless immigrant in Mobile and eventually built a banana empire in Central America. From his headquarters in New Orleans he not only gained an ever-increasing share of the market, but in 1911 had overthrown the Honduran government, using General Lee Christmas as his instrument. And in another coup, Zemurray would take over the United Fruit Company in 1932.[25]

The disputed territory was the floodplain of the Motagua River, a vast swampy tropical jungle that was good only for the cultivation of bananas. From the time of its discovery by the Spaniards in the sixteenth century the area had been virtually uninhabited because it was so unhealthy. This began to change dramatically in the early 1900s, when the Cuyamel company began establishing banana plantations there. The company derived title to its land both from purchases and from concessions secured from the government of Honduras. By late 1917 the Cuyamel company had built thirteen plantations and a rail line in the region. As A. G. Greeley, the local manager, freely admitted to Morley, the company held title to its property from Honduras and was engaged in a crash program of developing and improving their facilities in the disputed area just as rapidly as possible. The aim was to have as strong a case as possible of "actual possession" when the disputed strip came up for final adjudication. Therefore, the company was feverishly extending its railroad into the areas south and east of the Motagua River, the very heart of the territory claimed by both Honduras and Guatemala.[26]

Ever eager to see and decide things for himself, Morley determined to travel through the disputed territory. On December 23, Greeley took him to the end of the Cuyamel company's railroad line. A further three miles of right-of-way had been surveyed and partially graded. However, the Guatemalan dictator Estrada Cabrera had rushed in 225 troops, who deployed across the Cuyamel right-of-way. They dug in, laid a telephone line and hacked out a road back into Guatemala, and built huts to live in. Their commander notified Cuyamel to cease and desist. And on December 20, the Guatemalan soldiers began building a telegraph line and a road across the line of the Cuyamel railroad. It was this action that had given rise to the story of a Guatemalan invasion of Honduras that Consul Boyle and Morley had heard back in Puerto Cortés. Honduras had fewer than five hundred troops in the general vicinity, but to meet this Guatemalan aggression the authorities were frantically recruiting patriots. Honduras eventually moved in another five hundred soldiers, but later began withdrawing some of them.

Morley, accompanied by Greeley and Bradley, marched boldly up to the Guatemalan advance guard's positions and asked the commanding officer's permission to pass through his lines in order to reach the Guatemalan railroad and travel on to the capital, "of course in an archaeological capacity," as he smugly informed his ONI control.[27]

The Guatemalan captain quite frankly told Morley that he was rushing work on the telegraph line and the road, and that his orders were to complete them at all costs. A clash with the Hondurans indeed seemed imminent. The officer carefully scrutinized Morley's passport, telephoned his own superior for instructions, and announced that Morley could come through his lines under escort. He even allowed Morley to telegraph ahead for a motorboat that would take him partway. The archaeologist took his leave of Greeley and Bradley; escorted by two barefoot Guatemalan soldiers, he slogged and squished through mud for two miles to the nearest town. Despite his puttees, Morley was soon splattered in mud up to his waist. Morley was in very much of a hurry, for he wanted to get his information to the American legation in Guatemala and to ONI as soon as possible. His motor launch was waiting, and he spent a most unpleasant night chugging downriver in "that wretched little craft," while trying to sleep with a pillow improvised from a dirty shirt and his pajamas wrapped in a towel and with his raincoat for a blanket. But to his relief he reached the railroad station by 7 A.M. the next morning, in time to catch the one train a day to Guatemala City. By that night, December 24, he was at the legation briefing Walter Thurston, the secretary, on the disputed border situation:[28]

I believe this particular strip rightfully belongs to Honduras and will eventually be awarded to her, but that is not the important point now. On the contrary, as I see it, we must take no sides in the question at this time, but must prevent, if possible, any outbreak between the two countries which could require the sending of American troops down here to straighten it out, and correspondingly slacken our efforts in France. Moreover, taking sides now puts us in the disagreeable position of having to choose between the first two nations of Central America which declared against Germany, breaking diplomatic relations with her; in short it forces us to choose between declared friends with the certainty in advance that our decision must displease one side or the other.

As I see it, therefore, we should not force arbitration at this time but try in some other way for an easement of the very delicate situation which undoubtedly prevails in the region, and a withdrawal of the disturbing elements therefrom until the close of the war.[29]

Morley strongly urged this course of action on Thurston, who agreed and so cabled the State Department. The archaeologist made the same recommendation by cable to "Gustav Koch," the ONI accommodation address. When he subsequently submitted his written report to ONI, it included several maps of the disputed territory prepared by Held.

After that week of intense activity, Morley was looking forward to spending a pleasant and relaxed Christmas. Held, who had been sketching and measuring artifacts at Quiriguá, had gone off to spend the holidays with friends in Puerto Barrios. Morley's plans, however, were disrupted in terrifying fashion by that fearsome natural phenomenon— earthquake:

> The present "family" of earthquakes made its first demonstration in November, when on the 17th Guatemala City was given a good little shake. For the next five weeks there were only occasional tremors until the night before Christmas—the evening I reached the city—when about seven o'clock there was another brisk little shake.
>
> I had been out to dinner on Christmas night and was on my way to the American Club for a night-cap before turning in. I had reached a corner just one block from the club when suddenly without warning the ground lifted up under my feet and began to shake violently. My first thought was of the live wires overhead, and I darted into the shelter of a doorway, only to run back again into the street as [the] house to which it gave entrance shook like a leaf scattering plaster over my head.
>
> The electric wires were still spluttering furiously, and realizing my extreme peril directly underneath them, I set off running for the central plaza, three blocks off.
>
> As I passed the American Club there debouched through the doorway perhaps a dozen men, pell-mell into the street. These joined me and we all continued running towards the central plaza. People were already pouring into the latter from all sides by this time, some in pyjamas, some in night-shirts, and the ladies in robes-de-nuit, sketchily covered with blankets or overcoats, as it was cold.
>
> This first shock occurred at 10:32. It was followed almost continuously by tremors of decreased intensity for an hour when the earth again bellied up under our feet and rocked violently back and forth. Buildings around the plaza crashed to the ground, wires short-

circuited, flashed, sputtered, and the Indians all dropped to their knees and fell to droning their "Ave Marias" and telling their beads.

This second shock did the maximum damage. It cracked the walls and roofs, and loosened the masonry. Subsequent tremors have only tumbled this down. But to return to Christmas night.

Followed a longer interval of slight shocks, and then at 2:10 a.m. came the last heavy shock of that long night. It was of about the same intensity as the first and brought down many more buildings. I spent the remainder of the night between the plaza and the patio of a friend.

Only when the day broke could we begin to comprehend the real magnitude of the calamity. Guatemala City was in ruins. Nine-tenths of its houses were either destroyed, or else rendered unsafe for habitation; public buildings, churches and stores were either demolished outright or at best badly damaged. Light and water services were completely disrupted, and have so remained ever since. Telegraph lines were down and railroad communication with both coasts cut, and people began to pour out of the city to neighboring fields and open places.

The government promptly took the situation in hand—martial law was declared; free distribution of food inaugurated; and emergency hospitals established throughout the city. There were no disorders and less than a dozen people all told were shot for looting. The number killed by the shocks on Christmas night are [sic] estimated to have been about 70.

Slight tremors continued for the next four days, the 26, 27, 28, and 29, but only tremors. Public confidence was beginning to return, people were venturing into their houses to salvage what was left of their belongings and we all hoped—and indeed believed—that the worst was over.

Suddenly at two o'clock in the afternoon of the 29th another tremendous shock rocked the stricken city. The movement of this, unlike that of the others, was horizontal—that is from side to side, and as a result many more walls were toppled over. Because it was in the day-time also, many people were in their houses and the loss of life was therefore greater than it had been on Christmas night. More than a hundred people are estimated to have been killed by this one shock alone.

The inhabitants of the city were now thoroughly terrified. No one could predict when the thing would end, and in consequence a great exodus followed, people leaving the city by the hundreds and fleeing to the south coast.

Again we had an interval of five days during which only slight tremors worried us. These had decreased as to intensity but not in the least, as to frequency. The city was in fact slowly being shaken to pieces.

On the afternoon of January third Commander Brumby of "The Cincinnati" with three officers: Lieutenants Taylor and Fox and Ensign Purdy, and three bullies came up from the port of San Jose to offer what emergency relief he could.

The "Cincinnati" had been en route from San Diego, California to Panama and when within 200 miles of the latter had been recalled by a wireless message to San Jose.

It fell to me to accompany him in his call upon the President. This interview passed off satisfactorily. Commander B. offered his sympathies and aid to the President, both of which were gratefully accepted; and later he sent a cable to Washington enumerating certain medical supplies which were urgently needed.

One or two of the officers who came up with him had expressed the hope that they might feel a slight shock just for the experience. They had their wish all right, and more, that same night.

We had had a late dinner at the legation, which by the way is one of the very very few houses which escaped serious injury. At 10:30 we rose from the table and went into the corridor surrounding the patio, the only lights we had being candles.

Ten minutes later came the worst shock which the city has experienced. The earth again rose up beneath our feet and shook violently back and forth, short vicious jerks, which all but threw us off our feet. The glass doors of the corridor smashed, dust rained down on our heads, buildings in the immediate vicinity collapsed—happily the German Club where they had the champagne dinner the night the news of the sinking of the "Lusitania" came in—was one of these, and a fine impalpable adobe dust filled the air, choking us.

Naturally everybody broke for the patio. Ensign Purdy in his haste dived through an open door, ran afoul of a tub of bamboo, upset himself and the floral decorations and barked his shins. This shock by stop-watch lasted eleven minutes and was by far the most destructive of all. It brought down the two tall cathedral towers and the pediments between them; finished the railroad station; laid low the bullring and shook down about every other building the first shocks had left standing. About a hundred people were killed that night, including a number of soldiers who were sleeping in a cuartel which collapsed. The total mortality up to the time I left was about three hundred.

Two of my pictures show the railroad station as it was after the shocks of Christmas night and after that of the night of January third. The difference in the extent of damage between the two accurately measures the relative destructiveness of these two shocks elsewhere in the city. That of the third practically finished the place. It was even felt way over here in Belize as a violent movement of the earth.

Commander Brumby told me the next morning before he left that he had had enough of earthquakes and that he would be perfectly contented to be back on the "Cincinnati" again and headed toward sea.

I made myself known to him and also introduced him to [ONI Agent] No. 84 [J. H. Watts]. Held was in Puerto Barrios, as I have said, so did not meet him. The latter is now in Guatemala City but will be back here next week. I described to Commander B. the nature of my work and told him of our coming trip up the Yucatan coast. But to return to the earthquake.

Guatemala City is literally in ruins; 98 percent of the houses are either entirely destroyed or at best uninhabitable, and indeed I think at least half are flat on the ground. Guatemala City suffered far more than San Salvador did, both actually and relatively—actually because it is twice as large, and relatively because a higher percentage of it was destroyed.[30]

Faced with this catastrophe, the man to whom President Estrada Cabrera turned was General Lee Christmas, the dean of American filibusters in Central America. He appointed Christmas as commander of the "Sanitary Police" and gave him the job of cleaning up Guatemala City. At the head of what was presumably a crack body of sanitary policemen, Christmas went to work.

Christmas was a fabulous character. A large man with clear blue eyes, a ruddy complexion, and a mane of fine white hair, his life was something out of an adventure novel. He had been a locomotive engineer for the Illinois Central in New Orleans, but was fired in 1891 because he got drunk, dozed off at the throttle, and wrecked his train. He then drifted down to Honduras and became a mercenary. Christmas certainly qualified as "an old Central America hand," having first gone to that region in 1894. During his subsequent career he became the quintessential soldier of fortune in a period that produced literally hundreds of American soldiers of fortune. By 1904 he had attained the coveted rank of brigadier general in the Honduran army. But his adventures also included a stint in 1907–1908 as head of the Guatemalan dictator Estrada Cabrera's secret police. The single most spectacular feat Christmas performed occurred in 1910–1911 when, hired by the banana tycoon Samuel Zemurray of New Orleans, he overthrew the government of Honduras and installed the exiled politician General Manuel Bonilla as president.[31]

Morley was introduced to this larger-than-life figure in December 1917, in Guatemala City. Over drinks in the Hotel León where Christmas was staying, the archaeologist and the mercenary hit it off, and Christmas regaled Morley with anecdotes about his colorful career. He even invited Morley to his room to inspect a pair of French dueling pistols of which he was quite proud. Christmas was a spellbinding raconteur, and he kept the archaeologist enthralled as he ranged through a number of topics. He claimed, for example, that President Estrada Cabrera had promised him a lucrative shark-fishing concession, one of whose by-products, incidentally, would be shark-backbone canes. And he alluded to the Guatemalan dictator's request that he stay around for a while in case his military expertise were needed in countering the rumored Mexican-Salvadoran plot to invade Guatemala. The soldier of fortune also gave Morley a detailed account of how he had overthrown the Honduran government and installed Bonilla as president. The most intriguing part of this tale was Christmas's assertion that Bonilla was merely a pawn in an intrigue involving the floating of a loan to Honduras by J. P. Morgan; if the loan had gone through, the then American secretary of state, Philander P. Knox, would have received a $2,000,000 payoff. Morley was appalled and expressed his disgust if the story were true.

Morley was prepared to vouch for Lee Christmas's patriotism. The mercenary had lost his United States citizenship because of his role in overthrowing the Honduran government. But he had recently regained his citizenship, and Morley for one was quite impressed by the pride with which Christmas displayed his American passport. As far as Morley was concerned, whatever Christmas may have done or been in the past, at present he was a loyal American.

This view was not unique to Morley; it was shared by some people in the State Department. After the United States entered World War I, Christmas traveled to Washington in hopes of securing a commission in the army. He failed to get a commission.[32] But in his discussions in Washington, Herbert Stabler of the State Department had suggested that Christmas become a State Department secret agent in Central America. When he failed to become an army officer, Christmas became interested in State's offer. Presumably it beat being the Chief of the Sanitary Police, which he still was in January 1918. Christmas called at the American legation every day, while back in Washington various State Department officials asked each other's opinion on the advisability of hiring Christmas, who was, after all, notorious. Christmas, on the other hand, was anxious to learn how State would react were he to take an active part in what he felt was an inevitable clash between Guatemala and Honduras. While undoubtedly eager to win additional military laurels, Christmas was determined to do nothing to jeopardize his United States citizenship, "the re-granting of which seemed to have caused him great pride."[33] State finally decided to take the plunge. On March 12, 1918, Christmas was sent an application form—in duplicate—to fill out for the position of Special Agent of the State Department. At the same time, the American minister in Guatemala was asked for suggestions as to what tasks to assign Christmas.[34] Incidentally, one of the documents in the State Department file on Christmas was a lengthy extract entitled "Conditions in Central America," taken from Morley's Report no. 19 of February 1, 1918, which ONI had sent over to State.[35]

The American minister in Guatemala gave a favorable appraisal of Christmas, stating that he would be a valuable secret agent. The only problem was that Christmas was a celebrity; thus, his presence anywhere would require a plausible explanation. Fortuitously, such an explanation was at hand. One J. H. Burton, president of the Burton Lumber Co. in New York City, a firm that manufactured prefabricated houses, had recently been in Guatemala City. Burton was trying to sell his product to the Guatemalan government for housing earthquake victims. A substantial contract was at stake. When Burton returned to the United States he had entrusted his interests to Lee Christmas, who had acted as his interpreter and who, of course, had access to President Estrada Cabrera. He had arranged a personal interview for Burton with the dictator. Before hiring Christmas, though, the canny Burton had made discreet inquiries that reassured him that Christmas was a man of integrity—once he was bought he stayed bought. Accordingly, he hired Christmas for $250 a month.[36] The American minister pointed out that Christmas's job with Burton would provide excellent cover for his activities as a secret agent. As to what assignment Christmas should have, the minister came up with a choice bit of diplomatese: "As to the nature of the work to be assigned to him I would recommend that it be of a general character to cover everything going on secretly that would be likely to be of value to our purposes."[37]

On May 17, 1918, Lee Christmas was appointed as a Special Agent of the State Department, although he didn't get around to taking the formal Oath of Allegiance and Office until October 25.[38] He was paid $2,400 a year plus $4 per diem for expenses. Since he was not a bonded State Department officer, he would have to submit his accounts to the American minister in Guatemala, who paid him.[39] Christmas's assignments were to investigate the Guatemala-Honduras boundary dispute, then proceed to Tegucigalpa to evaluate rumors of close ties between President Bertrand and the Germans there. Christmas would next proceed to Amapala to ferret out any links between Bertrand and German commercial houses. Finally, he was to determine whether in fact there was a clandestine German radio station at the Bay of Fonseca.[40] In the late summer of 1918, he was ordered to make a reconnaissance in a small boat of the Honduran coastline from Trujullo to Cape Gracias a Dios, essentially duplicating what Morley and Held had done. This mission was subsequently canceled by the State Department.[41] Christmas's nominal employer, J. H. Burton, consented to the former's activities as an agent of State's Bureau of Secret Intelligence despite the business disruptions this arrangement caused Burton. Cables between State and Christmas were relayed through Burton's New York offices.[42]

This arrangement had unexpected consequences, however. In his capacity as Burton's representative in Guatemala City, Christmas hired an assistant, an American named Webb. The latter proved unsatisfactory and Christmas fired him in June 1918.[43] Christmas then discovered

Webb breaking into his office to steal his papers. The outraged Christmas had Webb arrested and thrown into prison. The hapless Webb then appealed for assistance to the American minister to Guatemala, Dr. William H. Leavell. When Leavell visited him in prison, he was dumfounded when Webb produced a document showing that he worked for the War Trade Board Intelligence Department. Leavell secured the release of Webb, who left immediately for the United States.[44] The whole episode was one of those instances of secret agents tripping over one another.

When Morley learned from Walter Thurston that Lee Christmas too would be performing his patriotic duty as a secret agent, the archaeologist was delighted. But in the aftermath of the devastating Guatemalan earthquakes, Morley was preoccupied with producing political intelligence. He firmly believed that "Guatemala is the keystone of the arch of peace from the Rio Grande to Panama, and so long as she stands firm, Mexico and Salvador cannot start much trouble in Central America. In short, I think he [Estrada Cabrera] may be counted upon now, more than before the quake, to remain friendly and 'right.'"[45] Estrada Cabrera was worried that Mexico and El Salvador would seize the occasion to attack him—precisely the same kind of fear the Salvadoran government had regarding Estrada Cabrera immediately after the devastating Salvadoran earthquake seven months earlier. In Morley's words, "the old President is in a blue funk over the whole business and anticipates trouble where none exists." Evidently the earthquakes had ratcheted the dictator's paranoia up a few notches.

Although neither Morley nor Thurston felt there was much danger of Guatemala being invaded, the archaeologist enumerated several disquieting factors in the earthquakes' aftermath. First, about 100,000 people were living in the streets, parks, and vacant lots under pitifully inadequate shelter. But the rainy season was still five months off, and six thousand tents loaned by the United States would soon be on the way, so this problem would be alleviated to some extent. Second, because of the crowded conditions, sanitation had collapsed. "Latrines have not been established, and people defecate wherever the spirit moves them. All the parks, plazas, and open lots already smell unto high heaven." Local relief committees were utterly incapable of coping, and Morley stressed that foreign assistance was absolutely necessary. "The situation demands a corps of experts under the direction of a capable executive officer, the latter certainly not a Guatemalteco."[46] Regarding the labor situation, Morley had some harsh things to say:

> The labor situation is completely demoralized. The Government issues daily rations of corn—about five ears the person per day— to everybody and consequently no one will work at any figure. Normally the Latin American laborer cares nothing for money so long as he has enough to eat and get drunk upon, consequently now that the government is feeding him, and since he can no longer buy drink—the cantinas are happily all closed by government order— he will not work. He is actually better off now than before the earthquake. He had no property to begin with, and therefore he has lost nothing; before he had to feed himself, and now the Government feeds him. Hence he refuses to work and the business of the capital is at a standstill.[47]

There was no shortage of food in the capital, but there was in the rest of the country. The government was seizing food supplies in the provinces and rushing them to Guatemala City. The result was a glut in the capital and scarcity elsewhere. "All this wants regulation of course, but there appears to be no Guatemalteco honest enough, or capable enough, or armed with sufficient authority to swing the job. In fact nothing short of a foreign commission backed by the President and the full authority of the military—which the people have been taught to fear—will turn the trick."[48]

The financial situation was critical. At present all the banks were operating under an emergency agreement by which they were allowing depositors to withdraw only twenty-five *quetzales* (Guatemalan dollars) a week regardless of the size of their accounts. This arrangement was causing business to stagnate. And even when normal banking resumed, several institutions, such as the Banco Colombiano and the Banco Americano, were said to be in precarious straits and might easily fail. Morley urgently recommended that the United States quickly provide financial assistance to Guatemala: "the present is a Heaven sent opportunity for crushing German commercial supremacy and with it, its invariable accompaniment of German intrigue and propaganda in the richest and strongest country of Central America." In order to rebuild Guatemala City an estimated $10,000,000 to $15,000,000 was needed.

Germany would happily lend that sum, but of course at present she could not. But if a strong American banking institution were established in Guatemala, it could not only be instrumental in obliterating German commercial supremacy in the country but would also provide the capital for rebuilding that the Guatemalans themselves simply did not have. As Morley put it, "In the future let interest on foreign loans be paid to New York, Chicago, and Philadelphia, instead of to Berlin, Hamburg, and Bremen as at present."

Morley reinforced his argument that the United States should act quickly and decisively to assist Guatemala by stressing that Estrada Cabrera was this country's best friend in Central America and the strongest guarantee against upheaval in the status quo. Therefore, American aid could head off destabilization, and possible revolution, arising from the earthquake disaster. He cited

> The moral effect throughout both Americas of standing by our friends in their hour of adversity. Guatemala was the first American Republic excepting Panama and Cuba which of course were wet-nursed into their positions and therefore do not count, to break relations with Germany and to endorse our action thereby. This is a matter of common knowledge, and I believe, even of comment throughout the chancelleries of Central and South America. How can we then afford to desert our first American ally of any consequence in the European war? It appears to me, that political necessity dictates a policy of real aid in the present crisis to convince the other American republics that uncle Sam stands by his friends. And aid to Guatemala now means generous and immediate financial assistance.[49]

It was essentially the same argument he had made to his superiors after the Salvadoran earthquake.

American assistance to Guatemala would have the additional benefit of influencing that country to settle the boundary dispute with Honduras peacefully. For a full week after the earthquakes the American legation in Guatemala was preoccupied with the disaster. When Thurston could finally take up the boundary question, he was instructed by the State Department to proceed along the lines he—and Morley—had suggested. Thurston promptly secured an interview with Estrada Cabrera, who said he welcomed the American suggestion. On January 3, 1918, the old dictator informed Thurston that he would withdraw his troops and discontinue any activity in the disputed region, provided Honduras did likewise. And on January 7, the Guatemalan foreign minister called at the legation and informed Thurston that the withdrawal order had been issued.[50] Morley was later disappointed to learn that Guatemalan and Honduran forces were still facing each other and no withdrawal had occurred. Besides his disappointment that Estrada Cabrera, "a wily old cove," had broken his promise to Thurston, Morley remained worried about the disputed territory:

> So long as Guatemala and Honduras maintain troops in this region drawn up opposite each other just so long will there be danger of a clash between the two countries. It is, in short, an ideal situation for German propagandists. It would not take much either to touch such a situation off: a few pesos worth of aguardiente, a few Teutonic lies, some shots in the bush and a genuine battle might be precipitated. I am not crying the wolf, Taro, I think you will agree I am not given to summoning the lupine visitor without cause; nor do I believe either that any German influence is behind this boundary dispute yet, but the powder and fuse are there and it only wants a spark to set it off.[51]

But someone else would have to deal with that problem.

On January 3, Morley had been a member of an official American delegation visiting President Estrada Cabrera. The archaeologist, acting as surrogate for Walter Thurston, escorted Commander Brumby of the cruiser *Cincinnati* who with several officers was calling on Estrada Cabrera at his presidential complex, La Palma, overlooking the capital. Ushered into that august presence by two Guatemalan generals, what the Americans experienced was anticlimax—Estrada Cabrera received them in a small khaki army tent. Two benches ran along the walls, and at the rear was a table at which the dictator was seated. The interview, in which Estrada Cabrera thanked Brumby for United States assistance and Brumby inquired as to what medical supplies were urgently needed for earthquake relief, lasted half an hour. Morley had the opportunity to study the president, who looked about sixty years old. Morley was struck by his appearance of mental fatigue. His most notable features were his piercing black eyes, and he exuded both cruelty and power. Returning to Guatemala City, Morley accompanied Commander Brumby to Watts's radio station. The president had given Brumby permission to use it, and the commander sent a message requesting the medical supplies to the *Cincinnati* for relaying on to Washington. The interview with Estrada Cabrera was one of the last things Morley did in Guatemala City. On January 8, 1918, the archaeologist left the shattered capital for Belize to prepare his Yucatán reconnaissance.

8. Belizean Interlude

Morley spent a good deal of his time in Belize at his battered portable typewriter finishing a comprehensive report to ONI of his activities since his arrival at Puerto Barrios nine months earlier. The report, dated February 1, 1918, evidenced Morley's typical thoroughness. He included a map by Held showing their travels, and a chronology taken from the archaeologist's diary listing where they had been every single day from April 14, 1917. A second map by Held illustrated the network of sub-agents that Morley had constructed, as well as wireless and telegraph stations, while a third displayed the railroad and steamship lines servicing British Honduras, Guatemala, El Salvador, Honduras, and the Atlantic coast of Nicaragua.[1]

The archaeologist reminded his case officer that when he had first arrived in Central America he had only a general idea of what kind of information ONI wanted and of where and how serious the German problem might be. Consequently, it took him several months to become oriented. Somewhat pedantically, Morley identified two principal problems and two principal fields of potential trouble, the two being, at least so far, unconnected. One problem and potential trouble area was "interior and south coast, political and German; and the other is north coast, political but as yet not German." The cable his ONI case officer had sent Morley in San Salvador in July 1917, ordering him to proceed to Trujillo, and Spinden to Bluefields, clearly indicated what ONI wanted done. Therefore, Morley and Held confined themselves almost exclusively to the second or north coast problem.

In May, Morley had already recruited two subagents, James Roach in Guatemala City and John Bennett in San Pedro Sula. Based upon subsequent observation of the two, however, Morley and Held had concluded that neither subagent was really satisfactory: "Roach, though of unquestioned loyalty—he is from good old American stock—is not an 'information getter,' in fact he is temperamentally inhibited from ever becoming one. And Bennett of equally unquestioned loyalty is at the same time too much of a talker and alarmist to be a success at our work. I therefore suggest that these two men be stricken from the list of our agents and not utilized in the future." Their loss would not be serious because their territory was being quite ably covered by ONI Agent J. H. Watts from Guatemala City. And whoever ONI decided to send—Morley had reluctantly recommended Arthur Carpenter—to cover San Pedro Sula should be a "live wire" because in Morley's opinion that city was the strongest German center from Bluefields to Belize.

With experience, Morley had assembled a much more capable group of subagents.[2] As he explained, these were, without exception, leading men in their communities. Most of them had large organizations under their direct control and were exceptionally well positioned to know what was happening in their territories. And each of these individuals was characterized by responsibility and superior judgement. Each had served his apprenticeship in Central America and was thoroughly familiar with local conditions. If any of them reported trouble, ONI should take the report seriously. Morley could recommend his subagents as being "dependable in the highest degree." Expounding on this point, the archaeologist stressed:

> This quality of good judgment of mental balance; when to S.O.S. and when to wait, seems to me to be one of the most vital to success in our work. Already there has been too much hysteria, too many false alarms and abortive warnings. We fritter away our slender energies in running down false clues, and dissipate our all too little strength over unessentials. Chronic pessimism in the end is likely to prove as costly as confirmed optimism, the one as dangerous as the other. These agents, however, are not the men to go off at half cock. They know their Central America inside and out, and should any of them send out a hurry call the occasion will be found to have justified it.

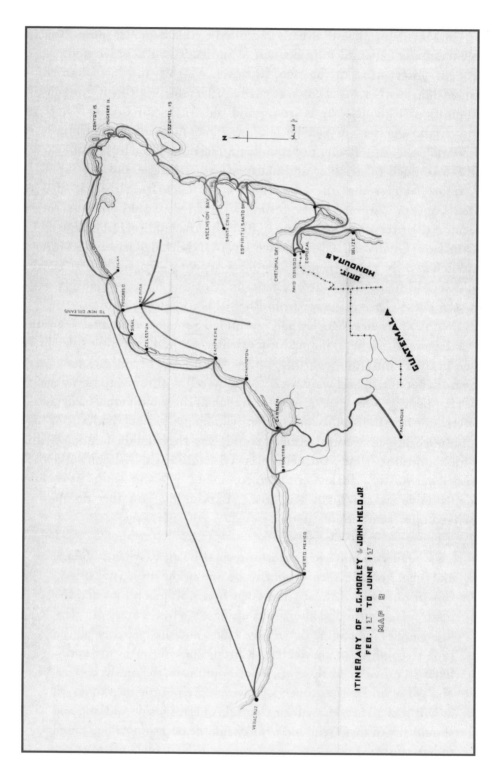

ITINERARY OF S.G. MORLEY & JOHN HELD JR
FEB. 1ST TO JUNE 1ST
MAP B

The members of Morley's network were:

1. Belize	Dr. T. Gann	Principal Medical Officer of British Honduras	The Belize Hospital, Belize, Brit. Honduras
2. Livingston	Mr. E. Reed	American Consul at Livingston, Guatemala	American Consulate, Livingston, Guatemala
3. Puerto Barrios	Mr. G. M. Shaw	Manager Guatemala Division United Fruit Co.	United Fruit Co., Puerto Barrios, Guat.
"	Mr. A. A. Pollan	Secretary to preceding	United Fruit Co., Puerto Barrios, Guat.
4. Oma & Cuyamel	Mr. A. G. Greeley	Manager Cuyamel Fruit Co.	Cuyamel Fruit Co., Cuyamel, Honduras
5. Tela	Mr. R. H. Goddell	Manager Tela R. R. (United Fruit Co.)	Tela R. R. Co., Tela, Honduras
6. Ceiba	Mr. D. H. McCullough	Leading American importer in Ceiba	Ceiba, Honduras
7. Rincon	Mr. H. D. Scott	Manager Trujillo R. R. (United Fruit Co.)	Trujillo R. R., Trujillo, Honduras
8. Cape Gracias a D.	Mr. P. A. Bischoff	Assistant Manager C. C Mengel Mahogany Co. Nicaragua	C. C. Mengel Mahogany Co., Cape Gracias a Dios, Nicaragua
9. Bluefields	Mr. B. M. White	Manager C. C. Mengel Mahogany Co. Nicaragua	C. C. Mengel Mahogany Co., Bluefields, Nicaragua

Map 3. Held's map covers four months of Morley's operations from Belize, British Honduras beginning February 1, northward along the coast of the Mexican territory of Quintana Roo, thence along the coast of Yucatán, inland to Merida, and beyond. Subsequently, Morley and Held covered portions of the states of Campeche, Chiapas, Tabasco, and Veracruz, before boarding ship to sail to New Orleans, June 1, 1918. Courtesy Office of Naval Intelligence, National Archives.

What is striking about this list is the presence of Morley's friend Dr. Thomas Gann of Belize. Gann was not merely a subagent as were the others—he was ONI Agent No. 242. This was noteworthy, but what was remarkable about Gann was that not only was the good doctor Our Man in Belize, he was also Their Man in Belize. Gann was the chief British intelligence officer in the colony. This arrangement was surely a most unusual instance of Anglo-American cooperation in the field of intelligence. But what Gann really represented was both cooperation and compromise between the two Allied powers.

In May 1916, the Counselor of the State Department, Leland Harrison, had been anxious to dispatch a Bureau of Secret Intelligence agent to Belize to investigate the arms traffic across the British Honduras border with Mexico. This was in connection with reports of a revolutionary movement against Guatemala being organized in Mexico, allegedly with support from within British Honduras. Harrison asked the British Ambassador, Sir Cecil Spring-Rice, for his government's reaction to the idea. The British government dealt with the overture in a charmingly urbane manner. The Foreign Office solicited the views of both the Admiralty and the War Office. The Admiralty replied that if the Americans pursued the proposal, then in the interests of reciprocity the American government be asked for permission to send a British agent to the Philippines to investigate rumors that they were a conduit for Germans supplying arms to subversive elements in India.[3] The War Office, for its part, raised no objection to the American proposal but as quid pro quo in arms traffic investigation suggested that the American government be asked for permission to send British agents to Buffalo, New York, and to Lima, Ohio, to investigate arms smuggling on behalf of the Irish independence movement Sinn Fein.[4] The Americans got the message and quietly dropped the idea.[5] British Honduras remained a hotbed of intrigue, and Gann's dual role was an imaginative solution to a delicate intelligence problem: this way the Americans and the British could not only keep an eye on the Germans but on each other as well.

Having discussed the acquisition of information, Morley turned to its transmission. Obviously, the region's radio stations offered the best means of communicating intelligence information quickly. Referring his case officer to Held's second map, Morley listed these stations, which were shown on the map as large red circles: Belize, Guatemala City, Tela, La Ceiba, Rincón, and Bluefields. Transmissions from these stations were all relayed through Swan Island, although Belize, La Ceiba, and Rincón relayed through Tela for commercial convenience.

The Belize wireless station was the property of the colonial government. Morley had arranged with the governor that if Dr. Gann needed to transmit anything urgently Gann would be permitted to communicate directly with "Dominus," the ONI cable accommodation address in Panama. In Guatemala City the government wireless station was operated by ONI Agent J. H. Watts. President Estrada Cabrera permitted him to send messages either in English or in code, provided they were signed by the American minister. But occasionally Watts was able to slip a message through unrestricted. The United Fruit Company stations at Tela and Rincón were directly under the orders of Morley's subagents Goodell and Scott, and both men had already been instructed to accept messages for "Dominus." Morley stated that he had personally tested this arrangement in December by sending a message from Tela to Panama. At La Ceiba the Vaccaro Brothers Company, owner of the wireless station, had given similar instructions. The company's local manager, Salvator D'Antoni, was a personal friend of Morley's subagent D. H. McCullough, and had been ordered to accept messages from McCullough for "Dominus." Morley had likewise tested this arrangement by sending a message to Panama. As for the Bluefields station, the day Morley had left Bluefields Mr. Easton, manager of the United Fruit wireless service at Swan Island and Limón, told Morley that the Bluefields station had been instructed to accept all messages for Panama.

Morley could take considerable satisfaction in having built a network of subagents and arranging communications for them. Yet the communications facilities were not completely satisfactory. Supplementing the wireless net was a chain of telegraph stations along the coast. But they were all government owned, so messages could not be sent as freely as by wireless. These stations, indicated in blue on Held's map were, from north to south:

1. Belize   British Honduras
2. Stann Creek   "   "
3. All Pines   "   "
4. Riversdale   "   "
5. Monkey River   "   "

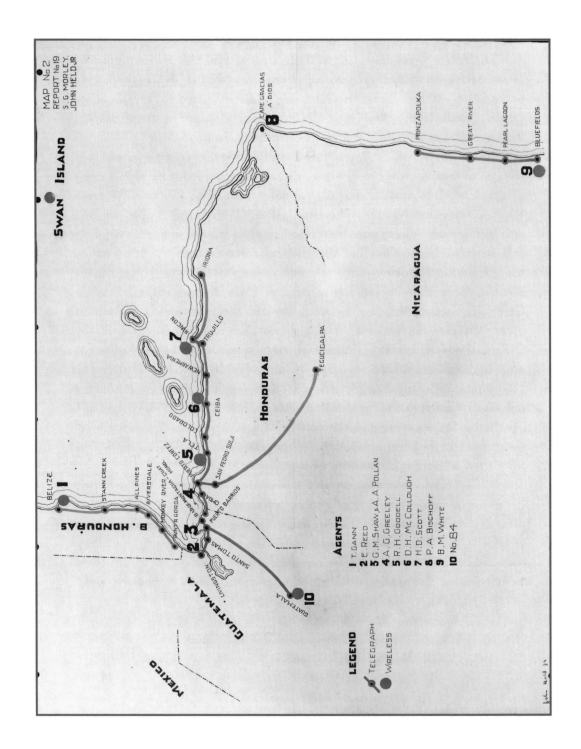

MAP No 2
REPORT No 19
S. G MORLEY,
JOHN HELD JR

SWAN ISLAND

MEXICO

B. HONDURAS

GUATEMALA

BELIZE
STANN CREEK
ALL PINES
RIVERSDALE
MONKEY RIVER
PUNTA GORDA
RIO HONDO
BASE-MANAGUA - CHAT
PUERTO TOPITZ
LIVINGSTON
SANTO TOMAS

HONDURAS

PUERTO BARRIOS
OHOA
SAN PEDRO SULA
TELA
TOLDRADO
CEIBA
NEW ARMENIA
RINCON
TRUJILLO
IRIONA
TEGUCIGALPA
CAPE GRACIAS A' DIOS

NICARAGUA

PRINZAPOLKA
GREAT RIVER
PEARL LAGOON
BLUEFIELDS

AGENTS
1 T. GANN
2 E. REED
3 G. M. SHAW, & A. A. POLLAN
4 A. G. GREELEY
5 R. H. GOODELL
6 D. H. McCOLLOUGH
7 H. D. SCOTT
8 P. A. BISCHOFF
9 B. M. WHITE
10 No. 84

LEGEND
TELEGRAPH
WIRELESS

6. Punta Gorda	British Honduras	
7. Livingston	Guatemala	
8. Santo Tomas	"	
9. Puerto Barrios	"	
10. Bar of the Motagua	"	
11. Bar of the Motagua	Honduras	
12. Omoa	"	
13. Puerto Cortez	Honduras	
14. Tela	"	
15. Colorado	"	
16. Ceiba	"	
17. New Armenia	"	
18. Trujillo	"	
19. Rincon	"	
20. Iriona	"	
21. Prinzapolka	Nicaragua	
22. Great River	"	
23. Pearl Lagoon	"	
24. Bluefields	"	

And there was a further complication. There existed one large gap in the facilities—a "dead zone" where there were neither wireless nor telegraph stations for transmitting information speedily. The center of this zone was Cape Gracias a Dios; the Honduran government telegraph extended eastward only as far as Iriona and the Nicaraguan government line extended northward only to Prinzapolka.

Not surprisingly, Morley recommended that a wireless station be constructed at Cape Gracias a Dios. Such a station could be relatively

---

Map 4. In only nine months Morley had recruited a formidable network of agents who covered the east coast of Central America from Bluefield's, Nicaragua to Belize, British Honduras. Held's map illustrates where Morley's ten agents were located and whether they had access to either radio or telegraph communication. Courtesy Office of Naval Intelligence, National Archives.

modest—a single small tower with a transmitter having a 250-mile radius would easily reach Swan Island, Bluefields, and Rincón. And the station might even be built at no cost to the United States government. The C. C. Mengel Mahogany Company of Louisville, Kentucky, which exported mahogany from that area, might be willing to erect such a wireless station to facilitate the operation of their business. In any case, Morley urged, the proposed station was urgently needed to plug this most serious communications gap extending for hundreds of miles along the isolated stretch of coastline.

A lesser priority would be the addition of a wireless station at either Omoa or Cuyamel. As things stood now, in the event of trouble Morley's subagent A. G. Greeley would have to use the government telegraph to communicate with the American legation in Tegucigalpa. The legation, in turn, would have to use the government telegraph to contact the nearest cable office, which was located in San Salvador. A wireless station at either Omoa or Cuyamel would obviate this slow and insecure transmission chain and, while not absolutely necessary, would thus be quite useful. In this connection, Morley mentioned that when he had been in Cuyamel, Greeley had said that had it not been for the war the Cuyamel Fruit Company would have installed a wireless station there. Moreover, Greeley was of the opinion that the company would install one now if the United States government asked them to do so and granted the necessary permission to export the apparatus required.

On the subject of wireless communications, Morley reported that his subagent at Puerto Barrios, G. M. Shaw, manager of the Guatemala division of United Fruit, had passed through Belize the day before on his way back from the United States. Shaw stated that while in New York he had tried to persuade the manager of the United Fruit wireless service to install a station at Puerto Barrios. Shaw felt that if United Fruit gave him permission, he could secure the necessary concession from Estrada Cabrera with little or no delay. To Morley, the advantages of such a station were obvious. It would constitute an important link in the coastal chain, but more importantly it would free the ONI subagents in Livingston and Puerto Barrios from having to communicate through Guatemala City. That channel was subject to interruption at any time, due to the frequent failure of telegraphic service to the capital. If these three stations were added, but especially the one at Cape Gracias a Dios, there would be a complete transmission system stretching from the northern frontier of

British Honduras to Limón, Costa Rica. All the ONI agents along the coast would be in wireless communication with the outside world.

Morley made a further recommendation, that his subagents receive official letters of commendation from someone high in authority—preferably the secretary of the navy—thanking them individually for their willingness to serve their country in this delicate but very important work. The archaeologist explained that these men were not motivated by any desire for gain or financial remuneration. In fact, each and every one of them was already earning at least twice what ONI could afford to pay; some of them, such as Goodell and Shaw, earned in excess of $10,000 a year, which in 1918 was real money. All these individuals were willing to accept the additional responsibilities only because they wanted to do their bit to win the war and saw in ONI service the best way of doing so. Morley stressed that his agents would not accept salaries, only reimbursement for necessary expenses. But official letters of commendation would be deeply appreciated and would bring home to them the importance of their work. "I sincerely trust you may be able to have such letters sent to them for, believe me, it will return compound interest in increased willingness, alertness and efficiency."[6] Even though he was an amateur spy, Morley grasped the fundamental concept that in intelligence work the psychological rewards for agents are sometimes more important than any monetary consideration. And, as a good leader, he was solicitous of the welfare of his men.

With regard to railroad facilities, Morley realized that this information was more useful to the military than to ONI, but he did make the point that Guatemala was at least theoretically vulnerable to simultaneous invasion by Mexico, El Salvador, and Honduras, all of which had strategic railroads that could be used to move troops rapidly for an attack.

Turning to maritime matters, Morley stated:

> The steamship lines, their routes and ports of call emphasize another important point in our work. They clearly demonstrate that security for us in these countries follows our merchant marine, and they define at the same time the zones of maximum and minimum danger, where intelligence service is most and least required.

Morley's discussion of the coast began with the port of Progreso in Yucatán, which was serviced primarily by the Ward Line. Then eastward

to Cape Catoche and down the Yucatán peninsula to British Honduras
there was a stretch of 450 miles of coastline where no steamers called
and where only the infrequent sailing vessel or fishing boat were found.
Four years earlier the Mexican government had maintained a trimonthly
gunboat service in these waters, but had abandoned the effort. "This
stretch therefore is a zone of potential danger, where trouble might log-
ically be anticipated."

Conversely, the zone of maximum safety was that section of coastline from British Honduras as far east as Trujillo, Honduras. These waters
were teeming with maritime traffic of all kinds—steamships, motorboats,
sailing vessels, and small craft. At Belize the United Fruit Company and
the Otis Company provided fairly regular weekly sailings. In addition,
from Belize there were weekly sailings to the smaller ports in British
Honduras. United Fruit also serviced Livingston, Santo Tomás, and
Puerto Barrios, as did many Bay Island schooners and a host of small
craft. The Cuyamel Fruit Company owned two or three steamers, which
constantly plied between Omoa and New Orleans. And United Fruit's
steamers called at least weekly at Puerto Cortés and Tela. The Vaccaro
Brothers Company's three steamships were engaged in making round
trips between La Ceiba and New Orleans. Finally, United Fruit ships
occasionally called at Rincón and Trujillo. This whole stretch of coastline, as well as the adjacent islands, was "constantly patrolled by an
extensive fleet of friendly craft, from whose ceaseless, if unintentional,
vigilance little escapes."

There was, however, a second zone of maximum danger—from
Trujillo east to Cape Gracias a Dios. Traffic along this desolate coast consisted largely of tramp steamers that called at the cape once or twice a
month to load mahogany. And there was a considerable trade in
mahogany along the coast of Nicaragua, with Prinzapolka, Wawa, and
Waunta being the principal centers. The steamers calling at these ports
to load lumber, together with the motorboats plying the coast, provided
a reasonably adequate surveillance of this part of the coast. Farther south,
Bluefields was connected to New Orleans by a weekly steamer. Morley
was not familiar with conditions south of Bluefields, but he had been told
there were no regular sailings between Bluefields and Limón, Costa Rica,
where there began another zone of safety extending to Colón, Panama
and patrolled by regular sailings of United Fruit steamships.

After this discussion of the coast, Morley gave a summary of political conditions in Central America. As he had already noted, there were two problems in the region and two possible areas of danger: the highlands of the interior and the Pacific coast, and, secondly, the Atlantic coast. Morley classified both El Salvador and Guatemala as being in the former category, while Honduras was in the latter. He explained that when the Spaniards colonized Central America in the sixteenth century they established their provincial capitals in the highlands of the interior, relatively close to the Pacific coast. After independence, these cities became the national capitals. "It is on the Pacific side, therefore, that the political cauldron seethes the hottest, and it is here that practically all the Germans . . . , with the exception of the colony at San Pedro Sula, are located. And it is in this region therefore where their machinations and intrigues are the most pronounced."

The archaeologist offered his considered opinion, that "Guatemala is safe, at least so long as the present regime prevails. The President is on our side through the strongest possible tie that binds these Central American people, namely, self-interest." Although the German colony in Guatemala was the wealthiest and most powerful in Central America, its members were under the closest surveillance by Estrada Cabrera's minions. Unless the Allies suffered some military catastrophe, or unless Mexico and El Salvador were to attack Guatemala, Morley envisioned no trouble from the Germans there. He went on to reiterate his earlier recommendations regarding ways the United States could use the situation arising from the recent earthquake to its advantage. He again stressed the advisability of providing emergency relief, for:

> Guatemala was the first American republic to break diplomatic relations with Germany (I discount Cuba and Panama as being national minors) and for this reason Pan-America, but particularly the four sister republics, is watching the situation closely to see whether it pays to be Uncle Sam's friend or whether Guatemala has drawn a blank.

A much different situation obtained in El Salvador. There, the population and government were frankly anti-American if not openly pro-German. "Happily their teeth were drawn some six months ago when the earthquake of June 7 gave them something else to think about besides plotting against their Tio Sam." Morley had recommended at the time that the United States apply economic pressure against El Salvador, if for no other reason than to show Honduras that it paid to be an American ally and that the Honduran breaking of relations with Germany had been a shrewd move. El Salvador depended on the United States, particularly on American steamship lines, for her foreign commerce; cutting off this service should quickly bring El Salvador to heel. Morley was very tough-minded insofar as dealing with Central America was concerned: "Please let me repeat, Taro, there is no such thing as altruism and statecraft in the politics of these countries; the business of state is done on a strictly quid pro quo basis."

Regarding Honduras, when Morley left there six months earlier, the situation was satisfactory except for German commercial dominance at Amapala. But since then the German firms of Koencke & Co. and P. Maier had been blacklisted. This was welcome news to Morley, who expressed "the earnest hope that the provisions of our blacklist will be vigorously, ceaselessly, and relentlessly enforced." It was, the archaeologist believed, the strongest weapon the United States had to crush German intrigue and propaganda, which invariably followed German trade. Its rigorous enforcement should be made a priority for American consular officers. The German firms at Amapala had had to turn their holdings over to one Dr. Gasteazoro, a Nicaraguan living in San Salvador who was an old friend of Morley's and "a very smooth hombre." Moreover, Morley understood that Pacific Mail steamers no longer called at Amapala, though on these matters "Taro" was much better informed than Morley because Joe Spinden had been reporting on developments in this part of Honduras. If there was an area of concern it was on the Atlantic coast, which Morley had already discussed. The likelihood of a German submarine base anywhere on this coastline was, to say the least, remote.

Yet there was another kind of danger on the north coast of Honduras—that of revolution against the present government, which was neither strong nor particularly popular. The previous December, in fact, a short-lived insurrection had occurred in the area between Trujillo and La Ceiba. And there was a rumor that Estrada Cabrera had supported the rising as a way of diverting attention from the boundary dispute.[7] Morley's view was that rebellions in the coastal area required the immediate and calming presence of American gunboats. He added that these insurrections were usually plotted and launched from Xcalac or

Payo Obispo, Yucatán, on the border with British Honduras. Morley planned to investigate this area on his forthcoming trip along the Yucatán peninsula, and he would try to leave a subagent there, for it was a strategic site. He pointed out:

> Our only safeguard against these activities is to know about them in advance through our agents so that we can discount their effect and [if] possible render them abortive. They are only a natural expression of the turbulent Central American temperament, the eternal struggle of the "outs" to get "in," and may be expected to continue throughout the war. They only become sinister and menacing, however, when they are backed by German brains and money, or have been allowed to gain too much headway.

Unfortunately for the historian, Morley chose not to commit to paper his key recommendation:

> I am reserving until I reach Washington the most important recommendation of all in regard to our intelligence work down here, the result of my observations for the past six months along the north coast. As I can lay this matter before you more advantageously in person, I will postpone mention of it until I see you in the spring.

To that end Morley was organizing his expedition to Yucatán, at the end of which lay the home leave for which he and Held were yearning.

Morley chartered in Belize a twenty-two-ton sloop, the *Lilian Y*, which had a thirty-six-horsepower Wolverine auxiliary engine, a forty-one-foot keel, a seventeen-foot beam, and a five-foot draft. The vessel carried a crew of six—captain/owner, engineer, oiler, two deckhands, and a cook. In addition, Morley's party consisted of himself, Held, Dr. Gann, a cook, and a servant. The servant, a youth named Hubert, had no passport photograph. No problem. Held simply sketched him in profile on the appropriate blank in Hubert's passport.[8] By the terms of the charter Morley paid $15 a day for the boat, and took care of all papers, clearances, bills of health and so on. The captain paid and fed his crew.[9]

This arrangement proved eminently satisfactory. The archaeologist would enthusiastically report: "We went where, when and how we pleased. There was no grouching over the fuel consumed; and the crew being fed by the owner did not bring their dietary troubles to me." Morley felt that short of owning one's own vessel, this arrangement was by far the best for intelligence work. Chartering a boat had already proved its value during his extended cruise on the *Lily Elena*; it did so again on the Yucatán trip. But chartering a boat was expensive, and it would consume most of the $1,000 ONI sent him in Belize. He requested that an additional $500 be waiting for him at the end of the trip, to be sent to him in care of the American consul at Frontera, Tabasco, Mexico.

Morley was pleased, for reasons both archaeological and intelligence-related, to have his friend Dr. Gann along. As we have seen, Gann was the ONI agent for British Honduras as well as being the principal medical officer of the colony. In order to secure the doctor's services for the trip, Morley had to obtain the governor's permission. This involved several cordial conferences in Belize with that official, the results of which were gratifying:

> A plan of close cooperation in this work was perfected and Dr. Gann was appointed Intelligence Officer for the colony with permission to act for us in the same capacity at the same time. He was given a two months' leave from his regular duties in the colony in order to make this trip, during which period I allowed him the customary salary of $100.00 (gold) a month and expenses.[10]

The only condition the governor imposed was that he be furnished with a copy of Morley's report on Yucatán; to reciprocate, a copy of Gann's report to the governor would be furnished to ONI. When Morley made his final report, on March 31, 1918, instead of sending the usual duplicate copies to ONI separately, a precaution in case of loss, he sent the report in triplicate, accompanied by Held's map in triplicate, so that ONI could duly forward one set to the government of British Honduras. The crowning gesture in the Anglo-American love feast going on in Belize occurred when Governor W. Hart Bennett graciously made available his yacht, the *Patricia*, to transport Morley's party in comfort to Corozal, on the northern frontier of British Honduras. There, on February 3, they boarded the *Lilian Y*, which had preceded them.

The timetable for the journey had been revised several times. In the latest version Morley expected to have completed his reconnaissance at Progreso, the port of Mérida, the capital of Yucatán, in April. By mid-

April he and Held would be on their way back to the United States, but instead of returning directly from Progreso they would continue down the Mexican coast to Laguna del Carmen and Frontera. That way they could investigate the Bahía de Términos and the Usumacinta River. This would delay their arrival in Washington by a month, but, as Morley wryly observed, what was another month added to the eleven they would have already spent in the field.[11]

9. The Naval District

While Morley was preparing for his Yucatán trip in the spring of 1918, significant changes had been taking place in the Office of Naval Intelligence's structure in the field. ONI shifted operational control over its agents in Central America to the 15th Naval District in the Panama Canal Zone. This command was responsible for Area No. 2, which included not just the waters adjacent to the Panama Canal but also Central America and northern South America; Area No. 1 encompassed the Mexican coast, from the Rio Grande to British Honduras.

The naval district system, established in 1903, originally consisted of thirteen districts covering the coasts of the United States, with their primary function being coastal defense. But in 1916, under the pressure of World War I, which included the increased use of submarines, several additional districts were created and all the districts were transferred from the Bureau of Navigation to the Office of the Chief of Naval Operations. The districts were also given full-time staffs and new operational and administrative responsibilities.[1]

The 15th Naval District was not established until November 28, 1917. Its headquarters were at Balboa, on the Pacific side of the Panama Canal Zone. The District's commanding officer held the title of "Commandant" and theoretically was to be a line officer holding at least the rank of Captain.[2] And under the revised district regulations of 1916, the District's staff included an "aide for Information" (Intelligence), and a District Intelligence Service.[3] Operational subdistricts, called sections, were also created; each section base conducted local operations.[4]

Presumably because of a shortage of captains and despite the obvious strategic importance of the Panama Canal, the Commandant of the 15th Naval District was not a captain as prescribed by regulations. He was Commander L. R. Sargent who was commander, naval forces, Canal Zone, with the cruiser *Tallahassee* as his flagship. Commander (later Captain) Sargent was assigned the additional duty as Commandant, 15th Naval District.[5] In August, 1917, the marine superintendent of the Canal Zone, who had been handling intelligence matters, had transferred this responsibility to Sargent (ONI Agent No. 176), along with a bank account of $1,000 and Agent J. J. Perdomo.[6]

Providing insight into the view from ONI headquarters in the fall of 1917 is the following "Personal and Confidential" letter from Lt. Commander O. W. Fowler to Commander Sargent:[7]

October 18, 1917.

My dear Sargent,

I am writing to you personally as there are so many things that I can take up in a personal note that are difficult to handle in an official communication. In the first place, I am in charge in this Office, under [Captain Edward] McCauley, of the work such as you are doing in that section for O.N.I. I consider that Area No. 2, as regards the Navy, is the most important section on this side of the Atlantic. I am very glad that you have consented to take charge of it and can assure you that this Office will give you all the money and men required. The letter requesting that you be given this duty, in addition to your present duty, has been sent to Navigation and you should receive your orders within the next few days. I believe that you have enough men, sent you from this Office, with the possible exception of someone for the Zone. Each of the men already placed should be in a position, by this time, to pick out on the spot such other men as may be needed. However, if you want any assistants please advise stating what sort of men you desire—gentlemen or men to mingle with the working classes.

Under an arrangement with the other departments the Navy is now handling all matters connected with shipping, arrivals, departures, etc., in general everything connected with the sea or along the coast. Captain Cone told me the method of handling suspects, arriving and departing from the Canal Zone, and it appears that it would be difficult for any agent to slip through. I understand that the enemy is now attempting to send mail carriers from Brazil and Argentina to Spain by way of Chile, the Canal, and Havana. I have informed the Attache to Chile of this and he will keep you posted regarding the sailing of suspicious passengers from the ports of the West coast of South America for the Canal Zone.

The work of this Office is continually increasing and there is now in addition to its former work the making of investigations of suspicious firms for the chief censor, the export board, war industry, etc. Probably the greatest part of the work this Office may send you will be investigating suspicious firms, cable messages and shipments requesting information regarding enemy agents or suspects.

When your organization gets sufficiently under way we would like to receive monthly reports showing a summary of work within the Area.

With kind personal regards, I am
Very sincerely yours,
[O. W. Fowler]
Commander L. R. Sargent, U.S.N.
Commander, Naval Forces, I.C.Z.

ONI later assured Sargent that "the Office will approve practically anything in the way of funds and personnel for which you can show reasonable proof of need."[8] Further, ONI proposed changing the way agents reported. Heretofore they had mailed their reports in duplicate, one copy for ONI in Washington and one to the 15th Naval District. As of August 1917, the 15th Naval District's accommodation addresses were: for mail—J. J. Perdomo, P.O. Box 202, Ancón, Canal Zone; for cables—Dominus, Panama. However, Dominus became compromised, so on August 22 the accommodation addresses were changed: for mail—American Forwarding Co., P.O. Box 698, Cristóbal, Canal Zone; for cables—Wilburjohn, Cristóbal.[9] ONI now suggested that agents report directly and exclusively to Commander Sargent, who would review their reports and forward on to Washington only the information he felt was pertinent. The overburdened Sargent disagreed: "The limitations of existing mail service are such that a delay as long as two months would not be unusual in getting a report to Washington if it were routed Via this office instead of direct."[10] The old system continued.

Commander Sargent had some strong views of his own about restructuring the agent network. As Sargent put it, "The Agents who were early in the field apparently had roving commissions of considerable scope; and certain of their investigations carried them for considerable periods away from the sphere of postoffices and cable stations."[11] Sargent intended to establish a clear organizational structure. He dispatched Alcibiades Antoine Seraphic (ONI Agent No. 94) on an inspection and organizational tour of ONI stations in Colombia and Venezuela. Because of the difficulty of communication with the Canal Zone, it was decided to have the naval authorities in Puerto Rico handle Venezuela. The 15th Naval District retained jurisdiction over Colombia, maintaining an agent in the port of Santa Marta.

He was Oliver Clay Townsend, whose career was considerably different from that of other ONI agents. In April 1917, ONI had found itself unable for lack of resources to cover the coast of neutral Colombia between Cartagena and Panama. There was concern because of the many Germans living in Colombia and widespread pro-German—really anti-American—sentiment in that country. The Colombians bitterly resented the way the United States had engineered Panama's independence from Colombia in 1903 in order to build and control the Panama Canal. What ONI desperately needed in order to cover the strategic portion of Colombia's coastline was someone who was familiar with Colombia and who was experienced enough to deal with the authorities and avoid any international complications. Furthermore, he must have a plausible excuse for operating in Colombian waters. And finally, he must furnish his own boat, since at that time ONI lacked the legal authority to take over and assign a boat for such duty.

Improbably, a man meeting these unusual qualifications was located. A forty-eight-year-old mining engineer from North Carolina with business interests in Colombia, Oliver C. Townsend, was recommended to Captain Edward Macauley, who interviewed him and asked him to take on the assignment "with the primary duty of policing the coast for protection against German submarine bases." Townsend agreed, and on April 6, 1917, he was commissioned as a lieutenant (j.g.) In the Naval Coast Defense Reserve (Class 4). Townsend was commissioned so that he could receive funds; by law only an officer could do so. Moreover, in case of embezzlement, he could be court-martialed.

Townsend (Agent No. 55) departed for Colombia on April 8, 1917, arriving in Cartagena on May 1. From then until November 1918 he received no orders from ONI headquarters in Washington. And, as Townsend stated: "In May, 1918, I was asked to confer with Commander Sargent, at Panama. It was then agreed that my work should remain independent, the effect of which was to practically leave me without any close affiliation with Washington Headquarters, and with only an occasional contact with Panama." Townsend, the Lone Sailor, remained in the field until December 8, 1918.

Left to his own devices, Townsend soon organized the effective surveillance of the three hundred miles of Colombian coast between Cartagena and Panama. This was accomplished initially at no cost to ONI. Townsend himself defrayed all the expenses between May 1 and October 1, 1917, because of the difficulty ONI experienced in establishing funding channels. Townsend was, however, subsequently reimbursed. The patrol system Townsend organized included four large seagoing powerboats, as well as his personal forty-eight-foot launch *Porpoise*. This improbable fleet "effectively shut off the possibility of any enemy base establishment or other activity in this locality, which by reason of its many natural base sites constituted, in the eyes of the Naval Authorities for a certain period at least, a genuine menace to allied shipping and the Panama Canal approaches." In addition, Townsend established a patrol system on the Pacific coast of Colombia to cover the area between the port of Buenaventura and the Canal Zone. One large powerboat and two sailing coasters performed this duty. Despite considerable opposition from Germans in Colombia, which took the form of attacks in the newspapers, secret appeals to the Colombian government, and the antagonism of petty customs officials who were recruited to obstruct his activities, Townsend doggedly carried out his lonely assignment. As per his request, he was honorably discharged on March 26, 1919.[12]

Colombia may not have been a priority with Commander Sargent, but Central America was. He dispatched agent J. J. Perdomo on an inspection tour lasting from October 14, 1917, to January 12, 1918, when he arrived back in the Canal Zone. During this tour, Perdomo made a complete circuit of Central America except for the east coast of Nicaragua. He managed to meet all the ONI agents, although some of these meetings had been difficult to arrange because of the perennial communications problem. For example, it will be recalled that Perdomo made contact with Morley quite by accident in a hotel lobby. But for all his efforts, Perdomo's organizational abilities were less than outstanding. Sargent informed the Director of Naval Intelligence: "While I cannot commend too highly his willingness and faithfulness, I feel that as an organizer, he hardly met with the success I had expected." By April 1918 Perdomo had been reassigned to Cartagena, Colombia. From there he was transferred to Rio de Janeiro, where he served under the naval attaché from June 20, 1918, to February 27, 1919. The change evidently did Perdomo a world of good, for the attaché wrote: "Excellent agent . . . Has been a most indefatigable and intelligent worker. In my opinion he has been the most valuable agent that has served under me during the war."[13]

Whatever might be thought of Perdomo, his efforts did help Commander Sargent to reorganize Central America. The secretary of the navy himself gave Sargent broad authority to do so: "All agents except Vice Consuls are wholly at your disposition as to locating them."[14] On April 1, 1918, Sargent divided Central America into five sections:[15]

SECTION No. 1
> *Costa Rica*
> Headquarters of Agent: San José.
>> East Coast Sub-Agent: Puerto Limón
>> West Coast Sub-Agent: Puntarenas
>> Active Helpers: 6

SECTION No. 2
> *Eastern Littoral of Nicaragua*
> Headquarters: Bluefields
>> Voluntary aids at Cape Gracias and among the
>> mahogany camps along this shore.
>> Active Helpers: 6

SECTION No. 3
> *Republic of Salvador, West Coast of Honduras,*
> *and West Coast of Nicaragua.*
> Headquarters: San Salvador, Republic of Salvador.
>> Sub-Agent: Amapala, Honduras.
>> Sub-Agent: Corinto, Nicaragua

SECTION No. 4
> Northern Coast of Honduras and adjacent islands and cays
>> Headquarters: Trujillo, Honduras
>> Volunteer aids at Belize, Puerto Barrios, Livingston, Omoa, Cuyamel, Ceiba, Rincón, and Tela, as well as available helpers and friends along the coast to Cape Gracias.
>> Active Voluntary Helpers: 9

SECTION No. 5
> *Guatemala- Headquarters: Guatemala City*
>> Sub-Agent at Puerto Barrios
>> Sub-Agent at Champerico
>> Active Volunteer Helpers: 5

The agents in charge of each Section were:

> Section 1   Cyrus Wicker (No. 165)
>
> Section 2   Samuel Lothrop (No. 173)
>
> Section 3   Herbert J. Spinden (No. 56)
>
> Section 4   Sylvanus Morley (No. 53) and John Held (No. 154)
>
> Section 5   Joseph H. Watts (No. 84)

The 15th Naval District had an intelligence office in Cristóbal, in the Hamburg Amerika Building, which had been seized by the United States government when war was declared.[16] There was also an Aide for Information, Lt. H. H. Henneberger, to handle intelligence matters. Nevertheless, Commander Sargent remained personally involved. He kept in close touch with the five section heads and expected them to monitor their agents closely.[17] But these personnel assignments quickly unraveled, to Sargent's dismay. A major problem was Cyrus Wicker, the ONI agent whom Morley and Spinden had found so congenial when they had met him in Bluefields. Wicker, who was being run by Commander Sargent, was not ONI's best agent. A notation in his file reads: "San Jose, Costa Rica—Did not make very good impression as he let his connection with Naval Intelligence be known." Worse still, Wicker was guilty of conduct unbecoming a member of the Cosmos Club. A chagrined Commander Sargent had to report that Section 1 was left vacant "due to the sudden and inexcusable defection of No. 165 [Wicker]; a defection which, had he been in the service in a capacity other than that of Agent, would have warranted exceedingly vigorous punishment."[18] Presumably Commander Sargent had in mind something more drastic than, say, a good keelhauling, since Cyrus Wicker had deserted his post during wartime. Continuing in the same vein, Sargent deplored the desertion of yet another ONI agent, A. S. Northrup (No. 85), who had abandoned his post in Colombia because he was homesick; Northrup had joined ONI on February 1, 1917, at a salary of $7 a day. In Sargent's words: "This undisciplined dereliction of duty cannot be too strongly condemned, as the strength of our organization depends upon its individual members; and if their calibre is so small as to make the desertion of a post seem a trifling matter, we are indeed liable to find our efforts in vain."

Despite Cyrus Wicker's desertion, the situation in Section 1 was not as bleak as it appeared. The subagents were filling in capably, and Section 1's relative proximity to the Canal Zone made communications comparatively easy. Moreover, Commander Sargent intended to transfer Samuel Lothrop from Section 2 to head Section 1. As for Section 2, the new head would be J. A. Connor (Agent No. 238), who had recently arrived in the Canal Zone and was still being briefed. On the way to his new headquarters in Bluefields he would make a survey of conditions in western Nicaragua and around Lake Managua. Connor would then function as a subagent of Section 3 until he was experienced enough to run Section 2 himself.

Section 3 would be the responsibility of "our newest recruit," Ensign Albert B. Pullen, who was en route to San Salvador from Costa Rica. Pullen had been recruited and commissioned into Naval Intelligence in the Canal Zone by Commander Sargent himself, who designated Pullen Agent No. S-30. Pullen had earlier been operating on the west coast of Colombia, where he had built a network of informants.

Morley and Held, who had worked together as a team for so long that they were now considered a single entity, were in charge of Section 4, but because they were off on their Yucatán reconnaissance, Commander Sargent assigned Joe Spinden to fill in during their absence. Spinden normally headed Section 3. He was, however, currently on leave in the United States.

The only stability in this game of musical agents was in Section 5. Here, J. H. Watts was placed in charge and remained in charge. He was quietly building a network of subagents. For instance, Commander Sargent offered an American businessman in Guatemala, P. W. Schufeldt, a position as agent. The latter, however, refused the offer to become a regular ONI agent, preferring to serve as an unpaid volunteer subagent reporting to Watts about conditions in the Petén region of Guatemala.[19] As we shall see, Schufeldt would not be Watts's only subagent.

As additional agents arrived in Area 2, there developed the problem of concocting a suitable "cloak," i.e., cover, for each of them. For example, in March 1918, the 15th Naval District was experiencing difficulty in the case of newly arrived Agent No. 238, J. A. Connor. As Commander Sargent's aide explained, at first glance cover as a mining man or mining engineer should be quite plausible to the locals. But there were three covers that were worn threadbare by now: "mining man, cattle man, and timber man." The only way any of these covers was of any use was if the agent had actually functioned in one of these jobs, besides which he should be connected with some firm in the United States to lend credibility to his story. In the case of Agent Connor, by no stretch of the imagination could he possibly pass for a mining man in a region where it was well known that only qualified mining engineers or experienced mining men were dispatched to the distant areas comprising Area 2. Furthermore, a mining man could be used only in a mining region, which would limit Connor's availability for the western part of Central America, or Sections 3 and 5.

It was suggested that the following "cloaks" be used for Area 2 if at all possible:

A. Moving picture owner—several reputable operators could be deployed to open and operate movie theaters, thus ensuring the showing of pro-American films, "which is undoubtedly one of the best kinds of propaganda." Most importantly, it would provide a credible reason for an agent's presence in any locality, and should his business appear to be failing, he could relocate elsewhere if necessary. But "in any event, his reason for being in the field would appear to be legitimate to the inhabitants."

B. Merchandise broker—some men really engaged in this line of business should be recruited by ONI. They could be stationed anywhere, handling from five to ten different lines of merchandise, and they could actually work at building up a business. "Cheap jewelry, cutlery, paper novelties, and notions would be a few of the more suitable lines to handle. As they would travel with samples only, their mobility would be ensured, and they could, without comment, work all the cities of a section."

C. Men connected with any company which had branches or agencies in Central America. This would of course require the cooperation of the companies' executives.

D. Bona-fide mining men connected with mining or steel companies.

It is also suggested that the men to be used as Vice-Consuls, under that plan, be given a short course in consular work before leaving Washington. This would make them useful in their ostensible office, and make their occupancy of the position seem legitimate to the inhabitants.[20]

Having agents such as Morley, who was not only what he professed to be, an archaeologist, but also an archaeologist with an established reputation in his field, was thus a godsend for ONI.

Regarding the vexing problem of communications, Sargent was pleased to report that the cooperation of the United Fruit Company was proving invaluable. For that reason, the 15th Naval District informed the Director of Naval Intelligence in May that "the plan of using the United Fruit Co. facilities can not be allowed to become known to more than a very few persons without jeopardizing our whole system. The same is true of our cable address."[21]

As an example of United Fruit's cooperation, Commander Sargent noted that Captain H. E. Powell, "traveling freight agent on all United Fruit Co. boats, continues to make safe communication with Colombian ports possible. He is entirely responsible, and is rendering valuable service." Commander Sargent's office paid him a salary of $50 a month plus expenses, which averaged $25 monthly.

More importantly, Sargent had also been dealing with Mr. Udell, the secretary to a United Fruit Company vice-president. As we have seen, Udell was the conduit for getting ONI expense money to Agent Watts in Guatemala City. Sargent reported:

On March 7th, Mr. Udell, of the United Fruit Co., arrived on [*sic*] the Zone, and I was greatly disappointed to find that the scheme for handling mail through the agency of the United Fruit Company's Masters could not be put in operation. At that time I wrote fully explaining the situation, and it need not be gone into here. Suffice it to say that it is practically the only way that mail can be speedily handled between the points on the East and North coast of Central America and Panama. The system of radio communication via United Fruit Co. stations is working well, and the spirit shown by the various station Agents employed by the United Fruit Co. is most commendable. Mr. Udell was untiring in his efforts to put the United Fruit Company's facilities at our disposal, and the result of his efforts is apparent in the prompt and courteous treatment we have received from all the confidential employees of this company.[22]

But speaking of Udell, there had evidently been some problem in delivering to Agent Watts his expense money in Guatemala City, for Sargent mentioned that "I have employed Mr. F. D. Duran as a special Agent at a salary of $90.00 per month. Mr. Duran arrived here with a letter of introduction from No. 84 [J. H. Watts], which stated that No. 84 had not received his funds from the home office, and was no longer able to retain the services of Mr. Duran, although he considered him a remarkably good man for this work." Commander Sargent was favorably impressed by Durán, who was a Guatemalan educated at the University of California at Berkeley.

I, therefore, enrolled him in the organization and sent him to the West coast of Colombia on a special mission, i.e., to run down the various reports I have had on enemy activity along that coast in the matter of shipments of electrical supplies from Puerto Colombia Eastward, which had the appearance of being suitable for wireless equipment.[23]

Unfortunately, Commander Sargent had also been favorably impressed by Ensign Albert B. Pullen, the man he had just assigned to take over Section 3, with headquarters in San Salvador. Pullen became an unmitigated disaster. To make things even worse, he was a disaster of Sargent's own making, for the commander had personally recruited him. Pullen had been the vice-consul at Puerto Limón, Costa Rica. He resigned that post planning to join the army, hopefully as a pilot.

Commander Sargent, who knew and liked Pullen, felt that his character, ability, intelligence, discretion, knowledge of Spanish and of Central

America could best be employed in a Naval Intelligence capacity. The commander therefore invited Pullen to the Canal Zone. Pullen arrived in Cristóbal on December 20, 1917. Sargent prevailed on the acting commander of the Canal Zone Naval Reserve District to commission Pullen as a reserve ensign on December 21, with orders to report to Commander Sargent, the Commandant of the 15th Naval District. On December 22, Sargent assigned Pullen to "special confidential duty," sending him off to reconnoiter the coast between Panama and Buenaventura, Colombia. Evidently the new ensign performed creditably enough in accomplishing this mission.[24] The trouble started after he returned and took up his new assignment as head of Section 3. As a section head, he was authorized to use his own judgment in investigating anything suspicious. He could not, however, leave his section without permission except in extraordinary circumstances when there was not time to request permission.[25]

Pullen was one of those people who just could not get over the fact that he was now a real, honest-to-goodness spy. This romanticized self-image made him a loose cannon of very heavy caliber. For example, on April 19, Pullen wrote from San Salvador to his father in Texas:

> Now this is absolutely necessary. If any of these governments should find out that I am a spy (and that is really all I am) they could easily put me out of the way and no one could say a word about it. At any rate I would have a lot of trouble and I know you don't want to see me get in trouble. Any one of your letters are [sic] liable to be opened and read by these people, so you must be careful what you write.[26]

This indiscreet communication was read by the American postal censor and set in motion enquiries about Pullen on the part of ONI and the State Department. In reply, the legation in San Salvador reported:

> Person named Albert B. Pullen, who claims to be Lieutenant in the United States Naval Reserve Force, detailed to the Intelligence Bureau at Panama and Panaman [sic] commerce, now in Amapala, Honduras. He states that he is secret agent for Justice and Navy Departments, to cover territory of Salvador, Costa Rica and south coast of Honduras and Nicaragua.[27]

Commander Sargent interceded for Pullen, who kept his job. Until, that is, he made an unauthorized voyage on the steamer *San José*, in August 1918, in pursuit of an imagined lead. Pullen's performance was truly memorable.

Back in June, Pullen had reported to ONI that a secret treaty between Honduras, El Salvador, and Mexico was under consideration. ONI informed him that up to $1,000 would be paid for that information, "but only if absolutely bonafide and treat[s] of international matters important to present war."[28] Evidently thinking he could score a real coup by securing at least a copy of the supposed treaty, Pullen suddenly left his post in San Salvador, raced to the coast, and took passage on the *San José*.

On September 7, 1918, a delegation of irate American citizens stormed into the branch office of Naval Intelligence in San Francisco, located at 202 Balboa Building. They had just arrived on the *San José* and were there to lodge formal complaints against Pullen. For starters, they charged that he had searched several people at gunpoint during the voyage. For example, Dr. J. P. Henderson, a physician from Chicago, indignantly related that

> when Ensign Pullen boarded the S.S. San Jose he made it known to all the passengers that he was a Secret Service operator representing the United States government; that he was not in uniform and produced no credentials; that he drank freely and was at times not in control of his normal faculties; that on one of these occasions he entered Dr. Henderson's room with a six-shooter in his hand and demanded to know why Dr. Henderson wore his waistcoat under his pajamas, to which Dr. Henderson replied that he kept his watch and his passports in his waistcoat.

Dr. Henderson was so outraged that he planned to complain personally to the secretary of the navy. Moreover, some passengers accused Pullen not just of drunkenness but also of taking drugs. The ship's radio operator stated that Pullen had not been "on the boat ten minutes" before he let the passengers and crew know that he was a secret agent. The radio operator added that Pullen drank regularly at the ship's bar and "associated with a woman on board the vessel whose character was not such as to merit the attention of a Naval Officer."[29]

But Pullen's most spectacular feat aboard the *San José* involved the Mexican ambassador to El Salvador. Pullen was convinced that the ambassador carried certain important papers, and that these papers needed stealing. The ensign evidently sought proof of the alleged secret treaty being negotiated between Honduras, El Salvador, and Mexico. Pullen confided his plan to carry out a "black bag" job to various other passengers and then, on the night of August 23, the intrepid secret agent sneaked into the ambassador's stateroom. Pullen proved to be a singularly inept burglar, for he managed to awaken the ambassador's wife, who began screaming hysterically and was quickly joined by her husband and child. Pullen fled and hid. The ambassador protested to the ship's captain, and since Pullen's plan was common knowledge among the passengers, it was likely that the ambassador would learn who the intruder was and would lodge a formal diplomatic protest.[30]

While the shocked ONI station chief, Lt. Commander William C. Van Antwerp, was trying to deal with this avalanche of accusations, he had the opportunity of sizing Pullen up for himself. That worthy showed up in the ONI office identifying himself as an ensign and requesting that he be vouched for with the Cable Censor's office so that he could send a coded cable to the American minister in Panama. Pullen, in civilian clothes and unable to produce any credentials, announced that he had just arrived on the *San José* and was a government agent operating in a confidential capacity. Under further questioning, Pullen stated that he was a government spy working under Commander Sargent. He readily admitted breaking into the Mexican ambassador's stateroom to search through his papers on his own initiative. He further admitted carrying a pistol, explaining that "spies generally went armed." Pullen also admitted drinking, but emphasized that although in the course of his work he often had to appear to be drunk, he was always in control of his faculties.[31]

While the San Francisco office of ONI tried to check out Pullen's story, Pullen went to the local navy medical facility for treatment. The doctor who saw him thought that he probably was not a dope fiend, but stated that Pullen was suffering from a venereal disease. Pullen acted so suspiciously that the doctor not only refused to treat him, but urged that he not be treated at any naval installation.

In view of the foregoing, the station chief's report on Pullen to the Director of Naval Intelligence concluded that "I am firmly of [the] opinion that he is not a suitable man to represent Naval Intelligence in any capacity." He planned to keep Pullen under surveillance while awaiting further instructions. Pullen's career was rapidly sinking by the bow as a result of his shipboard antics. The process accelerated when Pullen left San Francisco and proceeded to Washington without authority, in order to plead his case with the Director of Naval Intelligence.[32]

Commander Sargent had tried to save his protégé, Pullen, by requesting that he be returned to the Canal Zone and only be relieved of his intelligence duties: "His fault apparently is over zeal which can be utilized to advantage except in Intelligence field work." But the secretary of the navy was now demanding an explanation from Sargent, and when an astounded Sargent read the full report on Pullen, the mortified commander wrote to ONI that "it is all too apparent that Pullen, from whatever cause, has entirely left the track; and has terminated his usefulness not only in the intelligence service, but in any position of trust in any branch of the Navy." Commander Sargent recommended that Pullen be cashiered.[33]

W. E. Dunn (Agent No. 168) subsequently took charge of Section 3.[34] In November 1918, a Marine Corps officer, Major Harrison, designated as Agent S-50, was assigned to run Section 3. Harrison's code signature was "Harbo."[35] Offsetting the Pullen debacle, Commander Sargent could console himself with the knowledge that there were also some very good ONI agents in Area 2.

One was Samuel K. Lothrop. As of January 1918, he was operating out of Bluefields, Nicaragua. Lothrop, using the code name "Laposso," reported by cable to "Wilberjohn," i.e., the 15th Naval District. And among the things he reported was the disquieting news that Morley had been regularly betrayed by the crew on the *Lilly Elena*. Moreover, Spinden and Lothrop himself were under suspicion because, like Morley, they were American scholars.[36] Fortunately, nothing damaging resulted from these betrayals and suspicions. However suspect he may have become, Lothrop was kept in Bluefields until March, by which time he had enlisted a volunteer subagent, a local businessman named Henry Speers, of the Huddleston Marsh Co., to monitor Bluefields, especially violators of the American Black List.[37] Nothing much was happening in Bluefields, and Lothrop was ordered to the Canal Zone for reassignment.

Lothrop discovered that just getting from Bluefields to the Canal Zone to report to Commander Sargent took some doing. There was no direct steamer service, and the alternative was to charter a vessel, at enormous expense. So Lothrop sailed from Bluefields to New Orleans, and from there to Colón. On the Bluefields to New Orleans leg of the trip he carried a letter of introduction from S. H. Barker of the Bluefields Fruit and Steamship Co., a subsidiary of United Fruit, to Lt. Commander Manly of Naval Intelligence at New Orleans. Barker explained Lothrop's itinerary, identified him as the ONI representative in Bluefields, explained that Lothrop had no passport because he had been in the tropics since the United States's entry into the war, and requested Manly to expedite Lothrop's passage through New Orleans.[38] Manly did so, and Lothrop arrived in the Canal Zone on March 28.

As we have seen, Commander Sargent had intended for Lothrop to remain as head of Section No. 2, based in Bluefields. But because of Cyrus Wicker's defection, Sargent reassigned Lothrop to run Section 1—Costa Rica. This, by the way, was what J. J. Perdomo had originally recommended back in November 1917.[39]

Lothrop had some advantages as an agent. For one thing, he was imaginative; he devised a presumably unbreakable code using Mayan hieroglyphs. For another, he had help—his wife Rachel was enlisted as an agent. Besides being attractive, she was adventurous. She had accompanied Lothrop on archaeological expeditions to British Honduras, Guatemala, and Honduras; she would now accompany him in his intelligence assignment. Rachel Lothrop was also bright—she gently chided Charles Sheldon because his letters to her had "Navy Department" overprinted on the stamps. An embarrassed Sheldon assured her the matter would be corrected.[40] The 15th Naval District assigned Rachel Lothrop the designation S-32, and the code name "Andoran" for cables. She not only secured information, but she ran the base in San José whenever her husband was out of the capital.

By April, Lothrop was staffing his Costa Rican network. At Puerto Limón he had the local manager of United Fruit, one Chittenden, who was authorized to hire one subagent. Chittenden, however, was soon replaced by the newly arrived American vice-consul at Puerto Limón, Harry C. Morgan, who was also ONI Agent No. 186. Lothrop recruited another American vice-consul, John Saxe, as his agent in Puntarenas, paying him $75 a month; Lothrop coyly referred to him as "Mr. Bags." If Saxe so desired, he was authorized to enlist one subagent, to be paid not more than $50 a month. Lothrop also planned to recruit a volunteer subagent at Playa Real and, if possible, a Costa Rican to serve as subagent at large, with a salary of $75 a month.[41] Although an amateur,

Lothrop had a realistic view of the world of espionage. He hired A. Renaud de la Croix to assist him. De la Croix was an old French ex-soldier long resident in Costa Rica, and he had worked for Cyrus Wicker. The Frenchman's great quality was that he knew whom to bribe for information; Lothrop was confident that de la Croix could obtain any government record or private paper that might be needed. Lothrop paid him $2 a day and promised a bonus for anything extraordinary. Lothrop, however, did not trust de la Croix and gave the Frenchman no idea for what government department he was now working.[42]

In his organizational plan Lothrop not only discussed subagents but also specified communications links, both by mail and by radio. Part of his mail went through United Fruit channels. Because the Costa Rican government routinely opened all letters and read all overland cables, it was imperative that these messages be sent through the American legation or consulates. Lothrop also made some general observations and recommendations, the most important of which was that ONI in Washington and Panama not blow agents' cover through carelessness, as had happened in the past. He also observed that the agent network would always be limited by inadequate communications. Moreover, agents were sent into the field without special training, and this situation needed attention. ONI should not rely on volunteers too much; they had their own business affairs to deal with and were thus unable to give their secret work the meticulous attention it required. In addition, many of them became bored and lost their initial enthusiasm.[43]

Before Lothrop could function effectively as spymaster he had to deal with the Cyrus Wicker mess. Wicker had just returned to Costa Rica from a trip to Washington, and his very presence jeopardized Lothrop. The latter begged the 15th Naval District to get Wicker out of Costa Rica, for he could expose not only Lothrop's operation, but that of others as well. Lothrop himself had heard Wicker speak of Morley and Spinden in such a way as to leave little doubt about their being spies. While in Costa Rica, Wicker had let it be widely known that he was an ONI agent. When he left on his trip, his baggage was even marked "USN." Now that Wicker was back, he was busily ingratiating himself with the president, Federico Tinoco, whose regime the United States opposed. Wicker, who had once been secretary of the American legation in Nicaragua but had left the diplomatic service under a cloud, was currently offering to help secure American diplomatic recognition of Tinoco in return for Wicker being given valuable land concessions in Costa Rica. Lothrop's fears were confirmed. Not only was Wicker settling permanently in Costa Rica, but while in Washington he had learned Lothrop's true occupation.[44] Wicker, however, was quite cordial on those infrequent occasions when he encountered Lothrop.

ONI was concerned both about preserving Lothrop's cover and about recovering Wicker's codes, which were still in his possession. This ticklish job fell to Lothrop. He went to see Wicker, who told him all his troubles and expressed great willingness to perform intelligence work again in Costa Rica or, if necessary, in Honduras. Lothrop tactfully explained that this was not an option, and the conversation ended on a high note when Wicker reluctantly surrendered his code books. A relieved Lothrop reported to the 15th Naval District that the code books were now safely in the legation, and he was awaiting instructions for their disposition.[45] On June 25, 1918, Commander Sargent's aide informed Charles Sheldon, a.k.a. "Taro," back at ONI headquarters:

> As regards Wicker, I have to report that No. 186 [H. C. Morgan] is taking all of Wicker's codes to Havana where he will turn them over to the Naval Attache. Wicker, I understand, is still in Costa Rica. I have neither heard from him nor communicated with him since my wire to you, in which I advised sending him $500, provided you could get him out of Central America and keep him out. This office will have nothing more to do with Wicker under any circumstances, and considers the incident closed.[46]

Fortunately, although Wicker remained in Costa Rica he created no further problems. He formally resigned from ONI, devoting himself to Costa Rican politics and to the castor-oil business.

A final note about Wicker. In October 1918, he wrote the Director of ONI a letter justifying his allegedly unauthorized and personal trip to the United States in February, the trip that Commander Sargent had deemed desertion. Wicker began by stating that in July 1917 he had volunteered to become a civilian agent of ONI for a period of not more than six months. He had previously applied for a commission as an army reserve officer and had passed the physical exam. En route to his post in Costa Rica, he had stopped over in Panama and had informed Commander Sargent of his expected army commission. Sargent had allegedly stated that military service took precedence over civilian work, and that Wicker would have to return to the United States if commissioned. According to Wicker, Sargent gave him verbal permission to return to the United States. On August 20, 1917, Wicker was commissioned as an Ordnance captain but was not ordered to report to Washington for active duty until February, 1918. He tried to travel via Panama and report to Sargent, but couldn't; so, he went straight to Washington. There, he told his story to Lt. Commander Fowler, the executive officer of ONI, and offered to resign from that organization. Fowler, though, let Wicker continue working for ONI. On Fowler's authorization, Wicker resigned his army captain's commission, and, with Fowler's approval, waited in Washington until that resignation was accepted, on March 22. The next day Wicker left Washington, on ONI's orders, for his post in Costa Rica. No one raised any question about his being AWOL. He had done exactly what Sargent had told him to do. Wicker had since resigned from ONI.[47] That was his story and he was sticking to it.

Besides having to deal with Wicker, the Lothrops's assignment was to collect political intelligence and to thwart those persons trading with the enemy in violation of the American Black List. There were, however, occasional reports of German submarines to be forwarded to the 15th Naval District. For example, in May 1918, Rachel Lothrop passed along the assertion of a Costa Rican military judge that his government knew that somewhere in Mexico the Germans were assembling six submarines, which had been brought over from Germany in pieces. The submarines were to raid maritime traffic between the United States and the Panama Canal.[48] Most tidbits the Lothrops gathered were less delightfully imaginative.

The couple provided a steady flow of information about the Costa Rican government and political situation, such as an eighteen-page review in April of the Tinoco administration.[49] The Lothrops's case officer in the Canal Zone, John Steele, considered their work to be excellent. He mentioned that they were providing the best information on Costa Rica, and that ONI was sharing that information with others.[50] Lothrop was particularly intent on proving that British Consul F. Nutter Cox was involved in trading with the Germans, and that the United States chargé d'affaires, Stewart Johnson, was involved with Costa Rican revolutionists.[51]

The Lothrops and their case officer had a continuing problem in keeping their expense accounts straight; the navy's accounting procedures had not been devised with secret agents in mind. More importantly, ONI's security measures were still less than watertight. Compartmentalization and the concept of need-to-know had not yet taken hold. Steele stressed that all communications should be signed only with the Lothrops's code names or numbers, never with their signatures. This applied especially to messages sent to ONI headquarters in Washington, where communications passed through dozens of hands before they were filed. Steele himself had done some investigating on this point and had been shocked to discover that one file clerk was able, without any apparent effort, to rattle off the names of all the agents in Area No. 2. In a lighter vein, Steele bemoaned the hardships being endured by the personnel in the Canal Zone: a new law prohibited officers and enlisted men from crossing into Panama except on official business. So much for the fleshpots. And in a further blow, the Canal Zone was now officially bone dry.[52] War was just hell.

Lothrop's campaign to gather evidence against British Consul Cox for trading with the enemy took on new urgency when he learned that Cox had become a partner in Wicker's castor-oil business.[53] And Lothrop continued to build his case against the American chargé, Stewart Johnson, for consorting with revolutionists and for allegedly accepting bribes.[54] Lothrop finally secured eyewitness evidence and signed affidavits against Cox, and he dispatched the whole dossier to his case officer, John Steele, who congratulated him and forwarded the evidence on to Washington.[55] Lothrop's campaign against Johnson ended less happily, however. The State Department took great umbrage at what it considered Lothrop's disparagement of Johnson and demanded Lothrop's removal unless he reconciled with the chargé.[56] Lothrop refused; his wife continued to send in reports critical of Johnson.[57]

As for Lothrop himself, he was increasingly the center of bureaucratic controversy. Not only was the State Department upset with him, but some American friends of Johnson's in Costa Rica had launched a campaign of vilification against him.[58] ONI was extremely nervous about the flap and on August 24 ordered Lothrop to return as soon as possible to Washington to answer the allegations. He did so, and explained himself satisfactorily to the State Department as well as to ONI. State decided to close the legation in San José and recalled Stewart Johnson.[59] ONI decided to replace the Lothrops in San José. Lt. Henneberger, the 15th Naval District's intelligence officer, was to go there and select someone from among the

American residents, which was what Lothrop had suggested. Mrs. Lothrop traveled via Key West to Washington and joined her husband. Although he had been exonerated, Lothrop had had it with ONI. He resigned.[60]

But he didn't resign from intelligence work. He applied for an army commission. The army, unlike Secretary Daniels of the navy, was quite willing to commission a man of Lothrop's talents. On October 24, 1918, Lothrop became a 2nd lieutenant assigned to Military Intelligence. His orders stipulated that he was commissioned only for intelligence and would never be assigned to command troops.[61]

Lothrop's resignation was unquestionably a loss to ONI and the 15th Naval District, but Commander Sargent had other first-rate agents. He thought especially highly of Morley and Held, reporting to the Director of Naval Intelligence that

Nos. 56 [Spinden], 53 [Morley] and 84 [Watts] have continued as they began. Turned out finished work throughout. Nos 53 and No. 154 [Held] are especially to be commended for their thoroughness. As you are aware from their reports, the whole coast line of Northern Honduras is dotted with Active Volunteer Helpers, and an exhaustive study of every point of danger was made.[62]

Sylvanus Griswold Morley

Fig 2. Morley's offical ONI Agent No. 53 photograph taken either late March or early April, 1917. Morley was 33 years old and within a year he was easily the best intelligence agent the United States goverment had in WWI. Courtesy National Archives.

Fig 3. *Charles Sheldon, ONI agent No. 246, was Morley's Case Officer. Self-effacing, Sheldon spoke Spanish and was ONI's best spy master. Courtesy of Alaska and Polar Regions Archives, Rasmuson Library, University of Alaska, Fairbanks. Accession no. 76-42-2N, VFSP-William Sheldon Collection.*

Fig 4. Captain James H. Oliver, Director, Office of Naval Intelligence, January, 1914–March, 1917. Courtesy Wyman H. Packard, A Century of U.S. Naval Intelligence, *Official of Naval Intelligence, Naval Historical Center.*

Fig 5. Rear Admiral Roger Welles, Jr., Director, Office of Naval Intelligence, April, 1917–January, 1919. Courtesy Wyman H. Packard, A Century of U.S. Naval Intelligence, *Official of Naval Intelligence, Naval Historical Center.*

Fig 6. John Held, Jr., was 28 years of age when this photo was taken in April, 1917, for his official ONI Special Agent No. 154 file. Held, who barely looked 18 years of age, would become America's greatest cartoonist/illustrator during the 1920s. Courtesy National Archives.

Herbert J. Spinden

Fig 7. Herbert J. Spinden. With a Harvard Ph.D in anthropology, a published monograph on Maya art, and a position as assistant curator at the American Museum of Natural History, the scholarly-looking Spinden was a natural as ONI Special Agent No. 56. Courtesy National Archives.

Fig 8. John Alden Mason, ONI Special Agent No. 157. With a Ph.D. from the University of California, Berkeley, and a position as assistant curator of Mexican and South American Archaeology at the Field Museum of Natural History in Chicago, Mason should have made a first-rate intelligence agent. But, as he admitted himself, he was a terrible spy, and after only five months was recalled and discharged by ONI. Courtesy National Archives.

Fig 9. Only 24 years old, a Harvard graduate who would get his Ph.D. after the war, Samuel Kirkland Lothrop was recruited by his friend Morley. Accompanied by his wife Rachel (who became ONI's only female overseas field agent in WWI) Lothrop was assigned to Costa Rica. In 1918 he resigned from ONI over a spat with a State Department diplomat, and joined Military Intelligence. This is his U.S. passport photo. Courtesy Peabody Museum of Archaeology and Ethnology, Harvard University, Lothrop Collection.

Fig 10. Dr. Thomas Francis William Gann, a surgeon, was both the Principal Medical Officer for British Honduras and the Chief intelligence officer for the British Colony. He was also ONI Special Agent No. 242 and an old friend of Morley's. Gann, sporting a bow tie, is second from right, posing with the Governor of British Honduras, second from left, and two staff members of the British Museum. Photo from Gann's Discoveries and Adventures in Central America (New York : Charles Scribner's Sons, 1929), p. 103.

Fig 11. ONI Special Agent No. 143, William R. Rosenkrans, posing for his official ONI photograph, was a 42 year old college graduate who spoke fluent Spanish. Based in Veracruz, Rosenkrans was named a vice-consul to aid his cover. Courtesy National Archives.

Fig 12. Beginning in fall 1917, Joseph J. Perdomo, ONI Special Agent No. 93, was Morley's supervisor. Unfortunately, Perdomo not only looked like a spy, he acted like one. On several occasions Morley had to bail Perdomo out of trouble. Courtesy National Archives.

Fig 13. ONI Special Agent No. 219, Wilson Popenoe, looked more like a college freshman in his official ONI spy photo. But Poponoe, who bore the title "Agricultural Explorer" with the United States Department of Agriculture, was a most competent ONI special agent through 1922 and a friend of Morley's after the war. Courtesy National Archives.

Fig 14. Cyrus F. Wicker, ONI Special Agent No. 165, should have been a first-rate ONI spy. He had been a State Department diplomat based in Central America, spoke Spanish and knew who the players were. However, Wicker abandoned his post (although there is some confusion over the circumstances) and came to the United States in 1918. He and Morley crossed paths in Nicaragua. Courtesy National Archives.

Fig 15. General Lee Christmas, wearing the uniform of a Honduran General after the overthrow of that government in 1911. Morley and Christmas hit it off when they met in Guatemala City in December, 1917. Courtesy Howard Tilton Library, Tulane University, Hermann Deutsch Collection.

Fig 16. Manuel Estrada Cabrera, President of Guatemala (1898–1920) had ties with ONI, via the government radio station that was operated by ONI Special Agent Joseph Watts. Morley met the President following the December 1917 earthquake. Courtesy Tulane University, Latin American Library.

Fig 17. *A portrait of Honduran President Fancisco Bertrand, whom Morley persuaded to write a letter of recommendation. Morley put this letter to good use when he was accused, of all things, of being a spy.* Courtesy Enciclopedia Historica de Honduras, *with permission of Graficentro Editores.*

Fig 18. General Octavio Solis, the Governor of the Mexican Territory of
Quintana Roo, photographed standing beside a Mayan Indian. General Solis
was quite taken by Morley and Held, particularly after Held sketched the
general. From Thomas Gann, In an Unknown Land (New York : Charles
Scribner's Sons, 1924), p. 20.

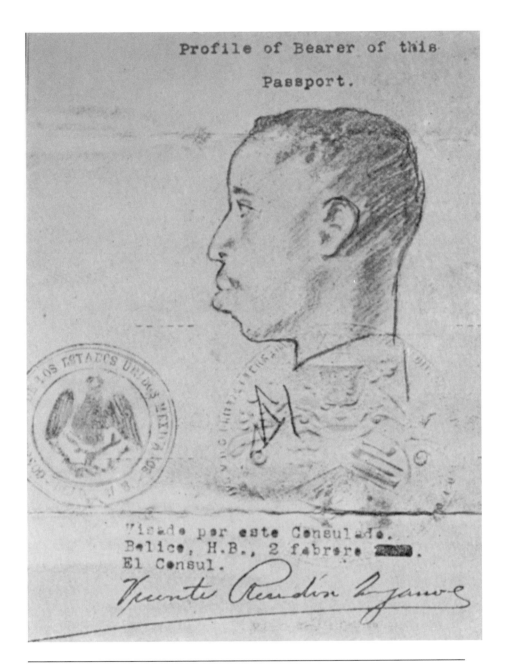

Fig 19. John Held Jr's talents were utilized when Hubert, a crewman on the Lilian Y, needed a passport photo. Held sketched Hubert in profile for his passport which was duly stamped on February 2, 1918, by a Mexican consular official in Belize. From Thomas Gann, In an Unknown Land (New York : Charles Scribner's Sons, 1924), p. 19.

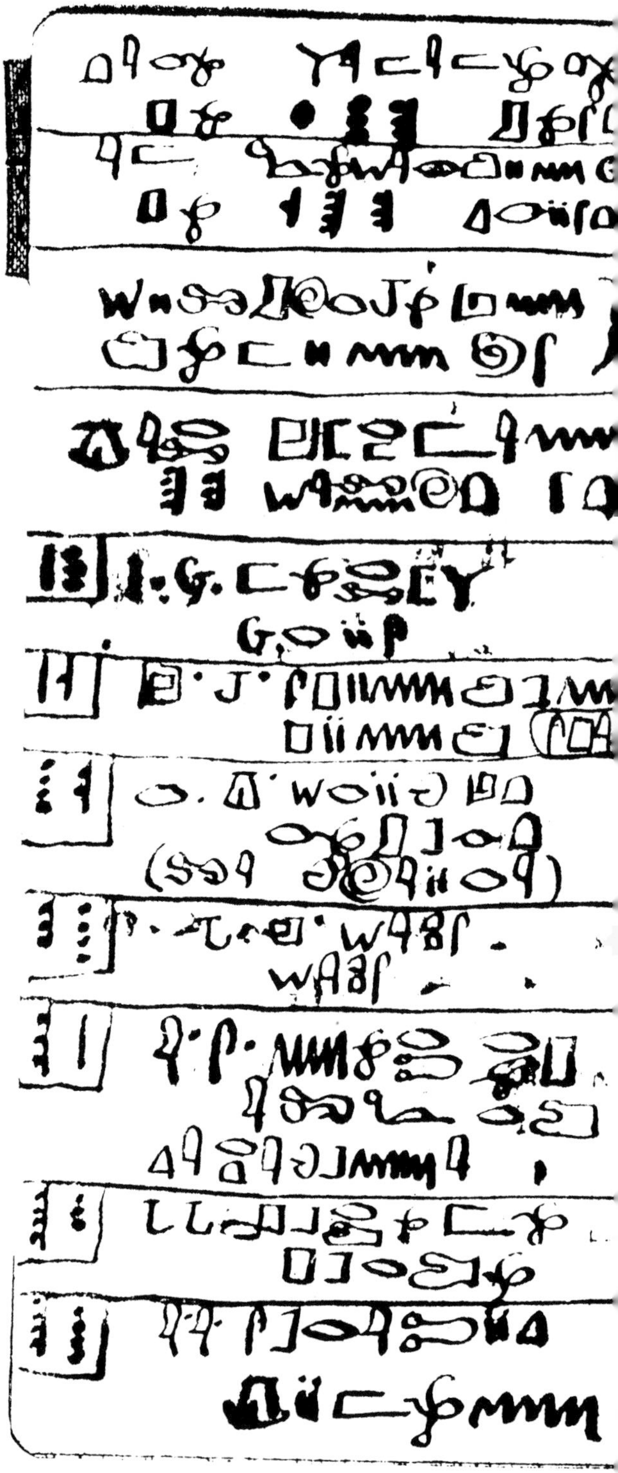

Fig 20A. ONI Special Agent Samuel K. Lothrop, in Costa Rica, used a unique method of note-taking, coding his notes with Mayan hieroglyphics. This illustration has only one block (middle of the right-hand page) that he wrote in English. It refers to a visit of the U.S.S. Marblehead en route to the Central American coast via the Swan Islands off the coast of Honduras. Courtesy Peabody Museum, Harvard University, Lothrop Collection.

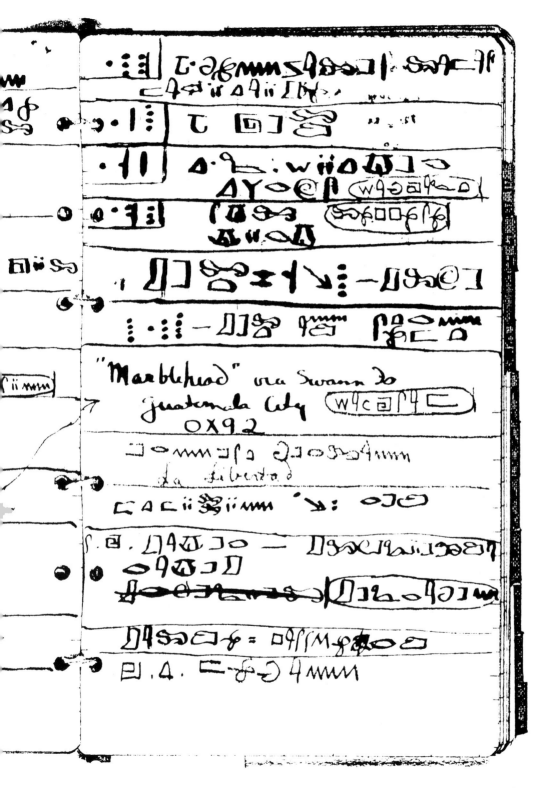

"Marblehead" via Swann to
Guatemala City

la libertad

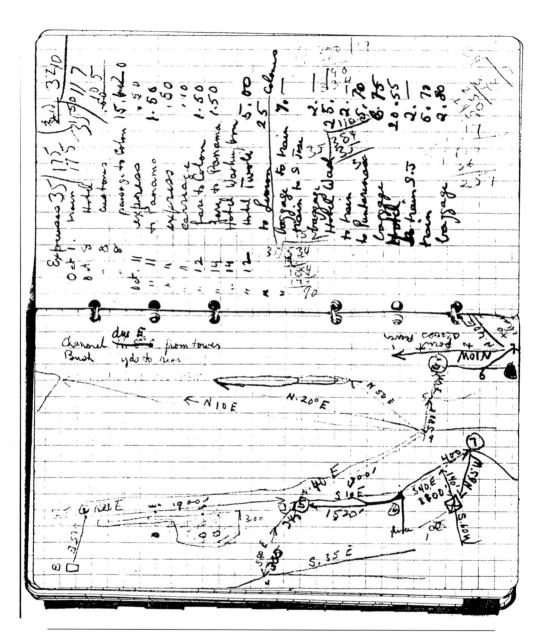

Fig 20B. *Morley's friend Sam Lothrop kept a notebook that bears evidence of some of his intelligence collection activities. At the bottom of the page is a drawing in which Lothrop provides directions and distances from what apparently is a tower (whether a radio transmitting tower or not is unclear), presumably on the Costa Rican coast. At the top of the page are his expenses for a trip in October 1917 from Costa Rica to Panama. Courtesy Peabody Museum, Harvard University, Lothrop Collection.*

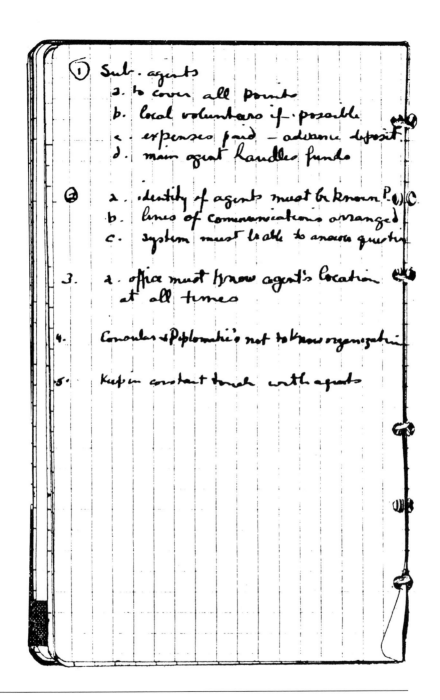

Fig 20C. Lothrop jotted down a list of instructions that he used with his sub-agents. Instruction No. 4 is worth noting: "Consuls and Diplomats not to know organization." Courtesy Peabody Museum, Harvard University, Lothrop Collection.

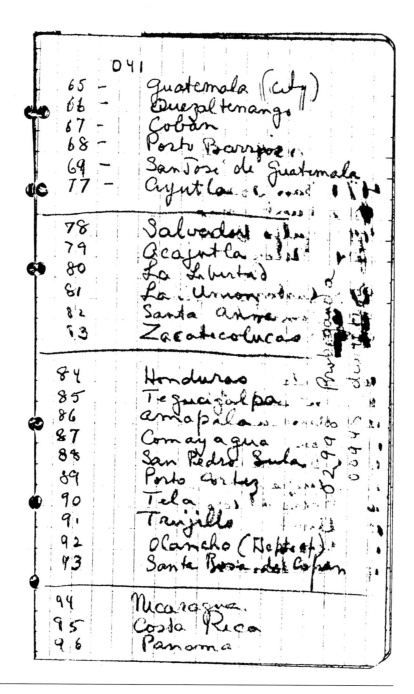

Fig 20D. *In the vernacular of the cryptanalytical community, the codes provided by the ONI to their agents were simply substitution codes. For example, Guatemala City was coded as 65. Courtesy Peabody Museum, Harvard University, Lothrop Collection.*

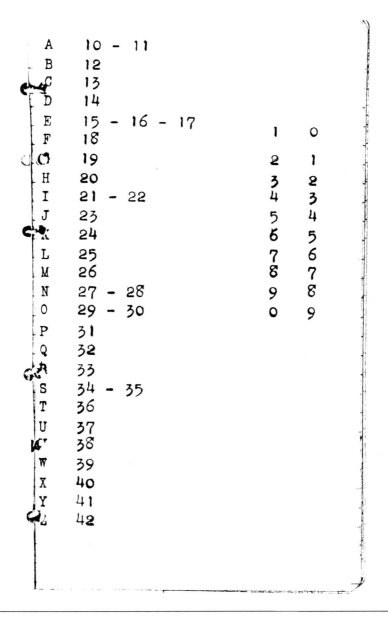

A	10 – 11			
B	12			
C	13			
D	14			
E	15 – 16 – 17			
F	18		1	0
G	19		2	1
H	20		3	2
I	21 – 22		4	3
J	23		5	4
K	24		6	5
L	25		7	6
M	26		8	7
N	27 – 28		9	8
O	29 – 30		0	9
P	31			
Q	32			
R	33			
S	34 – 35			
T	36			
U	37			
V	38			
W	39			
X	40			
Y	41			
Z	42			

Fig 20E. For writing coded messages, ONI provided numerical substitution codes. For example, the letter A would be coded either as 10 or 11. The letter A, E, I, N, O, and S, which are used most often in the English language, were given multiple numbers. Numbers were coded in the most elementary fashion. The number 1 was 0, 0 was 9, etc. It would not have taken even the most junior cryptanalyst long to break codes using these methods. Courtesy Peabody Museum, Harvard University, Lothrop Collection.

Fig 21. Profile of Dr. Franz Boas (1858–1942), considered the father of
American anthropology. He accused Morley and his colleagues of using
academic cover to conceal their intelligence operations for the U.S. Navy
during WWI. After surfacing his accusation in a letter to The Nation, Boas
was drummed out of the Council of the American Anthropological
Association. The spies who had crawled through the swamps of Central
America looking for German submarines were irate since Boas had
remained safely in New York. The spies won the battle and Boas was
humiliated. Courtesy American Philosophical Society, Franz Boas Papers.

10. Quintana Roo

Seldom has an intelligence mission been better documented than Morley's coastal reconnaissance of the Yucatán peninsula in 1918. Besides Morley's diary and his detailed reports to ONI, Dr. Gann would subsequently recount their journey in a book written for popular consumption.[1] Gann was deliberately vague about important aspects of the trip; for example, he never said when it occurred, he never explained who Held was, and only once (p. 196) did he refer to rumors of German spies. This reference, in fact, strikes the reader as a jarring note in what otherwise seems an entertaining account of an archaeological expedition.

As Morley and Gann already knew from their previous trip to the ruins of Tulum, the coast of Quintana Roo ranked as one of the more desolate and inhospitable regions on the face of the earth. An expedition along that shore faced both natural and human dangers. The coastline suffered periodically from hurricanes, such as the one in 1916 whose winds and tidal surge had obliterated much of what little human settlement there was. Although Morley and company were not traveling during hurricane season, they had to contend with hazards of a permanent nature.

Paralleling the entire coast was a coral reef, sometimes close to shore, sometimes as much as a mile out to sea. The coast has been described as a "nightmare" for small sailing craft; in a strong northeast or east wind they had to run for safety behind the reef, where they might be bottled up for a week or more, waiting for more moderate weather. And sometimes they were wrecked on false openings in the reef, where, because the water was a little deeper, the surf did not show up as

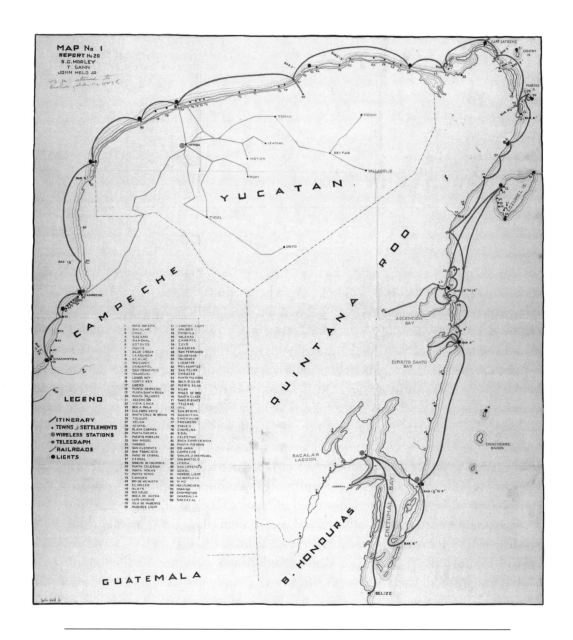

Map 5. Held's detailed map of the coast of the Yucatán peninsula from Belize to Champoton, Campeche which Morley and Held explored from February through March, 1918. The map contains the location of towns and settlements, radio stations, telegraph stations, railroads, and lighthouses. In addition, Morley and his crew measured the water depth at the mouth of each harbor and river to determine whether a submarine could "cross the bar." Courtesy Office of Naval Intelligence, National Archives.

conspicuously. And at Tulum, landing was always difficult. Boats had to negotiate a narrow opening in the reef, something that became impossible whenever there was a strong breeze. And even on calm days the surf pounded the rocky shore with incredible force, and a boat encountered a maelstrom of water with jagged shafts of limestone protruding from the sandy bottom. Moreover, the waters off Quintana Roo abounded with sharks and barracudas. And once ashore, travelers had to be wary of the numerous snakes, mainly rattlesnakes and coral snakes. Then there were the insect pests: ticks, sandflies, wasps, mosquitos, centipedes, tarantulas, and so on.[2]

There was also at least a potential threat from two groups of people inhabiting Quintana Roo. One was the lawless *chicleros* who, "in their immense wide-brimmed conical hats, machetes, revolvers, bandoleers, cotton shirt and trousers, red blankets, and sandals,"[3] presented a picturesque appearance but were ready to fight—and kill—at the slightest provocation, or even without provocation. Long after the time of Morley's trip, *chicleros* continued to inspire apprehension among travelers.[4]

Much more formidable, though, were the *indios sublevados*, or rebel Maya, who controlled part of the interior of Quintana Roo. They were the descendants of those Maya who had rebelled against their "Mexican" (i.e., non-Indian) masters in 1847, touching off the ferocious Caste War of Yucatán. This explosion of Mayan resentment at centuries of subjugation and oppression nearly drove the non-Mayan minority into the sea. Not until 1855 were the authorities able to regain a measure of control. Defeated but unconquered, the rebel Maya retreated into the forests of Quintana Roo, where they established an independent society and worshiped a "Speaking Cross." They carried on decades of guerrilla warfare, sometimes obtaining weapons and supplies in British Honduras.[5] These years of conflict with the "Mexicans" were characterized by atrocity and counter-atrocity.

Not until 1900 was the Mexican government able to mount a decisive campaign against the rebels. General Ignacio Bravo was assigned the mission of pacifying Quintana Roo. He did so in a brutally methodical fashion, establishing bases on the coast and driving on the rebel capital of Chan Santa Cruz. Bravo employed overwhelming technological superiority, and Indian machetes and shotguns were no match for an army equipped with repeating rifles, machine guns, and artillery, and supplied by the narrow-gauge railroad it built as it advanced. By the summer of

1901 it was all over. The Caste War had officially ended, and the Indian capital, Chan Santa Cruz, was renamed Santa Cruz de Bravo. In 1902, the federal territory of Quintana Roo was carved out of Yucatán.[6] Yet diehard bands of Mayan rebels still held out, and they had a nasty habit of killing intruders.[7]

It was, one suspects, with some trepidation that Morley and his companions set out on their journey. The reconnaissance formally began on February 4, when the *Lilian Y* sailed out of Corozal.[8] The sloop must have been quite a spectacle, for she was loaded to capacity, with oil drums, luggage, deck chairs, blankets, coils of rope, and crates of onions and potatoes crammed into every available space. The sloop proceeded up the coast for a few miles, crossing into Mexico at Chetumal Bay and docking on the west side at Payo Obispo—the present-day city of Chetumal—capital of the territory of Quintana Roo. Payo Obispo was also the base of the Southern Flotilla of the Mexican Navy, which consisted of two small steamboats of less than thirty tons each and a number of motorboats.

The ONI agents hoped to secure the cooperation of the Mexican authorities for their expedition and thus had prudently left Gann, a British official, behind in Corozal; Mexicans bitterly resented the aid that the Mayan rebels had for years received from British Honduras.

After clearing quarantine, Morley and Held were escorted by the governor's secretary to meet that personage, General Octaviano Solís. Solís was in his mid-thirties, and he was an example of revolutionary upward mobility. He had once been an illiterate political prisoner, yet through the Mexican Revolution had risen to become a general and governor.[9] But since he was the governor of a godforsaken Mexican territory, Solís had few visitors, and he outdid himself in hospitality. Morley ceremoniously presented his Carnegie Institution credentials to the governor. The archaeologist also broached—to Held's disgust—the idea of Held painting a watercolor portrait of the general. The general thought this a splendid idea and proceeded to don his dress uniform complete with medals. Held grudgingly painted the portrait, which Morley deemed a great success, for Held captured perfectly the general's luxuriant mustache, beetle brow, fierce gaze, and hooked nose.[10] Held's portrait delighted General Solís, which helped Morley succeed in his principal objective—to secure a letter of recommendation from Solís. In fact, Morley obtained two letters, couched in the strongest terms he had ever read. One letter was official and the other was unofficial, but both left no doubt in the reader's mind, whether he was a military officer or civilian functionary, that he was to give Morley every assistance within his power. The culmination of Morley's diplomatic triumph came when the governor not only accepted his invitation to dinner, but afterward invited him and Held to his home for a little champagne.

The next day, February 5, Morley awoke badly hung over, but hung over in a good cause. He was anxious to get on with his mission, but upon being informed of February 5's significance in Mexico—the date that the Liberal 1857 Constitution and the current 1917 Constitution had been promulgated—he thought it churlish not to stay over for the patriotic festivities. Accordingly, he and Held went to the governor's mansion, where they met assorted dignitaries. Morley photographed the governor and his staff and watched as the parade set forth. The parade consisted of the territorial band, followed by General Solís and his staff, and then a contingent of sixty-odd soldiers commanded by a lieutenant colonel. The procession marched to the schoolhouse, where a succession of patriotic speeches and poems went on for some time. As a signal mark of honor, Morley and Held were seated near the governor.

Afterward the governor invited them for cocktails at the naval headquarters, where for four hours they listened to the gramophone and consumed potent drinks. Held quickly became the man of the hour by drawing caricatures, which were immensely popular. Around 2 P.M. the cocktail party ended, and everyone adjourned to a restaurant for a banquet accompanied by much wine, and by a speech on Mexican-United States friendship. Morley had to rise and deliver an effusive response. By the end of the banquet everyone was quite mellow.

Mercifully, the banquet finally ended, and with many enthusiastic *vivas* for everything and everybody, the party adjourned for a visit to the Southern Flotilla's radio station. Despite his somewhat impaired condition, Morley made a careful study of this facility. The transmission tower leaned a bit, the result of the hurricane that, on October 15, 1916, had devastated the entire district. All the wireless equipment was of German manufacture, and the station was in regular communication with Mérida, Campeche, and even Acapulco. It could also tune in Mexico City, as well as the United Fruit stations in Honduras and on Swan Island.

Morley then accepted an invitation to tour the rest of the Southern Flotilla's installations: hospital, barracks, and machine shop. He found the machine shop to be quite modern, fully equipped, and capable of turning out rather elaborate parts. As the grand finale, the archaeologist was taken for a ride on a Mexican navy speedboat that had been built locally.

While all this was going on, Held had returned to town to participate in a game of baseball, one in which he and the governor played on the same side. Held was a much better cartoonist than athlete; he was yanked from the pitcher's mound for wild pitching that let four runs in, and he also struck out twice. Despite Held—and not coincidentally—the governor's team won by a handsome margin.

Following the afternoon's activities, Morley and Held begged off for an hour's rest before their next engagement—dinner at the governor's followed by a dance that lasted until 3 A.M. The life of a secret agent could be a demanding one. But their social investment paid handsome dividends. Not only did Morley rank their reception at Payo Obispo as one of the most enjoyable he had experienced in his ten years of coming to Latin America, but his intelligence mission was greatly facilitated. The territory of Quintana Roo covered the entire eastern side of the Yucatán peninsula, and the governor's friendship and glowing letters of recommendation ensured that Morley and Held would have carte blanche to poke about as they saw fit.

Not that Morley and Held particularly felt like poking around. When the dance at Payo Obispo ended at 3 A.M., the exhausted travelers were conveyed by government motorboat across the Bay of Chetumal to the settlement of Xcalak on the coast. Xcalak was a miserable little place languishing on an isolated stretch of barren sandy shoreline. Its few inhabitants were Mexican sailors, soldiers, and government officials, whose depressingly monotonous existence was enlivened only by the infrequent arrival of a gunboat from Veracruz bringing replacements.[11] Xcalak had been practically obliterated by the 1916 hurricane, which demolished the wireless tower, blew five vessels ashore, and drowned a number of people. It was at Xcalak, on February 6, that Morley and Held were reunited with Thomas Gann, who observed with amusement that they "showed distinct signs of wear and tear." The *Lilian Y* had returned to pick up the doctor at Corozal, and had brought him to Xcalak. As Gann informed his companions, the reconnaissance had nearly ended before it had really begun. On the way up from Corozal, the *Lilian Y* had run aground on a reef at night because of the helmsman's carelessness. With considerable effort, the vessel had finally scraped over the reef into deep water. Then the next morning the *Lilian Y* had nearly been wrecked on a false opening in the reef, shearing off just in time to avoid having her bottom ripped out.[12]

After this inauspicious start to the voyage, a relieved Morley was doubly glad to have the charts he had requested from ONI because

> The east coast of Yucatan is the most dangerous littoral from the Rio Grande to the Isthmus of Panama. It is fringed with a very steep-to-barrier-reef for almost its entire length, with 100-fathom water outside and 1 to 3 fathoms inside. The anchorages within, moreover, are none too trustworthy. The bottom is rocky in places and the holding qualities are poor.
>
> There are many openings in the barrier-reef giving soundings up to 18' but they are narrow for the most part (100' to 300') and their passage should not be attempted without an experienced local pilot. In rough weather (i.e., any gale from the northeast, east or southeast) they are impassible and local seamen prefer to stand out rather than to take the chance running the gauntlet of such perilous gateways to safety as these.
>
> The prevailing winds for 6 months are from the east and even a slight breeze from this quarter will pile up a high surf.
>
> We enjoyed exceptionally fine weather in the month of February and yet everywhere along this stretch we noted a long swell which pounded the barrier-reef with a noise that could be heard a half mile off.
>
> The beach is strewn with wreckage: life-bouys, dories, paddles, doors, ships' timbers, mahogany logs etc., eloquent if mute witnesses of the dangerous character of this shore.[13]

Morley and his companions methodically worked their way north along the coast. (See Appendix 2) It was, as had been the expedition to the Mosquito Coast, slow, hot, frustrating, and dirty work. Where the *Lilian Y* could not go for fear of running aground, they took to the vessel's jolly boat. Dr. Gann described it as the "'pram'—an invaluable little boat, which without her Evinrude engine did not draw over 6 in., and was absolutely impossible to upset in any sea . . ."[14] Where the boat could not go they explored on foot. On one occasion they had to struggle through ten yards of malodorous mud that reached above their knees in order to reach the shore. Some twenty-five miles up the coast from Xcalak, the *Lilian Y* reached Punta Herrero, where the Mexican government maintained a small lighthouse. The landscape was depressing in the extreme: a flat scrub-covered plain having no sign of civilization except for the lighthouse. As Morley explored along the brush lining the shore, he stumbled across two corroded iron bands that had heavy handmade iron spikes through them. These half-buried relics were mute evidence of some tragedy at sea, and set the archaeologist to musing. From what vessel had they come? Perhaps a Spanish galleon, or a pirate ship, or maybe some anonymous fishing boat. How long had they been rusting away on this desolate beach? There were no answers, and he left to rejoin his companions.

They spent the night at the lighthouse, and Morley commented approvingly that the equipment was of French, not German, manufacture. The hospitable lighthouse keeper told Morley of some ruins nearby. Of course, nothing would do but that the archaeologists go inspect them. After hacking their way through heavy brush they reached the site and found a small platform with a modest late Mayan temple of crude plastered masonry whose roof had collapsed. Although the site was disappointing, Morley and Gann happily took detailed measurements as well as several photographs.

As the *Lilian Y* neared Ascención Bay she was intercepted by a small sailing vessel flying the Mexican flag. Aboard was the local Customs official. When Morley showed him General Solís's letters, the official immediately placed himself at their service; they obligingly towed his craft into port. The settlement of Ascención was located on a sandbank on the northern shore of the bay. It had been founded in 1902 as a Mexican Army encampment, boasting a pier and many substantial buildings. Whereas it had once housed a population of some twenty-five hundred, Ascención had fallen into decay, and the 1916 hurricane had finished it off. Ascención currently had a population of eight: the lighthouse keeper and his family plus two minor Customs officials. There was not a lot to do in Ascención. Morley noted that a local pastime was going to the beach to stomp on Portuguese men-of-war in order to hear them burst.

The expedition next sailed across the bay to Vigia Chico, the terminus of the railroad running inland some thirty miles to Santa Cruz de Bravo, today the city of Felipe Carillo Puerto. Vigia Chico had been built as a port by General Bravo. It was a depressing collection of ruined dwellings, barracks, whorehouses, and pens for convict labor, all centered on a rather impressive stone wharf. Despite the railroad and telegraph line to Santa Cruz de Bravo, and occasional visits from ships, Vigia Chico was an isolated and repelling place. The chief point of interest was the rusting hulk of a Mexican gunboat, the *Independencia*, beached near the pier. Vigia Chico had suffered most severely from the devastating 1916 hurricane: freight cars were blown off the pier into the bay, a barge was flung a quarter mile inland, and virtually every structure was demolished. One writer has observed that the quality of life in Vigia Chico was suggested by the glass floors in several of the buildings: floors made by shoving empty rum bottles upside down into the sand. A lieutenant and a dozen soldiers were all that remained of a once-substantial garrison, and the civilian population consisted of a few *chicleros* and chicle contractors.[15]

Ironically, when Morley and his companions went ashore, the entire male population—some fifty—were waiting on the wharf to meet the travelers, whom they suspected of being Germans. Once the question of nationality had been straightened out, Morley was anxious to visit Santa Cruz de Bravo. The only way to get there was on the railroad, which really wasn't much of a railroad at all. It was a Decauville two-foot-gauge line with small flatcars, each pulled by a mule. The railroad was another of the Mexican army's projects. Santa Cruz de Bravo had been a military base for campaigns against Mayan rebels as well as being a penal colony. The railroad, built by convict labor, linked this advanced base with the coast. The whole enterprise was a strictly military operation; to provide a clear field of fire against Maya attacking the trains, the brush had been cleared for thirty yards on each side of the track. The project had been completed by General Ignacio Bravo, in whose honor the settlement of Chan Santa Cruz had been renamed Santa Cruz de Bravo. By 1911, however, General Bravo had left the peninsula and the government was no longer much concerned with disaffected Maya, for the Mexican Revolution was convulsing the country. In 1915 the railroad was abandoned.

Morley's party[16] traveled at mule pace on the railroad, passing through some inhospitable terrain, which to the archaeologist appeared indescribably poor. Limestone outcrops were everywhere, broken only by sparse low brush that was thorny and almost impenetrable. After an overnight journey they reached Santa Cruz de Bravo. The town was abandoned, and vegetation was rapidly taking over. At one corner of the plaza rose the huge barrel vault of the church, which dated back to the colonial period. The unfinished structure lacked its towers, and the facade was without decoration. In 1848, this entire region of the peninsula was abandoned because of the Caste War. The Maya occupied what was then Chan Santa Cruz and converted the church into a Mayan oracle. Not until 1901 did Mexican troops under General Bravo reoccupy the town. The church was converted into a prison that quickly developed an appalling reputation—convict laborers consisting of criminals and political prisoners, both men and women, were locked in at night, and robbery, rape, and murder were commonplace. Convicts and immigrants built Santa Cruz into a bustling town, with a hospital, school, shops, electric lighting, and a public market. But because of developments stemming from the Mexican Revolution, Santa Cruz was abandoned in 1915, with the inhabitants leaving by train for Vigia Chico. Mayan rebels, who had continued their guerrilla warfare, reoccupied the town, destroying much of what their enemies had built.[17]

At the time of Morley, Held, and Gann's visit only two Indian families inhabited the place. The visitors measured and photographed the church and other features of interest, then left the town to its slumber. Morley and his associates returned down the railroad, a trip made exasperatingly slow by the recalcitrant mule pulling their car. They reached the small station of Central, where a number of "sullen, swarthy, unclean Mexican *chicleros*"[18] were about, but fortunately nothing untoward occurred.

Morley had been told that General Francisco Mai, the principal chief of the rebellious Santa Cruz Maya, was expected at Central, and the archaeologist was anxious to talk with him. But while awaiting the chief's arrival, Morley and Gann decided to visit some ruins in the vicinity. There, in the middle of the heavy brush, Morley came upon one of the most perfect small Mayan temples he had ever seen. Two stories high, it stood on a low platform; the whole structure was slightly under nine feet high. The second story rose from the first like a smaller block placed on a larger one. The two archaeologists photographed and measured the temple, then they explored other ruins nearby. These, however, were of small temples that had been substantially demolished by Mexican soldiery years earlier.

Returning to Central station, where Held had been amusing himself by sketching, Morley and Gann decided that General Mai would not be coming after all, so the party started back down the track to Vigia Chico. On the way they encountered two Indians walking up the track. Morley's mule driver recognized one of them as General Mai's "first captain." Through an interpreter in their party, Morley learned that General Mai had not come because he was suffering from chills and fever. Doctor Gann seized the opportunity and supplied the Maya captain with quinine and cough medicine for the general. The interpreter reinforced the growing cordiality by telling the Indian that Morley and company were bearing gifts for the general and were searching for ruins. The Maya mentioned that there were sizeable ruins inland from Tulum, which of course piqued Morley and Gann's interest. The talks were carried on, according to Dr. Gann, "to the accompaniment of American ragtime on the horrible, cheap little gramaphone, the delight of Morley's heart, which accompanied us on all our travels by land or sea."[19] In what must have been a sacrificial gesture, Morley informed the first captain that the gramophone was a gift for the general. Dr. Gann must have been ecstatic. Morley worked out a rendezvous with the first captain for February 16 at Tulum, and urged him to bring the general along. As evidence of their goodwill, Morley and Gann plied the first captain with whiskey and cigars and sent him on his way. The travelers finally reached Vigia Chico after dark, their journey having been delayed by uncooperative mule motive power.

On February 12, the expedition left Vigia Chico to complete their examination of Ascención Bay. As Morley later reported to ONI, not only was the coast of Yucatán dangerous for sailors, but the very nature of the rivers, bays, and lagoons made them unfit for use by the Germans. The rivers really amounted only to small creeks, the lagoons were mere shallow basins filled with sandbanks, and of the three large bodies of water—Chetumal, Espíritu Santo, and Ascención bays—only the latter was even theoretically suitable for use by the enemy. No vessel drawing more than six feet of water could even enter Chetumal or Espíritu Santo bays. Moreover, Espíritu Santo was a shallow lagoon with a maximum depth of just ten feet. The bay was very shallow around the edges—the water was less than three feet deep a quarter of a mile offshore—and there were but six feet of water at the bar leading into Espíritu Santo.

With regard to Ascención Bay, Morley stated that, with the possible exception of the Caratasca Lagoon in Honduras, Ascención offered the best possibility for a German submarine base than anywhere else between the Bahía de Términos and Bluefields, that is, for about two thousand miles of coastline in Mexico and Central America. Not, he hastened to add, that there was the least sign of German activity there. Still, at the entrance to Ascención the water was twelve to fourteen feet above the bar, and inside the bay there was a considerable area with water sixteen and seventeen feet deep. Mexican gunboats drawing twelve feet had called at Ascención regularly from 1905 to 1915. For purposes of comparison, the largest vessel that ever navigated the Caratasca Lagoon was the *Yulo*, property of the Emery Mahogany Company, which drew only eight feet. On the other hand, Ascención was remote, off the main Caribbean sea-lanes, little frequented, and the shore of the southwestern three quarters of the bay was uninhabited. Yet Morley was confident that anything suspicious would be speedily reported. There were a number of men from Belize working at Vigia Chico on the west shore of the bay; from February to May fishermen from British Honduras camped on the Culebra Keys, at the entrance to the bay, to hunt for turtles. Moreover, a British subject from Belize named Peter Moguel living at Vigia Chico represented the Allies and had instructions to report anything unusual immediately to Dr. Gann.[20]

From Ascención Bay the ONI agents sailed to the island of Cozumel. The sea was rough, and Morley—always a wretched sailor—avoided eating and took to his bunk in utter misery. His spirits revived when, the next morning, the *Lilian Y* docked at San Miguel de Cozumel. Morley had not been there since April 1913, and he was eager to reacquaint himself with the town. After going through the formalities with the port and Customs officials, Morley set out in search of a pilot who knew the coast intimately. A business acquaintance recommended a candidate, and upon interviewing him Morley soon realized that the man knew every reef and anchorage between Cozumel and Progreso, Yucatán. Morley was so pleased that he hired him on the spot for two dollars a day.

After a delicious lunch—a welcome change from the greasy fare produced by their cook on the *Lilian Y*—Morley and his friends wandered off to inspect the ruins of a large church, now roofless, built by the Spaniards. After that, however, the day went downhill. Morley was outraged at learning that it would cost $32.34 to secure clearance papers for the *Lilian Y*. His frustration increased when it became clear that even after paying the fee the papers wouldn't be ready until sometime the next day.[21] A glum Morley resigned himself to attending a dance that evening organized by the port captain; the archaeologist suspected that not only was he attending the dance, but he had also paid for it through the extortionate clearance charge. Held tried to lighten the mood by drawing caricatures of everybody, but Morley was still out of sorts. The archaeologist thoroughly enjoyed dancing, but whatever pleasure he got from this was offset by the "unspeakable" native rum his hosts kept forcing on him.

The following morning the necessary papers were obtained, and the *Lilian Y* set sail, the principal residents of the village having gone down to the dock to see her off. The expedition had made a major change in plans, however. The pilot had informed Morley that he knew of some extensive ruins between Ascención and Espíritu Santo bays. He described them in such glowing terms that Morley's interest was aroused. Although it meant retracing the route some sixty-five miles, the archaeologist in Morley prevailed over the secret agent; the coastal reconnaissance was put on hold. All day the *Lilian Y* battled adverse winds and currents, but because of the late start they failed to reach their destination on schedule. At dusk Morley insisted that they go ashore to sleep, as just the thought of sleeping on board made him seasick. Gann accompanied him, whereas Held was quite comfortable sleeping aboard the sloop. While they were making camp, Gann noticed a fresh jaguar spoor next to where they had broken out their cots. In view of this unsettling development, they sent back to the boat for weapons—Gann's shotgun and Morley's .45-caliber automatic. Fortunately, the firearms were not needed. Within a ring of hurricane lamps, Gann and Morley slept the sleep of the just in their cots—decorously attired in their pajamas.

The next day, after several false starts the pilot succeeded in guiding Morley, Held, and Gann across mud flats and through heavy brush to the ruins. According to Morley, they were of an unknown Mayan city of considerable importance. The archaeologists' enthusiasm was fired, and they promptly set about mapping and photographing the site. To speed the work, they offered extra pay to the *Lilian Y*'s crew to come with machetes and clear brush and trees from in front of the main temple; the crew responded eagerly. Morley commented that the site had a feature he had never seen before: an arch or gateway leading directly to a temple. Another innovative feature was a Chac Mool figure reclining under the arch directly in line with the main temple. While most of the party were digging out the partially buried Chac Mool so it could be photographed, Morley and Gann went off to inspect a large structure: it proved to be a tremendous colonnaded hall like the two at Tulum, 102 feet long. Morley and Held carefully measured it. But the Chac Mool figure was the salient feature of the ruins. In fact, Morley named the site Chac Mool.[22]

When the archaeologists had finished their investigations, the *Lilian Y* weighed anchor and the expedition proceeded northward up the coast to Tulum. Morley noted that on the entire east coast of Yucatán Tulum had the worst reputation among sailors, for even in the calmest weather a heavy surf crashed against the rocky coast; according to their pilot this resulted from the strong coastal current. As if to bear out this observation, the *Lilian Y* had a potentially fatal accident. As the sloop passed through the fifty-yard break in the reef, the engine suddenly quit. With the vessel drifting helplessly toward certain destruction, the captain frantically hoisted sail. The *Lilian Y* recovered just in time to negotiate the break and anchor safely inside the reef.

Morley was bitterly disappointed because neither the Mayan general Mai nor his first captain appeared at Tulum, as agreed. So Morley and Gann employed their time in inspecting and measuring the ruins.[23] In addition, they searched for a stela Morley had left on the beach two years earlier. Morley soon had men digging up the beach for the vanished monument. It was Held, however, who found four of the seven missing fragments. They were scattered along the edge of the brush, where the 1916 hurricane had hurled them. To Morley's further joy, the critical top piece of the stela was also located. One of the last things the expedition did was to bury the fragments of the stela in a safe place and meticulously record the location. Both Held and Morley felt that the scene was like something out of *Treasure Island*.

On the next leg of the journey, the sloop put in at Playa del Carmen, a small village of pacified Maya south of Puerto Morelos. The expedition was running short of provisions, and Morley recorded that he and Gann went ashore to replenish their stock. Held, who was reading a book, could not be bothered to accompany them; Morley testily called him lazy and blasé. By a combination of barter and purchase, the two archaeologists restocked the larder. They also clambered over some small Mayan ruins in the neighborhood. As they were preparing to leave, they were asked to examine a sick villager. Doctor Gann did so and diagnosed chronic malaria. When the travelers returned to the boat they sent back some quinine for the poor wretch, but Gann thought he would probably die. Morley commented that conditions appeared to have improved little since John Lloyd Stephens had traveled through the area in the 1840s.

After a brief stopover at Puerto Morelos, where the Mexican government maintained a lighthouse and the only telegraph station on the entire east coast of the Yucatán peninsula, the *Lilian Y* headed for Isla Mujeres. There, they inspected the lighthouse and a little Mayan temple built on a high bluff. The shrine was gradually toppling into the sea, but through measurements and photographs they preserved at least some data about it. Perhaps the most remarkable thing the travelers found on Isla Mujeres was a covered shed with a wooden commemorative tablet erected by the Mexican government on February 18, 1917, to commemorate the four-hundredth anniversary of Juan de Grijalva's discovery of the island. It struck Morley as both admirable and pathetic that the elderly president Venustiano Carranza, careworn and assailed by enemies such as the *Villistas*, the *Zapatistas*, and the *Felicistas*, should have found time enough in his harried official life to order the tablet to be erected, and even more so that the order had actually been carried out.

At Isla Mujeres the expedition made another archaeological detour. A local boy told Morley of some ruins on Cancún Island, which today of course is a major tourist resort; at the time it was just "a long, flat bank of sand covered with stunted brush."[24] Morley promptly hired him as a guide. The boy promised to lead the party to the figure of a "king." When they reached the site, however, they found that the figure had toppled from its niche in the facade of a building, and its head had broken off. Fortunately, the head was still in good condition; Gann and Morley photographed it, and Held made a drawing of it. On the way back to the boat, the trio paused to measure another large colonnaded hall.

Getting back to their intelligence mission, Morley and his friends checked the coastline, lagoons, and mangrove swamps all the way north to the tip of the peninsula, rounding Cape Catoche and entering Yucatán proper. In addition to Morley's reconnaissance, the USS *Salem* landed a party, in August 1918, at Isla Mujeres and Cancún to investigate reports of supplies being stockpiled for German submarines. A party from the same warship also reconnoitered the entrance to Ascención Bay under cover of darkness for signs of enemy activity.[25]

West of Cape Catoche the barrier reef gave way to sandy shoals extending far offshore. These shoals made for water so shallow that even a boat like the *Lilian Y*, drawing only five feet of water, had to stand between two and three miles offshore. At Progreso, the principal port of the Yucatán peninsula, large vessels stood from two to five miles off, and it was claimed that a battleship had to lay ten miles out. Sailing westward along the low and barren coast, they touched at the villages of Holbox, El Cuyo, and Río Lagartos. After yet another detour to investigate some ruins and a henequen-producing hacienda, a large landed estate, the expedition started on the last leg of their journey, their destination being Progreso.

On the way, the *Lilian Y* intercepted a large motorized schooner heading for Belize. The schooner hove to, and Doctor Gann was able to give her captain his report for the governor of British Honduras. On April 24, 1918, Captain Roger Welles, the Director of Naval Intelligence, sent to Captain V. H. Haggard, the British naval attaché in Washington, a copy of Morley's report and acknowledged the governor of British Honduras's cooperation. Haggard then forwarded the report to the governor.[26] The United States Navy also contributed to the defense of British Honduras in a more tangible way, by selling two field radio sets to the British for $4,000 and shipping them to the colony.[27]

11. Yucatán

On February 25, 1918, the *Lilian Y* reached Progreso.[1] Because of their late arrival, the bureaucratic port formalities had to wait until the next morning, much to the displeasure of Morley, who couldn't wait to get off the *Lilian Y*. He complained that although the captain secured her with two anchors, the craft still rocked all night. As far as he was concerned, the *Lilian Y* would rock in a millpond.

Morley's letter from General Solís helped clear their path through Customs. The only delay came when Morley had to turn in the weaponry he and Held carried—four pistols, plus belts and bandoliers of ammunition—because no one was permitted to carry firearms in the state of Yucatán. The Mexican officials required an inventory including the weapons' make, caliber, and number of cartridges for each. Morley did, however, manage to smuggle through Customs his last six bottles of claret. This was fortunate, for under the existing revolutionary regime Yucatán was dry.[2] After getting through Customs, Morley and Held looked up American Consul Gaylord Marsh. Morley's initial impression was not favorable. The consul had evidently heard of them and affected a very knowing air. Morley and Held played dumb until Marsh dropped his air of mystery. Morley initially thought him a bit of a fool.

Having made contact with the American consul the ONI agents eagerly inquired about their mail. To their great disappointment, the only mail that had accumulated for them at the consulate was second-class material: scientific publications, the *New Republic*, and so on. The reason for the absence of correspondence was that the Ward liner, which should have arrived the previous week, had collided with a torpedo boat in New

York harbor and had to put in for repairs. There would be no mail for at least another week. To men who had been on the fringes of civilization for the past month, this was bitter news indeed. But since nothing could be done about it, the trio boarded the train for the twenty-mile ride to Mérida, the capital of Yucatán. Dr. Gann waxed positively eloquent about the place:

> Merida is one of the prettiest, cleanest, gayest little capitals it has been my good fortune to visit. In many ways it reminds one of Monte Carlo in the season. The warm climate, the scrupulous cleanliness of the streets and plazas, the flowers, music, and sunshine, the crowds of pretty, well-dressed girls, the numbers of prosperous-appearing idlers, the absence of poverty, squalor, and ugliness, and the perpetual air of festa [sic], are all common to both.[3]

Checking into the Grand Hotel, they reveled in the amenities, such as a leisurely lunch, baths, and fresh clothing. Then Morley took his companions to look up old acquaintances. He had last been in Mérida in 1913, but his gift for making friends meant that he had a wide circle of friends and acquaintances there; these people would prove to be of great assistance in both his intelligence and archaeological endeavors. Perhaps the most useful was Juan Martínez, a prominent citizen who was intelligent, cultured, spoke good English, and was strongly pro-Ally. Until recently he had been the representative in the United States for the Yucatecan government commission controlling the henequen industry, with henequen being Yucatán's principal export. As we shall see, he provided Morley with a wealth of economic intelligence. Before his involvement with henequen, Martínez had been government Inspector of Ruins (archaeological sites) in Yucatán, a post now held by his son. Martínez shared Morley and Gann's passion for Mayan archaeology, and he was the principal authority in Yucatán on the ancient Mayan language.[4] In this first of several visits he discussed the Maya for hours with his three guests, and he allowed Morley to read an unpublished paper of his. Martínez also acceded to Morley's request that he arrange an interview with the governor for himself and Gann.

After supper Gann retired early, but Held and Morley were determined to see more of Mérida. They toured the city in a new seven-passenger Overland auto owned by a friend of Morley, and then they went to the theater. They repeated this pattern several times during the succeeding days.

On February 28, Morley and Gann had an audience with the governor. Reflecting the revolutionary tenor of the times, Carlos Castro Morales had been a master mechanic on the railroad for twenty-three years before being installed as governor of Yucatán. He was an impressive physical specimen—not very tall but quite broad. The chain-smoking governor prided himself on being a freethinker, a socialist, and an archaeology buff. Morley's friend Juan Martínez gave the American archaeologist a glowing introduction, after which Morley presented his Carnegie Institution credentials and described his archaeological plans. The meeting was a great success. The governor, who was surprisingly knowledgeable about the history and archaeology of Yucatán, issued them a letter instructing local officials to assist them in their research and he even put the railroad's automobile at their disposal.[5] As usual, Morley had demonstrated his ability to move easily in important official circles.

But he also secluded himself in a friend's villa on the outskirts of Mérida to write his report to ONI. It was certainly not a moment too soon, for he had last reported two months earlier from Belize. After describing their voyage along the coast to Progreso, Morley turned to political intelligence. With his typical thoroughness, he explained that the Yucatán peninsula was divided into the states of Campeche on the west coast and Yucatán on the north coast, and the territory of Quintana Roo on the east coast. Morley referred his case officer to the enclosed map drawn by Held and showing all the railroads, cities, towns, and haciendas. As was obvious, the commercial life of the peninsula was centered in Campeche and Yucatán, while Quintana Roo, by far the largest entity, was but sparsely populated.

The few small settlements in Quintana Roo were either on the coast or on some body of water emptying directly into the sea, such as Chetumal Bay or Bacalar Lagoon. The interior was the domain of the Santa Cruz, an independent tribe of Mayan stock who had been waging guerrilla war against the Mexicans since 1848. Until the Mexicans withdrew from Santa Cruz de Bravo in the heart of the Santa Cruz country, which the Indians had claimed since 1848, killings, atrocities, and reprisals on both sides were the order of the day. In 1915, General Salvador Alvarado, the military governor of the peninsula, ordered that the capital of Quintana Roo be moved from Santa Cruz de Bravo to Payo

Obispo on Chetumal Bay, and most of the five-hundred-odd Mexicans in the territory now lived there.[6] Since the withdrawal there had been relative peace in Quintana Roo.

The Mexican retreat had left the Santa Cruz in undisputed possession of Quintana Roo's interior as far north as Puerto Morelos; there were no Mexican settlements in this region. Within the last two years, though, the principal chief of the Santa Cruz, General Francisco Mai, had permitted a few chicle contractors to operate along the line of the abandoned Ferrocarril Nacional de Quintana Roo, which ran from Vigia Chico to Santa Cruz de Bravo. But the contractors' operations were very limited and they were very much on their good behavior.

The Santa Cruz numbered between five and ten thousand. Their head chief, General Mai, lived at Chunpup, twenty-five miles northwest of Vigia Chico. There were two secondary chieftains, whose place of residence Morley also specified. As he had mentioned, the Santa Cruz had little love for Mexicans, having left off killing them less than three years earlier. But they were quite friendly to the inhabitants of British Honduras, going there frequently to trade. In fact, two summers earlier General Mai had sent a delegation to Belize, headed by his own brother, to ask the governor to annex the Santa Cruz and their territory to the British Empire.

Morley explained that he was reporting in such detail to demonstrate that not only the coastal strip but also the interior were unsuited for German activities. Yet ever since the beginning of the war, the specter of a German-engineered invasion of British Honduras from Yucatán had worried the authorities in Belize. And the desire for accurate information as to the possibility of this happening was the main reason Dr. Gann had been given a leave of absence to accompany Morley. The possibility of such an invasion was extremely remote. For one thing, there were fewer than two hundred Germans in the entire peninsula. For another, any invading force would have to contend with dense jungle, no roads, and very inadequate trails. Unless Mexico were to cooperate on a large scale with supplies and transportation facilities, such an attack would simply be impossible.

Ironically, Morley had heard while in Mérida that the Mexican government feared that the British would strike from British Honduras and seize Quintana Roo! These mutual fears of invasion paralleled those existing between Guatemala and Honduras. He commented that "in our business, as in everything else, history repeats itself."

Morley postponed an analysis of the political situation in Yucatán and Campeche until his next report, since he was still collecting material and familiarizing himself with local conditions. He could already see, however, a general discontent by Yucatecans against the Carranza government. They felt they were being exploited, as in fact they were. Their single crop, henequen, from which binder twine was made, was being bought by the government at the low fixed price of seven cents a pound; the government, in turn, sold the henequen in the United States through the government-controlled Comisión Reguladora de Henequén for the highest price it had ever commanded—nineteen cents a pound—and pocketed the difference. Hacienda owners felt that they, not the government, should be reaping this extraordinary wartime profit. But the chances of that were slim since the Carranza regime desperately needed the income from henequen sales.

Another source of discontent was that even though wages were phenomenally high, the cost of living had increased so enormously that real purchasing power had eroded to the point that the masses were worse off than they were before the days of their present prosperity. Another destabilizing element was that General Alvarado had freed the Indians from peonage, or indenture for debt. Laudable as this measure might be, the Indians were now reluctant to work. They were deserting the haciendas, flocking to the cities in search of a better life but finding that food was scarce and the cost of living distressingly high. Lastly, Morley reported disapprovingly that "there is a sort of state socialism in operation down here now, and the country is flooded with spellbinders, soapbox orators, labor organizers, etc. It is a confused business all around but I will try to present its essential elements in my next." His conclusion followed:

Taking into consideration all the different factors I have outlined, it does not appear to me probable that this region can, or will be used by the Germans for the establishment of submarine bases, certainly not without the active cooperation of the Mexican Government. Even Ascencion Bay, the most naturally favored spot on the Yucatan littoral for such a purpose, could hardly be thus utilized without the direct assistance and participation of the Mexican authorities, and clandestinely not at all.

Similarly the idea of a Mexican-German attack on British Honduras by land or by sea is equally improbable. Either offers great natural obstacles, and the Santa Cruz in the event of the latter would not cooperate and might frustrate.

Finally the increasing dislike of the Yucatecans for the Mexicans makes it extremely likely that any such madness on the part of the Mexican Government as this would be immediately followed by a secessionist movement down here; and an appeal to us for a protectorate. The Yucatecans thus appealed to the Republic of Texas for a protectorate in the early forties of the last century, and they are ready to do it now with any kind of encouragement from us.

Yucatan's economic future is indissolubly connected with the United States, a fact generally recognized by the Yucatecans themselves. They need us, and we need them, or rather their henequen to make our binder-twine; and any declaration of war against us by Mexico would almost certainly be followed by the establishment of an independent government here in the peninsula, which would seek to place itself under our protection. But of this more in my next.[7]

While in Yucatán Morley conspicuously maintained his archaeological cover, and he did so in style. He took full advantage of the assistance graciously provided by the younger Juan Martínez, the current Inspector of Ruins. The latter provided letters of introduction to all the caretakers of archaeological sites, who were his subordinates. Martínez also introduced Morley's party to the hacendados, or owners of large landed estates, on whose properties ruins were located, and had these hacendados provide letters to their foremen to provide food, lodging, transportation, and anything else Morley and his companions might require.[8] The archaeologist and his two friends spent weeks traveling by car and on foot to visit major Mayan sites, places such as Chichén Itzá, Kabah, and Uxmal, which Gann had not seen.[9] At Uxmal, Morley and Gann uncovered several hieroglyphs that made it possible to date the ruins with precision. The jubilant archaeologists also prevailed on Held to assist them in their inquiries—he became a kind of poor man's Michelangelo. To obtain copies of the glyphs and paintings on the capstones in several rooms, they built a rickety scaffold, and an apprehensive Held lay on his back some fifteen feet above the floor copying the material. Not the least of their accomplishments was the discovery of several new Mayan sites.

The three ONI agents also embarked on a reconnaissance of the western shore of the Yucatán peninsula. Gann and Morley left Mérida by train, on March 1, for the port of Campeche. In that decaying colonial city, surrounded by massive walls and a moat built in the seventeenth century to protect Campeche from marauding pirates, they were reunited with Held, who had sailed aboard the *Lilian Y* down from Progreso, examining the coastal towns as he went. The trio stayed at the Hotel Guatémoc, which had once been the Spanish governor's palace. They experienced their share of frustration while in Campeche. First, they couldn't even get the shallow-draft *Lilian Y* all the way to the wharf because the harbor was silting up so badly; Gann observed that unless dredging operations were undertaken soon, the port would be unable to carry on even what little business it currently conducted. Then there was the hassle and protracted delay involved in clearing the *Lilian Y* through Customs because she was an English-registered vessel.

From Campeche, the ONI agents sailed down the coast to Champotón, a town of some fifteen hundred inhabitants located at the mouth of the Champotón River. Their objective was to investigate rumors of a German wireless station. According to what they'd been told in Yucatán, Champotón was a hotbed of German spies, who brazenly operated a radio station. What Morley and company experienced was anti-climax. They discovered that the "wireless" rumors originated in two sixty-foot posts carrying the government telegraph line across the mouth of the Champotón River high enough to permit boats to pass underneath. Viewed from the sea, the posts resembled supports for a wireless aerial. As for Germans, there simply were not any to be found. Having laid yet another rumor to rest, the trio returned to Mérida. They spent the next several weeks in their tour of Maya ruins. Then Morley and Held parted company with Gann, who sailed the *Lilian Y* back to British Honduras.[10]

After Dr. Gann's departure, Morley and Held remained in Mérida, where Morley was amassing a considerable amount of political and economic intelligence. He presented his findings in a lengthy report to ONI.[11] The operative word was "henequen," for it was the key element in both the economic and political fortunes of Yucatán. During most of the nineteenth century Yucatán had been a struggling backwater state with few exports—some sugar, a few cattle. The state was "poverty-stricken and down-at-the-heel." All this changed virtually overnight in the course of a single year, 1898, and because of the rise of a single industry—the cultivation of sisal fiber (*agave sisalense*), or henequen.

It was the Spanish-American War that began transforming Yucatán from one of the poorest states in Mexico to one of the wealthiest. During the war the supply of Manila hemp was disrupted; consequently, the price of substitute fibers soared. For example, Morley stated, sisal was selling for 4³⁄8 cents a pound in April 1898; by June the price was 11 ¹⁄8 cents. After the Spanish-American War the reappearance of Manila hemp produced a corresponding slump in the price of sisal, which reached its nadir of 4¹⁄2 cents a pound in 1911. But sisal cultivation increased because a demand had been created and a market was established. There was continuing demand in the United States for binder twine for use in the wheat harvests. The Yucatán peninsula with its rocky limestone surface and shallow soil—in order to plant trees in Mérida it was necessary to blast holes in the limestone and fill them with soil—was the natural habitat of sisal, which it was soon discovered made the best, and cheapest, binder twine.

Fortunes were made overnight, especially among hacendados, who were delighted to find their hitherto-marginal estates suddenly transformed into veritable gold mines. To illustrate the Golden Age of Yucatán, Morley included the following table:

YEAR	PRICE PER POUND IN CENTS	NUMBER OF BALES EXPORTED	VALUE OF CROP (U.S. CURRENCY)
1898	$6\frac{3}{8}$	418,972	$9,459,037.13
1899	$7\frac{1}{3}$	445,978	10,105,620.68
1900	$6\frac{5}{8}$	499,634	11,308,016.35
1901	7	523,000	11,591,726.86
1902	$9\frac{1}{8}$	540,000	18,216,395.81
1903	$7\frac{1}{2}$	613,165	16,665,577.27
1904	$7\frac{1}{3}$	631,216	16,011,290.72
1905	$7\frac{1}{4}$	641,833	14,812,715.15
1906	7	615,910	13,623,761.39
1907	$6\frac{1}{4}$	639,822	12,437,158.78
1908	$5\frac{1}{4}$	687,262	10,388,508.33
1909	$5\frac{3}{4}$	593,843	10,107,313.97
1910	$5\frac{1}{4}$	636,744	8,833,237.34
1911	$4\frac{1}{2}$	730,500	10,965,907.00
1912	$5\frac{1}{8}$	846,151	14,574,209.37
1913	$6\frac{5}{8}$	836,950	20,889,826.36
1914	$5\frac{1}{3}$	964,862	13,973,511.05
1915	$5\frac{7}{8}$	949,639	16,040,947.62
1916	$12\frac{5}{8}$	1,291,433	[sic] 11,633,003.55
1917	$19\frac{1}{4}$	733,832	[sic] 19,612,843.28

But practically all of this enormous wealth was concentrated in the hands of some seventy-five "old families," a closely knit oligarchy who owned virtually all of the land. The Indians, who made up the majority of the population, were bound to the land by peonage, which in effect resembled slavery. As long as he was in debt, an Indian could not leave a hacienda. Since hacendados kept the books at the *tienda de raya*, or company store, it was virtually impossible for a peon to work his way out of debt. Most of these unfortunates were born, lived, and died on the same hacienda, thus providing a steady labor supply.

Yet there was some justice, in a perverse sort of way. The hacendados exploited the peons, but International Harvester Company exploited the hacendados. About 90 percent of the entire Yucatán sisal crop was exported to the United States to be made into binder twine; 80 percent of this was purchased by International Harvester. For years the company arbitrarily fixed the price it would pay and when it would buy. Since there was no competition in the field and the hacendados in Yucatán had no cash reserves, they could not withhold their crop from the market in expectation of prices rising. They spent every cent they had and even borrowed against future crops. International Harvester pretty much had things its own way.

In 1912, the hacendados tried to free themselves from International Harvester by organizing in Mérida an agency to market their sisal—the Comisión Reguladora del Mercado de Henequén. The Comisión tried to raise the price of sisal, but failed miserably. It had no financial backing and its members repeatedly cut prices behind each others' backs. So International Harvester retained its monopoly and continued to dictate prices.

The traditional view has been that the situation in Yucatán changed dramatically on March 19, 1915, when one of Venustiano Carranza's generals, Salvador Alvarado, captured Mérida, for the Yucatán peninsula had been largely unaffected by the Mexican Revolution, which began in 1910. Because of its isolation, Yucatán was a kind of oasis of peace during the subsequent years of civil war that devastated Mexico. Yucatán for all practical purposes was an island, the only feasible means of communication being by sea from the port of Progreso. This reinforced the strong separatist tradition that had characterized Yucatán all the way back to the colonial period. But all this changed when Venustiano Carranza dispatched General Alvarado and six thousand troops to occupy Yucatán. The Great War had already increased the demand for sisal, and the Carranza regime urgently needed the revenue that its sale would produce. The Yucatecans attempted to repel the invasion but were quickly overwhelmed, and the elite families fled into exile in Cuba and the United States. General Alvarado was now proconsul of Yucatán; while professing allegiance to Carranza, he ran Yucatán to suit himself. A man of considerable ability, he was ambitious, idealistic, had boundless self-confidence, and harbored a deep hatred for capitalism and the Roman Catholic Church. Yet this traditional interpretation of "revolution from without" has recently been revised by historians Allen Wells and Gilbert M. Joseph, who suggest that Alvarado found considerable local support for his revolutionary program.[12]

Alvarado's first act was to confiscate the property of those who had fled. But he still needed money to finance his administration, and in the Comisión Reguladora he had a ready-made instrument for raising cash. Through forced loans from the planters he quickly amassed a war chest, and by April 1915 he compelled them to sign contracts with the Comisión Reguladora to deliver all their sisal to it for the next five years at a fixed price. By the simple expedient of making the Comisión Reguladora the only legal buyer of sisal, planters either sold to it or watched their crop rot in the fields. And since Alvarado controlled the railroads and the docks at Progreso, hacendados either joined the Comisión Reguladora or faced ruin. By November 1915 Alvarado was in complete control of the sisal market and began dictating to International Harvester. When the company balked, Alvarado cut off the supply until International Harvester capitulated. By the time Morley was reporting—April 1918—Alvarado's profit margin was 11 3/4 cents a pound—compared to the 2 cents in November 1915, when he first gained control of the market. Morley estimated that Alvarado and the Carranza administration had made nearly ten million dollars in 1916, even more in 1917, and if the present high price of sisal held for the rest of 1918 their revenues would exceed fifteen million; and these were conservative estimates.

In Morley's view, Alvarado's efforts to create a "socialist utopia" in a land with a historically feudal tradition and a 25 percent literacy rate had resulted in the creation of a "socialist despotism with himself as the fountainhead of all authority."

> He liberated the peons; dismantled the churches; drove out the priests; closed the cantinas; prohibited the sale or manufacture of liquor in the state; abolished bullfighting; opened schools; fixed an 8-hour working day and minimum wage scale. An enlightened program you will say. Yes, but as in Russia, one that is ruining the country.
>
> Take for example the labor situation, and its relation to the sisal industry, which affects us vitally as I will show presently. The

abolishment of peonage and the increase in wages i.e., from .25 cents for 1000 leaves in 1915 to $1.25 in 1918, 500% increase in five years, has made the Indian virtually independent. He will only work one to two days a week and during which time he makes more than enough to support him for the remaining five, and since he has no use for money beyond the immediate demands for living expenses, and corn, his staple, is still cheap, he prefers idleness to the accumulation of any monetary margin above the bare cost of living.

In consequence of this condition the sisal leaves are dying on the plants for want of labor to cut them. In the past month I have been all over the henequen belt and I can assure you that the plantations are in a deplorable condition. Many plants—some estimate as high as fifty percent—are a total loss, and everywhere the fields are choked with bush and brush. There is practically no new planting being done and as it takes five years after planting before the leaves can be cut, it is evident that unless conditions change soon the entire sisal industry will be a thing of the past.

Already as the accompanying tables will show, the annual supply has suffered a serious curtailment because of all these new "reforms" and this in the face of the highest price ever paid for the fibre, which should have stimulated production to a maximum.

Take for example the figures for the last five complete years: 1913–1917:

YEAR	NUMBER OF BALES EXPORTED
1913	856,950
1914	964,862
1915	949,639
1916	1,291,433
1917	733,832

This shows that 1917 was the lowest year in the previous five, notwithstanding the fact that the current price was the highest ever paid for the fibre; and that it was more than a half million bales lower than the 1916 output or 43% off that maximum.

The outlook for 1918—when we will need more binder-twine than ever before in the history of the country—is even more disquieting. I give below the production for the first quarter (January–March) for the last six years including that of the quarter just closed:

First quarter

JAN–MARCH	NUMBER OF BALES EXPORTED
1913	151,234
1914	279,505
1915	114,902
1916	385,144
1917	147,281
1918	121,500

These figures speak for themselves. They require no comment of mine to show how serious is the present shortage of sisal. The production for the first quarter of 1918 is already 68% behind that of the corresponding quarter of 1916 and 17% behind that of 1917.

If the same proportionate loss is sustained in the remaining three quarters as sustained in the first, the 1918 crop will be under 500,000 bales, or a quarter of a million less even than the low 1917 crop. There literally will not be enough to go around and where also is all the binder-twine for the 1918 wheat crop coming from?

It is freely asserted here by the Yucatecans that Carranza and Alvarado are desperately trying to ruin Yucatan financially so as to crush out once for all the possibility of her ever attaining independence. Whether this be true or not it is of course impossible to say but what is certain is that the sisal industry is slowly being ruined.

The price of labor has been forced up to such a high level by the socialistic government that the cost of production of sisal is now almost if not quite equal to the prevailing price of the fibre as fixed by the government, i.e., 7½ cents. And what with the scarcity of labor for harvesting the crop and the consequent loss of thousands of plants, a shortage of cars to move the crop to Progreso, the high

freight rates and dockage charges and the depreciation of machin-
ery, plants, and equipments, the planters are surely being ruined.

Morley stated that socialist agitators, professional labor organizers, and
American draft dodgers were abroad in the land inciting the Indians
against their former masters. The result: the Indians refused to work. And
there had been sporadic rioting.

> And this at a time when Yucatan should be enjoying an unprece-
> dented prosperity like Cuba and Hawaii, when her single crop is
> three times more valuable than it has ever been before. In short, the
> present condition here constitutes the most scathing arraignment of
> socialistic govermentary control that I ever knew of anywhere, and
> except for Russia is the blackest case against socialism on record.

The domestic troubles of Yucatán were of no particular interest to the
United States except as they affected the supply of sisal, "which at present is a vital necessity not only to the American people but also to a successful prosecution of the war."

Turning to the political situation, Morley reported that two months
earlier, just before the ONI agents arrived, General Alvarado had left
Mérida for Puerto México, Tabasco; he was now commander of the
entire Southeastern military zone of Mexico. Alvarado left as governor
of Yucatán Carlos Castro Morales, who for twenty-three years had been
master mechanic on the Yucatán railroad, and who was another socialist. Castro Morales, however, was only a figurehead, and Alvarado
remained the real power in the peninsula.

During Morley's travels throughout Yucatán in the past month, he
had been able to verify the depth of dislike that all classes of society had
for the despotic Alvarado. Even the peons whom he had liberated had
no use for the general, while all over the state flags had hung at half-mast
on March 19 as an expression of sorrow for the day Alvarado had made
his triumphal entry into Mérida in 1915. The hatred of the planters was
understandable. They could only dream of the fortunes they would be
making if they could sell their sisal directly in the United States. As for
the lower classes, not only was inflation destroying their meager standard of living but, being deeply religious, they bitterly resented Alvarado's
anticlerical policies. Finally, just as the Maya had a visceral hatred of

"Mexicans," Yucatecos as a whole despised their fellow citizens from outside the peninsula. In particular, they resented the hundreds of Mexicans who had entered Yucatán in Alvarado's wake.

Morley even speculated that the resentment at being exploited was so pronounced in Yucatán that the citizens might well prefer American intervention and an American protectorate to their present intolerable situation. He stressed that he had come to this conclusion only after "conversations with all kinds of people: planters, mestizos, Indians and foreigners." In this connection, Arthur Pierce, the British consul in Mérida, had told Morley that he had been approached several times in the last two years by Yucatecans who wanted Britain to establish such a protectorate. Morley became rather enthusiastic as he discussed the subject:

> These of course are only trifling matters, but after all they are the straws that show which way the wind is blowing, and I believe that with any sort of encouragement from us the Yucatecans would throw off the Mexican yoke, separate themselves from the rest of the republic and declare themselves an independent state.
>
> If Mexico should force our hand by allying herself with Germany and declaring war on us I am confident that such a separation could easily be effected. A gunboat at Campeche, another at Progreso to prevent the Mexicans from sending any reinforcements over here, and the Yucatecans themselves could easily take care of the thousand-odd Mexican soldiers now maintained here.
>
> A condition not unlike that which confronted us in Panama, it seems to me, may be developing here in Yucatan. In Panama owing to the repeated double-crossing and deliberate procrastination of the Colombian Government we were eventually forced to countenance if not actually connive at the establishment of a separate state on the Isthmus. Here if the supply of sisal is cut off altogether our hand may be similarly forced. We have got to have binder-twine and any step necessary to enforce the permanence of the supply can only be regarded as a measure of self preservation.

While the independence of Yucatán might not be feasible just yet, Morley had an immediate solution to the current shortage of binder twine in the United States. He had just learned something interesting from his friend Juan Martínez. The latter had formerly been the director of the Comisión

Reguladora, and he had been a friend of Morley for the last five years, both in Mérida and in New York. It was Martinéz who presumably had supplied Morley with the wealth of statistical data concerning henequen. Martínez had informed Morley that there were 516,000 bales of sisal stored in Yucatán. If steps could be taken in Washington to secure the immediate shipment of this stock, it would greatly alleviate the shortage. But speed was essential, for in only ten weeks the American wheat harvest would be at its height.

> Finally in summing up the political condition here, I may say that all my information as well as my personal observation indicates that if such an extreme step as intervention in Mexico should become necessary we could count upon the active cooperation of the Yucatecans themselves in any movement looking toward the separation of the peninsula, i.e., Quintana Roo, Yucatan and Campeche from the rest of the republic and the erection thereof into an independent state, so disgusted are the Yucatecans with the Mexican regime of robbery and mismanagement. Sisal is the very life of the country, the single export and source of wealth, and the gradual destruction of the industry is raising a smoldering discontent everywhere.

With regard to the foreign population, "the Chinese, Syrians and Spaniards (in the order named) are the most numerous; the Germans, the best organized." There were about one hundred Germans, and the German Club was the center of their organizations in Mérida, as it was everywhere else. All the influential Germans belonged, and they were quite active in spreading propaganda, which found a receptive audience given Mexicans' historic resentment of the United States.[13]

There had been a German newspaper in Mérida, *El Boletín de la Guerra*, published by the leading daily, *Voz de la Revolución*, but by threatening to apply the Black List, Consul Marsh had forced them out of town. The German newspaper was currently being published in Progreso, but it was in precarious financial condition.

Morley heartily approved of using the Black List, deeming it a most effective weapon in the Latin American countries, which were dependent on the United States for supplies. Morley was upset that the Black List had not yet been applied against the biggest German business in the peninsula—the hardware firm of Ritter and Beck, which employed some ten

Germans. The American and British consuls in Mérida were, in the archae-ologist's opinion, "good men and they keep the Germans jumping." They had recently secured the dismissal of Germans from the English-owned power plant and from the Comisión Reguladora. Morley felt confident that the two consuls were capable of keeping the Germans under control.

Speaking of Germans, Morley included a list of twenty-six Germans in Mérida, giving brief descriptions of them and paying particular atten-tion to the six most important, and hence potentially most dangerous. In addition, the archaeologist appended a list of the membership of the German Club. Before the war the German Club had many Yucatecan members, but these resigned as soon as the Black List was issued for fear of being blacklisted.

Morley was happy to report that not all propaganda activities were carried out by Germans. Pro-Allied propaganda was also being produced, principally by most of the Syrians, who constituted the largest foreign colony in Mérida. They had formed a Syrian League to support the Allies, and both the American and British consuls had attended the inauguration banquet. The leading Syrian propagandist was currently said to be in hiding, though, for an order had allegedly come from Mexico City to deport him for breach of neutrality. To Morley, if this were true it demon-strated the pro-German sympathies of the Carranza regime, which permitted German propagandists to operate with impunity. As far as Morley was concerned, Yucatán was ripe for American propaganda, and he recommended that a skilled practitioner be sent down from the United States. It was unwise for Morley and Held to participate in such activities because of the resulting unwanted publicity. Aside from letting it be known they were loyal Americans, they had assiduously avoided engaging in propaganda.

There had occurred a truly bizarre incident during Morley's stay in Mérida:

> An extraordinary Englishman by the name of Major L. O. Burnett arrived here from New York just after we did, and only left for the same port last week. He took no pains to conceal that he was in the British Secret Service, which not only put him under suspicion with Held and myself but also with Gann and Pierce, Gann even going so far as to say he was not an Englishman, and Pierce was at his wit's end to establish his real identity.

The man's credentials from the British Foreign Office—which by the way were not stolen from him by one of our people—were all right, and in addition Pierce received money and code messages from the British Consul in New York for him. The man by his talk had obviously been on the Western Front and the most charitable construction to put on his yarns was that he was suffering from shell-shock, so impossible were they. He told me himself that he had been retired from active service on account of his wounds, but then he told everything to everybody. He had plenty of money, Pierce paying over to him $2000.00 gold from the British Consul-General in New York while he was here, and he was always sending off expensive telegrams in code through Pierce. During the six weeks that he was here we were all working on him: Pierce, Marsh, Watkins, Gann, Held and myself, and we all reached the same conclusion regarding him, namely, that as extraordinary as he was, he was as he presented himself to be. He made foozle of everything down here and left in disgust. If he is a fair example of the British Secret Service, all I can say is that it is a wonder the Huns have not carried off the Crown Jewels from the Tower of London.

The mysterious Englishman's name was actually Sidney Charles Burnett. The British consul in Mérida had reported that Burnett claimed to have been sent to investigate German activities. Burnett further stated that his passport had been stolen. The consul forwarded the passport serial number and a physical description of Burnett, who declared that he was known to the British consul general in New York City. The consul in Mérida asked in bewilderment, "Who is he?" Nobody in the Foreign Office seemed to know, nor was there any record of Burnett's passport having even been issued.

The mystery was finally cleared up when, on April 10, 1918, a chagrined Admiral Sir W. Reginald Hall, director of British Naval Intelligence, sent a SECRET letter to the Foreign Office requesting that the British consul in Mérida be instructed to inform Burnett that his orders to proceed to British Honduras were canceled and his employment terminated. Burnett was to deliver to the consul a report on his activities as well as his expense account and the balance of funds in his possession. The consul, in turn, would refund him the money for his passage back to England and issue him an Emergency Certificate for the journey. Further investigation by the Foreign Office revealed that Burnett's passport had been issued at the request of M.I. 1C.[14] The latter was the shadowy War Office section dealing with secret agents and liaison with MI 6. The British Office of Naval Intelligence and MI 6 maintained a very close relationship, with their directors meeting almost daily.[15]

A much less flamboyant secret agent than the Englishman Burnett was the man whom Morley had recruited to cover Yucatán and Tabasco. Morley reminded his ONI case officer of the importance of this region, with Ascención Bay on the east and the Bahía de Términos on the west, with a strong German colony in Tabasco[16] and in Mérida the strongest German center west of San Pedro Sula, Honduras.

A good man was needed to monitor this strategic region, and Morley believed he had found him in the person of Lewis Hunt Watkins. The latter was young for such a responsible assignment—only twenty-three years old. He was an American citizen, had registered for the draft, and had a brother who was a major in the Medical Corps serving with the American Expeditionary Force in France. Watkins had attended Eastern High School in Washington, D.C. He was a civil engineer, a graduate of the Carnegie Institute of Technology in Pittsburgh, and had worked for the Hydrographic Department of the United States Coast and Geodetic Survey. He spoke Spanish fluently and was currently working for the Laguna Corporation of Philadelphia, purchasing hardwoods and dyewoods in southeastern Mexico. Not only had his employment taken him through virtually all of Chiapas, Tabasco, Campeche, Yucatán, and Quintana Roo, but his job provided excellent cover for his clandestine activities. Morley gave him a glowing recommendation:

> Although he is a little under the age for our service, his peculiar qualifications, his already-established alibi (The Laguna Corporation), his excellent record as a "news getter," for which I can vouch myself, and finally his intense loyalty make him peculiarly qualified and adapted for our service.

Watkins was quite knowledgeable about the area from Ascención and Espíritu Santo bays in the east to the Isthmus of Tehuantepec in the west. And his business trips during the last year had brought him into close personal contact with the leading Germans of the region.

Because of his peculiar qualifications and his experience—Watkins had been carrying out secret missions for Consul Marsh at Progreso for the past year—Morley had enlisted him as a regular ONI agent on the usual terms: $100 a month and all expenses to begin May 1. Watkins would be designated as Agent No. 99. Morley mentioned that he could not give Watkins a code book because he and Held had only one copy between them, but ONI could communicate securely with Watkins through letters delivered to either Captain Jones of the Ward liner *Esperanza* or to Captain Smith of the Ward liner *Monterey*, which vessels sailed monthly from New York to Progreso. Either of the captains could be handed a sealed package for Watkins with the "A" and "B" code books inside, with instructions to deliver it to Watkins personally— they both knew him well—or to bring it back if they couldn't make personal contact. Held had instructed Watkins in the use of both codes, and Morley had given him a keyword, so ONI should have no difficulty working with him through this channel. Morley would provide additional information orally once he reached Washington. It says something about Morley's stature as an agent that he was able not just to recruit Watkins but to instruct him in the use of ONI codes.

On another subject Morley reported that the governor of Yucatán had just issued a warning directed at the German newspaper in Progreso, *El Boletín de la Guerra*, threatening drastic action against it if the newspaper continued attacking Consul Marsh. Although the warning mentioned no names, the public understood that it referred to *El Boletín* and Consul Marsh. Morley believed the move was an attempt to offset the deportation order for pro-Allied Syrian propagandists, and it showed that the local government was certainly more friendly than the Mexican government.

The archaeologist ended by saying that he was just recovering from another severe attack of malaria. He still intended to reconnoiter the coast as far west as Frontera, Tabasco. Therefore he requested that ONI transfer by the first week in May $500 in care of Consul Bowman in Frontera. Morley also asked that the captains of those American steamers that regularly called at Frontera be instructed to receive him and Held as passengers. Otherwise, they would not be allowed to embark from Frontera for New Orleans because of the quarantine regulations, and this would greatly delay their return to Washington. A tired Morley wrote:

Truth is, Taro, we are fed up with traveling all the time and we both
need a rest. As you know, this kind of work is a constant strain even
if one accomplishes nothing at it. It is a 24-hour working day and
no shift, and we both need and want a relief from responsibility for
a bit.

12. The Journey Home

As soon as Morley had recovered from his latest attack of malaria, he and Held left Mérida.[1] They sailed from Progreso on April 28, 1918, touching at Campeche, and the next day landed at Ciudad del Carmen, at one of the two entrances to the Laguna de Términos. (See Appendix 3) The archaeologist reported that although on the map that body of water might appear favorable for a German submarine base, in reality it was not, for three reasons. First, at each of its two bars there was less than fourteen feet of water; inside the lagoon the average depth was only six feet, with nine-foot channels. The shores were flat, low, and marshy, and in the rainy season the shoreline was completely submerged. Second, there was a sufficient number of "wide awake" Americans in the vicinity, and especially at the deeper entrance to the Laguna at Ciudad del Carmen, to keep the American government advised of any hostile activity. Six or seven American corporations engaged in the mahogany and chicle business owned extensive properties in the region and had their headquarters at Ciudad del Carmen. "The resident managers are all loyal Americans with little to do but routine work, and plenty of time to think about the war." Their motorboats were constantly crossing the Laguna and traveling up the rivers that emptied into it. These men were always on the lookout for any suspicious activity, and should any occur Morley was confident that he would be notified immediately. Third, there were hardly any Germans in the region: two at Ciudad del Carmen, one up the Usumacinta River at Balancán, another at Palenque, and three at Frontera. Morley doubted whether there were more than twenty-five Germans in the entire state of Tabasco.

In closing this matter, therefore, I repeat what I said at the beginning, that I think there is little danger to be apprehended from the Laguna de Terminos unless, indeed, local conditions change greatly and Mexico should declare war against us. In the latter event, I have already reported in my No. 21, it is probable that the States of Quintana Roo, Yucatan and Campeche, with a little encouragement from us, would separate themselves from the rest of the republic and set up an independent government. If such a time ever comes, it is to our interest, and should be seen to, that the "line of split" comes as far west as the Usumacinta River, so that all of Campeche and the Laguna de Terminos district would be included in the new and friendly state.

As for the political situation in Tabasco, it was being monitored by a man named Dunn, whom Morley did not meet. The archaeologist did not know whether Dunn was working for ONI or some other intelligence organization: in all probability Morley was referring to W. E. Dunn, ONI Agent No. 168.

Politics in Tabasco were complex. The current military governor, a native of the state named Luis Felipe Domínguez, was maneuvering to be elected constitutional governor, which civil office was at present being occupied by one of his henchmen. Domínguez was an elderly hacendado who was quite popular. General Salvador Alvarado, commander of the southern military zone encompassing Quintana Roo, Yucatán, Campeche, Tabasco, and Chiapas, was supporting a rival candidate. According to American Consul Bowman at Frontera, Domínguez claimed that he had the support of President Carranza. Morley felt that Carranza was trying to curb Alvarado's power. And further, Morley understood that Carranza opposed Alvarado's return to Yucatán on grounds that he wanted the states to return to civilian government as quickly as possible.

At the moment, though, Alvarado was not having everything his own way in Tabasco, as he had in Yucatán. He had his hands full battling the rebel *Felicistas*, the followers of the conservative General Félix Díaz. On April 30, Alvarado had captured the town of Ocosingo, in the highlands of Chiapas, a town that had been a *Felicista* stronghold for the last two years. The defeated rebels fled northward over the mountains to Palenque, entering that village on May 4. But a detachment of Alvarado's

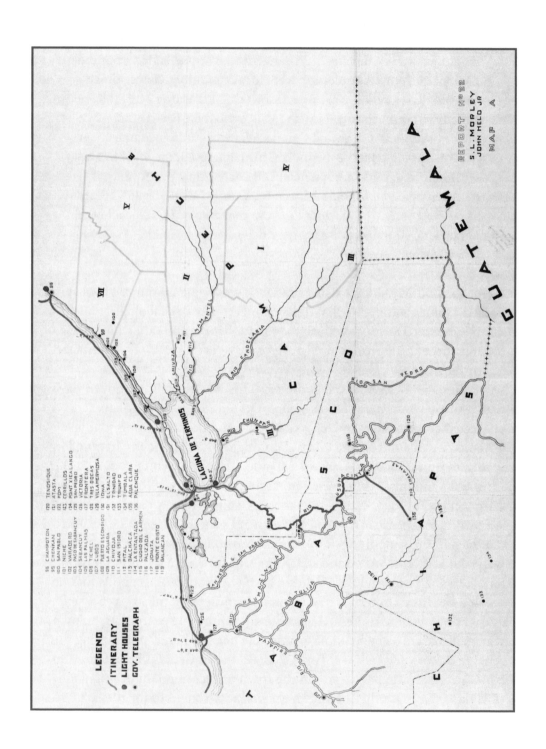

federal troops was in hot pursuit, and the rebels retreated to Agua Clara, a day and a half's journey to the south.

Morley and Held, meanwhile, had been reconnoitering up the Usumacinta River as far as Monte Cristo. They were quite anxious to visit the magnificent Mayan ruins at Palenque some thirty-five miles west of Monte Cristo, but had almost abandoned the idea because of the dangerous conditions. But the lieutenant colonel commanding the federal detachment sent word that the area had been cleared of rebels and that the Americans could travel to Palenque in perfect safety. They did. When Morley and Held reached the town of Palenque, they found that the contending forces had stolen everything that was not nailed down:

> I was told that each one of them had led off a string of 3 or 4 horses and mules. And as for food, clothing and the like, there was none left in the village when we got there. What the rebeldes had left the Federales had finished. The women took to the woods and the place was gutted after the most approved Latin-American fashion. But this is only a minor matter. Truth is, the whole State of Chiapas is in an unsettled condition. Rebel bands roam at will, and only where the Federales are concentrated can they make any headway against them. Guerilla warfare goes on everywhere unchecked, and the Federales are little more than able to hold their own.

Leaving Palenque on May 13, the two ONI agents returned to the coast and made their way to Frontera, where Consul Bowman brought them up to date on the situation in Tabasco. Compared with Chiapas, the state was relatively peaceful. And public sentiment had shifted toward the Allies in the last few months. For one thing, the Germans had overadvertised their huge March offensive in France. When, for example, they failed to capture Paris as promised, the public in Tabasco had become more skeptical about Germany's chances of victory. More importantly, though, was the effect of the Black List on the Tabascans:

Map 6. This map covers the travels of the two intrepid ONI agents, Morley and Held, from the coastal town of Champoton, Campeche, along the coast of Tabasco, and into the interior of Chiapas from the end of March 1918 through May 1918. The map delineates the location of lighthouses, telegraph facilities, and rivers and towns in the three Mexican states. The cartograper was, of course, John Held Jr. Courtesy Office of Naval Intelligence, National Archives.

a rigorous enforcement of the Black List is bringing even the pro-Germans of them to a whining submission—doubtless as insincere as it is unwilling—but effective nevertheless, in that they dare not help, or sell to German houses for fear of going on the Black List themselves. It is self-preservation with them of course, and not any real sympathy with and for the allied cause, but it works out the same way so far as German isolation down there is concerned.

Morley commented that one Robert Boyd of Ciudad del Carmen, who had lived in Tabasco for more than fifty years and had previously been American consular agent at Ciudad del Carmen, had given him additional insights into Mexican politics. A "close and intelligent observer of native affairs," Boyd believed that before the summer ended there would be a major upheaval in Mexico.

> He says the Carranza Government has no real strength, and that the increasing irritation against us caused by German propaganda plus the grave situation in France may cause the Mexican pot to boil over. This, of course, is only one man's opinion, but one who has been in close contact with the Mexicans for more than fifty years and knows the national character intimately from its love of power to its hatred of the foreigner, particularly the American, perhaps the two ruling Mexican passions.

Events would prove Boyd an indifferent prognosticator. Mexico did not explode against the United States and there was no major upheaval before the end of summer. The upheaval would come in the spring of 1920, when a rebellion overthrew Carranza, who was assassinated while fleeing.

Morley took up another matter, the alleged existence of a secret German wireless station at Triunfo, Chiapas. Morley and Held had first heard of the alleged station at Triunfo in April, while they were still in Mérida. Agent Watkins told them the story, which he had heard at Ciudad del Carmen in February: a German on the plantations of the German-American Coffee Company in northern Chiapas was operating a clandestine wireless station. When Morley and Held arrived in Ciudad del Carmen in late April, they too heard the same vague story but could learn no corroborating details. The desire to investigate the matter was one of the reasons they had made the trip to Palenque. On the way they stayed with an American, Henry Snead, who owned a ranch near Palenque. When Morley asked him about the station, Snead replied that he had heard the story, but could supply no additional details. As it happened, Snead was selling off his cattle, preparing to return to the United States and enlist. He was on the verge of taking a month-long trip through the highlands of Chiapas to San Cristóbal and Tuxtla Gutiérrez, the state capital. Morley seized the opportunity to acquire firsthand information about that relatively obscure region, so he recruited Snead on the spot. Morley guaranteed any unusual expenses that Snead might incur and instructed him to write a comprehensive report on the region, to include population and activities as well as local sentiment. Snead was eager to "do his bit" for the war effort, and Morley informed him that this was his chance. Snead was to mail his report on board an American ship at Frontera. The report would be addressed to Morley at the Carnegie Institution, in order to avoid suspicion.

And on the subject of Chiapas, Morley had just learned from one H. N. Cook, sales manager for the Aguila Oil Company for all of Central America, who had returned from Guatemala the previous week, that Alfred Clark, Jr., son of the general manager of the Ferrocarril Internacional de Centroamérica, had been enlisted as a subagent by ONI's man in Guatemala City, J. H. Watts, Agent No. 84. Morley was pleased. He reminded his case officer that he himself had recommended Clark as a potential ONI recruit in a report from Guatemala City nearly a year earlier. In Morley's view, Clark was exceptionally well fitted for secret work:

> He is able, has good judgment, knows the country and people thoroughly, speaks Spanish fluently, and moreover makes frequent business trips over into Chiapas selling oil for the Aguila Oil Co. which he represents in Guatemala. He goes more or less regularly to Tapachula, claimed by some to be the strongest German center in the state, and will cover the southern part of Chiapas for us. This with Snead's report on northern and central Chiapas should give us a pretty good idea of one of the least known and most inaccessible parts of Mexico.

Returning to the subject of the alleged German radio station, Morley made a point of asking Snead to make a special effort to learn what he could about it during his forthcoming trip. As luck would have it, however, Morley and Held got that information themselves through a chance encounter. In Frontera, they happened to meet C. T. Bleuel of 97–99 Water Street, New York City. It so happened that Bleuel was the manager of the German-American Coffee Company, 56 Pine Street, New York City, on whose property the clandestine wireless was supposedly hidden, and he was on his way back from Triunfo to the United States. Bleuel told them that the previous resident manager at the plantation in Triunfo was a German named Wilhelm Farholz, who was such a swine that even his own countrymen disliked him. According to Bleuel, Farholz cheated the company for years, lived like a feudal baron at company expense, let the plantation deteriorate to a shocking degree, and was even alleged to have tortured the Indian workers. Everyone seems to have hated Farholz. Bleuel's Company had run afoul of the American authorities, who stopped the firm's drafts; soon its shipments of coffee also ceased. Morley speculated that it was "for having continued to employ such a notorious Hun as Farholz after the President's decree."

At all events, Bleuel had been dispatched from New York to Triunfo in March with instructions to fire Farholz and do whatever else he thought necessary to rehabilitate the Company. Bleuel took with him an American named K. X. Downing, whom he was to break in as the new manager. Bleuel told Morley that he first heard at Frontera about the wireless on the Company's property, and he investigated the rumor thoroughly. He stated that the most powerful generator on the plantation only developed twenty-five horsepower. In short, he was certain the whole story was a myth. Bleuel did fire Farholz and replace him with Downing, "who is a loyal American, so even if there was such a plant, it can hardly be worked under his nose so to speak." As for Farholz, he left Triunfo and went to Frontera. Morley speculated that perhaps the wireless story had arisen because of the Company's German name, the unsavory reputation of its German manager Farholz, and the isolated location of the plantation. The archaeologist stated: "In conclusion I believe it is not going too far to say that this wireless station may probably be relegated to the same ephemeral realm as the Champoton one, in a word that it never existed."

Morley next discussed Consul Marsh, for whom he had developed great admiration:

I am enclosing two extras published at Progreso excoriating Consul Marsh. He is the liveliest anti-German wire we have met yet. He hounds the Huns and draft-dodgers out of positions as quickly as they get them by means of the Black List and is a veritable scourge to these gentry. I think he probably exceeds the strict limits of his authority at times, but if so, it is always in the right direction, and he should be supported just as far as possible if they try to oust him from his position, a movement to effect which is probably on foot. He earnestly and honestly believes he has a special and divine mission to castigate the Hun, and believe me Taro, he loses no opportunity however small, of so doing. It is no wonder that they hate him so, and will try to secure his removal. He should be kept at Progreso by all means however. We need a good man there.

The archaeologist also enclosed a "report on the Economic, Financial and Monetary Situation in the Republic of Guatemala," prepared by the aforementioned H. N. Cook, whom Morley described as a close observer of the financial situation in that country.[2] Morley indicated that he would have more to say about Cook when he reported to ONI in Washington.

There was one topic on which Morley had strong views—propaganda. He urged the immediate launching of a vigorous pro-Allied propaganda campaign in Mexico, to offset the strenuous efforts the Germans were making in this field. Morley was concerned not so much for the Yucatán peninsula as for the rest of the country. He described German propaganda as being pervasive in Mexico. To support this contention, he enclosed a copy of an "extra" that the pro-Allied Mexico City newspaper *El Universal* had published some time ago, composed exclusively of headlines from the strongly pro-German daily *El Demócrata*. Morley pointed out that the headlines were not just lies, but were cleverly calculated to inflame the already hostile Mexican attitude toward the United States.[3]

While in Tabasco, he and Held had repeatedly been mistaken for Germans. When Morley finally asked why, he was told by a Spaniard in Monte Cristo that no less than three German propagandists had passed through that isolated little village in the previous month, distributing German war literature, inciting the villagers against the United States, urging that Mexico break diplomatic relations with her northern neighbor, and proclaiming that Germany was winning the war.

Morley declared that it was not the function of ONI agents to counter German propaganda. Such an undertaking should be the job of a commission or special press bureau, and he felt the situation was sufficiently acute to warrant the establishment of such an agency. German propaganda was of necessity based on lies, while American rebuttals need only state the truth, such as, for example, the huge sums being voluntarily subscribed for Liberty Loans, the numbers of men pouring into the armed forces, the increasing numbers of ships being launched, and the vast resources of the United States compared with Germany's bankruptcy and her dwindling manpower. The Mexicans were no fools, and if they were presented with the truth they would see that Germany could not win the war in the face of the United States's financial, industrial, and manpower superiority.

> The British, I understand are spending $5000.00 a month on propaganda work in Mexico. Our drive should be larger. Mexico is not only nearer our borders, and we are thus perforce more vitally interested in her, but also she is actually the most pro-German anti-American nation on this side of the Atlantic, the gravest menace to the status quo in the New World. Propaganda may not save the situation, but as yet is a sadly neglected field by us, though not by the Huns. But more of this also in Washington next week.

After their travels in Tabasco and Chiapas, Morley and Held eagerly returned to Frontera to start their long-awaited journey home. They were heartened to find a $500 draft from ONI awaiting them at the American consulate. Unfortunately they just missed the boat, and since there was a steamer leaving for Veracruz the next day, they took it.

The weary agents were on their way home, but the hunt for German submarine bases went on, and not just by the navy. MID (Military Intelligence Division) had one of its best agents investigating both coasts of Mexico for secret U-boat refueling facilities. He was, improbably, an Austrian chiropodist, Paul Bernardo Altendorf. The Austrian had performed brilliantly as a double agent, frustrating German plots and exposing German agents in Mexico. In June 1918, he was operating on the Gulf coast of Mexico checking out rumors of clandestine supply bases. The rumors proved to be unfounded.[4]

Morley and Held sailed from Veracruz on April 21, aboard the small Volvin Line steamship *Harald*, and it took them a week to reach New

Orleans. Being back in the United States took some getting used to, as Morley explained to his case officer:

> Home again at last and devilish glad to get back; we were begin-
> ning to feel like a couple of expatriates after our 13 months'
> absence. And how changed everything is—uniforms everywhere,
> flags, war-posters, Liberty Loan drives, Red Cross dittos, etc. etc.
>
> Our first taste of it was at [the] mouth of the Mississippi where
> a particularly efficient-looking submarine chaser circled round us
> suspiciously. Coming up the river we saw our first camouflaged ves-
> sels, bizarre looking cubist affairs, which had an amazing trick of
> breaking down into nothingness, actually disappearing against the
> dock backgrounds. So it has been all along. We feel we are in a dif-
> ferent country. When we left, everything was confusion, disorgan-
> ization, duplication of effort. Today it seems to us that we are
> effectively organized on a war basis. But all this is aside the point,
> intensely interesting to us but an old story to you.

A tired but elated Morley was finally home. In April, he had written to the Carnegie Institution from Mérida asking that his and Held's mail be sent to the St. Charles Hotel in New Orleans pending their arrival. They planned to continue on to Washington, and Morley had requested that Carnegie make reservations for them at the Cosmos Club; if that were not possible, then at the University Club, of which he was also a member. Realizing that accommodations were scarce in wartime Washington, Morley facetiously said he was prepared to camp out on Carnegie's lawn if necessary.[5]

The most significant result of returning home was that Morley's asso-ciation with John Held ended. Despite their occasional differences, they had constituted a formidable team and had gathered an impressive mass of geographical, political, and economic intelligence during their four-teen months together. Through these often-difficult months, Held had been Morley's faithful sidekick. But now it was time to part. Held had experienced enough adventures and had gained enough artistic inspira-tion to last him for a good long while. He returned to New York to resume his career.

As for Morley, he badly needed rest. On June 8, 1918, he asked to be relieved from active duty for two months. Morley justified the request by explaining that for the past fourteen months he had been on duty in the tropics working under ONI and needed to recuperate "from the effects of malaria and kindred ailments contracted while on duty." The request was granted. The Director of Naval Intelligence gave him leave until August 10, 1918, on which date he was again to report to the director for duty.

When Lt. Commander O. W. Fowler of ONI sent Morley these orders, he expressed the hope that the archaeologist would rest and recuperate during the summer "so that this Office may continue to avail itself of your valuable services."[6] Morley's recuperation during the summer included visiting friends in New York City and his mother in Cambridge. In addition, he made a month-long trip in July by rail to visit relatives and friends. He went from Boston to New York; Cleveland; Hanley Falls, Minnesota; Kansas City; Wagon Mound and Santa Fe, New Mexico, returning to Boston via Philadelphia. The noteworthy aspect of this journey was that Morley traveled in uniform. Besides whatever gratification wearing a uniform may have provided a secret agent, it made Morley eligible for a reduced railroad fare.[7] One of the first things he'd done upon arriving in Washington, on June 3, had been to purchase a full set of uniforms, both blues and dress whites, and he had been wearing them at every opportunity ever since. But even while enjoying his furlough, Morley was an ONI talent scout, notifying his superior that "I am keeping on the lookout for good men for our service, and if I run across any will advise you."[8]

In August a reinvigorated Morley was back in Washington, ready for his next ONI assignment.

13. The Second Tour

Morley was so highly regarded as an agent that he could practically write his own ticket. Reflecting the organizational changes that had occurred in the spring of 1918, it was the 15th Naval District that would run Morley, and that organization was anxious to keep him happy—and for that matter Held, if he chose to return. On June 25, 1918, while Morley was still on furlough, Commander Sargent's aide wrote to ONI in Washington:

> I am delighted to hear that Mr. Morley, and possibly Mr. Held, will be back here in August. Prior to their setting sail for this port [Balboa, Canal Zone], I should appreciate it if you would advise me as to the nature of any conversation you may have had with them relative to their desires concerning their posts. They have both done excellent work for the service and it is not my intention to send them to any particular place where they would dislike going, provided I can do something better for them. A foreword, therefore, in regard to them will help me.[1]

On August 10, 1918, the day Morley reported back in Washington for duty, ONI cabled the 15th Naval District: "Morley here ready to return. Held will not go back. How will you use Morley? Unless you have important reasons for him can use him elsewhere."[2] Fifteenth Naval District did have "important reasons" to use Morley, for ONI later cabled Commander Sargent that "Morley may correspond Gitaro Ando. Matter of cabling must be decided by you. This Office does not know how you will use him. It may possibly assist with United Fruit."[3] The name "Gitaro Ando," P.O.

Box 91, Philadelphia, was now the accommodation address for ONI agents operating outside the United States.[4] On August 24, the Office of Naval Intelligence notified the 15th Naval District that Morley would be leaving Washington shortly. ONI also offered to send another agent to Commander Sargent—an "able scientific man who collects marine invertebrates and paleontological material experienced in Latin American Countries. Answer quick if you want him." Commander Sargent answered quickly, saying he couldn't use the scientist.[5]

Morley was going back to Central America basking in the approval of both ONI and the 15th Naval District. All this approval was nice, but Morley wanted it translated into something tangible, so on the day of his departure from Washington, August 31, the archaeologist formally requested promotion from ensign to lieutenant (junior grade).[6] The request was strongly endorsed by the Director of Naval Intelligence, who "urgently recommended" the promotion. The director recapitulated Morley's services:

> He was assigned to duty with the Office of Naval Intelligence, Area No. 2, now Section A-7, on April 7, 1917, and served continuously therewith in foreign countries until June 10, 1918, when he was granted sixty days' leave of absence to recuperate from illness contracted while on duty.
>
> He left Washington on April 22, 1917, and returned on June 3, 1918, having traveled for thirteen months in Guatemala, Honduras, Salvador, Nicaragua, British Honduras and the southern part of Mexico (in States of Quintana Roo, Yucatan, Campeche, Tabasco and Chiapas).
>
> During this period he made two intensive coast reconnaissances along the Atlantic Littoral of southern Mexico and northern Central America: (1) from Bluefields, Nicaragua, to Trujillo, Honduras, the Mosquito Coast; and (2) the entire coast line of the Peninsula of Yucatan, an aggregate of about two thousand miles. In addition to the foregoing coast reconnaissance work, he traveled extensively in the interior of Guatemala, Honduras, Salvador and Southern Mexico, covering not only the activities of alien enemies, but also the local, political and economic situation as well.
>
> This young man has an excellent record and surely deserves the promotion recommended.

In view of the fact that he is leaving Washington this week, it is requested if the promotion is granted, that notification of the action taken be sent to him care of the Commanding Officer, Fifteenth Naval District, Balboa Heights, Canal Zone.[7]

Anticipating that the request for promotion would have a happy outcome, Morley had taken the oath and filled out the paperwork for the rank of lieutenant (j.g.) on August 18. And indeed, in due course the promotion came through; Morley's date of rank would be December 10, 1918.[8]

By September 3, Morley was aboard the steamer *Metapan* bound, via Havana, for Colón in the Canal Zone. During the eight-day voyage he worked on the manuscript of his forthcoming book, *The Inscriptions of Copán, Honduras*.[9] He arrived at Cristóbal, the Atlantic terminus of the Panama Canal, on September 14 and traveled across the isthmus to Ancón, checking into the Hotel Tivoli, which was operated by the American government. While enjoying the splendid hilltop view from the Tivoli, Morley remarked on the stupendous accomplishment represented by the Canal and its ancillary facilities:

all have made me realize as no amount of reading ever could have done, what a really man sized job we have done down here, and further, what a brilliant future could be anticipated for the other Central American Republics and Mexico, if they were only under our aegis.[10]

Morley expected to be stationed in San José, Costa Rica, at least through October and possibly through December.[11] As of October 18, however, he was still in Ancón; on that date, he learned that instead of going to San José he was being sent to Tegucigalpa, Honduras. He planned to leave Panama on October 19, on the Pacific Mail steamer *San Juan* for Amapala, Honduras. Morley anticipated reaching Tegucigalpa by November 5.[12] In the event, Morley arrived in Tegucigalpa on October 30 and presented his ONI credentials to the American minister, who extended all the courtesies of the legation.[13] This was a far cry from the problems the archaeologist had experienced with American diplomats at the beginning of his intelligence career.

While conditions in the field had thus improved for Morley, one problem continued. Although World War I was nearly over, both ONI's and Morley's security measures still left quite a bit to be desired—and his cover was again blown. On October 18, the Carnegie Institution received the following letter on Navy Department stationery:

> Ens[ign] Sylvanus G. Morley has requested the Navy Department to advise the Carnegie Institute [sic] that mail forwarded to him by the Carnegie Institute [sic] should be sent to him in care of American Legation, Tegucigalpa, Honduras.
>
> Very truly yours,
> ROGER WELLES REAR ADMIRAL U.S.N.
> Director Naval Intelligence
> C. Sheldon
> By direction[14]

The Carnegie Institution duly thanked ONI for providing it with Morley's most recent address.[15] Furthermore, when Morley's mother, concerned at not hearing from her son, inquired of the Carnegie Institution as to his whereabouts, Carnegie sent her a letter quoting the above communication from Admiral Welles.[16]

By then of course it hardly mattered, for the war would be over in another two weeks. As soon as it was, Commander Sargent began dismantling his intelligence apparatus. On November 18, 1918, he recommended to ONI that all volunteer unpaid agents in Area No. 2 be retained but expenditures for their expenses be sharply curtailed; that cooperation with United Fruit be maintained; that all paid agents in Sections 1, 2, and 4 be eliminated; that Section 3 be placed under a marine officer from the detachment stationed at Managua; a Major Harrison received this assignment, being designated Agent S-50, his code name "Harbo." Sargent recommended that emphasis be placed on Section 5 (Guatemala), retaining W. H. Watts (Agent No. 84) and providing him with a $200 sinking fund, but instructing him to use unpaid volunteer assistants as much as possible. Commander Sargent further suggested that Herbert Spinden (Agent No. 56) be retained in his present assignment to cover Colombia, providing ONI thought it necessary; otherwise, Spinden could be discharged. Morley (Agent No. 53) would complete his current special assignment and then return to the Canal Zone for further orders.[17]

Morley's special assignment was to gather political intelligence, now that German activity was irrelevant. In particular, he was closely monitoring the situation in El Salvador. ONI was still concerned about El Salvador because of her anti-American administration and her ties to Mexico, whose nationalist president, Venustiano Carranza, was no friend of the United States. El Salvador was approaching a presidential election that, in true Central American fashion, promised to produce bloodshed and a political crisis. Morley's reports provide a fascinating glimpse into the Byzantine world of Salvadoran politics.[18]

It should be noted that the political machinations in El Salvador mirrored those in the other countries of Central America. The British minister to Guatemala, an experienced diplomat, frankly admitted to the Foreign Secretary his inability to follow the cabals among Central American politicians. In his opinion, a desire to intrigue against each other and the United States seemed the only reasonable explanation for the incessant missions and visits that, among other things, kept American secret agents busy trying to sort out which ones constituted "Mexican-German intrigue."[19] There was a lot to sort out. American agents had been especially concerned about political and economic ties between Mexico and El Salvador, things such as the Salvadoran president's fulsome praise of Venustiano Carranza, and Mexico's gift of aircraft and a radio installation to the Salvadoran regime. By February 1918 El Salvador was in regular radio contact with Mexico.[20]

In preparing his reports Morley relied heavily on three informants.[21] One was Edwin E. Huber, whom Morley had interviewed in 1917 as a potential ONI agent, finally deciding against recruiting him. The 15th Naval District had found Huber more attractive; Commander Sargent had enlisted Huber and had assigned him to cover San Salvador, replacing Ensign Pullen of painful memory.[22] Morley reported that Huber, who had been living in San Salvador for the past year, "appears to have an intelligent grasp of the situation." Morley's second informant was Dr. José C. Gasteazoro, who was thoroughly familiar with Central American politics in general and with Salvadoran affairs in particular. Gasteazoro was a close friend of the leading presidential contender's brother, and was pro-American to boot. Morley referred his case officer to Boaz Long, the American minister to El Salvador and to Dr. Charles Bailey of the Rockefeller Foundation on this point. Bailey was Morley's third source. Bailey got his information from one of his employees, John Wright. Wright was a young man in his mid-twenties, educated in the United States, pro-American, son of an American father and a Salvadoran mother, and the nephew of the Salvadoran president. Morley stated that Wright was "to be trusted as a reliable source."

What Morley reported on was something resembling a soap opera with a political plot. There were two candidates vying to succeed incumbent President Carlos Meléndez. One was Dr. Tomás Palomo, who was not only minister of the interior but private physician to and close friend of the president. The rival candidate was Dr. Alfonso Quiñones, who was not only the vice-president but the brother-in-law of the president. From all accounts there was no doubt that in a free election—that is, one without military coercion—Quiñones would win, for he had the enthusiastic support of the masses. Dr. Palomo, on the other hand, was supported by the great majority of landowners, by the leading families of El Salvador, and, toward the end of the campaign, by the departmental governors. Moreover, the cabinet supported Palomo three to one, the minister of foreign relations being the only *Quiñonista*.

To muddy the political waters even further, the division existed in President Meléndez's immediate family. The president's young and beautiful wife, Doña Sara Meléndez, strongly supported Palomo, and the president's brother, Guillermo, was also a *Palomista*. Bitterly opposing them were the rest of the president's family. His mother, the seventy-five-year-old matriarch Doña Mercedes Meléndez was a fervent *Quiñonista*, as was the president's youngest brother, Jorge, who managed his brother-in-law Quiñones's campaign. Morley clearly understood the real nature of the political conflict. It was a family fight:

> In the President's immediate family it became a woman's fight, a young, vivacious, lively, society-loving, frivolous wife arrayed against a deeply religious, austere, pious, unpretentious, but powerful mother. These two influences pulling the President first one way and then the other led I believe to much of his apparent indecision in the past six months and finally to his non-interference in the municipal elections on December 8 which so far as he personally was concerned were held without presidential interference.
>
> This enmity between these two ladies has been of long standing, and had reached the point where Don Carlos's mother no longer came to her son's house. It arose through the opposition of the old lady to the marriage of her son Jorge with Ester Meza the sister of the President's wife. She is said to have put her foot down

firmly saying that one Meza in the family was enough, Sara being already married to Don Carlos. Jorge like a dutiful son in these parts gave up the young lady upon his mother's opposition and thereby brought down the ire of Dona Sara. It is said too that old Dona Mercedes objected to Don Carlos's marriage but was unable to prevent it. At all events Don Carlos's wife has been arrayed against her husband's family all along and she has been working for Doctor Palomo, the rest of the family working for Leonor's husband Alfonso Quinones. Other leading Palomistas were Florentino Sosa, the Director of the Post Office and the President's closest friend; General Rodolfo Cristales, the Governor of Santa Ana; General Tomas Calderon, the Governor of San Miguel and General Anibal Santos the Governor of Sonsonate, the second, third and fourth largest cities respectively in the republic, Sosa being the leader of the Palomistas.

Since each of the two candidates had powerful support both within the president's family and in the country at large, for a considerable period of time no one was quite sure what the president would do. Although in his speech at the opening of the National Assembly on February 18, 1918, President Meléndez had declared that he didn't propose to have himself reelected and had given assurances that the forthcoming election would be impartial and free, few took him at his word.[23] Would he support one or the other candidate, or might he try to get himself reelected? By July it was evident that he was planning his own reelection. Two plans to accomplish this were proposed: one involved amending the constitution to permit the immediate reelection of the president; the other, even more imaginative, proposed nothing less than the union of El Salvador and Honduras into one country of which Carlos Meléndez would be the first president.

The American chargé d'affairs in El Salvador took the proposal for union with him to Washington in July. It met with an unenthusiastic reception. Back in El Salvador, a new political party, the *Constitucional Reformista*, was launched to give the proposed amendment to the constitution some semblance of popular enthusiasm. Morley mentioned that these maneuvers had already been reported by "our man Huber" and by the American legation in San Salvador, as well as by Morley himself in his Reports 23 and 24, which unfortunately are not available.

Thus, by the fall of 1918 there were three presidential contenders—Quiñones and Palomo openly and President Meléndez sub rosa. The president's supporters, of course, metamorphosed as *Reformistas*. Moreover, several newspapers were founded to promote the president's reelection; the best editorial talent in El Salvador was mobilized to stress the inadequacy of the existing constitution and the imperative necessity of amending it to secure the future prosperity of the nation. And in early October, twenty-five thousand campaign buttons ordered from the United States arrived, bearing the legend "Constitutional Reformist Party, Citizen Don Carlos Meléndez Candidate for the Presidency."

Morley had informed ONI, in his Report no. 25, which is also missing, how the mayor of Santa María de Santiago sent an open letter to every municipality in the country urging them to pass resolutions demanding the convening of a constitutional convention. These ploys flopped. There was virtually no public response to the reelection maneuvers, and the two announced candidates were quietly trying to scuttle the whole campaign. They were each spending considerable amounts of money, and neither intended to be defeated by some academic exercise in constitution writing. But, curiously, Morley had been told that both of the announced candidates had assured the president that if he would publicly announce his desire for another term, both were willing to withdraw from the race.

At some point, it occurred to somebody that the existing constitution explicitly stated that any amendments to it would not take effect until a year and a half later, so it was unclear how amending the constitution would legally allow the president to reelect himself in December.[24] By the end of October the Reformist Party was allowed to die a natural death, and the president and his followers shifted their efforts to implementing Plan B—the union of El Salvador and Honduras. Morley heard from Agent Huber that the chief of staff of the Salvadoran army had confided in Huber that the real object of the proposed union between El Salvador and Honduras was to contain Guatemala between Mexico and the new country in order to depose Estrada Cabrera and establish a liberal regime in Guatemala. A British diplomat speculated that in proposing the union the presidents of El Salvador and Honduras were just twitting the paranoid dictator of Guatemala, who considered any such alliance as a threat to himself.[25]

In his earlier reports Morley had outlined the activities on behalf of the union, activities that grew more frantic in November as the

Salvadoran presidential election neared. Morley was in Tegucigalpa as of October 30, but Huber kept him posted on the maneuvering in El Salvador in favor of the proposed treaty of union. It began to appear as though the treaty might go through after all. The government mouthpiece newspaper *La Prensa*, which was also subsidized by Mexico, published a whole series of articles extolling the economic benefits of union. In addition, the government assisted in the convening of a union congress early in November. Nevertheless, the Salvadoran public continued to view the proposed union as merely the centerpiece of President Meléndez's reelection strategy.

Meléndez had already begun replacing departmental governors with men personally loyal to himself, a move generally interpreted as indicating his determination to reelect himself. But the disintegration of the Reformist Party due to lack of popular response, coupled with the now dimming prospects of union, due to Honduran President Bertrand's adamant stance that he, not Meléndez, should be the chief executive of any united country, created a climate of uncertainty in El Salvador. By the time Morley returned to San Salvador on December 5, it seemed that everything was up for grabs.

President Carlos Meléndez was reported to be gravely ill, although in fact he had had a slight stroke. Members of the president's family talked darkly of poisoning and insisted that two other physicians be called in to treat the president besides his personal physician Dr. Palomo, who was, after all, a candidate to succeed Meléndez. The president's formidable mother entered his home for the first time in years and announced that she was now in charge. The only people allowed to visit the president were members of his immediate family. John Wright, the president's nephew, told Morley's friend, Dr. Bailey, who in turn told Morley, that either Wright, his uncle Jorge Meléndez, his aunt Leonor Meléndez Quiñones or the matriarch Doña Mercedes Meléndez were constantly by the president's bedside, and Wright himself gave the chief executive all his medications.

Although the president was incapacitated, he was still active politically. Some days prior to the municipal elections, Meléndez had telegraphed a list of names to the fourteen departmental governors asking them to assist those candidates insofar as they could within the law. Since the governors were mostly *Palomistas* and especially since the governors of the three largest departments—Santa Ana, San Miguel, and

Sonsonate—were fervent *Palomistas*, the president's action was generally interpreted as evidence that his wife, Doña Sara Meléndez, had won the familial power struggle and that Dr. Palomo would be elected. This view prevailed down to the municipal elections.

The day before the municipal elections, however, the president sent another telegram to the governors ordering them to ensure that an absolutely fair election was held. Eleven of the fourteen replied affirmatively. This telegram was generally interpreted as canceling the previous one, and as evidence that the president's mother and brothers had won the familial power struggle, and that Quiñones now had the president's support. After all, as one observer reported rather cynically, the elections were supposed to be free, but the president possessed the only vote that really counted.[26]

Nevertheless, the *Palomistas* remained confident of victory, enjoying the support of most governors and relying on the military to control the elections. Morley was reliably informed that just before the elections Quiñones made several propositions to Palomo: that they both withdraw in favor of President Meléndez; that they both agree on some third candidate; that Palomo become president and Quiñones vice-president and select the cabinet. Palomo rejected these overtures, stating that the most he was prepared to do was pay half of Quiñones's campaign expenses to date. Quiñones, in turn, rejected this offer.

In San Salvador the threat of armed conflict was very real. The municipal police, who took their orders from the mayor, were *Palomista*, and the *cabildo*, or city hall, itself was occupied by *Palomistas*. The federal police, on the other hand, were *Quiñonista*. The national guard were ostensibly neutral but were actually *Quiñonista*, at least in the capital.

The night before the municipal elections, December 7, the police occupied city hall, where the voter lists were kept and where voting would take place the next morning. Throughout the night armed *Palomista* supporters were smuggled in through a hole in the back wall—all this without the knowledge of the *Quiñonistas*.

On election morning, December 8, the president's brother, Jorge Meléndez, proposed that the *Palomistas* and *Quiñonistas* each appoint ten of their number to constitute a joint board that would deal with electoral challenges. His proposal was accepted. The main doors of the city hall were opened wide enough to admit the *Quiñonista* delegates. But after only five had entered—among them, Jorge Meléndez himself—the doors were suddenly slammed shut. Inside, the outraged *Quiñonistas* protested this act of what they considered treachery. In the heated argument that ensued, Jorge Meléndez's bodyguard ordered a prominent *Palomista* not to get so close to his master, whereupon the *Palomista* whipped out a pistol and blew the bodyguard's brains out.

The furious *Quiñonistas* milling around outside, most of them unarmed, heard the shot and naturally assumed that their colleagues were being massacred. They charged, breaking down the doors and pouring into city hall. At this juncture the municipal police inside the building opened fire on the crowd. The federal police, who were stationed outside to keep order, returned the fire. Eventually the national guard restored order, but by then three or four more persons had been killed and twelve to fourteen wounded.

The result of this bloody melee was that the *Quiñonistas* took control of city hall and the polls. For the rest of the day they permitted only their own partisans to vote. The *Palomistas* of course protested, claiming that this travesty was illegal. The *Quiñonistas* ignored them and kept right on voting.

Morley found himself caught up in the election mayhem:

> I was crossing the Plaza in front of the National Theatre when the fight took place. I heard shots but thought they were fire-crackers which they interminably shoot off down here on every fiesta. Indeed it was not until I saw a brave officer with his sword between his legs in imminent danger of tripping over it, running swiftly and efficaciously for the nearest shelter that I too suddenly realized what was afoot and joined him in flight. People screaming and yelling poured out of the streets leading from the cabildo and there was quite a confusion.
>
> Similar scenes attended even with greater bloodshed were enacted elsewhere throughout the republic. Where the Palomistas gained control as in Santa Ana, San Miguel and Sonsonate etc. they prevented the Quinonistas from voting at all and consequently all those departments went Palomista. In Nahuizalco one particularly brutal Palomista comandante opened fire on a crowd and killed 49. This is authentic. I reported in my cable of Dec. 9 that more than one hundred had been killed. I now find that the correct figure is nearer if not quite two hundred, with perhaps five or six hundred

wounded. Indeed I have just received this morning (Dec. 30) a new casualty list from Salvador [Morley had left San Salvador for Tegucigalpa on December 21] through the hands of Stormont, the British Consul at Amapala, which gives much higher figures:

Nahuizalco	71	killed
Sonsonate	1	killed
Turin	49	killed
Estahzuelas	176	killed
Santo Domingo	19	killed
Sensentepeque	200	killed
Total	516	killed

I must confess however that I believe these figures are too high unless many of the wounded have died since. As upwards of 90% of the killed, I am reliably informed, were Quinonistas blame for these outrages would appear to attach principally to their opponents, which seems probable from the fact that most of the departmental governors were Palomista.

Morley cabled ONI that in the week following the elections the country seemed almost equally divided, with Quiñones enjoying a slim lead. But each side claimed that its candidate had won and threatened dire consequences unless the victory were acknowledged.

With El Salvador sliding toward civil war, the American legation asked for a United States warship, and the cruiser *Marblehead* arrived off the coast of El Salvador on December 16. But two days before its arrival, the electoral deadlock had been broken. President Meléndez had assembled the leading politicians, including Palomo and Quiñones, for a conference at his residence. He asked them to agree on a compromise candidate, which they were unable to do. Morley was told by his informant, Dr. Gasteazoro, that the *Palomistas* wanted the minister of war, while the *Quiñonistas* supported the foreign minister. Neither was acceptable to the other side.

Since compromise proved impossible, the president declared that it was his duty to pick the more popular candidate, whoever that might be, and he asked the advice of those present. Then General Miguel Batres, a leading *Palomista*, spoke up and said that Quiñones appeared to be the more popular of the two. With this, President Meléndez declared that Quiñones had been elected as his successor. The jubilant *Quiñonistas* left the conference proclaiming a sweeping victory, and by that evening the word on the street was that Quiñones was the president-elect and that the *Palomista* ministers would resign immediately.

In the days following, several *Quiñonistas* were appointed to the cabinet, and they announced that their first order of business would be to investigate certain irregularities alleged against Palomo himself, who resigned as minister of the interior. Furthermore, both outgoing President Meléndez and defeated Dr. Palomo were leaving the country. The Palomo political machine collapsed, and Quiñones was in complete control. On December 21, Meléndez formally turned over his office to Vice-President Quiñones, who thus became the acting president. That same evening Morley again left San Salvador for Tegucigalpa.

In his report Morley stressed that the arrival of the *Marblehead* and the visit to San Salvador by her officers had an extremely salutary effect. "A marvelous calm settled down over everything at once and while it was given out that the visit was only one of courtesy as our friends the French say, 'all the world' understood that the good Tio Sam was watching the situation closely." In Morley's view, the common people resented the killings that had accompanied the election, and the presence of the American Navy was considered a safeguard against a repetition.

Although Morley was now in Tegucigalpa, he continued to stay abreast of the Salvadoran situation through Agent Dunn and through Dr. Bailey, with whom he communicated in a private code. Bailey still received news about President Meléndez and his private circle from John Wright, and he forwarded the information to Morley. Morley thought it very significant that Wright had told Bailey that President Meléndez had said "that whatever was done or whatever step was taken they must be careful to do nothing that would offend the United States government." "This," Morley commented, "I am sure you will agree, is much different from the fire-eating anti-American attitude of less than a year ago."

Morley had previously told both Bailey and Dr. Gasteazoro that, in his opinion, the United States would disapprove of any action that would violate the Salvadoran constitution. Morley's two informants then relayed this view to Salvadoran government circles as coming from "an unofficial but well informed source."

Morley planned to return to San Salvador to observe the presidential election and to report on the economic situation, which was acute. The government had not paid any salaries since September, and the accumulated arrears totaled a million dollars. Sadly, the treasury was empty. In closing, Morley urgently recommended that Boaz Long be speedily returned from leave to his post as American minister to El Salvador:

> . . . his presence would be most desirable at this most delicate time when the new administration is formulating its new policies.
>
> The anti-American administration of Melendez is over and the new man is at least friendly to Americans and is moreover a close friend of Mr. Long. It is not improbable that Salvador could be induced to withdraw her objections to the Fonseca Bay Naval Base if properly approached. I have this on reliable authority, and if someone like Mr. Long were on the ground who knows the situation as well as he does, and who is as universally liked by the Salvadoreneans as he is, to take the matter up, at least to sound it out, I believe something might at last be put over. At least I am confident that what is done in the next few months will determine Salvador's attitude on this all important question for the rest of the Quinones administration. I earnestly hope therefore for the good of the service and for a better understanding with Salvador, Mr. Long may be permitted to return to his post as soon as possible and the sooner the better. If we want that Naval Base now is the time to strike for it before Quinones' policy becomes fixed as against it.

Morley next reported from Tegucigalpa, on January 6, 1919.[27] He was still monitoring the efforts to effect the union of Honduras and El Salvador, but his focus was once again on the election situation in El Salvador, which was heating up again. He planned to return to San Salvador for a couple of weeks. The archaeologist had developed yet another source of information in that capital: Rene Kilheuer, a Frenchman who represented the Minor Cooper Keith interests in that country. The presidential imbroglio in El Salvador continued. On January 1, the Salvadoran chargé d'affaires in Tegucigalpa presented the American legation with a trial balloon, inquiring if the State Department would extend diplomatic recognition to acting president Quiñones if he were to reelect himself, explaining that even though immediate reelection violated the letter of the Salvadoran constitution, Quiñones was clearly the popular choice as evidenced by the municipal elections of December 8. The point became moot, however, because on January 3 a new ticket was put forward: Jorge Meléndez for president and Alfonso Quiñones for vice-president. This seemed to Morley a satisfactory solution to the problem, since Jorge Meléndez, the former president's brother, had not only managed his brother-in-law Quiñones's campaign but was at least as popular among the public. By mid-January the compromise was hammered out and the crisis in El Salvador abated.[28]

Morley's special assignment was now at an end, and ONI saw no point in keeping him in Central America since the wartime intelligence network was being closed down as rapidly as possible. Accordingly, Morley was ordered back to Washington.[29] This development was not entirely to Morley's liking. Though he was doubtless eager to go home again, there were also compelling reasons to remain in Central America, as he explained to the 15th Naval District:

San Salvador, El Salvador
February 1, 1919

My Dear Mr. Wilbur [15th Naval District]:

Your cable of last week instructing me to close up our work here and return to Washington did not surprise me, I had anticipated some such a step for some time and had been making my plans accordingly. To lay these before you properly however and—as I hope—to secure your approval and cooperation therefor, there was required a longer communication than was possible by cable, hence my message last week advising that an important letter would follow on the next boat south.

As you know, ever since taking up my work with you I have maintained at the same time my connections with the Carnegie Institution, and indeed I have had to carry on numerous archaeological investigations during this period in order to the better facilitate the other work.

Your recent cable leaves me free to continue my scientific researches again, and at the same time, finds me down here in the field of my investigations during the best season of the year for archaeological work, and finally provided with sufficient Carnegie

funds to carry out these studies—in short everything is favorable to
my getting in a good field season, provided, of course, you can
secure from Washington permission for me to remain down here
until the close of the present dry season i.e., June.

This arrangement, please understand at the outset, would free
our friends in Washington from any further financial responsibility
for my work. My expenses from now on would be borne by the
Carnegie Institution exclusively, and as for my salary, I could be
placed on inactive duty without pay until I return; or until such a
time as I am finally retired from the service or placed on a reserve
or whatever is to be the ultimate disposition of such men as myself
after the war.

Aside from the interests of the Carnegie Institution and any personal wishes of my own in this matter, I may add that advantage
will accrue to our friends in Washington from such an arrangement
since I would continue to make reports to them until I returned to
the United States, whenever that would be, just as though I were
still on active service. Indeed so far as that part is concerned this
change need make no difference in my present activities for Mr.
Ando, the only real difference being that I would be drawing my
salary and expenses from the Carnegie Institution instead of from
our friends in Washington.

To put such a plan through, however, it will of course be first
necessary to secure from Washington permission to remain down
here, without further cost to themselves however until June; and I
am therefore laying this matter before you with the request that you
take it up direct with Washington. At the same time I am sending a
copy of this letter to Washington by the legation pouch which leaves
today.

If this request should be approved, I plan to visit Costa Rica,
Nicaragua, Guatemala and possibly even Yucatan before returning
to the states and I would continue to report as before on matters of
interest not only to ourselves but also to the Department of State.

I am returning to Tegucigalpa next week as quickly as I recover
from an attack of fever which I have had for the past ten days now
on and off, and may I ask you to be so kind as to let me know there
the outcome of what you have been able to do for me in this matter?

I earnestly hope this request may be granted as I can get in four months of field work down here before the rainy season commences and at the same time I will be able to continue the other work without further cost to our friends in Washington. Awaiting your reply in Tegucigalpa and thanking you for any help you may be able to give in this matter I close.

Very faithfully yours
Sylvanus G. Morley[30]

This arrangement was agreeable to Morley's naval superiors: "This officer was relieved from all duty and detached from Naval Intelligence at Tegucigalpa, Honduras on March 1, 1919."[31]

While leading a double life as scholar and ONI spy, Morley had "covered nearly 2000 miles of Atlantic littoral in the republics of Nicaragua, Honduras, Guatemala and Mexico, as well as a great deal of the interior of the first three, and some work on the Pacific."[32] In the course of doing so, he had endured "ticks, mosquitos, fleas, sandflies, saddle-sores, seasickness, bar-running, indifferent grub and sometimes no grub at all, rock-hard beds, infamous hostelries and even earthquakes."[33]

It had been a grand adventure.

14. Postwar Developments

The wartime role of scholars such as Morley and his ONI associates erupted into a heated controversy in 1919. At issue was a question that persists even today: Is it ethical for scholars to use their profession as cover for gathering intelligence? What precipitated this firestorm in anthropological circles was an open letter to the editor of *The Nation* by Franz Boas, written on October 16, 1919, and published in the magazine's December 20 issue.

Boas was born into a liberal Jewish family in Prussia in 1858. He received a Ph.D. from the University of Kiel, but found that his professional prospects in his native land were dim because of his liberal views, which included opposition to prewar German imperialism. He emigrated to the United States and in 1895 was appointed assistant curator of anthropology at the American Museum of Natural History. He held that position until 1905, when he left to teach at Columbia University, where he would number Margaret Mead among his students.[1]

Boas was the country's most distinguished anthropologist when he wrote his memorable letter to *The Nation*. In the letter, Boas sounded a lofty tone of righteous indignation, decrying what he considered to have been the prostitution of science. He began by reminding the reader that despite President Wilson's declaration to the contrary, the United States government indeed employed spies. He then protested vigorously against the actions of a number of scientists, men whom Boas now refused to consider as scientists any longer, who had betrayed science by using it to cover their nefarious activities as spies.

Boas did condescend to excuse the soldier, whose business was murder; the diplomat, whose profession was based on deceit and secrecy; the politician, who lived by compromising his conscience; or the businessman, whose aim was to maximize profits within the limit of lenient laws, if they valued patriotism above decency and served as spies. But not the scientist, whose very life was the pursuit of truth. Therefore, anyone using science to cover spying, who was unscrupulous enough to pose before a foreign government as a researcher and ask that government's assistance while clandestinely conducting espionage, committed an unpardonable offense against science and forfeited the right to be considered a scientist.

Boas stated that he had accidentally learned that at least four anthropologists, while serving as government secret agents, had introduced themselves to foreign governments as representatives of reputable American scientific institutions engaged in legitimate research. By doing so, they brought discredit on the whole scientific community and caused great harm to the very process of scientific inquiry. Because of their actions, foreign nations would henceforth look with suspicion on the visiting researcher engaged in honest work. Because of their actions, a new barrier had been raised against friendly international cooperation.[2]

An account sympathetic to Boas states that in the summer of 1917 Boas had learned that several anthropologists had engaged in espionage in Mexico while conducting anthropological research. Two of them had used contacts they had made through Boas while studying at the International School of American Archaeology and Ethnology in Mexico City. After seething for two years at what he considered their reprehensible conduct, Boas exploded in the 1919 letter to *The Nation*.[3] There was, however, more to it than that.

The two miscreants who had abused their association with Boas were the failed ensigns William H. Mechling and J. Alden Mason. Boas had indeed on occasion furthered their scholarly careers prior to World War I. And it was through Boas that Mechling had met the leading Mexican anthropologist, Manuel Gamio, head of the government Directorate of Archaeological and Ethnographical Studies.[4] In July 1917, Gamio wrote to Boas, mentioning that Mechling and Mason had requested permission to conduct archaeological work in Yucatán. Boas, who planned to publish a paper by Mason, was surprised by Gamio's statement and asked German-born Berthold Laufer, curator of anthropology at the Field

Museum in Chicago where Mason had been employed, about him. Laufer replied that all he knew was that in April Mason had left on a special mission for the government and was prohibited from discussing the mission or his destination. His interest now thoroughly aroused, Boas suspected that Mason and Mechling might be involved in some kind of sordid political mission, something Boas abhorred. He therefore implored Alfred Tozzer at Harvard to tell him everything he knew about the matter. Tozzer, who knew quite a bit, replied in a confidential letter that he was not prepared to make any comment regarding Mason and Mechling's trip.[5] A frustrated Boas then made the same request of Pliny Earle Goddard at the American Museum of Natural History, saying that Gamio had written Boas that Mason and Mechling were in Yucatán working for the Peabody Museum and the Field Museum; Gamio assumed that Boas knew all about their activities.[6]

Meanwhile, Berthold Laufer of the Field Museum had been having second thoughts. He suggested that Mason and Mechling might be on a harmless political mission just using "archaeological research" as cover, as a way to justify their presence in Mexico. In fact, they might not even do any archaeological work at all. Laufer asked Boas not to disclose to Gamio the political mission of the pair, as this might embarrass the United States government and get Mason and Mechling into serious trouble. He urged no action pending further developments. But the next day he changed his mind again because of further information just received from Boas. Laufer was surprised and outraged at the possibility that Mason and Mechling had secret dealings with the Peabody Museum. He promised a thorough investigation and legal action, if warranted. Laufer further stated that Mason had left the Field Museum on April 7 on a summons from the War [*sic*] Department. Mason was on an indefinite leave of absence without pay. Mason, moreover, was not only on a political mission but had talked about it a lot before leaving, so the rumor had spread all over town. Belatedly, from Washington, Mason had asked people at the Field Museum to maintain strictest silence. As for Mechling, he had been hired by the Field Museum in March or April, to begin on July 1. But in late April he had written to Laufer that he was a reserve officer and might be called to active duty. Laufer had not heard from him since. Laufer ended by saying that for two weeks he had tried to dissuade Mason from "his plan," but to no avail, and Laufer felt that Mason had been taken in by a so-called friend. In any case, Mason had no connection with the Field Museum, which was not responsible for his actions. Laufer planned to write directly to Manuel Gamio.[7]

Boas also wrote to Gamio that Gamio's news about Mason and Mechling had been a complete surprise to him. He informed Gamio that Mason was not employed by the Field Museum and was now working for the United States government. Gamio of course already knew this, since Mason had told him about his and Mechling's intelligence mission. Boas stressed that he had absolutely nothing to do with Mason and Mechling's trip to Mexico. He asked Gamio to confirm that he had received Boas's letter.[8]

Boas informed Berthold Laufer that he was willing to give Mason the benefit of the doubt, although he found it incredible that any self-respecting scientist would stoop to spying on a country with which the United States was on good terms. Boas invoked high moral principals, but there was a considerable element of self-interest involved. He stated that he could not allow even the shadow of suspicion to fall upon himself, for it would ruin the work he was doing in Mexico. And he summarized his letter to Gamio.[9] Boas was also busily writing to other colleagues informing them that Mason was in Mexico on a mission for the United States government and assuring them that he had nothing to do with it.[10]

Manuel Gamio was unperturbed by Boas's revelations. Replying to the latter, he said that several months earlier Mechling had come to see him in Mexico City and had stated that he was commissioned by the Field Museum. Mechling remained in the capital about a week and then left for Yucatán. Mason had accompanied Mechling to Veracruz, waiting for him there while Mechling went to Mexico City; they had then traveled together to Yucatán. Gamio had offered Mechling a job as an ethnologist, but Mechling had declined. He had subsequently corresponded with Mechling, again in connection with a position for him.[11]

What is clear is that Franz Boas did everything he could to blow Mason and Mechling's cover, which, along with their own indiscretion, helps to explain why their mission failed so miserably. But Boas by no means confined himself to exposing Mason and Mechling. He informed a colleague at Berkeley that Spinden was engaged in spying, the same as Morley and Mechling and Mason.[12] Since neither Morley nor Spinden were beholden to Boas, and Spinden never spied in Mexico, and Morley had not yet spied in Mexico, the explanation put forth by Boas's apologist rings hollow. And Boas was not just interested in preserving his scholarly virginity; he was pro-German. Although he had become an American citizen he retained a deep cultural attachment to the Fatherland.[13] Boas made no bones about his position. On January 8, 1916, he had written a lengthy letter to the editor of the *New York Times* entitled "Why German-Americans Blame America." It was an expression of what "we who sympathize with Germany and Austria . . ." thought. Nothing got by Boas—he noted: "It is perfectly obvious that the belligerents have at heart effective warfare rather than international law." Having provided that keen insight on the war, he went on to oppose the popular demand for preparedness.[14] It would appear that the United States won World War I despite Franz Boas.

His 1919 letter was a lightning rod that attracted thunderbolts from those who despised Boas on patriotic, professional, and personal grounds. Presumably Morley and Spinden did not weep bitter tears of remorse on learning that Franz Boas no longer considered them scientists. They must have been furious at the self-appointed conscience of their profession, who had sat out the war safely as a civilian in New York City while they were serving their country. Someone who was certainly furious with Boas was W. H. Holmes, the head curator of the Department of Anthropology at the U.S. National Museum. He denounced Boas's "reprehensible" letter to *The Nation* and called for a concerted effort to end the "Hun control" of anthropology in the United States. He reported with great satisfaction that Boas's position of Honorary Philologist at the Bureau of Ethnology had been abolished. Further, if Boas or any of his minions were selected to fill the $6,000 position in the National Research Council, Holmes would resign from the American Anthropological Association and work to organize a new association that would be truly American.[15] With this kind of counterattack brewing, Boas was vulnerable on several counts: he had impugned the actions of patriotic Americans; he was a German; and he was despised by many of his fellow anthropologists.

The whole affair came to a head on December 30, 1919, when the American Anthropological Association's governing council met in Cambridge, Massachusetts, with Clarke Wissler presiding. Morley's friend, Neil M. Judd, introduced a resolution:

> That the expression of opinion by Dr. Franz Boas contained in an
> open letter to the editor of The Nation under date of October 16,

1919, and published in the issue of that weekly for December 20, 1919, is unjustified and does not represent the opinion of the American Anthropological Association. Be it further resolved:

That a copy of this resolution be forwarded to the Executive Board of the National Research Council and such other scientific associations as may have taken action on this matter.

When the resolution was put to a vote, Wissler and one other member of the council abstained. Ten members, including Morley's old Harvard professor Alfred Tozzer, who had been a captain in the Signal Corps,[16] voted against the resolution. But twenty members, including Morley, Spinden, Lothrop, and Marshall Saville, anthropologist of the Museum of the American Indian in New York City and ex-captain in Military Intelligence,[17] voted in favor. By a two-to-one margin, Franz Boas had been repudiated by the governing board of his professional organization.[18] Not only was Boas censured, but he was removed from the Council of the American Anthropological Association, and was forced to resign from the National Research Council.[19] The humiliation of Boas, who had dominated his profession for some twenty years, was complete. In essence, the Germans lost and the spies won.

Morley's connection with American intelligence continued even after his discharge on March 1, 1919. In his capacity as an archaeologist, he spent some time in the capitals of all five Central American republics between March 15 and June 15, 1919, and he periodically reported to ONI. His reports culminated in his No. 32, written on July 16, 1919, after his return to Washington.[20] The report was in two parts, the first dealing with the current political situation in Central America. Morley focused on the prevailing instability and corruption in the region, mentioning, for instance, that the government of El Salvador was a "family affair," with the Meléndez family exercising dynastic control, and that in Honduras seventy-six members of the president and his wife's family were occupying important government posts. He concluded that unfortunately the histories of Mexico and the Central American republics demonstrated that they alternated between military despotism and revolution, and therefore the United States should take forceful measures to impose stability. He strongly recommended that the United States, under the Monroe Doctrine, establish protectorates until such time as those countries gave evidence of being able to govern themselves.

The second part of Morley's report concerned the establishment of a permanent United States intelligence service in Central America. During the war, ONI, MID, and the State Department's BSI had at one time or another maintained agents in Central America. ONI had been first in the field, deploying half a dozen agents in Guatemala and Honduras within a month after the declaration of war. By war's end, ONI had built an intelligence organization covering all of Central America, with headquarters in Balboa in the Canal Zone. The War Department, on the other hand, had not gotten organized until the war was nearly over. Not until October 1918 had it stationed military attachés in El Salvador, Guatemala, Honduras, and Nicaragua, with intelligence headquarters in Tegucigalpa, Honduras. The State Department never maintained a definite intelligence unit in Central America, relying instead on the legations and a few special agents such as General Lee Christmas, and most of these special agents were not in the field until late in the war. So it had been ONI that had almost single-handedly gathered intelligence for Central America and southern Mexico throughout World War I. Morley pointed out, however, that if the war had lasted another year, ONI would have been supplanted by MID, which had the military attaché structure and was much better funded.

As for the postwar era, ONI was at a serious disadvantage because it had decided to rely solely on voluntary unpaid agents who would have the privilege of reporting by using the diplomatic pouches. But there was no longer the wartime patriotic incentive for these people, besides which the legations resented their access to the diplomatic pouch, as was the case in Honduras.

Morley decried the shift in intelligence from ONI to MID, stressing that Central America would continue to be the navy's responsibility. In the unlikely event that the army would be called on to operate in Central America, it would have to rely on the navy for support. Furthermore, any situation requiring troops could be handled more effectively, promptly, and economically by the marines. Finally, Morley objected to MID on the grounds that military attachés were in uniform, which in itself severely hampered their ability to collect intelligence, for in Central America every American was under suspicion.

He strongly recommended that Central America be turned over to ONI, which could cover the region with three professional agents—one for Guatemala, one for El Salvador and Honduras, and one for Nicaragua and Costa Rica—reporting to the Director of Naval Intelligence. Agents should be paid a salary of $300 a month—the same as the State Department was paying its intelligence officers—and $10 per diem in lieu of expenses (which would come to a total of less than $22,000 per year). Agents should be selected from scientific and professional rather than business circles, "unless a business man would agree not to try to make money on the side," as had often been done in the consular service. Agents should work closely with the legations and have the privilege of using the diplomatic pouch and cable when necessary. To improve the efficiency of such an intelligence service, ONI's headquarters for Central America should be changed from Balboa (15th Naval District) to New Orleans (8th Naval District) because all the steamship lines to the Atlantic ports of Central America converged on New Orleans. Morley concluded by stating that this kind of intelligence service would cost little more than was currently being spent on military attachés in Central America.[21]

For the next few years Morley conducted fieldwork, mainly in the Petén region of Guatemala, but remained in contact with American intelligence. The State Department consulted with him in 1919 about what to do with its agent Lee Christmas.[22] That same year Military Intelligence was compiling handbooks with information of military value for all parts of the world, and Samuel Lothrop suggested that MID contact Morley for data on southern Mexico. In June 1919, MID not only asked to borrow Morley's documents and maps on a confidential basis, but also interviewed him personally. Further, in January 1922, Morley provided MID with intelligence and current maps of the Petén.[23] It would appear, however, that 1922 marked the end of his involvement with intelligence.

Between seasons of fieldwork, Morley managed to stay quite busy. In 1920 he put in a marathon stint at the Cosmos Club, reviewing the proofs for his monumental *The Inscriptions of Copán*, which appeared that same year. Morley was also much in demand as a speaker, for he had a positive gift for explaining the splendors of Mayan civilization to an appreciative public. He also helped to raise public interest through his articles, such as the five he published in *National Geographic* between 1922 and 1936, and the cover story he wrote for the June 30, 1947, issue of *Life* magazine. Morley's thesis was that the Maya were the Greeks of the New World, the preeminent pre-Columbian culture.[24]

Morley maintained his connection with the Carnegie Institution, a connection that had begun with his hiring in 1914. It was in 1923,

though, that he scored a professional coup by negotiating a contract
between the Carnegie Institution and the Mexican government for the
excavation of the important Mayan ceremonial center of Chichén Itzá.[25]
The agreement would subsequently be broadened to include other sites,
but directing the work at Chichén Itzá remained the focus of Morley's
efforts for many years. In Yucatán Morley continued to expand his
already impressive circle of friends and acquaintances. Most improbably,
he developed a close friendship with the governor, Felipe Carrillo Puerto,
who was a flaming socialist and thus represented everything Morley
despised. The archaeologist also knew Alma Reed, the American reporter
who was desperately in love with Carrillo Puerto.[26] The latter's life ended
prematurely, for he was captured and executed during a revolution in
1924, one which, incidentally, also resulted in the execution of General
Salvador Alvarado, who had been Carranza's proconsul in Yucatán.
During the years that Morley worked at Chichén Itzá, he received a
steady stream of visits from colleagues, among them Dr. Gann, Joe
Spinden, J. Alden Mason, Marshal Saville, and J. Eric Thompson. In
1924, Morley and Gann traveled to Europe together to attend professional meetings and examine Mayan materials in several museums.[27]
Morley also found time to marry again, in 1927. His second wife, Frances
Rhoads, was sixteen years his junior, but theirs proved to be an enviably
happy marriage.[28] She was a gracious hostess at the comfortable home
they shared at Chichén Itzá, and she accompanied her husband on his
expeditions, such as one to Uaxactún in 1928.[29]

Perhaps the most unusual aspect of Morley's years at Chichén Itzá
was his involvement with the rebel Maya. Morley not only had a passionate interest in the ancient Maya, but he also had a great affection for
their contemporary descendants. The latter evidently reciprocated the
feeling, for in January 1934 small groups of Maya from Quintana Roo
began visiting him at Chichén Itzá. Gradually, the purpose of their visits
emerged: the Maya wanted his help in an armed struggle against the
Mexicans who were encroaching on their remaining lands. Morley
explained as tactfully as possible that as a foreigner in Mexico he could
not embroil himself in political affairs, but that he would be happy to do
what he could to help them. Although the Maya did not fully understand
Morley's position, he visited them as their honored guest.[30]

Until 1940, Morley lived at Chichén Itzá, directing the Carnegie
Institution's work there as well as at other sites in Middle America. In

1940 he moved to Mérida. As Morley's biographer put it, "Morley had brought fame to the Carnegie Institution and distinction to himself."[31] He engaged in his last extensive excavation in 1941–1942, at Uxmal, and in 1944 he and his wife spent two months traveling in Central America and Mexico in what proved to be his last long expedition.[32]

During World War II the Carnegie Institution asked Morley to write his autobiography, which promised to be most interesting given the multitude of events he had witnessed and participated in during his decades of Latin American involvement. Morley's principal source would be his voluminous diaries and notebooks, which were sometimes quite candid. For instance, he mentioned that he did not like to have a wet bed because he had been a bed wetter as a child.[33] Regarding the autobiography, the archaeologist Edwin Shook gives the following account: Morley's notebooks also reflected his interest in the ladies, for between marriages he had recorded his conquests as though he were recording Mayan hieroglyphs. But his second wife, Frances, who was keenly aware that she was married to a personage, was so concerned about Morley's reputation that she kept expurgating the salacious parts of his manuscript. Morley became so exasperated that he finally abandoned writing his autobiography and instead wrote *The Ancient Maya*.[34] Still, problems continued. The Carnegie Institution editors were furious when Morley delivered the manuscript of *The Ancient Maya*; Carnegie had envisioned a volume on the ancient Maya as the culminating work of a series of monographs detailing Mayan research, but Morley had incorporated both his own research and some of that performed by other Carnegie staffers. Carnegie refused to publish Morley's book. After Carnegie disassociated itself, Morley approached Macmillan, but that publisher rejected *The Ancient Maya* as being too technical and having too many illustrations. Morley then turned to Stanford University Press, which was delighted to publish *The Ancient Maya*, and the work quickly became a classic.[35]

Morley retired to Santa Fe, New Mexico, to a house he had purchased in the early 1940s. He enriched that city by donating his valuable collection of Spanish colonial ecclesiastical art to the Museum of New Mexico. In a sense, Morley's life came full circle; in 1947 he agreed to become both director of the Museum of New Mexico and the School of American Archaeology, where he had begun his career in 1908. He occupied those posts for the next fifteen months, until he died of a heart attack on September 2, 1948.[36]

Morley evidently did not maintain contact with his wartime assistant, John Held. Upon his return from Central America, Held moved into a large apartment on 40th Street in New York City. He lived with Ada "Johnny" Johnson, who was ten years older than Held and who had been an ambulance driver during the Great War.[37] In 1918, she became the second Mrs. Held. The changes Held was making were not only matrimonial but artistic as well, developing the "roundheaded, big-footed, one-eyed girl who later evolved into the famous Flapper of the '20's."[38] The Twenties was a golden decade for Held, bringing him fame and fortune, for as a caricaturist he invented the flapper, the symbol of modern youth. His drawings were featured in leading magazines, he had syndicated cartoon strips, and he could frequently name his own price for his work. He also took a flier into politics, running for Congress. He lost, in large measure because he never made a speech or even bothered to leave his home.[39]

In the early Thirties he lost most of his money to a world-class swindler, Ivar Krueger. Perhaps not coincidentally, he also had a nervous breakdown. Held illustrated books, produced a variety show, designed theater sets, and turned to sculpting. In 1940, he was artist-in-residence at Harvard. During World War II he worked for the Signal Corps as an illustrator, and he wrote and illustrated children's stories. John Held died on March 2, 1958. His reputation as an important American artist grew in the 1960s, with exhibitions of his work in Indianapolis and Newport. And from 1969 to 1972 the Smithsonian Institution had a nationwide traveling exhibition of "The Art of John Held Jr."[40]

Morley's ONI superior, Charles Sheldon, a.k.a. "Taro Yamamoto," performed capably as a case officer: he ran a total of sixteen agents in Latin America.[41] Sometime after the war Sheldon evidently weeded his papers, for they contain but one letter written on ONI stationery.[42] Sheldon was well thought of in ONI; he was the only civilian whom the Director of Naval Intelligence, Rear Admiral Roger Welles, recommended for a decoration in 1919.[43] He was also well thought of at the State Department. In 1919 he was one of the three men recommended by the diplomat Boaz Long to become permanent chief of the Division of Mexican Affairs.[44] But, instead, Sheldon became once again a conservation activist. He lobbied for comprehensive game regulations for the Alaska territory and had the satisfaction of seeing such a bill passed by Congress in 1924. When the law was implemented in 1925 it was hailed as a model of progressive legislation. But Sheldon still loved to hunt, and in 1921–22 he made an expedition among the Seri Indians on the west coast of Mexico, and he hunted bighorn sheep in the American Southwest.

During the 1920s he continued to make his home in Washington, adding to his impressive personal library and entertaining naturalists and explorers.[45] He remained active in the influential Boone and Crockett Club. In 1925 he coedited *Hunting and Conservation: The Book of the Boone and Crockett Club*.[46] He began working on another book, which was published posthumously as *The Wilderness of Denali* in 1930. Sheldon died of a heart attack at his summer home in Nova Scotia on September 21, 1928. He was buried in Rutland, Vermont. It would have pleased him to know that in 1980 Mount McKinley National Park was renamed Denali National Park and that a plaque honors Charles Sheldon as the park's founder.[47] His Southwestern journals were published in 1993 under the title of *The Wilderness of the Southwest*.

After his 1917 ONI debacle in Mexico, the anthropologist John Alden Mason returned to the Field Museum in Chicago and resumed his post as assistant curator of Mexican and South American Archaeology. Still smarting under Franz Boas's disapproval, Mason, in February 1920, sent him a letter in which he gave a dignified explanation of the patriotic motives for his wartime service as a spy. Predictably, Boas replied that Mason's conduct had been indefensible and proceeded to lecture him about professional ethics. Despite their fundamental disagreement about whether it was honorable to spy, they remained on reasonably friendly terms.[48]

Mason left the Field Museum in 1924 for a similar position at the American Museum of Natural History in New York. Two years later, he became curator of the American section in the University of Pennsylvania Museum at Philadelphia. He remained there until his retirement in 1955, when he was named curator emeritus, a title he held until his death in November 1967. Mason conducted research in the American Southwest as well as in Latin America. He maintained his friendship with Sylvanus Morley, visiting the latter's excavations in Yucatán on occasion.[49] From 1945 to 1948, Mason edited the *American Anthropologist*. His book *The Ancient Civilizations of Peru*, published in 1957, remains a standard work in the field.[50] Mason proved to be much more successful as a scholar than as a spy.

Samuel K. Lothrop, by contrast, excelled in both areas. As we have seen, after his work for ONI ended, he secured an army commission. His army career proved to be brief. During his tour of duty in Military Intelligence he functioned as an analyst, preparing strategic studies and special reports on various Latin American countries. His performance received warm commendation from his superior officers.[51] But with the war over, Lothrop yearned to return to civilian life. As he explained in requesting a discharge, his army salary did not cover his expenses, and he was anxious to return to archaeology as soon as possible. Lothrop received his discharge on March 15, 1919.[52]

He remained in Washington for a while, staying at the Cosmos Club, where he was an associate member.[53] His immediate interest was in lobbying for a congressional investigation of the United States diplomatic corps in Central America, a body which, with a few exceptions, he considered incompetent and corrupt. To that end he held discussions with Congressman John Jacob Rogers, of the Fifth District in Massachusetts, and with Senator Henry Cabot Lodge. Although both politicians showed interest, Lothrop finally decided that too much time had passed for a successful investigation. He did express a willingness to testify about events in Costa Rica, but someone else would have to conduct the investigation and compile the evidence.[54] The matter was dropped.

Thereafter, Lothrop devoted himself primarily to archaeology. He returned to Harvard, receiving his Ph.D. in 1921. From 1919 until 1924 he was affiliated with the Carnegie Institution of Washington; in 1924 he left to join the staff of the Museum of the American Indian, in New York. In 1930, he resigned to join the Peabody Museum at Harvard, where he became a research associate and subsequently curator of Andean archaeology. His official connection with the Peabody Museum continued until his retirement in 1957, and unofficially until his death in New York City on January 10, 1965. Since he was independently wealthy he didn't have to worry about teaching, and he could spend much of his time in the field. Lothrop had a distinguished career, publishing four scholarly books and a number of articles. He was one of the founders, in 1937, of the Institute of Andean Research.[55]

Dr. Thomas Gann resumed his duties as principal medical officer in British Honduras. As a sideline, he owned a *cocal*, or coconut plantation, some ten miles north of Corozal. But even before his retirement in 1923, he continued his archaeological research. In fact, between 1919 and his death in 1938 he was lecturer in Central American archaeology at the University of Liverpool, enjoying the distinction of being the first person in England to hold such a position.[56] Gann also found time to engage in considerable fieldwork. Among other trips, he accompanied Sylvanus Morley to the ruins of Copán in 1922 and again visited the site in 1926; he also worked at Cobá and Uaxactún in 1926. Between 1924 and 1926, he participated in several expeditions to Lubaantún with the flamboyant English adventurer Frederick A. Mitchell-Hedges.[57]

In 1923 Gann visited Harvard University; the visit was marred by news that he had boasted of having bought in Mexico and smuggled into the United States a magnificent Mayan jade plaque. Since this was by no means the first time somebody had smuggled a pre-Columbian artifact out of Mexico in violation of that country's laws regarding antiquities, one wonders whether the uproar in archaeological circles was over Gann's action or because he was indiscreet enough to publicize it. The result, however, was that the flap cost Gann the appointment as physician at the Carnegie Institution's Chichén Itzá project, whose director, his old friend Sylvanus Morley, was eager to hire him. Further, in 1926 Gann visited Tulane University and proposed to Frans Blom, director of Tulane's Department of Middle American Research, that the department join with the British Museum, whose advisory committee included Gann among its members, to excavate the ruins at Copán. The proposal was allegedly rejected because of Gann's notoriety. That may have been the case, but, interestingly enough, Blom subsequently made Gann an honorary associate on the staff of the Department.[58] Gann was anything but a professional pariah. Besides his association with the British Museum, he belonged to the American Geographical Society, was a Fellow of the Royal Geographical Society, a Fellow of the Royal Anthropological Institute, and belonged to the Maya Society. During his lifetime and in his will Gann presented the British Museum with several important collections of Mayan material—including his extensive collection of jade carvings.[59]

Gann was also a prolific writer. Besides a number of scholarly articles, he produced *The Maya Indians of Southern Yucatán and Northern British Honduras*.[60] But he is perhaps best known for a series of popular books recounting his archaeological experiences: *In An Unknown Land* (1924); *Mystery Cities* (1925); *Ancient Cities and Modern Tribes* (1926), which, incidentally, is dedicated to Sylvanus Griswold Morley,

"The Little Friend of All the World" (the quotation from Rudyard Kipling's *Kim* seems most appropriate); *Maya Cities* (1927); *Discoveries and Adventures in Central America* (1928); and *Glories of the Maya* (1938). In 1931, he and the respected British archaeologist J. Eric Thompson published *The History of the Mayas from the Earliest Time to the Present Day*. Besides his scholarly contributions, Gann was instrumental in raising public awareness about the Maya. Not bad for a self-taught archaeologist.

Herbert Joseph Spinden, on February 1, 1919, requested to be relieved of active duty and placed on the navy's inactive list. He stated that with the demobilization the duties he had been performing had lessened significantly, and his service could be easily spared. Spinden, who was ill with malaria, wanted to resume his position in the American Museum of Natural History in New York City. The request was granted and on February 8, 1919, Spinden again became a civilian.[61]

He resumed his post as assistant curator of anthropology, to which he had been appointed in 1909.[62] Spinden had developed useful contacts; in 1920 he persuaded his friend Minor C. Keith, the banana baron, to extend the loan to the museum of Keith's impressive Costa Rican collection for another three years.[63] Spinden remained with the American Museum of Natural History until 1921, when he joined the Peabody Museum at Harvard. He served as curator of Mexican archaeology and ethnology at the Peabody until 1926. From then until 1929 he was curator of anthropology at the Buffalo Museum of Arts and Sciences. Yet he found time to lead an expedition to Mexico with Gregory Mason in 1926.[64] In 1929, he joined the Brooklyn Museum, where he remained until 1951, as curator of American Indian art and culture. Failing health forced his retirement, and he settled in Croton, New York. Herbert J. Spinden died on October 23, 1967.

His distinguished career included serving as president of the American Anthropological Association and the Explorers Club. He was a visiting professor at the National Autonomous University of Mexico and delivered lectures at universities in Chile, Peru, and Argentina. Spinden wrote several important books: *Maya Art*, 1913; *Ancient Civilizations of Mexico and Central America*, 1917; and *Maya Art and Civilization*, 1957.[65]

Like Morley, some of the other people he had dealt with during the war remained in intelligence for a time after the end of the conflict. One was Lewis Hunt Watkins, whom Morley had recruited to cover Yucatán and Tabasco as Agent No. 99. Watkins worked for ONI from December 6, 1919, to December 15, 1920, in Tampico, Mexico. His cover name was "Lewis," and he communicated with ONI by navy radio and through consular offices. Watkins received $200 per quarter for expenses such as hiring subagents, "entertaining for the purpose of procuring information," and travel.[66]

Morley's friend General Lee Christmas proved to be something of a disappointment as a Bureau of Secret Intelligence agent—he was simply too notorious. In October 1917, for example, Mexican agents were tracking his movements from New Orleans, suspecting his involvement with antigovernment Mexican exiles. The Mexican agents' cipher telegrams were intercepted, however, and turned over to the Riverbank Laboratories, which deciphered them and sent the clear text and translations to the State Department.[67]

Two weeks before Christmas officially became a Bureau of Secret Intelligence agent in October 1918, he wanted to return to New Orleans to investigate what he alleged were the machinations of a British firm, Pearson Oil, to loan $50,000,000 to the Guatemalan government in return for an exclusive petroleum concession. Although the American minister was skeptical, because there had never been indications of oil deposits in Guatemala, he considered the matter important. Should Christmas's allegations be true, it was imperative to have an American oil company at least match Pearson's offer.[68]

Because of his notoriety, Christmas needed a plausible reason for going to New Orleans, and he suggested that the State Department have his ostensible employer, the Burton Lumber Co., urgently summon him for an important conference. Burton did so, and on November 4, 1918, Christmas arrived in New Orleans by steamer.[69] He was met by Military Intelligence and ONI officers, who interrogated him and, over his heated protest, seized all his papers, which included confidential reports for Leland Harrison, Counselor of the State Department. The outraged Christmas asked his friend Forrest C. Pendleton, head of the Bureau of Investigation's New Orleans office, to vouch for him. Accompanied by Pendleton, Christmas proceeded to the local ONI office, to find that the matter had already been resolved; Lt. Commander Manley returned his documents and soothed his ego.[70] But the incident underlined the fact that Christmas was a marked man.

The aging adventurer reported that in New Orleans he met with Pearson's confidential representative, General Francisco Altschul, who offered Christmas a $50,000 bribe to help Pearson with the loan and oil concession. Christmas agreed, and after the meeting called his friend Pendleton of the Bureau of Investigation to his room in the Monteleone Hotel, informed him of what had transpired, and asked Pendleton to notify the State Department, which Pendleton did. And upon returning to Guatemala, Christmas informed not only the American minister but also President Estrada Cabrera of Altschul's proposition. According to Christmas, in exchange for an exclusive petroleum concession, Pearson would loan Guatemala $50,000,000 to settle her foreign debt, establish a bank to finance the rebuilding of Guatemala City, build public utilities in the capital, and build a railroad to Estrada Cabrera's hometown. In any event, none of this came to pass. The other reports in Christmas's Bureau of Secret Intelligence file are fragmentary, making it impossible fully to reconstruct his activities.[71]

With the end of World War I, the State Department felt it could dispense with Christmas's services, as of January 31, 1919. The American minister was instructed to so inform Christmas, to thank him orally for his services, and to assure him of similar employment in the future should the occasion arise.[72] Either the State Department changed its mind or it again required Christmas's services. On July 16, 1919, none other than Sylvanus Morley, recently returned from Central America, called at the State Department on Herbert Stabler, head of the Division of Latin American Affairs. Morley conveyed a message from Walter Thurston at the American legation in Guatemala City to the effect that Thurston didn't think Christmas was doing enough to warrant a salary of $300 a month, and that even Christmas admitted this. Morley suggested that the State Department inform Christmas that it could only afford to pay him $100 a month, but that his services were much appreciated and it would be desirable if he would continue to report to the State Department. Stabler concurred with Morley and Thurston.[73] Furthermore, in August 1919, the State Department squelched a proposed trip by Christmas to the United States because it wanted him to remain in Guatemala to report if need be on conditions in that country and in Honduras.[74] As far as can be determined, Christmas's connection with the State Department ended in late 1919.

His intrigues continued, however. He was determined to make a big score in oil. To that end, he reached an agreement with the Richmond Levering Company in New York City, whose president was Bruce Bielaski, former head of the Bureau of Investigation, for a lucrative contract if he could secure oil concessions and get the petroleum laws changed in Guatemala. Christmas sailed to Guatemala, where his old employer President Estrada Cabrera readily agreed. The only problem was that the president was insane. In April 1920, the congress declared him mentally incompetent and elected a replacement. Estrada Cabrera took offense and had the army shell Guatemala City for five days. Estrada Cabrera was finally arrested, and he died in prison.

Christmas quickly ingratiated himself with the new regime. To his great joy, his attorney managed to get the petroleum laws changed. In April 1921, the Richmond Levering Company gave Christmas a contract—$500 a month and a substantial percentage of the royalties on production. A syndicate was formed to begin exploring for oil.[75] But Christmas couldn't break his habit of intrigue. In 1921, the Honduran government became quite uneasy about Christmas's dealings with Honduran exiles in Guatemala.[76]

It soon ceased to matter. In December 1922, the army overthrew the Guatemalan government, and the new regime revoked the Richmond Levering concessions. Sick and broke, Christmas returned to New Orleans, where he died on January 24, 1923.[77] He was buried in his Honduran general's uniform.[78]

Wilson Popenoe, the Agricultural Explorer who had operated in Mexico in 1918, continued his association with ONI after the war. On September 10, 1919, he was hired by ONI as a confidential agent in Central and South America at the rate of $1 an hour for work performed outside his regular employment, provided that the time charged did not exceed four hours in any one day. Further, ONI agreed to reimburse reasonable expenses incurred in his ONI work. Under this contract, ONI had the option of severing its connection with Popenoe at the director of ONI's discretion. Popenoe agreed to these terms and prepared to leave for Latin America.[79]

Traveling as Agricultural Explorer for the Department of Agriculture, he reported to ONI on political conditions and transportation facilities in Guatemala, Costa Rica, and Nicaragua through the summer of 1920. Yet the lines of communication between an agent in the field such as Popenoe and ONI back in Washington still left some-

thing to be desired. ONI contacted Popenoe by writing to him in care of
Dr. David Fairchild, Bureau of Plant Industry, Department of Agriculture,
who then had the letter forwarded by diplomatic pouch. But besides this
cumbersome arrangement, Popenoe complained that his reports were not
being acknowledged and that he was uncertain whether he was even
reporting the kind of material ONI wanted (shades of Sylvanus Morley).
ONI reassured Popenoe of the value of his work, and he continued
reporting during his trip to Colombia, Ecuador, Peru, Bolivia, and Chile.
Returning via the east coast of South America, with a stopover in the
French and British Caribbean islands, Popenoe arrived back in
Washington in November 1921. His trip was not without excitement.
While taking photographs in a small town in southern Ecuador, he was
arrested as a Peruvian spy and had to use all his eloquence to talk his
way to freedom. Popenoe carried out another assignment for ONI in
Colombia in 1922, the year that his connection with that organization
evidently ended. A frequent topic of Popenoe's reports was his unhappi-
ness with the military attachés, whom he felt were not interested in compiling geographical data and who, as in the case of the attaché in Ecuador,
were anxious to secure copies of Popenoe's reports so they could amend
them slightly and send them to MID as their own work.[80] Interservice
rivalry was alive and well.

During the postwar period Popenoe maintained his friendship with
Sylvanus Morley. He and Morley spent a winter in adjoining rooms at
the Cosmos Club in the early 1920s, and on occasion they attended scholarly functions together. Popenoe related how he, Morley, and Joe Spinden
managed to get themselves lost in the subway while going to a meeting
of the Maya Society at the Brooklyn Museum. Morley, immaculately
attired down to spats and a walking stick, startled his fellow passengers
when he stood up and loudly proclaimed that it was a hell of a note for
three explorers to get lost in the subway. In later years they met infrequently at the Cosmos Club whenever Popenoe returned from living in
the tropics. As of 1948, Popenoe was employed at the Escuela Agrícola
Panamericana, established in 1943 on a plantation outside Tegucigalpa,
Honduras, with a grant of $800,000 from Samuel Zemurray's United
Fruit Company.[81]

Joseph H. Watts, who performed so capably in Guatemala City, eventually cracked under the pressure. This was reflected in his 1918 expense
accounts, which caused increasing concern in ONI headquarters. From

February 15, 1917, to March 1, 1918, his expenses were quite reasonable—less than $150 a month. This, of course, gratified his superiors in Washington, with Lt. Commander O. W. Fowler stating that Watts's expenses were a bargain compared with the valuable information he was providing. Then, in May and June 1918, Watts began hiring subagents, and his expenses increased. In August 1918, he submitted expenses of $905.03, mostly incurred by his subagents. From then on his expenses rarely fell below $1,000.00 a month, culminating in October, when they reached $2,490.58, which included a second-hand Hupmobile that Watts had bought for $956.65, a purchase for which he had no authority. Neither was he authorized to spend $94.00 for office furniture in November. And in December 1918 he submitted a claim for $668.00 for the salary and expenses of his subagent Thomas Nestor, but included no supporting documentation. Pending such corroboration, ONI disallowed the car, the furniture, and the subagent. The officer handling Watts's account commented that he seemed "exceedingly liberal" with ONI's money and recommended that Watts be grilled about his subagents and their expenses. On balance, Watts owed ONI $1,062.81. In late March, 1919 he was recalled to Washington to explain himself.[82]

As it happened, Watts was already in Washington, ostensibly on a mission to purchase field radio apparatus for Guatemalan President Estrada Cabrera. He had left Guatemala City on March 1 with $10,000 advanced by Estrada Cabrera, money that Watts would later claim was really for buying ammunition. While in Washington, he acted strangely, took a trip to New York, and upon returning claimed that he'd been drugged. Watts then went to Philadelphia, where he reportedly went on a spending spree, squandering some $3,000 of Estrada Cabrera's money. Watts was suffering a nervous breakdown. His brother informed the authorities that Watts had been sent to an asylum in Connecticut, then to the Windsor Sanitarium in Cleveland.[83]

The Bureau of Investigation was promptly called in, and two of its agents interviewed Watts, finding him to be a suspicious person who claimed to be working for ONI, but couldn't prove it. Rear Admiral A. P. Niblack, the Director of Naval Intelligence, advised the Bureau that until recently Watts had indeed been an ONI agent, and that because of his mental condition steps were being taken to return him to Washington.[84] Watts himself sent a despairing message to the State Department saying he was being held at the City Hospital in Cleveland. He had suffered a "nervous breakdown as result earthquake or overwork. Doctors will not release me to come to Washington or sanitarium thinking I am insane."[85] Naval personnel were dispatched for Watts. They took him to the Washington Naval Hospital, but he was transferred to St. Elizabeth's Hospital for the insane in the capital for observation and treatment.[86]

Watts escaped from St. Elizabeth's Hospital on July 14, and went to New York. ONI was desperate for him to be apprehended and returned to the Naval Hospital for interrogation. And ONI was most anxious to retrieve Watts's papers, requesting that the Bureau of Investigation send them all the papers and effects gathered from Watts in Cleveland.[87]

The fugitive ONI agent was finally arrested in Fall River, Massachusetts, and was brought back to the Naval Hospital under naval escort.[88] The escort, incidentally, had to borrow a pair of handcuffs from the Fall River police.[89] To ONI's enormous relief, Watts's papers were recovered. They included his ONI code books and the contract between Watts and the Guatemalan government for the purchase of the field radios.[90] The troubled ONI agent was again transferred to St. Elizabeth's Hospital for observation and treatment.

Again the resourceful Watts escaped, on the night of August 22, 1919.[91] He fled to his sister's home in Philadelphia, where he was joined by his wife and two children. The family then moved to Ocean View, Virginia. It was there that the navy at last caught up with him in October, and he was returned under guard to St. Elizabeth's Hospital in Washington.[92]

But from that point on, things began looking up for Watts. Having retrieved the code books, ONI was no longer interested in Watts. He was discharged from the navy. More importantly, he was discharged from St. Elizabeth's because his mental condition was improving. He rejoined his family in Philadelphia. In December 1919, his financial accounts with ONI were finally settled.[93] There matters might have ended, but remarkably, by 1923, Watts was back in Guatemala and was again cooperating with American intelligence.[94]

The intelligence careers of Morley and his associates ended in the early 1920s, but the need for intelligence of course continued. Unfortunately, ONI was unable to do very much, for in the rapid postwar demobilization it was largely dismantled. ONI's wartime director, Rear Admiral Roger Welles, was reassigned on January 31, 1919, to command Battleship Division One, Atlantic Fleet.[95] Furthermore, ONI's manpower was slashed, and the agency had to operate with a much-reduced budget. Taking a page from MID's book, ONI now relied primarily on naval attachés. Reflecting this priority, there was money to buy Cadillac touring cars for the naval attachés in London, Peking, Madrid, Rio de Janeiro, and Buenos Aires,[96] but little for intelligence.[97]

During these lean years, ONI officers made the rounds of corporate America, strengthening contacts and arranging for the delivery of information. In May 1919, Commander Fred P. Rogers conferred in New York City with the superintendent of the Far East Division of Standard Oil, the presidents of National City Bank, the International Section of Westinghouse Electric, U.S. Steel, and General Electric, and the old standby, United Fruit.[98] The agency also developed other sources of information. For instance, in 1919 Tracy Barrett Kittridge, formerly Intelligence Officer on the staff of the Force Commander, London, and lecturer at the Naval War College, went to Poland as a representative of the League of Red Cross Societies (International Red Cross). He was also an agent (No. 290) of ONI, reporting to Washington through State Department channels.[99]

But ONI operated without the services of one of its most flamboyant alumni—the naturalist Roy Chapman Andrews, whose career further illustrates the connection between intelligence and cultural institutions. Andrews was a celebrity who gained international fame by discovering fossilized dinosaur eggs in the Gobi desert. He was on the staff of the American Museum of Natural History for most of his adult life, beginning in 1906 by mopping floors and culminating in 1935 as Director of the institution, a post he held until 1941.

Andrews was born in Beloit, Wisconsin, on January 26, 1884. He received a B.A. from Beloit College in 1906, and almost immediately went to New York and applied for a job with the American Museum of Natural History. Andrews worked in the Museum in 1906–1907, then in 1908 went on the first of what would become a long series of expeditions, initially to places such as Alaska, the Dutch East Indies, Borneo, and Korea. He became a recognized authority on ocean mammals. Andrews was also studying at Columbia University, receiving an M.A. in 1913.

But increasingly it was Asia that attracted Andrews. Having explored in Korea, he envisioned expanding his field of operations to Mongolia and other regions of Central Asia. Accordingly, he launched a campaign at the museum for such an expedition. His efforts succeeded, and in 1916 he led the First Asiatic Expedition of the American Museum of Natural History, exploring Tibet, Burma, and southwestern China. He returned to New York in 1917, spending the following year organizing his collections and publishing his findings as well as making preparations for a second expedition, to Mongolia.[100] It was at this point that he entered the world of intelligence.

In his autobiography, Andrews states that, being anxious to do his patriotic duty, he offered his services to the secretary of war, whom he had known for years. That official offered him a desk job with Military Intelligence in Washington and a commission as a major. But Andrews craved action. Disconsolate, he went to the Cosmos Club for lunch and was hailed by none other than Charles Sheldon, who disclosed that he was in Naval Intelligence and promptly offered Andrews a job with that organization in the Far East just as fast as Andrews could get there. There would be plenty of action. After lunch, Sheldon took him to meet "the Admiral." A week later Andrews was on his way to Peking, his headquarters for the rest of the war.[101] He was reticent about his role:

> It is not permitted, even now, to tell what part I played in the war. Suffice it to say that it was exceedingly unimportant although interesting and at times exciting.[102]

An inkling of what he was doing comes from a letter his wife Yvette wrote to her aunt on December 1, 1918. The letter was intercepted by U.S. Postal Censorship. Written on "Second Asiatic Zoological Expedition of the American Museum of Natural History" letterhead, Mrs. Andrews disclosed that the letterhead was "mere camouflage" and that Andrews was really on a secret government mission in China.[103] She wrote a similarly indiscreet letter to another relative on the same date, saying that Andrews had made trips to Mongolia and to Shantung province. The ensuing flap resulted in Andrews being ordered home on January 24, 1919, to report to ONI.[104] Andrews later stated:

> I am quite familiar with the Tsingtau-Tsinan-Fu Railroad in Shantung and spent some time there on investigations for the Naval Intelligence. I was in Shantung at the time the armistice was declared. I made a fairly extensive report to the Naval Intelligence Bureau regarding my investigations.[105]

Roy Chapman Andrews indeed served in ONI under deep cover during World War I. He took the oath on June 10, 1918, becoming ONI Agent No. 241. Andrews was a civilian employee, receiving $4 a day in salary and $4 per diem for expenses. He went to China ostensibly to make comparative zoological studies of Chinese mammals. There was a cloak and dagger air about Andrews's trip to China. He sailed from San Francisco on June 29, 1918, aboard the S.S. *Ecuador*, bound for Shanghai. But Andrews's cabin mate was one Matias Arbolcya, a suspected spy. So, before sailing, Andrews was searched by officials of Military Intelligence, Customs, and the local ONI office. Since they found nothing of an incriminating nature, he was allowed to depart. Andrews carried with him a letter of introduction to a "John Rankin," and signed by "Allan Fraser." But written in invisible ink between the lines was an unsigned message dated June 12 from Captain Roger Welles, Director of Naval Intelligence, to Commander Gillis, naval attaché in Peking, introducing Andrews, who would be acting under Gillis's orders. The latter was instructed to report Andrews's arrival by cabling in code the phrase "Conditions unchanged." ONI would reply "Situation understood," which would serve to authenticate the invisible message. Commander Gillis was cautioned: "Under no circumstances should his name ever be transmitted by mail or cable, at any time. Designate him when necessary by the name of Reynolds."[106]

During his stay in China, Andrews developed an intense dislike for the Japanese. Although Japan was an ally of the United States, her agents continually tampered with American diplomatic pouches to the point that diplomatic mail had to be sent only on American ships. In his autobiography, published in 1943, Andrews referred to the Japanese as "little yellow traitors," a phrase few objected to since in 1943 the United States was having some trouble with the Japanese.[107]

What Andrews neglected to mention in his autobiography was that he continued to be an ONI agent after World War I. His card in the agency's files reads:

Andrews, Roy Chapman   Far East

(Has always been designated as "Reynolds" in cables and connection with O.N.I. carefully guarded).

Official of American Museum of Natural History, New York, writer and whose articles have been widely published. In March, 1919,

Naval Attache, Peking, advised that he would remain in China and
work for the Museum, making his headquarters at Gaga, Mongolia,
and recommended retaining him at Four Dollars per day only, Mr.
Andrews to pay all his other expenses. This request was approved
by O.N.I. March 14, 1919. Payment is made by Naval Attache,
Peking. Contract in secret file, Section B. Reports to Naval Attache,
Peking.

Approved:
A. P. Niblack[108]

Andrews himself would later inform Military Intelligence that "from
June, 1918, until March, 1919, I was in the service of the Bureau of Naval
Intelligence and did a good deal of running around in Mongolia and
China."[109]

Recklessly risking the wrath of Franz Boas, Andrews became
involved with Military Intelligence in 1920. Interestingly enough, his
involvement began in part through the National Geographic Society.
Maynard Owen Williams of the editorial staff sent a list of the Society's
contributors of material on China and Japan to Lt. Col. Nicholas W.
Campanole, MID's expert on Japan. Among those "especially worth
attention" was Roy Chapman Andrews, who had just returned from
Mongolia. In addition, Williams offered to provide MID with a monthly
list encompassing the entire world outside the United States. Williams,
an MID veteran himself, made suggestions as to how MID could keep
tabs on Americans traveling abroad and offered to help in any way he
could. MID should not hesitate to contact him, and if a more extended
interview were desired, he would be happy to go to MID's offices, and
while there to "renew old acquaintances."[110]

Not only was the National Geographic Society assisting Military
Intelligence, but so was the American Museum of Natural History. The
director, Dr. Frederick A. Lucas, cooperated cordially with MID and suggested that Andrews have a talk with that organization. Andrews himself, at the time associate curator of mammals, offered to assist MID.[111]
Military Intelligence immediately sent Andrews a list of matters pertaining to China and Mongolia, about which it was eager to learn his views.
MID included a personal questionnaire that Andrews filled out, and he
also answered MID's other questions about conditions in Mongolia and
China.[112]

MID wanted not just information but participation, and inquired of Director Lucas whether it might select a member of Andrews's forthcoming Third Asiatic Expedition. When the American Museum's Third Asiatic Expedition took the field in Mongolia during the 1925 summer season, 1st Lt. F. B. Butler of the Corps of Engineers was its topographer. Andrews had arranged with the Commanding General, United States Army Forces in China, for Butler to be placed on detached service with the expedition. Butler produced for his army superiors a detailed report on Mongolia, complete with photographs.[113] And when, in 1930, the Central Asiatic Expedition explored Outer Mongolia, its topographer was 1st Lt. Willard G. Wyman, Cavalry. As leader of the expedition, Andrews thanked the American military attaché on behalf of the American Museum of Natural History for lending him Wyman. Andrews added that MID would receive copies of all the expedition's maps as soon as they were printed.[114] In addition, Wyman prepared the usual reports and maps for Military Intelligence.[115] That organization, incidentally, sent copies of these materials to the Smithsonian Institution with the understanding that they not be published.[116] As an example of unexpected consequences, it was later reported to Military Intelligence that Andrews's expedition to Outer Mongolia was largely responsible for the Sovietization of that territory. The Mongolians regarded the expedition as the spearhead of some sort of foreign invasion. Furthermore, soon after Andrews dug up his famous dinosaur fossils some of the lakes began drying up. The Mongolians were convinced that Andrews represented malevolent influences, and they looked to the Soviet Union for protection.[117]

The 1930 expedition was evidently Andrews's last involvement with American Intelligence. The year 1930 also marked the end of Andrews's Gobi expeditions. Five times between 1921 and 1930 he had led teams of the Third Asiatic Expedition, or as it became known, the Central Asiatic Expedition, to explore Inner and Outer Mongolia.[118] Andrews remained with the American Museum of Natural History until he resigned as Director in 1941 in order to devote himself to writing. He died in 1960. And no, he was not the model for Indiana Jones, as claimed by Don Lessem in a rather gushy article in *The Boston Globe*.[119] The Director of Public Relations for Lucasfilm, Ltd. specifically refuted that allegation, stating that Indiana Jones was fictional and commenting that George Lucas named Indiana after a dog of his.[120]

As for ONI, during the interwar years the agency employed most of
its scanty resources to collect intelligence on the mysterious Japanese-
mandated islands in the Pacific. In addition to ordering aerial reconnaissance by marine seaplanes based at Guam (which drew Japanese protests
and had to be halted), ONI launched a major operation to infiltrate a
senior Marine Corps officer posing as a German copra trader. This officer, Lieutenant Colonel Earl H. "Pete" Ellis, who is widely credited as
being the father of amphibious operations, was able to tour some of the
mandated islands in 1922–1923, but turned up dead on May 12, 1923,
on the island of Palau in the eastern Carolines. The Japanese government
had his body cremated, and it was widely believed both by senior U.S.
Navy and Marine Corps officers that Ellis had been murdered by the
Japanese. The most recent scholarship, however, suggests that Ellis, who
had a serious drinking problem, essentially drank himself to death.[121] ONI
persisted throughout the remainder of the 1920s and 1930s in attempting to infiltrate American scientists with plausible cover into the
islands.[122]

Given the funding limitations during the interwar years, ONI was
forced to rely more and more on part-time spies. Some of these individuals, such as Whitney Hart Shepardson, proved to be winners.
Shepardson, a prewar Rhodes Scholar, was a lieutenant in the field
artillery in World War I, but never got to France. After the war, however,
he served as an assistant to Colonel Edward House in 1919 during the
Versailles peace negotiations. In February 1921, Shepardson was recruited
as an ONI volunteer agent, and left for a nine-month trip to England,
France, South Africa, Australia, and New Zealand. He was designated as
Agent No. 291, was given Universal Pocket Code No. 684 (a commercial
code), a Washington post-office box (J. W. Morrow, P.O. Box 1814), and
allowed $300 to cover the purchase of books, maps, and photographs.
What Shepardson returned with is unknown. However, what we do know
is that Shepardson had contracted a virulent case of the intelligence bug.
In 1931 he became vice-president of the International Railways of Central
America, the United Fruit railroad subsidiary. He subsequently helped
found the Council on Foreign Relations and coedited their yearbook, *The
United States and World Affairs*. It was following the German invasion
of Poland in September 1939, and the Wehrmacht's blitzkrieg through the
Low Countries and into France, that Shepardson assisted the British Secret
Intelligence Service in the United States in helping mobilize American

public opinion behind the British. He drafted "A Summons to Speak Out," which was given widespread coverage in the *New York Times* and the *New York Herald Tribune*.[123] Within a year Shepardson was on the ground floor as a new American intelligence service was created.

Interestingly, several of the people with whom he would be associated also had their first taste of intelligence with ONI when, during World War I, Assistant Secretary of the Navy Franklin D. Roosevelt named them as honorary ONI agents. This group was designated in the files as "volunteer agents: Mr. Roosevelt's friends."[124] It included William J. Donovan, future director of the Office of Strategic Services in World War II; his assistant director, G. Edward Buxton, Jr.; Bronson Cutting, future U.S. senator from New Mexico; newspaper publisher and future Secretary of the Navy Frank Knox; and William C. Bullitt, World War II Ambassador to the USSR and France. While it would certainly be a stretch to suggest that Donovan and Buxton cut their eyeteeth on intelligence as ONI volunteer secret agents, it does seem fair to suggest that their interest in intelligence began with ONI in World War I. It should be noted that Shepardson, who spans the period from the end of World War I through the Cold War in intelligence, became the first head of secret intelligence in London in 1942 before returning to Washington as Donovan's secret intelligence chief. He stayed in this position until OSS was dissolved on September 30, 1945, and remained with the Strategic Services Unit and the Central Intelligence Group (CIG) until his resignation in late February 1946. He then became the director of the British Dominions and Colonies Fund of the Carnegie Foundation and served as President of the Free Europe Committee in the 1950s, both of which were CIA cover corporations.[125]

By the late 1920s, John A. Gade, who had been ONI agent No. 60 during World War I, when as a lieutenant commander he had served as the naval attaché in Oslo, Norway, had become an enthusiastic proponent of intelligence; he had remained in the Navy Reserve and proposed that ONI become a major worldwide "full service" intelligence organization. Gade campaigned at least as late as 1934 in favor of ONI becoming that type of agency. CIA historian Thomas Troy notes that Gade's original recommendation in the late 1920s was the first substantive proposal to establish an American intelligence organization such as the Central Intelligence Agency would become.[126]

By the summer of 1940, following the German onslaught into France, it was the Office of Naval Intelligence that first proposed recruiting secret agents and deploying them overseas. Between June 1940 and September 1941, ONI established the Special Intelligence Section (SIS), which recruited thirteen ONI agents. They were spotted, assessed, vetted, and deployed outside the United States, principally to Europe, Asia, and the Middle East during a fifteen-month period. Not only did ONI recruit OSS's first thirteen secret agents, but OSS also copied certain distinctive security characteristics from ONI. For example, it is clear that the OSS agent number scheme was borrowed directly from ONI—during World War II Allen Dulles was No. 110 and Donovan was No. 109. And something as simple as requiring agents to number their reports sequentially was apparently borrowed from ONI. In 1940, ONI established a secret intelligence collection organization in Mexico that operated until the end of World War II.[127] But it would be the OSS (or technically the COI until 1942), that became the overarching American intelligence service in World War II and was the precursor of the CIA. However, the first tentative beginnings of the emergence of a major United States intelligence agency that deployed secret agents worldwide was not the OSS. It was the Office of Naval Intelligence.

By the time of World War II archaeological cover was wearing thin. In a watered-down version of how Morley and his associates had been employed decades earlier, the FBI recruited Edwin Shook and several of his fellow American archaeologists working in Guatemala to keep the Germans in that country under surveillance. The Americans traveled extensively, conducting "archaeological surveys." But this was only a temporary expedient until the FBI could deploy its own personnel. More significantly, the FBI also used an American archaeologist working in Peru—the ONI World War I veteran Samuel K. Lothrop.[128] What gave Shook, Lothrop, and their colleagues credibility was that they really were archaeologists. It was riskier trying to pass off intelligence agents as archaeologists, as when the Germans sent an SS mission to Tibet under archaeological cover in 1938–1939.[129] In 1941, an American intelligence official confronting the problem of inserting an agent into Vichy French North Africa commented:

> far as Anthropology or Archaeology is [sic] concerned the British and Germans have used this cover so hard that membership in any such expedition entitles you to a firing squad without the delay of a trial.[130]

15. Conclusion

The German U-boat fleet posed the most serious threat to the vital interests of the United States in World War I. Not only was American shipping at risk, but German submarines could potentially prevent the American Expeditionary Force from even getting to France. An important aspect of the United States Navy's problem was the possibility of Germany being able to establish secret submarine bases, or at least resupply points, on the coasts of Mexico and Central America. Indeed, Washington continually received reports and rumors to that effect. What lent credibility to these reports was the historic hatred of the United States by Latin American countries. It was therefore imperative that the navy move aggressively to neutralize this threat. Only by dispatching agents to conduct repeated on-the-spot reconnaissance of the coastlines, especially little-known areas such as the Caratasca Lagoon in Honduras and the large bays on the Yucatán peninsula, could these reports be checked out.

It is indisputable that the Imperial German Navy's strategy included the establishment of secret submarine bases. For example, intercepted communications in 1917 and 1918 revealed German efforts to construct at least two resupply points in the region. German plans were predicated on the acquiescence of the governments of Mexico and Central America. Several of these regimes, notably those in Mexico and El Salvador, were outspokenly anti-American. Furthermore, there was a substantial German presence in these countries; German subjects could presumably be counted on to assist the Fatherland.

The German strategy proved overly optimistic. It turned out that the littoral of Mexico and Central America simply did not lend itself to secret submarine bases. And the principal mileage that Germany derived from anti-American sentiment was in terms of receptivity to her propaganda rather than any concrete wartime actions. When, under American pressure, Guatemala, Honduras, Costa Rica, and Panama broke diplomatic relations with Germany, this effectively crippled even propaganda activities in those republics. Granted, Mexico and El Salvador remained anti-American and/or pro-German, but they were incapable of providing meaningful assistance to Germany's schemes. And the 1917 earthquake that devastated the capital took the steam out of El Salvador's defiant attitude, making her even more dependent on the United States. As for Mexico, not only did geographical proximity facilitate American surveillance of German activities there, but the United States had already demonstrated, both in 1914 by seizing Veracruz and in 1916 by dispatching the Punitive Expedition, that if necessary it was prepared to use force in its dealings with Mexico.

Thus it is easy for the historian to conclude that the German menace was greatly exaggerated.[1] Yet one should keep in mind the difference between perception and reality. The perception at the time was that German submarines indeed constituted a grave threat to United States shipping. So the rumors had to be checked out, no matter how improbable they seemed. In this connection, it should be remembered that Japan proved incapable of invading California during World War II, yet in 1942 the perception was that such an invasion was not only possible but imminent, and the population on the West Coast was terrified. Even Admiral Ernest J. King, commander in chief, U.S. Fleet, firmly believed that the Japanese were coming.

In retrospect, of course, the Germans never had a chance. They were, after all, trying to operate in a region already dominated by the United States. This fact has led some to argue that there was really no German threat and that American efforts to combat this nonexistent threat really masked the United States's determination to expand its hegemony.[1] For example, use of the American wartime Black List proved an effective weapon in crippling German business interests in Central America. In the postwar years, American businesses would supplant many of their German competitors. This has sometimes been presented as being somehow reprehensible. Yet there is evidence that nations act in their perceived self-interest. It would be remarkable indeed if the top priority of the United States government was to advance the interests of, say, Albania.

Fortunately for the United States, Sylvanus Morley and his associates were eager to do their patriotic duty. ONI welcomed these volunteers. Since providing cover for its agents was a principal consideration, ONI was delighted to enroll scholars who had established reputations and were familiar with the region where they would be operating as secret agents. It is easy to look with amused condescension on these amateur agents and their frequent lack of tradecraft. But, and this is the crucial point, they were loyal. Today's highly sophisticated technology and intelligence techniques prove useless when traitors such as Aldrich Ames at the CIA and Robert Hanssen at the FBI are busy for years selling the country's most sensitive secrets on a wholesale basis.

As for Sylvanus Morley, he demonstrated a remarkable ability to gather intelligence. His effectiveness stemmed in large measure from his gift for dealing with people, for he moved easily through various strata of society, from peons to presidents. Morley had an omnivorous curiosity about virtually everything, yet this curiosity was coupled with a strong sense of mission. As it became clearer that there were no German submarine bases to be found, increasingly he provided economic and political intelligence, making use of his wide circle of friends and acquaintances. In the process, he established a network of subagents, the network covering much of Central America and southern Mexico. This was arguably the best American intelligence network in World War I. Admittedly, Morley was not politically correct. This is hardly surprising, since virtually no one of his generation was; it would be decades before political correctness was concocted. Morley hated Germans. He referred to them pejoratively as "Huns." This was unquestionably insensitive, but there is considerable evidence that belligerents quite often manifest a shocking lack of sensitivity toward the enemy. While every generation writes its own history, it is all too easy to adopt a presentist point of view, condemning people who lived in the past for not having the values of the present. Were one to reverse this, Morley would have thought it inconceivable that a draft dodger could ever be elected president of the United States, or that Americans would develop an insatiable appetite for porn, drugs, and rock-n'-roll.

Historians of American intelligence have generally dismissed out of hand the early twentieth century, when the emerging American intelligence community was taking its first faltering steps. But by the time of the United States's entry into World War I, there had developed a

considerable amount of intelligence expertise, although some of it had not
yet been institutionalized. During World War I there was an impressive
buildup, particularly in ONI, which was the first organization in American history to deploy agents worldwide. As soon as the war ended,
though, most of the country's intelligence apparatus was dismantled.
Ironically, what happened to ONI mirrored what happened to Morley—
both came full circle. Morley ended by becoming director of the institution where he began his archaeological career, whereas ONI reverted to
its prewar condition of having to rely on contacts in the corporate world
for much of its intelligence. ONI would figuratively have to reinvent the
wheel when World War II came.

Regarding the whole question of the scholar as spy, Franz Boas lost
the ethical battle, but he won the war, at least in anthropological circles.
In his intellectually arrogant and sanctimonious position, Boas was to
some extent merely reflecting the tenor of the times when he asserted that
spying was an indefensible occupation for scientists. Even the United
States Navy viewed spying as an unsuitable occupation for gentlemen;
during World War I not a single career officer functioned as secret agent.
And in 1929, Secretary of State Henry Stimson, in effect, abolished the
Department of State's code-breaking operation, allegedly declaring that
gentlemen do not read each other's mail. That said, Boas's view that scientists are not like other men has remained the prevailing view in the field
of anthropology. For example, the anthropologist Paul Sullivan, writing
in 1989, disapproved of Morley's spying and was dismayed that Boas's
peers had voted to censure him.[2] He cited approvingly the American
Anthropological Association's enjoining its members:

> Do no damage—either to those whom we study or to the reputation
> of our professional community. . . . Do not deceive. Explain the pur-
> poses of your presence and your research, as well as the possible
> consequences for the people whom you study. No surreptitious or
> covert research, and no secret reports to sponsors, especially those
> whose purposes are other than scientific (such as the State
> Department, the Army, the CIA, the Drug Enforcement Agency).[3]

Sullivan's position is interesting, for at the time of writing he was a
professor at Yale University. Yale has probably provided the American

government with more spies—beginning with Nathan Hale—than any other institution of higher education in the United States.[4]

The real issue, of course, is whether American anthropologists in particular and scholars in general can legitimately operate as spies in wartime. Not only did Morley and his associates think so, but so did the directors of the Carnegie Institution of Washington and the American Museum of Natural History, among others. The "others" included the Soviet Union. If Franz Boas was upset by "scientists as spies," he presumably would have had a fit upon learning of the American scientists who spied for the Soviet Union during World War II and after, whether they were atomic scientists such as Ted Hall or social scientists like Maurice Halperin. If wartime spying is legitimate, then does the definition of "war" include a Cold War? Some American academics obviously thought so, since they participated in Operation Camelot, a 1967 CIA operation in Chile that involved social scientists using questionnaires to measure Chileans' susceptibility to communism. When Operation Camelot surfaced, it caused a furor in academic circles, as did the revelation that some social scientists had been supplying cultural information for the American war effort in Vietnam. As a result, the American Anthropological Association in 1967 adopted the above code of ethics strictly prohibiting, among other things, intelligence gathering of any kind. Since then, the American Anthropological Association has somewhat softened its stance, but the ethical controversy rages unchecked.[5] So does the recent acrimony over the study of the Yanomami Indians in the Amazon rain forest.[6] In a postmodern society increasingly governed by situational ethics, it will be instructive to see to what extent anthropologists adhere to their code in the future. And one can state with some degree of certainty that there will always be scholars who spy, whether on behalf of the United States government or against it.

Appendix 1

Report No. 11: "List of Rivers, Bays, and Lagoons on the Mosquito Coast from Trujillo to Bluefields"

Chapaqua River	Closed months. Feb 15 to Oct. 15	
	Maximum depth at bar when open	9'
	Minimum " "	3'
	Average " "	5' to 6'

Small Hondurenean settlement, 3 or 4 houses on W. bank Navigable about 10 miles for boats drawing not more than 5'

Aguan River	Open all year	
	Maximum depth at bar 9' Nov. Dec. Jan.	
	Minimum " "	3' April, May
	Average " "	4' to 5'

Small settlements both sides. W. bank: Bar of the Aguan, Caribs and several whites. Charles Kirkonnell and family from island of Guanaja. One Austrian, Alois Egelsee, uncultivated, and not dangerous. E. Bank: Santa Rosa de Aguan, commandancia, no whites. 24 miles up stream at Tablon an English family by name of Duvall.

Navigable for about 36 miles in the rainy season for Boats drawing not more than 5', and for 14 miles in the dry season.

Limon River	Closed 8 months. Feb. 15 to Oct. 15
	Maximum depth at bar when open 9'
	Minimum " " 3'
	Average " " 4' to 5'
	Small Carib settlement: Limon E. Bank. One American: Austin Gabriel and family. Navigable for about 15 miles in the rainy season for boats drawing not more than 5' and for 10 miles in The dry season.
Salada River	Closed almost entire year.
	Maximum depth when open 5'
	Usual " " 1'
	No settlements. Navigable for pitpans about 30 miles.
Paya or Vallecito River	Same as Salada
	Hondurenean ranch W. bank
Miel River	Same as Salada
	No settlement
Sangrelayn River	Same as Salada
	Iriona, small town on W. bank, population about 250, mostly Hondureanean. There is a commandancia and the last telegraph station on the north coast. Commandante: Dr. Lobos. No Americans or English or Germans. 2 whites: Gabriel Pinseau (French) and Antonio Ylla, Spanish (Catalan). Carib village: Sangrelaya, 4 miles above Iriona on E. bank.
Tocomacho River	Same as Salada
	Small Carib settlement 1/2 mile above mouth. 3 or 4 Germans:
	Dr. Bordenhiever, a physician, 50
	Fred Vitt, a cocoanut planter, 50
	? Chuker, " " 40
	and possible one or two others.
	An Englishman by the name of Bluett has a small plantation and lives in the immediate vicinity.

Black River	Open all year		
	Maximum depth at bar		8'
	Minimum " "		4' 6"
	Average " "		8'

Small settlement: Palacios, W. bank. 2 Americans Riplinger and Downell.

1 mile above mouth W. bank H. E. Dunning an American Carpenter.

5 miles above mouth E. Bank E. A. Bruner an American planter.

Navigable for about 15 miles in the rainy season to the junction of the Paulaya and Sigai rivers for boats drawing not more than 5', and for 10 miles in the dry season. Navigable for pitpans as far as Paya Falls 30 miles up.

Plantain River	Open all year		
	Maximum depth at bar		6'
	Minimum " "		3' 6"
	Average " "		4'

Indian settlement at mouth. 2 Americans, L. T. Potter and Ed Edwards both cocoanut planters, latter on W. bank.

After leaving Plantain river the mountains fall away to the SE until just N of Bluefields. The intervening country is low and flat.

Bruss or Brewers Lagoon	Sept. to Jan.		
	Maximum depth at bar	16' Sept. To Jan.	
	Minimum "	" 6' May to June	
	Average "	"	9'

Mouth 200 yards wide.

Average depth of lagoon 5'. This is reduced to 3' in many places by oyster beds.

An 8" channel passes around W end of lagoon and E of Cannon Islands thence E by S, to Sicri Point on S shore, thence E to cutoff at E end leading to Patuca River.

Small settlement at mouth on W bank. Commandancia. Peter Marin a Belize negro and British subject lives here. He is thoroughly familiar with all parts of the lagoon.

4 small islands, the Cannon Islands, 2 miles S of the mouth. 2 Americans: Willy and John Wood, brothers, 45 and 50 respectively live here with their Negro women.

Indian settlement: Bruss Lagoon, on S shore toward the E end, population about 250.

Ranch on N shore toward E end, an American, Dick Riplinger, 44, lives and manages a big cocoanut plantation which extends from the E side of the mouth of the lagoon, along the shore as far as the Patuca river. His house is visible from the sea, 7 or 8 miles [?] of the mouth as it is built on a narrow spit of sand between the lagoon and the sea. This property belongs to a Frenchman: D. Alvarez, of Ceiba, and is managed by Riplinger. It is called the Bruss Lagoon Cocoanut Company. The land at the W end of the lagoon is poor and swampy. The best land is at the E and S sides where the savanna, or open grassy plain come clear down to the shores of the lagoon.

There is an inland connection or cutoff between the E end of the lagoon and the Patuca river, which has a fairly deep channel, 9' to 10' but a low bar of 3' where it empties into the lagoon.

Patuca River	Open all year		
	Maximum depth at bar		7' Aug. To Dec.
	Minimum " "		4' March to June
	Average " "		5' to 6'

Mouth a quarter mile wide. Bar shifts constantly. 2 channels, deeper one to the E. This enters the river at right angles to it. W channel is shallower and narrower and is only used when the wind is from the E. The water of the Caribbean is discolored for a distance of 7 or 8 miles out to sea at the season of the floods.

The Patuca is a very large river, second only in size to the Wanks. Its bar is the worst on the entire coast W of Cape Gracias and it extends for more than a mile out to sea, and is practically impassible in any strong blow from the NNE or NW. Navigable for about 40 miles for boats drawing not more than 5'.

Tapacunta River

Open all year

Maximum depth at bar   5'

Minimum   "   "   3'

One old man from Haiti, John Benny, lives on W side at mouth.

In the Navy chart of 1877 this bar is shown as having had a depth of 7'. It is not regarded as a channel now, however, by the coast captains and is only used by small Carib boats.

This river which runs out of the W end of Caratasca Lagoon is not only closed at times, but is also shallow and narrow.

Caratasca Lagoon

Open all year

Maximum depth at bar   18'

Minimum   "   "   6'

Average   "   "   8' to 9'

Mouth about a quarter mile wide. After passing mouth of lagoon there are large shallows on each side along N shore, but on S side, particularly in front of the commandancia (Tansin or Ahuiayeri) i.e., just S of the mouth of the lagoon, there is another shallow not over 3' deep extending for a quarter mile off the shore. The largest steamer which had ever navigated on the lagoon is the "Yulu" drawing 8', formerly belonging to the Emory Mahogany Co. Who cut wood on the shores of the lagoon at one time. This was sold by them to the Nicaraguan Government some years ago, and has very recently been purchased by people in the states, after having been laid up here at Bluefields for some years.

The shores of the lagoon are low. The N side is separated from the sea only by a narrow strip of sand covered with low tropical bush. The S side has open rolling savannas covered here and there with scattering groves of pine. This savanna extends for 3 days journey to the S and as far E as the Wanks river.

There is a maze of connecting lagoons on the S and W sides of the large lagoon or Caratasca proper, Guaranta being the largest of those on the W, Tansin of those on the S and Kowkers of those on the E. There is no water connection with the Patuca, although with a small portage the trip can be made in pitpan or cayuca. The Guarunta and Tansin Lagoons are sweet water, which permits the growth of a rank water grass that fouls propellers and renders navigation even by small motor boats almost impossible. These 2 lagoons have a depth of 15', much deeper than salt-water Kowkera, which only has 8'.

The shores of these interlocking lagoons are indented with small bays and there is a maze of channels and islands, the shores of which are for the most part low mangrove swamps.

On the shores of these lagoons and their immediate vicinity there are upward of 1000 Mosquito Indians. The only whites on the lagoon are the Hunter and Haylock families, Island people from Guanaja, who live on the E shore of Kowkera Lagoon, and the occasional residence of 2 Americans, Johnson and Alexander who have ranches E of Kowkera Lagoon. Johnson is manager of the Richard Lehmann Co. at Cape Gracias and Alexander works for the United Fruit Co. at Tela. The only other foreigners on the Lagoon are those employed by the American Chicle Co. The commissary of this company is located on the S side of Tansin Island. The actual chicle camps however are 2, 3 and 4 days journey up the Ibentara River which flows into Tansin Lagoon from the S. The 60 to 80 employees of this company are chiefly Belize Negroes and Mexicans, all chicleros from British Honduras.

The settlements about these lagoons are distributed as follows:

Kaskera	just above point inside	9 people approx.		
Prumetara	1 ^{1}/2 leagues E of mouth	10	"	"
Dapat	1 league from the preceding			
Kowkera	" "	500	"	"
Laca	3 " " and 1 league back from shore	" 250	" "	" "
Nacunta	3 leagues from the preceding	10	"	"
Ahuiayeri or Tansin	3 " " this is the commandancia	"	"	"
Natabila	1 league from the preceding	12	"	"
Mistru	1 ^{1}/2 " " on or near Ibentara River	30	"	"
	Island or Tansin S Side			
Aguastara	2 leagues from the preceding	20	"	"
Kokota	1 " "	12	"	"
Dambila	^{1}/2 " "	10	"	"
Olisanta	^{1}/2 " "	8	"	"
Unuya	^{1}/3 " "	25	"	"
Pueblo Nuevo	^{1}/2 " " Commissary of the Am. Chic. Co. N Side			

| Palaca | Only settlement of N side | 20 | " | " |

After leaving Pueblo Nuevo, there are no
settlements on the SW or W, none in fact
until the house of John Benny is reached at
the mouth of Tapacunta River. See shore.

Huji	8 leagues E of Tapacunta River	7	"	"
Crata	3 " preceding	25	"	"
Yauravila	1 1/2 " "	30	"	"

Cruta River	Open all year	
	Maximum depth at bar	7'
	Minimum " "	4'
	Average " "	5'

2 channels, W one larger and deeper.

Small Hondurenean settlement W bank, commandancia.
Nicaragua claims as far W as this river and has a
commandancia on the E bank at the mouth.

1 mile above mouth on E bank is trading-post of John Border
a British subject from the Cayman Islands. He is very loyal
and only white man on the river.

Many Indian settlements up the river. Land between the
Cruta and the Wanks is low and marshy.

Navigable for 30 miles, as far as Indian settlement of Tipi for
boats drawing not more than 5'.

Just beyond mouth of the Cruta is Cabo Falso or False Cape.
This has a light—the only one of the Hondurenean coast E of
Puerto Cortez, and there is a small Indian settlement at the
same place, only one white—a Spaniard by the name of
Castillo.

| N. Channel Wanks River | Practically closed in March, April, May. | |
| | Maximum depth when open | 6' Sept. |

This is not the main channel or mouth of the Wanks. It
carries less water than the other mouth and is less used.

S. Or Main Channel	Open all year	
Wanks	Maximum depth at bar	6'
	Minimum "	3'
	Average "	4' to 5'

This is the main channel and carries out a tremendous body of water.

Settlement W bank at mouth: Cape Gracias a Dios or on some older charts: Port Dietrich.

The town is administered by Nicaraguan officials, i.e., commandancia and the customs house. Honduras however claims as far E as the Wanks and the site of the place more properly falls in her jurisdiction. Population about 400, mostly Mosquito Indians; there are a number of Negro, Nicaraguan and Island half-breeds however.

There are perhaps 2 dozen whites in all, chiefly Americans and Germans employed by the different mahogany companies which have their headquarters here. This number is constantly changing.

Practically the only large buyers of mahogany here now are the Mengel Bros. Co. of Louisville, Kentucky, the Freiburg Lumber Co. of Cincinnati, Ohio, and the Huddleston and Marsh Co. of New York. These three firms employ a number of subcontractors who do the actual cutting of the mahogany. Some of these are Germans as for example, the von Kurnatowski who sells his wood to the Mengel Co. and the Richard Lehmann Co. which sells its wood to Huddleston and Marsh.

There follows a fairly complete list of the whites although a few names may be missing:

AMERICANS

	[Age]	
J. L. Rogers	30	Manager Freiburg Lumber Co.
E. H. Johnson	35	Employee R. Lehmann Co.
Willie Seat	40	Represents United States Nicaragua Co. Captain of "The Zelaya" riverboat
P. A. Bischoff	28	Represents Mengels (the manager, B. M. White, is absent in the states on his vacation, expected to return about the middle of November.
Kid Green [?]	33	Works for von Kurnatowski, probably cannot return to the states.
W. W. O'Farrell		Representing Huddleston and Marsh
J. E. Williams		" " "
Walter Siler		Works for Mengel Bros. Co.
T. A. Frame	31	Had worked for the Mengels but was discharged.

GERMANS

[Age]

Otto Lehmann	45	Manager of Richard Lehmann and Co. (his cousin). His wife lives in New York and has recently been in trouble with our government.
Th. Von Kurnatowsky	45	Largest mahogany contractor on the river, said to be a decent fellow, who minds his own business. Mengel Bros. Co. is buying about two million feet of mahogany from him this year. He is married to a Nicaraguan.
Willie Drescher	35	Another Mengel Bros. Co. contractor, said to be all right.
Eduardo Kattengill		Works for the R. Lehmann Co.
? Borst	25	Works for Th. von Kurnatowski
? Fuchs or Fox	25	" " "
Max Otel or Ortel	25	" " Bordas mahogany exporters. He is a fanatic and bitterly anti American. The other Germans fear him because they do not know what he will do next. He is a hot head and a featherweight.
Adolfo Omer		{Will investigate these on my return
? Meissner a German sailor		{N and report on them later.

ENGLISH

[Age]

Henry Blakesley	45	British Consul. Claimed by some to be an American named Crawford, who changed his name to Blakesley as a result of some bank scandal in Albany, N.Y. Talks very English and has lived in England. Appears to have money some allege suddenly acquired. He is perfectly loyal.

UP THE WANKS RIVER

[Age]

125 miles above—Richard Eble	40	A German rancher
Mouth 210 miles up—Albert Fagot		Three American brothers keeping
Edwin "		a general store and trading-post
Conrad "		
John Asmussen		A German Dane who also runs a small store
G. R. Heath		An Englishman and the Moravian Missionary of this place
Mouth 350 miles up—? Bergson		A German representing R. Lehmann and Co.

POWER BOATS AT THE MOUTH OF THE WANKS RIVER

I. Boats that go outside

Baldwin	27 H.P.	Mengel Co.	good condition		
Imp	18 "	"	"	"	
Dorothy	52 "	R. Lehmann Co.	poor	"	
Move	10 "	"	"	"	
Lesambre	56 "	"	fair	"	
Consort	10 "	Henry Blakesley	"	"	
Cabo	27 "	"	"	"	
Patria (twin-screw)	48 "	Freiburg Lumber Co.	poor	"	
Rapide	12 "	Williams, an Islander	"	"	

II. River Boats

Deutschland	18 H.P.	Th. von Kurnatowski	fair	"
Fatherland			poor	"
Zelaya		United States Nic. Co.	good	"
		This is the only steam boat on the river. It is a large old stern-wheeler drawing 2'6." It runs as far as Waspock Mouth 210 miles.		
Sea Horse			no good	"
Herald			poor	"

two old hulls belonging to R. Lehmann "

The Wanks is navigable in the rainy seasons as far as Waspock Mouth 210 miles up, for boats drawing not more than 4'. Just beyond this point is Kipliphihini [?], the head of power navigation; pitpans, dories and cayucas can go much farther up. In the dry season navigable as far as the boom, 60 miles up, for boats drawing not more than 5'. Zelaya canal, an old artificial cut for taking out mahogany, runs from the E bank opposite the town to the middle of Sunbeam Bay. On W bank 6 miles above mouth and a little way back is the settlement of Ilaya. Opposite this on E bank there is a small artificially made waterway, through which boats drawing not more than 2' can pass in the rainy season. In the dry season it is practically closed. Formerly it was much deeper.

Land is building out rapidly at the mouth of this river, perhaps as high as 200' a year, and the town is being left farther and farther inland. The bar is constantly shifting, being pushed forward, and the space behind being filled in and becoming parts of the mainland. The former settlement of Cape Gracias a Dios, and the original cape of this name (dating from the visit of Columbus in 1502) is now 4 or 5 miles to the SW.

S. of Cape Gracias a Dios the tide is an important factor in the depths of the bars at any given time, making a difference of as much as 2' between high and low tides. The channels are also uniformly deepest on the S sides of the openings, due to the prevailing winds which are E, and the usual direction of the river currents, SE.

Old Cape Lagoon	Open all year	
	Maximum depth at bar	14'
	Minimum " "	6'

Just inside the lagoon there is a second bar or shoal not more than 2' deep with only a 3' channel through it. Beyond, the lagoon has 6'.

An Indian settlement (the original town of Cape Gracias a Dios) is on the S Bank of the lagoon. Population about 400 or 500, mostly Indians. One white family, all English: L. Taylor, wife and child. T[aylor] is a Moravian Missionary and is well educated. Very loyal. He lives at E end of the village, which stretches for more than a mile along the shore.

The lagoon is pear shaped 4 miles long and 2 miles wide. Originally it was much deeper, indeed 50 years ago an English fleet anchored inside where now there is only 3' to 4'. This silting up was due to the opening of a canal from the Wanks to the lagoon, which caused the latter to fill up and ultimately brought about the change of the principal settlement of the region from here to the mouth of the Wanks.

The E lagoon is even shallower. It extends N of the other and has a tidal channel to within 25 yards of the Zelaya canal.

Bemuna Bay &	For the description of these bodies of water
Wauni Sound	see page 11.

Sandy Bay	Maximum depth at bar	5'
	Minimum " "	3'

A narrow river or creek leading from Sandy Bay proper opens into the sea flowing SE. A shoal not more than 2' deep extends for a half a mile out to sea around the mouth. The channel is on the S side. Just inside the bar the water is 8' or 9' deep but behind i.e., W of Sandy Bay proper has a depth of 6' practically everywhere, and if it were not for this secondary bar of 3' it would be navigable for boats drawing up to 5' or even 6'.

Indian settlement of Sandy Bay on the W side. 2 whites: an old American named Wade who is thoroughly demoralized by the country, i.e., many times a squaw man, and a German Moravian Missionary.

Hausen, Hudson, Huero or Krokera River	Open all year		
	Maximum depth at bar		5' Sept.
	Minimum " "		3' June

Fairly deep channel as far as Tuapi where there are shallows.

Wawa and Karata Lagoons	Open all year		
	Maximum depth at bar		7'
	Minimum " "		3' 6"
	Average " "		5'

Shallow water extends farther out to sea here than at any other bar on the Mosquito Coast, breakers having been noticed as far as 3 miles out.

The bar itself is a mile and a half off shore. The main channel passes through the S side of the bar, although a new and much narrower channel has recently been made farther N. The latter goes almost due E from the mouth of the river. It had 6' of water this Sept.

Once over the bar the lagoon has a good deep channel until it opens into Karata Lagoon where it is 6' deep again. This quickly shallows to 5' the average depth of the lagoon, And to 4' off the village of Karata.

Small settlement S side of mouth: Wawa, population about 50, a commandancia. Just S of this on the coast

Outside is Kiah, population 150.

Indian settlement S side Karata Lagoon, population about 300. One white, a Swede Karl Bunsen, who runs a general store and trading post, and owns a motor boat.

There are two Indian villages on the savanna behind Karata having a population of 100 and 250 respectively

The Wawa River flows into the NW side of Karata Lagoon.

The bar and channel are both deep and the river is navigable as far as the settlement of Ahuiapihini, 30 miles above the bar.

There is considerable mahogany cut on this river, the largest company operating being an English firm, Belanger Incorporated. The manager, a Scotch Canadian by the name of Lauder, lives in Bluefields.

Waunta Lagoon	Open all year		
	Maximum depth at bar		7' Sept., Oct.
	Minimum	"	"	4' July
	Average	"	"	5' to 6'

The channel is again at the S side of the mouth. Shallow water extends quite a distance out, the 2 fathom curve being more than 2 miles off shore. A mahogany steamer "The Paraiso" went ashore there on Sept. 27 and got off. The captain made a survey of these shoals, he told me. Office and Commissary of the Wawa Commercial Company on S bank at mouth. The main logging camps are 30 miles up the river and 5 miles beyond is their boom and the end of power navigation.

The company has 22 miles of railroad.

Richard Lehmann is manager of the concern and he has just returned from the states—Sept. 27—I was told at Cape Gracias that he had been detained there some time pending the investigation of his case by the Federal authorities. He employs a number of Germans, perhaps a half dozen all told, as sub-contractors etc.

Walpasiza River	Open all year		
	Maximum depth at bar		9'
	Minimum	"	"	3'
	Average	"	"	6'

This river is used chiefly when the bar of the Prinzapalka River silts up, and boats drawing 4' or 5' cannot get in there. By using the Walpasiza, however, and going 25 miles up stream, entrance can always be made into the Prinzapalka through an interior connection which is always open.

Prinzapalka River	Open all year		
	Maximum depth at bar		9' Sept. Oct.
	Minimum	"	"	3'
	Average	"	"	6'

Town of Prinzapalka S side of mouth largest settlement on coast since Trujillo, a number of Americans and a few Germans. The chief businesses are mining and mahogany.

The large American mining companies whose mines are located from 100 to 150 miles inland all maintain offices here. The principal companies are The Eden Mining Co. of Philadelphia and the Luz y Angeles—the latter I think—of

New York. These companies employ young Americans, mining engineers, superintendents, managers and doctors, and nothing could start in this region without knowledge thereof quickly reaching our nationals.

The Mengel Bros. Co. have a representative here also.

This is the farthest point N reached by the telephone and telegraph in Nicaragua.

The river is navigable for about 100 miles in power boats. It is a big stream at its flood tide in Sept. and Oct. but shrinks to 3' at the bar in the dry season.

Great River	all year		
	Maximum depth at bar		10'
	Minimum " "		5'
	Average " "		8'

Settlement N bank Great River population 200 or 250. A commandancia. 3 whites: an Englishman ex-soldier by the name of Cooper who teaches the local school and 2 brothers named Sinclair also British subjects from Cayman Brac. [sic] The latter keep a general store and trading-post at the W end of the village.

Across the river is a large two story hotel in fairly good condition built by the same man (Detrick) who built the one at Cape Gracias. It is now owned by the Sinclair Bros. It was never opened. There are two chief industries Mahogany and Banana. There are a few Americans up the river managing banana plantations but no Germans. I was told all the latter had left.

The river is navigable for boats drawing not more than 6' for 100 miles. It was found to have the highest average depth at its bar of any river, bay or lagoon examined except Pearl Lagoon.

Pearl Lagoon	Open all year		
	Maximum depth at bar		10'
	Minimum " "		6'
	Average " "		8'

Small settlement S side of mouth: Pearl Point, population about 30; commandancia and commissary of the Atlantic Fruit Co. here. A few Americans but no Germans.

Principal settlement W side lagoon: Pearl City of Brautigams, population 600 or 700, commandancia, telephone and telegraph. A half dozen Americans live here employed by the Atlantic Fruit Co. The manager is a Swede named Brautigam. No Germans.

The lagoon is very shallow in most places because of the oyster beds, there is however a tortuous S shaped channel from the bar to Pearl City, having a depth of 10'.

Boats drawing 5' or 6' go into the wharf at Pearl Point but there is only 3' of water off the wharf at Pearl City.

The Pearl Lagoon bar was the best examined on the entire trip, and with the exception of bar at Bluefields it is said to be the best on the Mosquito Coast.

Omitted from page 8

Bemuna Bay and Wauni Sound	Open all year

Maximum depth at bar   4'
   Minimum   "   "   3'

Shoals about 3' deep extend for nearly a mile out to sea.

Channel is at the S side. There is a small island, just in the middle of the mouth.

Inside the bar the water varies from 6' to 12'

3 Indian villages on or near Wauni Sound

NW side Wauni 50 people about 6 miles from bar

NW side on Krackpakia Creek: Krackpakia 100 just above preceding: Auyapihini 30

N side Bemuna Bar: Bemuna

There is an interior connection between Bemuna and Sandy Bays.

Sylvanus G. Morley

Appendix 2

Detailed Report of a Coast Reconnaissance of the Peninsula of Yucatan from Xcalac Quintana Roo to Champoton Campeche.

Payo Obispo.   **Capital of Territory of Quintana Roo.**

PRINCIPAL OFFICIALS

Governor: General Octaviano Solis

Commander of troops: Lieutenant-colonel Florentin de la Rosa

Commander of the Flotilla del Sur: Lieutenant-major Edmundo Elizondo

Chief-engineer: Vicente Parrilla

Secretary to governor: Enrique Barragan

Assistant secretary: Armando Zapata Vera

Payo Obispo is located on the western shore of Chetumal Bay at the mouth of the Rio Hondo, 2 /12 miles north of Consejo, the northernmost settlement in British Honduras (pop. about 30) and 12 miles northeast of Corozal, the second largest city in British Honduras (pop. about 2000)

There are two wharves one used by the Flotilla del Sur, and the other by the Custom-house and general public. There is 4' of water at the end of each, and 6' a quarter of a mile off shore.

The electric-light plant and ice-factory are owned and operated by the government, and with the exception of a few store-keepers, chicleros and transients almost the entire male population is employed by the government in one capacity or another.

There are no Germans here or for that matter anywhere else in the Territory of Quintana Roo so far as I could learn.

There is a wireless station with a single tower 45 meters high. It communicates directly with Merida, Campeche and Xcalac all the time, and occasionally with Acapulco Mexico. The operator told me he could hear Swan Island Belize and the U.F.Company stations on the north coast of Honduras but that he did not work with them. The equipment is a 10 kilowatt Deutz Otto (German make), I was told that all the Mexican Government equipment was the same. I was also told that another wireless station was in course of erection at Puerto Moreles, (No. 31) but when we called there I saw no signs of it

Formerly Payo Obispo was the center for a large mahogany, log-wood and chicle export business. But since the C.C.Mengel Mahogany Co. of Louisville, Kentucky was driven out of there three years ago in the Garcilasso revolution the place has been of little importance and has been maintained by the Mexicans more through national pride and necessity than as a source of revenue.

The governor is an illiterate man of 34 from Puebla de los Angeles, and is said to be absolutely just. He has obviously risen from the rank and file, in, and with the revolution. He impressed me as a strong man, and in a military way, capable. His policy seems to be to mind his own business and keep out of trouble, that is to say he is not the intriguing kind so common in these countries. His assistant-secretary, Zapata Vera, told me that several months before he had given some "Guatemaltecan" revolutionists, who were at Xcalac, 3 days to clear out of there. I judge this to have been the same outfit which landed at Rio Esteban on the north coast of Honduras in the latter part of December, a matter already reported both by Held and myself (see my No. 18). This would again appear to indicate that our friend Manuel Estrada Cabrera had his finger in that particular pie.

*   *   *

The actual governing brains however are supplied by his two secretaries but more particularly by the senior Enrique Barragan a young man of 25 from Mexico City. He is very quick alert keen and intelligent without much education; does not speak English but plays baseball and was very friendly to us if indeed not downright pro-American, a very rare thing in a Mexican.

I could see for myself during the two days that we were there that the governor deferred every important decision to him even the matter of giving us a letter of recommendation.

Next in influence comes the assistant secretary Zapata Vera, also from Mexico City, a young man of 21, mother of Scotch parentege,father a Mexican and Under-Secretary for Foreign Affairs under President Diaz. Zapata Vera was educated at Philips Exeter Academy and speaks English fluently and was very friendly too. In fact he was specially delegated to look after us while we were there. He is the chap who is erroneously reported in Belize to be "the German secretary of the governor." This alleged Hun in the Belize story was named Zapata also. His hair is reddish and he has blue eyes on which evidence the credulous Belize creole has made him into a Hun.

These three men govern the territory. Solis provides the strong arm, the executive end as it were, and Barragan and Zapata Vera the brains or legislative and judicial end if I may stretch my simile so far.

About 200 troops are maintained at the capital and in the surrounding region distributed as follows: Payo Obispo 100 (we counted 60 privates in the parade on February 5 here); Bacalar 25 (No. 2); and about 5 each at Chac (No. 3); Sacxan (No. 4); Ramonal (No. 5); Esteves (No.6); Pucte (No. 7); and Blue Creek (No. 8), the last five being small chicle camps on the Rio Hondo, the boundary between Mexico and British Honduras.

In addition to being the capital of the territory Payo Obispo is the headquarters of the Flotilla del Sur which employs about 100 men including machinists, workman, sailors and officers. Most of these are stationed in the machine shops or on the boats at Payo Obispo though a few are at Xcalac. The salaries of these men alone cost the Mexican Government $10,000.00 gold a month.

The Flotilla del Sur consists of three steamboats: the Guatemoc, the Coatzecoalcos and the Explorador (the last being kept at Xcalac for towing purposes) about 28 or 30 tons each. 6 small motor boats (one of these makes 15 miles an hour) 3 stern-wheel river boats and several light draft bungays. There are also several privately owned motor boats in the town.

The commander Lieutenant-major Elizondo speaks English and appears to be very pro-American and certainly is very pro-President Wilson. He seems to be an able officer. The Chief engineer Vicente Parilla also speaks English and is a clever mechanic and machine man.

The Flotilla maintains a fairly well equipped machine and repair shop turning-lathes, drop-forges etc.an ice factory and electric light plant, the last three in charge of Parrilla, a thoroughly capable young man of 28. We saw some of his repair work on broken motor-boat parts that indicates fairly good machine work is being done here. The Flotilla also maintains its own hospital, office buildings and quarters both for officers and men.

In conclusion I should state that notwithstanding the fact that we were Americans and frankly came as such the atmosphere here was distinctly friendly and the allusions to our President were both friendly and flattering. They said quite freely that the election of Mr. Hughes would have meant intervention, and they were glad he had lost. There was a feeling of cordiality expressed which surprised me, and we were taken all over the place, shown everything, and wined and dined and feted, and for once in our long wanderings were made to feel that even as gringoes we were welcome.

I left as agent to cover this vicinity, i.e., Payo Obispo, Bacalar and Xcalac one Mariano Vasquez, who lives at Corozal but who goes over to Payo Obispo trading three or four times a week. He is thoroughly (trustworthy) having been working for Gann for ten years at least, as a collector of his rents. He will work through Gann at Belize making reports to him there and should be paid through Gann as he knows nothing of us, and thinks he is working for Gann only in this matter. He will cost about $15.00 or $20.00 a month.

*   *   *

Motor-boats run from Payo Obispo to La Aguada (No. 9) on the east side of Chetumal Bay, a distance of 30 miles and from there a Decauville Railroad 7 kilometers long runs across the point to Xcalac on the outside.

Held and I came across this way, Gann going around Ambergris in the "Lilian Y." See the itinerary on the accompanying map. Chetumal Bay is very shallow, about 12' deep in the middle but not more than 11 or 12 deep around the edges even a mile or so off shore. There are no houses or people at La Aguada everything having been destroyed by the great cyclone of October 1916, and never has been rebuilt. There is a telephone box and line running over to Xcalac for summoning a mule-drawn tram-car to take one over the Decauville railroad to Xcalac.

*   *   *

10. Xcalac.   The town of Xcalac is 6 miles north of Bacalar Chico Creek a small body of water (1 1/2' to 4' deep) which runs from Chetumal Bay to the sea and separates Mexico from British Honduras here. Xcalac has a pop. of about 150. There is 8' of water inside the reef a quarter of a mile off shore.

There is a small wireless station which however only has a

radius of communication as far as Payo Obispo, a small light house, a broken-down dredge, a ship-repair shop and a few rotting hulls. The place is very much run down, and indeed is largely in ruins having been directly in the main path of the great cyclone of October, 1916 which devastated this whole region.

The steamboat "Explorador" is kept here to tow boats in and out through the opening in the barrier-reef which was enlarged by dynamite some years ago by the Mexican Government to make it safer. It is still an ugly place however, and in any kind of a wind from the north-east, east, or northwest is downright dangerous. Local pilots will not attempt its passage at such times preferring to wait several days if necessary for the sea to go down.

This barrier-reef, which borders the entire east coast of the peninsula is a dangerous business. For example Gann was detained at San Pedro on Ambergris Key for 24 hours waiting for a north-east wind to subside and sufficiently to allow him to come out through the reef in the "Lilian Y." And about a year ago when the Mexican Government sent a troop-transport from Coatzecoalcos to Xcalac it was so rough when the boat got off Xcalac that the captain was afraid to try and run her through the break in the reef, but instead proceeded on to Belize and asked permission of the Governor there to land the troops and send them in smaller boats through British waters behind the keys (Ambergris, Congrejo, Corker and Long Keys) on to Payo Obispo.

The Mexican Government cut an 8' channel from the sea into a small lagoon behind Xcalac to make a safe anchorage for vessels up to that draft, but the mouth of this was filled in with sand in the cyclone already mentioned.

I give these few instances to show that the principal port of the territory, and the gateway to its capital is only an open road-stead, dangerous at best, and frequently altogether impassible.

*   *   *

The coast between Xcalac and Punto Herrero (No. 18) is low flat and sandy; there a few fishing villages and cocoanut plantations, the inhabitants being Maya Indians with an occasional Mexican. There are no foreigners. A list of the settlements follows:

11. Rio Guach	Pop.	30	to	40
12. Chauaixol	"	12	"	15
13. San Francisco	"	8	"	10
14. Majagual	"	25	"	30

17. Ubero   "   50   " 75 This is a cocoanut plantation owned by the
                                             firm of Caldwell and Bonastre of San Miguel
                                             Cozumel.

15. Lobos Key   These two points mark the southern and northern extremities
16. North Key   respectively of the dangerous Chinchorro Banks. Formerly the
                 Mexican Government had light-houses at each point but the one
                 on Lobos Key—the southern extremity-was destroyed in the
                 cyclone of 1916 and has not yet been rebuilt although I heard at
                 Payo Obispo that it soon would be.

18. Punto Herrero.

                 This is the southern point of Espirtu Santo Bay. Pop. about 13 (3
                 light-keepers and their respective families). This light is one of the
                 three most powerful in the territory and consumes $2^{1/2}$ gallons of
                 kerosene nightly. The head-keeper told me two shipments of oil are
                 received annually from Mexico. His light received on each ship-
                 ment: 600 gallons of oil, which was sufficient for 8 months. After
                 such a semi-annual shipment there is quite a quantity of oil stored
                 along this eastern coast of the peninsula. The equipment: lamps,
                 tower, lenses, etc. here and throughout the rest of the light-houses
                 on the coasts of the peninsula is French. There are 11 light-houses
                 in the territory as follows, No. 2 having been destroyed in the
                 cyclone of 1916 as already mentioned:

                        1. Xcalac (No. 10)
                        2. Chinchorro Banks, Lobos Key (No. 15)
                        3. " " North Key (No. 16)
                        4. Punto Herrero (No. 18)
                        5. Ascencion Bay, Punto Allen (No. 21)
                        6. Cozumel Island, Punto Celerain (No. 39)
                        7. San Miguel (No. 32)
                        8. Punto Molas (No. 40)
                        9. Puerto Moreles (No. 31)
                       10. Mugeres Island (No. 50)
                       11. Contoy Island (No. 51)
                       12. Cape Catoche (No. 48)

                 Of these the ones at Punto Herrero, Punto Celerain and Contoy
                 Island are the most powerful. We found all 11 burning regularly.
                 The inspector of light-houses for the territory is a young man
                 named Vidal who was educated at the Van Renssalear Polytechnic
                 Institute and speaks English fluently. He makes his headquarters at
                 San Miguel on the island of Cozumel.

Espiritu Santo
Bay

Just north of Punto Herrero are three very shallow entrances to
Espiritu Santo Bay all of them having less than 3' of water, The
deepest channel into the bay is over against the northern point
(Punto Fupar). This has a 6' depth over the bar. In heavy weather
entrance is dangerous here.

Inside the entrance a depth of 10' may be obtained but this
shades off very quickly to 9', 8', 7', 6', and 5'. The shores are very
very shallow and shoals of l' depth extend a long way out. There
is less than 3' of water a quarter of a mile off shore. The shores are
bordered particularly on the west and south sides by a 10 yard strip
of stinking soft mud almost impossible to wade through, which
makes landing a difficult, laborious and unpleasant process.

There are no people of any nationality not even Maya Indians
living on the shores of the bay, so poor is the surrounding country
and so difficult is it of access both by land and sea.

The soil is a shell-sand mixed with a little earth, which supports scrub growth of salt water pimento palm, sour-grass, mangrove and buttonwood.

Although on the map this body of water appears extremely
well adapted for exploitation against us, the following factors practically negative the possibility of its ever being thus utilized:

1. Very shallow bar, maximum depth 6'

2. Maximum depth inside only 6' and this only in the very
middle.

3. Very shallow water around sides, less than 2' almost
everywhere

4. Strip of soft mud 10 to 15 yards wide around south and
west shores

5. No inhabitants of any nationality on shores or in
immediate vicinity

6. Prevalent winds make the bar rough the greater part of
the year.

There are no people living on the coast between Espiritu Santo and
Ascencion Bays. The shores are low with sand dunes thrown up
just back of the beach line. We put ashore at two places: Punto
Santa Rosa (No. 19) and Punto Pajaros (No. 20) and did a little
exploring behind, as far back as the arm of Ascencion extending
south, which nearly connects it with Espiritu Santo Bay. We saw
no signs of recent human habitation however, and indeed one very
good sign that this littoral is visited but infrequently. The beach
was strewn with more or less valuable wreckage all along: life-pre-
servers, paddles, dories, mahogany logs etc; which would have been

picked up and salvaged if anybody had passed that way recently. We ourselves picked up an excellent little dory in good condition marked "Ti-Tani." One letter more and we would have had the Titanic only the word was hyphenated as I have written it.

I should report here also, the finding of a circular life-buoy in good condition belonging or at least marked: S.S.IAQUA S.F.

The only visitors to this shore, in fact the only inhabitants of the region save the Mexican settlements enumerated here and the Indian villages in the interior are fishing-folk from the Island of Cozumel or from San Pedro on Ambergris Key who come infrequently, and stay only for short periods in the fishing and turtle season—February to March—and Indians who come down to the beach in May-August to collect turtle-eggs.

The barrier-reef continues all along with frequent breaks giving 12' 14' 16' and 18' depths.

Ascencion Bay

The main channel into Ascension Bay is between Point Allen and Culebra Keys and passes just north of Buoy 224. This channel is 14' deep at high tide and 12' deep at all times. Within toward the center depths of 16' and 17' are found everywhere. This shallows down to 6' a quarter of a mile off shore, and to 1' close in. The shores are either rocky or sandy having none of the sticky mud noted in Espiritu Santo Bay.

There are only two permanent settlements on Ascencion Bay: Ascencion on Allen Point (No. 21) and Vigia Chica on the western shore (No. 22). There is a small temporary settlement of fishermen at Boca Paila (No.23) and another on the southeasternmnost of Culebra Keys (No.24), the last two only being occupied during the fishing season from February to May.

Formerly the Mexican Government maintained a small convict camp on the northwestermost of the Culebra Keys but the convicts escaped on a raft in 1911 and the place has since been unoccupied.

21. Ascencion.   Pop. 8, a light-keeper and 2 celadors or under Customs officials and their respective families. The place was formerly the largest town in Quintana Roo boasting a population of 2500. It was founded in 1902 by General Jose Maria de la Vega and was the first Mexican settlement in the region. The wharf is 40 yards long but is now in ruins. It has 6' of water at its end. The Mexican gunboats which formerly made tri-monthly sails to this port and which drew 12' of water used to anchor at Buoy No. 8 which is 5 miles

west by south of Allen Point and 1½ miles southeast of Vigia Chica. There is an abandoned two-masted Mexican gunboat "La Independencia" about a quarter of a mile off Vigia Chica.

22. Vigia Chica. This settlement is the tide-water terminus of the narrow gauge railroad (Ferrocaril Nacional de Quintana Roo) to Santa Cruz de Bravo. Formerly it was a town of 100 people now it is scarcely a third that size.

There is a Mexican lieutenant (Cristobal Sanchez) and a guard of 14 soldiers. These with a few transient chicle-bleeders constitute the present population.

The town suffered heavily in the cyclone of 1916, a barge being washed an eighth of a mile inland. Few of the houses are now habitable, and the whole place: stone wharf, railroad repair-shops, rolling-stock, etc. has already gone to rack and ruin. The wharf has 5' of water at its end at low tide.

26. Santa Cruz de Bravo. The inland terminus of this railroad is Santa Cruz de Bravo 56 kilometers west southwest from Vigia Chica This place was an old Spanish town abandoned in 1848 during the War of the Casta and occupied by the Santa Cruz Indians, a Maya tribe, from that time down to about 1902 when the reconquest of the region was undertaken by General De la Vega, and the town was reoccupied by the Mexicans and made the capital of the territory of Quintana Roo.

It was used for the double purpose of furnishing a convenient base from which the reconquest of the region might be effected and also for the purpose of establishing there a penal colony for the whole of the Republic, a sort of Mexican Botany Bay as it were. In fact the railroad from Vigia to Santa Cruz as well as all the Mexican improvements in both places were built by convict-labor.

The town was at its height in 1908 under General Bravo when it numbered close on to 3000 people. After the success of the Madero revolution the place began to decline and in August 1915 its final abandonment was ordered by General Alvarado then Governor of Yucatan on the grounds that it was too inaccessible and too costly to be maintained further as the capital of the territory. The capital was then removed to Payo Obispo on the shores of Chetumal Bay and Santa Cruz itself was turned over to the Santa Cruz Indians who had claimed it ever since 1848.

This step greatly relieved the tension between the Indians of the region and the Mexicans who had been at war with each other ever since 1848 and there is now in operation between them a sort of "live and let live non-interference with each other" sort of an arrangement.

When I visited the town on February 10 I found it entirely

abandoned save for two families of Santa Cruz Indians; and the fairly extensive improvements of the decade of the Mexican Regime (1905–1915) : electric-light and ice plants, water pumping station, telegraph-lines government offices, stores, restaurants, clubs, hospital, and plaza were fast falling into decay and the jungle was rapidly reclaiming all. The place and its equipment are now a complete ruin, and the millions of dollars spent there by the Mexican Government from 1905 to 1915 is a total loss.

Ferrocaril Nacional de Quintana Roo

The Ferrocaril Nacional de Quintana Roo is a narrow gauge railroad (size of gauge 2' between rails) and about a 20 lb. rail (1¼" wide). Formerly there were 5 small wood-burning locomotives and 30 cars; now there is nothing. All are piles of scrap iron at Vigia Chica. The rolling stock for this railroad was all supplied by Arthur Kopple of Berlin. The line is 56 kilometers long and when the road was in use the bush was kept cleared for a distance of 30 meters on each side of the right-of-way (campo del tiro) so that the Santa Cruz Indians could not attack the trains without being seen. There were six stations, not towns or villages in any sense, but armed military camps:

Station	A	at Kilometer	1	from Vigia Chica
"	B	"	"	10	"	"
"	C	"	"	18	"	"
"	Central	"	"	34	"	"
"	D	"	"	42	"	"
"	Laguna	"	"	52	"	"

There are wells at all these stations but all except Central are now abandoned and are returning to the bush.

When the Mexicans abandoned Santa Cruz two sections of the railroad were torn up in order to prevent the Santa Cruz Indians from attacking Vigia Chica, one near Santa Cruz and the other near Vigia Chica.

The former is between Kilometers 48 and 50 and is slightly over a mile in length, and the latter is between Kilometers 9 and 11 and is slightly under a mile in length. The rails from these two sections have not only been removed but sold.

Within the past two years (1917–1918) three chicle contractors: Julio Martin, a Cuban; Eusebio Alamilla, a British Hondurenean,; and Juan Jerales, a Turk have reached an understanding with the Santa Cruz Indians and an agreement with the Mexican Government and are bleeding in the region.

They have repaired the telephone line as far a Central (Kilometer 34) where Martin has his main camp now, and they use small trucks drawn by mules with the one carry at Kilometers 9–11 to haul out their chicle. Martins camp manager at Central is a Spaniard named Rosendo Villa who was very kind to us.

Returning to Ascencion Bay after leaving Allen Point we put in three miles above to pass the night but saw nothing or nobody. We passed San Juan Point, a rocky promontory with a few deserted fishermens huts in a small inlet behind. Three miles beyond is Chuyum Point and beyond this Boca Paila where we put in again. The shore all along here is low and sandy, and supports a low bush.

23. Boca Paila.   This is the opening of a large arm of Ascencion Bay, and is 25 yards wide. There are two bars, the first a 100 yards off shore has 3' of water and the inner one just where the channel narrows is 4' deep. At this latter point there is a 3 knot current.

Inside there are many arms of the lagoon and depths of 5' may be obtained if the channels are known. There are many shoals however, and if an experienced local pilot is not along even a boat drawing only 3' will ground.

This arm of Ascencion, Boca Paila, extends 8 miles north of here to a canal cut by chicle operators 5 years ago. This extends 4 miles north to Chunyaxche, a long freshwater lagoon which is said to reach almost as far north as Tuluum (No. 26). Maya Indians live around its shores.

In summing up the conditons in and around Ascencion Bay I must confess that physiographically it is not unadapted for use against us. There is a fairly deep channel (minimum 12' at the bar) and the whole western three-quarters of the bay is uninhabited. Lonesome as this part is however, I believe it scarcely possible that even a small sailing vessel could slip either in or out without being detected either by the inhabitants of Vigia Chica or Ascencion. A strange sail is a rara avis in these waters. The Lillian Y for example was the object of everybody's curiosity. Nevertheless physiographically considered Ascencion Bay is the best bet of this kind between there and Caratasca Lagoon on the north coast of Honduras, and as such should be kept under observation.

Politically considered the conditions are more favorable to us. There are no Germans in the entire Ascencion Bay district, and barring the 3 chicle contractors at Vigia Chica; Martin, Vila and Jerales

already mentioned there are no foreigners at all except colonials—
negroes and near negroes from Belize. Of the last there is relatively
a large number engaged in bleeding chicle or in fishing. The rest of
the limited population is Mexican or Indian.

Those colonials working at Vigia Chica or fishing all around
the bay as well as up and down the coast would quickly learn of
any unusual activity in the region and news thereof would quickly
reach Belize and our agent Gann there. The Belize creole is painfully
pro-ally and sees a German in every strange white man he meets,
as Spinden and Held found out to their cost in Belize nearly a year
ago. News of any hostile Teutonic activity in the Ascencion Bay
region would therefore be carried by them to Belize at once.

Then too the temper of the Mexicans in the region appeared
at least neutral and at Payo Obispo as I have already said almost
friendly. At least with Martin, Alamilla and Vila in the region I
think we would get an even break. Finally I am leaving as agent
there a Belize creole Peter Moguel. He will report to Gann at Belize
and indeed knows nothing of his connection with us. He will cost
us in the neighborhood of $25.00 a month.

Continuing up the coast from Ascension Bay we put ashore at three
places between Boca Paila and Puerto Morales: Tuluum (No. 26),
Playa Carmen (No. 29), and Punta Marona (No. 30). There are no
villages or even single ranchos between Ascencion Bay and Acumal
(No. 28) and indeed this part of the coast is the most deserted of
all.

Tuluum.

A large ancient ruined Indian city with a prominent tower on the
top of Kilbride or Ynan cliffs. The city is surrounded on the three
land sides by a high stone wall (15' high and 25' thick). On the sea
side the vertical wall of the cliff forms an adequate protection. This
wall encloses an area 1500' long (N. and S.) by 650' wide (E. and
W.) approximately 22 acres. Just south of the north wall in a shallow cave under an old stone building is a well of very brackish
water. There are openings in the barrier-reef both north and south
of the stone tower, but even in the calmest weather there is always
a heavy surf running here, and great breaker pounding the strand.
All the old captains and pilots of the east coast of the peninsula
agree that Tuluum is the most dangerous landing south of Cape
Catoche. The current here runs very swiftly and old hands venture
within the reef warily. The bottom inside is covered with rock and
the holding qualities of the available anchorages are poor. We
anchored in 18' of water a quarter of a mile off shore.

27. Xelha.

8 miles north of Tuluum there is a narrow opening giving access to
an equally narrow arm of the sea called Xelha which extends inland

for 3 miles. It has 6' of water at the bar. There are no people living on its shores or in fact in the vicinity and there is no protecting barrier reef here, which makes entrance thereto dangerous.

28. Acumal.   Small village of Santa Cruz Indians, Pop. 8 or 10, 4 miles north of Xelha. The opening here in the barrier reef is very narrow—not more than 12 yards wide and its passage is correspondingly hazardous.

29. Playa Carmen.

Village of Yucatecan or pacificado Indians. Pop. about 50. There is no barrier-reef in front of this place but as it is well under the lea of the Island of Cozumel the ordinary surf is not high. There is only 1 small row-boat here and no sail-boats, and the people are as nearly self-supporting as anywhere on this coast.

30. Punto Maroma.

A few fishermen's huts occupied only occasionally during the fishing season. These were deserted when we passed the night there on February 18. There is a dry reef in front of this place which gives it a protection unusual for this coast. The shore is everywhere low and sandy. On chart No. 966 Punta Maroma is incorrectly located north of Puerto Moreles. The point marked Chachatal on Chart No. 966 is probably Punta Maroma.

31. Puerto Moreles.

This place has the only telegraph station on the east coast of the peninsula. Pop. about 20, light-keeper, telegrapher, celador, agent of the chicle company working in the interior and their respective families. The Celador and light-keeper are under the jurisdiction of their respective head officers at San Miguel Cozumel.

The place is on a low sandy shore behind a dry reef which gives it excellent protection against the prevailing easterly winds. We anchored in 18' of water close in.

The wharf was formerly 100 yards long with a depth of 9' at its end, but the middle 100' was destroyed by a hurricane and now only the section adjoining the land is in use.

There is a small light which is raised and lowered on a low steel tower, telegraph office, customs house and two or three dwellings. The Mexican Government keeps a small bungay here for delivering telegrams from Merida and the interior to Cozumel and Ascencion Bay.

40 kilometers from the port and connected with it by a Decauville tram-line is Santa Maria, formerly the headquarters of the Banco de Londres de Mexico's chicle operations in the region. At the beginning of the revolution the Mexican Government took

over the establishment at Santa Maria but are now cutting no chicle there. The 20 odd men in the vicinity of the place are being used to cut wood.

There is considerable travel through Puerto Moreles in both directions, both to Cozumel from Merida and Vica versa. The route followed is railroad Merida to Dzitas and Tizimin, 90 miles mule-back Tizimin to Santa Maria and thence Decauville tram to Puerto Moreles 40 kilometers, and last 18 miles by boat to San Miguel Cozumel.

30 kilometers due west of the port is a large Indian village named Santa Maria Canche. There are no foreigners at Puerto Moreles only Mexicans and Yucatecans.

Cozumel Island

Cozumel Island is about 24 miles long and 8 miles wide at the widest place. It is 9 miles from the nearest point of the mainland, very flat and low and is covered with a thick growth of bush and trees. The chief industries are henequen, cocoanuts and turtle fishing.

The population of the island is about 1800 all living on the western coast or in the interior. No one lives on the east or sea side. There are no foreigners on the island.

32. San Miguel. The principal settlement is the village of San Miguel on the west side, a little nearer the northern than the southern end of the island. Pop. about 1400. The inspector of light-houses for the territory, Vidal makes his headquarters here. There is also an administrador de Aduana here. There are no soldiers and only a few police of the village. There is a small light-house. The wharf is 70 yards long and receives boats up to 5' and 6' draft at its end. The anchorage here is good in all weather save a "norther."

In addition to San Miguel the following settlements are found on the west or lea side of the island.

33. Paraiso.	Pop.	2
34. San Clemente.	"	8
35. San Francisco	"	10
36. Paso de Cedral	"	6
37. Cedral.	Pop.	
38. Rancho de Colombia.	Pop.	100
39. Punto Celerain	Pop.	6 Light-house
40. Punto Molas	"	6 " "

Returning to the mainland between Puerto Moreles and Punto

Nisuc (No.41) there are no settlements on the coast. There is a dry reef along the greater part of this stretch, but no openings in the coast-line proper which continues low and sandy.

Cankuen Island

Cankuen Island is formed by an arm of the sea cutting it off from the mainland. It is 7 miles long and perhaps a quarter of a mile wide at the widest place.

Both mouths Punto Nisuc (No. 41) and Rio de Nichucte (No. 43) are narrow, but within the body of water enlarges to quite a good sized lagoon. This lagoon is known locally by the name of its northern entrance "Rio de Nichucte," or more commonly El Rio.

At this end it is very narrow and with the tide running out has every appearance of being a river. It is salt water throughout however. The bar at the northern entrance at its mouth is $2^{1}/_{2}'$ at low tide and $3^{1}/_{2}'$ at high tide. For nearly a mile the entrance continues narrow, like a river, and then opens into the lagoon proper, which is about 6 miles long. The secondary bar where the lagoon narrows at its northern end is only 2' deep at low tide.

Within the lagoon we got depths of 6' and 7' but we had a local pilot from Isla de Mugeres who was thoroughly familiar with the channels. We were in a row-boat equipped with an Evinrude engine, and in all we drew about $2^{1}/_{2}'$. And with this light draft we only just managed to scrape through.

The bar at the southern end of the lagoon, Punto Nisuc, is about 3' deep. There are no settlements on the east side of the island which is composed of a continuous line of high sand dunes between 40' and 60' high.

42. Cankuen.   On the west or lea side 2 miles north of Punto Nisuc is a small settlement of Mexicans and Indians from Isla de Mugeres. This is called Cankuen and has a population of about 25. There are cocoanut plantations on the lea side and these form the principal industry of the place with fishing as a side line. The principal owner is Vicente Coral from Isla de Mugeres.

44. El Mecco.   Continuing up the coast we put in at El Mecco where there is a prominent tower of stone 40' high. There are fairly high sand dunes close to the shore. There is no barrier-reef here but the place is protected by Mugeres Island. We anchored in 8' of water 200 yards off shore. The shore along here has no permanent habitations only a few fiisheremns huts occupied irregularly in the fishing season.

Laguna las Blancas

This bay is only about 3 miles long. The length of 10 miles given in The Central American and Mexican Pilot (East Coast) p. 292 includes Blanquilla Island which however is separated from the mainland by a good sized stretch of water.

It affords safe anchorage for boats up to 8'. At the end is a small stream—Rio Blanco—navigable for a short distance in canoes and a cocoanut plantation named Islote (No 45) owned by Nicolas Martinez of Merida. It is operated by a Yucatecan named Hilario Canto. Pop. 8.

46. Rio Viejo.   The next settlement on the coast is the rancho of a Yucatecan named Lorenzo Moreno at Rio Viejo. This is located on the north side of the mouth of a small inlet called Rio Viejo, which is northwest of Cayo Sucio, incorrectly given as Cayo Lucio on Chart no. 966. It has $1^{1}/_{2}'$ at its bar and its total length is less than a half a mile. It is navigable only for the very smallest canoes. Pop. 8.

47. Boca de Iglesia.

Between Rio Viejo and Cape Catoche there are no settlements on the mainland. We put in at Boca de Iglesia (No. 47) which is the entrance to a long narrow and very shallow lagoon which extends from this point clear around Cape Catoche and Bolbox Island and is continuous with Yalahau Lagoon. The bar at the mouth is 3' deep but inside the lagoon shallows down quickly and in many places sand banks appear at low tide. We had great difficulty in reaching the ruins of the old Spanish church marked on Chart No. 966, in a shallow draft dory, and we very nearly were left stranded there by the falling tide.

This lagoon is very shallow even at high tide and it could hardly be used against us in anyway. The shallowest draft rowboats would find themselves entrapped at every low tide.

48. Cape Catoche.

Cape Catoche is the northeasternmost point of Yucatan or more properly speaking it projects from a low sandy island separated from the mainland by the lagoon just mentioned. There is a lighthouse and the only inhabitants are the keeper his two assistants, and their respective families, 8 or 10 people in all.

Very shallow shoals extend for a long distance out and even with such a light draft boat as the Lilian Y (5') we could not get any closer in than 2 miles.

Mugeres Island

Mugeres Island is 3 miles distant from the nearest point of the mainland, is 4^1/$_2$ miles long and ^{3}/$_5$ of a mile wide at the widest point. The northern end is sandy and low and the southern end rocky and elevated. There are two settlements on the island: Isla de Mugeres at the northern end and the Mugeres Light-house at the southern end.

49. Isla de Mugeres.

Pop. 300 now dwindling through lack of business to keep the place alive. Fomerly it numbered 400 to 450, when the Mexican gun-boats used to call there regularly. The only industry is fishing though some of the inhabitants have cocoanut plantations on the mainland opposite. There is a celador here. There is a short wharf with 8' of water at its end. We anchored in 10' to 12' of water 100 yards off shore. There are no foreigners on the island, only Mexicans, Yucatecans and Indians.

Gann heard an interesting story here which however we have been unable to verify either through our Consul in Progreso or our man here in Merida, and which I therefore pass on to you only for what it is worth as hearsay.

A man in the village told Gann that sometime during the first half of 1916 3 Germans had come around from Progreso in a sailing vessel about the size of the "Lilian Y," had touched at Mugeres only for 3 or 4 hours and then had gone on down the coast, and were seen no more. Further the informant knew that they were Germans because they did not speak either English or Maya or Spanish but some language unknown to him. I did my best to run this story to ground both in Progreso and in Merida but without success. Consul Marsh at Progreso knew of no Germans having gone up the coast from Progreso in the past two years and in spite of the fact that we inquired everywhere for 'estranjeros" we seemed to have been the only ones in the region for the past two years.

If 3 Germans did come along this coast in 1916 (you will note before our entrance into the war) they must have reported upon it as unfavorable to their purposes because I feel confident no German activities are going on along this coast at present. However I very much doubt the accuracy of the whole story or at least the German part of it.

I also heard at Isla de Mugeres that 3 Americans had come around from Progreso in December (1917) in a sail-boat looking for ruins, and that they had put in at Mugeres for a pilot to take them over to El Mecco on the mainland. They did not return to Mugeres.

Consul Marsh at Progreso could throw no light on this party either. My informant was sure this last party was Americans. At least they were our friends and we had to let it go at that. Before I finally leave Yucatan I shall make further efforts to find more out about these two "entradas."

One of them I believe must refer to a party of 3 Americans who were up this coast in 1911 exploring the archaeological remains and Gann's informant got the date mixed.

50. Mugeres Light-house.

On the high rocky promontory on the southern end of the island is Mugeres light. The keeper's name is Jose Sanchez and he with his family of 8 are the only people living at this end of the island. His oldest son is his only assistant.

51. Contoy Island.

Contoy Island is 4$^{1}/_{2}$ miles long by $^{1}/_{2}$ mile wide at the widest point. It is low and sandy with a line of dunes along its eastern side, The west side has many small lagoons. The coast is skirted by a nearly dry-reef 200 yards off shore. The only settlement is the light-house at the northern end and the only people its keeper, Sabino Reyes and his 2 assistants.

After rounding Cape Catoche several noticeable changes appear. In the first place the barrier-reef of the east coast does not occur, nor indeed the tremendous depths just off it, so characteristic of the east side of the peninsula. Sandy shoals on the other hand giving shallow soundings extend far out and even in a slight draft boat like the "Lilian Y" both our captain and the local pilot advised standing 2 to 3 miles off shore. There are many banks and we bumped on the bottom whenever we tried to run in close.

A second difference is that the sea does not usually run so high along the north and west coasts of the peninsula as along the east coast; and except in a norther or a hurricane little danger is to be apprehended on the north and west coasts.

Finally shallow lagoons (probably due to the land building out as along the Mosquitia)—which in some places entirely disappear in the dry season, January to May—parallel the entire north coast practically from Cape Catoche (No. 48) to Boca Canio Venecia (No. 82), so that with few exceptions most of the places shown on the accompanying map between Nos. 48 and 82 are on a narrow strip of land which is occasionally separated from the mainland by shallow lagoons.

52. Holbox.   Small fishing village Pop. about 150 all, Yucatecan or Mexican. It is located on the northern shore of Holbox Island near the western end. (There is a celador, a judge and several minor officials.)

There is no wharf. We anchored in 9' of water 200 yards off shore. The only business is fishing.

53. Chiquila. South of Holbox Island on the mainland. One man Mercedes Cettina and his family of 6 or 7 live here. He is the local agent for the Compania Comercial de Fincas Rusticas (described under No. 56). There is a Decauville tram-line 5 miles long from here to the interior to the sugar and rum plantation of Ingenio and another extending westward along the coast 25 miles to El Cuyo (No. 56), the headquarters of the company.

Yalahau Lagoon

The main channel into this lagoon (Boca de Conil) is just west of Holbox Island. From here 8' of water may be obtained to Yalahau. (No. 54) on the southern shore of the lagoon. From Yalahau eastward 6' of water is found to within $1^{1}/_{2}$ miles of Chiquila. For the rest of the lagoon is filled with sand banks showing 6' to 3' soundings and in places are even exposed at low tide. In some places on the other hand 12' depths may be found.

54. Yalahau. The town of Yalahau was formerly a thriving place but now it is entirely abandoned not one soul living there. All the inhabitants have emigrated either to Chiquila, or Holbox or to Cayo. There are the remains of a wooden wharf with less than 2' of water it its end. We anchored in $6^{1}/_{2}'$ of water 300 yards off shore. There is an old Spanish fort and a white stone house, the latter appearing from the roadstead.

Between Yalahau and Cuyo (No.56) at Chipepte (No.55) the boundary between Quintana Roo and Yucatan comes down to the sea. No one lives here. From El Cuyo the first settlement in the state of Yucatan the coast is more thickly settled and there is more coast-wise traffic.

Our problem also changes somewhat. Practically all the settlements in Quintana Roo including the capital are either directly on the seashore or upon the shores of bodies of water emptying thereinto, such as Chetumal Bay or Bacalar Lagoon. This is true because the independent Maya Indian tribe of the Santa Cruz hold the interior of the territory and will not permit the Mexicans to open it up and to settle there. A coast survey therefore of Quintana Roo covers the whole territory from the Mexican point of view, the interior being an all but trackless jungle held by unfriendly not to say hostile Indians.

General Francisco Mai at Chunpup 25 miles northwest of Vigia Chica (No. 22) is the supreme chief of this tribe. There are secondary chieftans at San Antonio Muyil west of Acumal (No. 28), and another at Chan Santa Cruz north of Bacalar (No. 2). The Santa Cruz Indians mistrust and dislike the Mexicans, and no coop-eration between them against us may be feared under any circum-stances that are likely to arise. Less than two years ago this same General Mai sent a delegation to Belize to ask the governor there if they could transfer their allegiance from Mexico to Great Britain and place themselves and their territory under the protection of the British flag. They hate the Mexicans and it has only been since Santa Cruz was returned to them 3 years ago that they have left off murdering them whenever they could catch them out in the bush.

The problem in the states of Yucatan and Campeche on the other hand is interior and political rather than coastal, but in order to present a complete survey of the coast clear around the penin-sula from Xcalac to Champoton, the coastal features of both Yucatan and Campeche will be included here, while their political conditions will be reserved for a later report.

56. Cuyo.   Cuyo or Monte de Cuyo is so named for a large ancient mound, 26' high a few hundred yards back from the beach, The light-house now rises from its summit. The town has a population of 250 and is located on a very narrow strip of land between the sea and the Rio Lagarto a salt water lagoon. There is a celador and several other minor officials.

The wharf is 350' long with a depth of 7' at its end. The head-quarters of the Compania Comercial de Fincas Rusticas, a branch of the Banco Nacional are located here, and the various activities of this company give rise to about all the business of the place.

This company raises sugar, cuts wood (cedar) and formerly made rum but since the state of Yucatan went dry, as well as Campeche, this best paying branch of the business has had to be discontinued. They also have large salt pans on the shores of the Rio Lagartos for evaporating salt.

The company employs about 150 men distributed among their five plantations: Ingenio, Santo Eusebio, Moctezma, Otzceh and Solferino. These are connected with Cuyo by a Decauville tram-line which crosses the shallow Rio Lagartos just behind the town and then divides, one branch going east some 30 miles to Chiquila and Ingenio, and the other south some 25 miles to Otzceh, whence a 25 mile mule-back ride brings one to Tizimin and the railroad line to Merida.

There are five light-houses along the coast of the State of Yucatan as follows, all of which we found running regularly:

    1. Cuyo (No.56)

    2. Punto Yalkubu (No. 65)

    3. Progreso (No. 77)

    4. Sisal (No. 80)

    5. Celestun No. 81)

Between Cuyo and Rio Lagartos there are four more salt works or evaporating pans each in charge of a single man as follows:

57. Alegrias.   5 miles West of Cuyo

58. San Fernando.

    8 " " " Alegrias

59. Coloradas. 5 " " " San Fernando

60. Mulsinik.   5 " " " Coloradas

62. Rio Lagartos

This arm of the sea is known locally as a river but it is really a salt water lagoon. There is only 2' of water over the bar at low tide and 3' at high tide. Inside depths of 6' and 7' are found. For the most part it is very shallow however as for example behind Cuyo where it is only 1' deep.

There are extensive salt beds along its shores and this forms one of the chief sources of employment for the limited population of the region.

It extends eastward as far as the boundary of Quintana Roo where it opens out into a large and shallow body of water. Westward it extends more or less continuously to Boca Canio Venecia (No. 82).

61. Lagartos.   Just inside and to the east of the mouth is Lagartos on the north side of the lagoon. Pop. about 200 all Yucatecan. Principal industries saltworks and fishing.

63. San Felipe.   Just inside and to the west of the mouth is San Felipe also on the north side of the lagoon. Pop. about 100 all Yucatecan. Principal industries salt-works and fishing. There is a celador at San Felipe who also does for Lagartos. There is a 3-masted schooner wrecked off San Felipe.

She has been there more then a year and is said to be in good condition.

64. Chisacab.   Some 12 or 15 miles west of San Felipe there is a cocoanut plantation with 4 or 5 caretakers.

65. Yalkubu Point

There is a light-house here.

66. Boca de Silam.

> This is another mouth of the same lagoon which is known farther east as the Rio Lagartos. There is 7' of water at the bar and 6' for a short distance within. Nobody lives here.

67. Puerto de Silam.

> Pop. about 350. Principal industry the exportation of henequen which is shipped here. There is a celador and one or two minor officials, all Yucatecan. The approach is very shallow. We grounded repeatedly 1 1/2 miles out looking for the channel. There is however a 6' channel clear in to the end of the wooden wharf.
>
> The port is connected by a Decauville tram-line with the town of Silan (No. 68) 8 miles inland which in turn is connected with the town of Chemax by the same tram-line, which Is connected with Merida by railroad. (See map)
>
> Between Puerto Silan and Progreso there are 8 small villages and settlements as follows:

69. Minas de Oro.

> 5 miles from Puerto de Silam pop. about 100 tram-line to interior.

70. Santa Clars.	3	"	"	Minas de Oro	"	"	300	" " " "
71. San Crisante	10	"	"	Santa Clara.	Very few people only industry salt-works			
72. Telchac	5	"	"	San Crisante	pop.about 800 tram-line to Motul, R.R.to Merida			
73. Ixil	5	"	"	Telchac	Very few people henequen			
74. San Benito	5	"	"	Ixil	" " " only industry salt-works			
75. Uaimitun	3	"	"	San Benito	" " "			
76. Chicxulub	5	"	"	Uaimitun	" " "			

77. Progreso. Pop. between 7000 and 8000. The principal port of the Peninsula of Yucatan. There are two railroads to Merida the capital of the State of Yucatan 25 miles south, one standard and the other narrow gauge. There are 3 trains daily each way. There is a telegraph office, light-house customs-house etc. but no wireless station. There are three wharfs and the following lines have more or less regular sailings to this port:

> 1. New York & Cuba Mail S.S. Co. (Ward Line) sailings both to New York and New Orleans.
>
> 2. Kerr S.S. Co. sailings both to New York and New Orleans.
>
> 3. Compania de Fomento del Sureste S.A. (formerly Compania de Navegacion de Mexico) operates from Progreso along

the gulf coast of Mexico, Campeche, Laguna del Carmen, Frontera, Puerto Mexico and Vera Cruz.

4. Wolvin S.S. Co. occasional sailings only.

5. "The Frontera" owned by a Yucatecan Manuel Sosa, operates along the Gulf coast of Mexico and occasionally as far around as New Orleans.

6. Occasional tramp steamers from Cuba and elsewhere.

The larger boats, like those of the Ward Line, all have to anchor from 3 to 6 miles off shore. The port is only an open roadstead and in the norther season is dangerous particularly for small boats. The Mexican Government has heavy sunken chains in the roadstead and small vessels may anchor to these at a cost of $5.00 gold a night.

The chief exports are henequen, hides and chicle, the last two being far behind the first in importance. Henequen is the substance from which binder twine is made and is an absolute sine qua non for the harvesting of our great grain crops. The terrific price to which it has risen under war conditions—20 cents the pound—has given rise to an extraordinary economic situation down here which I will cover in my next report as it has a very definite bearing not only on the politics of the State of Yucatan but also on the whole republic of Mexico since it is from this state that Carranza draws his chief revenue.

Neither will I go into the extraordinary labor conditions prevailing here now, reserving that matter also for a subsequent report. I may say in passing however that owing to the existence of an extremely well organized union of dock hands and stevedores this class of labor at Progreso is now receiving from $10.00 to $22.50 gold per day. These laborers are mostly Yucatecan and Mexican. The cost of living is enormous even compared to our war prices at home, sugar for example in a sugar country is .60 cents gold a pound, and except for the grandiloquent sound of their wages the laborers are worse off than under the old regime where if wages were lower the cost of living was even lower still. The keeper of the wharfs is a British subject from Corozal British Honduras and lately in the service of the government of that colony. In Belize he never earned more than $75.00 gold a month. Here he earns $225.00 gold the month. His name is Fernand Villamar.

The Collector of the Customs is a Mexican Francisco Ramos. The commandante is also a Mexican and said to be a decent fellow.

The entire foreign population numbers about 100 distributed about as follows:

Americans	4
Italians about	6
Spaniards "	20
Syrians	15 to 20
Chinese	20 to 30
Germans	6

The remainder are British subjects, chiefly negroes and creoles from Belize.

The Germans are all men of little or no education and no ability, Consul Marsh tells me. They are employed on the docks as stevedores, baggage handlers etc. One works in the Custom-house. One by the name of Kellar is rumored to have blown up a munitions plant at home.

Of a different class and probably more dangerous is a young German about 23 years old who has recently come from Mexico City. His name is Ernest Kentzler and his father is on the American Black List in Mexico City.

He came to Progreso with a letter of introduction from his father in which the relationship between them is deliberately concealed, and he is referred to as a friend, Consul Marsh is keeping his eyes on him and all his movements are closely watched.

I will speak of but one more thing at Progreso at this time namely the German newspaper there "El Boletin de la Guerra." The editor is a Yucatecan named Herman Lopez Trujillo. It was formerly supported largely by its advertisements, but Consul Marsh has frightened most of these out of it and it is now supported to quote its own words "by friends of the cause." It probably receives help from the Boletin de la Guerra in Mexico City. Marsh reports that it has dwindled in size from a four page to a one page affair and he believes that it is on its last legs.

Marsh appears to be a live wire and our interests are being well looked after. He has doubtless covered all this ground and much more besides but I am including the few points I have made here to make this report complete.

78. Chelen.	Fishing village 6 miles west of Progreso pop. 150 no celador.
79. Chuvelna.	" " 2 " " " Chelen " 50 to 100 no celador.
80. Sisal	" " Pop. about 100. Formerly Sisal was the chief port of Yucatan, but since the establishment of Progreso 60 years ago it has been almost entirely abandoned. Formerly there was a telegraph station here but this has been removed to Celestun (No. 81). The nearest railroad is 12 miles distant.

There is 12' of water 200 yards off shore and 3' at the end of the piling which was formerly the wharf. The anchorage is bad in a norther. Few boats call there now. Previous to the visit of the 'Lilian Y" there had not been a boat in the port for a year.

The light-house is a red tower which rises from the northwest corner of the old Spanish fort. The single keeper A. Erena a man about 52 years old claims to be a Hollander. He was a ships carpenter in Pacific waters for 23 years. He has been in the Mexican light-house service for 6 years in other Gulf stations. He speaks English, has lived in the states and claims he has great trouble in collecting his wages. ($3.75 Mex. a day) He claims this pay is insufficient to live upon with the prevailing high prices, and he appeared to be greatly dissatisfied with the present regime, mourning the vanished glories of the Diaz Administration.

81. Celestun.   Pop. about 600 all Yucatecan and Indian. Nearest railroad point Chanchucmil 20 miles distant. There is a light-house and telegraph station here. We anchored in 6' of water 100 yards off shore. The town is supported by a natural salt deposit which runs parallel to the coast about a quarter of a mile inland. It is 9 miles long. Celestun is the last settlement in the State of Yucatan, the boundary line between Yucatan and Campeche passing 2 miles south of the town.

82. Boca Canio Venecia.
6 miles south of Celestun. This is the mouth of the same lagoon which extends north and east as far as Progreso in the rainy season. It is dry for most of the year however except for the lower 12 miles. There are a few fishermen's huts -not occupied—and a cocoanut grove on the northern side of the mouth and one man living on the southern side. No one lives on the shores of the lagoon. (There is 6' of water over the bar).

83. Punto Piedras.
A few fishermen's huts occupied only during the fishing season.

84. Rio Jaina.   A small river 15 miles north of Campeche. It has 1 1/2' of water at the bar. The river extends only a few hundred yards inland and ends in a swamp. There are a few fishermen's huts and a white stone house, these are only occupied in the fishing season. 9' of water 200 yards off shore.

The coast between Progreso and Campeche is low and sandy, scrub bush, mangrove and occasional cocoanut grove. The bights along the shore have a maximum depth of 3'.

The low range of hills which traverses Yucatan from northwest to southeast comes down to the shore about 5 miles north of

Campeche and from here south follows the coast as far south as we went, i.e., Champoton (No. 96).

85. Campeche. Capital of State of Campeche Pop. 25000. It is connected with Merida by telegraph and also with the rest of the republic. It is also connected with Merida by railroad (5 hours). There is a wireless station located on the summit of the hill of San Miguel Castle (320' high) 3 miles south of the city (No. 86). We did not have an opportunity of seeing the station and I can give no information as to its equipment.

So far south as we went we encountered 3 lighthouses in the State of Campeche all burning regularly:

San Miguel Castle (No. 86)

Morros Point (No. 91)

Champoton (No. 96)

There is a wharf but the roadstead is so shallow that even the Lilian Y could only get within 200 yards of shore.

There are about 12 Germans in the town of which I give only the names of the most important.

1. Robert Alcantrop or Archentrupp is the Norwegian Consul, an officer in the German Army and manager of the electric light plant of Campeche and runs the newspaper. He is regarded as an able man.

2. Henry Luis Cramer is probably the ablest German in Campeche. He was described to me by an American named Watkins who worked for Mason and Mechling when they were down here as "a Mexican spy." Consul Marsh tells me that this name Cramer is probably only a nomme du guerre. He is an expert machinist, speaks English fluently, pretends to be very friendly with Americans but is crooked. He spends a great deal of his time in Progreso.

3. Henry Berger, a mechanic fairly skilled.

4. Adolf Hinze works in the electric-light-plant. Of these the first two are by far the most important.

We had less than a day in Campeche and as most of that was spent in the Custom-house in the vain endeavor to expedite the clearing of the "Lilian Y' for Champoton we did not see much of the town. Then too the American upon whom I had relied upon for most of my information about the place was away, and I did not know a soul there. As I expect to have to return to Campeche before finally leaving Yucatan I will defer further report upon the place until later.

When we finally got the "Lilian Y" cleared for Champoton only 33 miles distant it cost me $25.00 gold! When I complained they dragged out a lot of dusty tomes and read me "leyes" until my head reeled. And all expenses everywhere in the peninsula are up in proportion.

You will not wonder when you see my expense account that I had to cable you for a thousand gold muy pronto, and I will have to have another five hundred before I get away.

86. San Miguel and San Luis Castles.
The former is on the high hill 3 miles south of Campeche where the single wireless tower is erected, and the other is at the foot of the same hill.

87. San Bartolo. Wood, charcoal and cattle plantation.

88. Lerma. Small village 4 miles south of Campeche.

89. San Lorenzo.
Pop. 20 to 30 Henequen and corn plantation owner a Yucatecan named Pedro Aguirre who lives at Campeche. There is a private telephone line connecting the plantation with Campeche.

90. Uoxel. Pop. 20 to 30 Henequen plantation owned by Spaniard named Francisco Vetancourt of Campeche. There is a private telephone line connecting the plantation with Campeche.

91. Morros Light-house.
This light is fairly well elevated on a rocky promontory and is watched by two keepers.

92. Seibaplaya. Fishing pop. about 800 all Yucatecan or Indian, one negro in the place. No telephone or telegraph. The water is very shallow off the town. We anchored in 8' of water about a mile off shore.

93. Siho. Henequen plantation, a branch of the next described.

94. Haltunchen. Large henequen and sugar plantation, a great deal of rum was formerly made here, but since Campeche has gone dry this has been discontinued. It belonged formerly to the Banco de Londres de Mexico. The Mayordomo or manager is a Yucatecan. This is perhaps the largest plantation on the west coast of the peninsula.

95. Paraiso. Sugar plantation on the north bank of the Champoton river just across from the town of Champoton.

96. Champoton. Pop. 1200–1600. Telegraph station and light-house. The town is located on the south bank of the Champoton River at the mouth and just across from No. 95. The Champoton River has a depth at its bar of 3' to 3$^{1}/_{2}$' at low tide a never more than 5' at any time.

Inside it varies from 18' to 24' deep and so continues for about 20 miles to Kanasalla (No. 97) the head of navigation. The chicle companies working in the interior i.e., the eastern part of the state and over into Quintana Roo land their supplies at Champoton send them up the river by boat to Kanasalla and thence overland by mule to the various camps.

The approach to the town is very shallow. We anchored in 8' of water a mile off shore.

The only foreigner of any nationality that we were able to locate in the town was an ex-priest, a Spaniard by the name of Rodriguez (Felix). Alvarado seems to have had a particular grudge against the Roman Catholic Church, and he allowed but one priest for the whole state of Campeche. This threw a good many of the padres out of jobs, and our friend Rodriguez himself looked a bit down at the heel.

The Government telegraph line from Merida and Campeche running south to the rest of the republic comes down to the beach between Seibaplaya and Champoton. It carries four wires entering and leaving Champoton, and after leaving follows south along the beach.

These four telegraph wires are carried across the Champoton River by 2 high poles one on each side perhaps 100 yards apart and each 60' high. From any distance out at sea these look like the two towers of a wireless station, indeed Held so identified them, before we came ashore and discovered their true function. This resemblance is probably the foundation upon which the story of a wireless station here rests, a rumor which crops up from time to time and has had rather a wide dissemination. It even reached as far as Belize where it appeared as a story that Germans were operating a wireless station at Champoton. Held got an even more circumstantial account from Consul Marsh at Progreso to the effect that there were two high towers at the Champoton River with wires between them. This story was brought in by Indians. Marsh also told me of vague rumors of a wireless plant at Champoton.

Diligent questioning at Champoton failed to develop any suspicious characters or in fact any foreigners in the region except the 2 Germans at the plantation of Saccacal (No. 98) next described; and the chance resemblance of these two high telegraph poles with four wires stretching between across the river to the antennae of a wireless installation seemed more than sufficient to account for the vague rumors already mentioned, especially since we saw no other poles or steel towers in the town.

For the rest the place is very much down at the heel like its ex-padre. The export of chicle was the chief business, but since the

American Chicle company was driven out of this region in the Manuel Castillo Brito revolution several years ago the place has been steadily declining. There is a Custom-house and an Administrador.

98. Saccacal. A henequen plantation 15 miles south of Champoton. It is owned by the American Manufacturing Company of Brooklyn. The manager until very recently was a man named Kosbiel, a German-American I believe, whom I knew fairly well five years ago before there were such pestiferous things. I understand that during the first years of the war-that is before we went in-he was pro-German. He has been in the states now for some 7 or 8 months, and the British Consul here in Merida told Gann last week that he had heard from K. recently to the effect that he (K.) had made a lucky strike in oil and would therefore not return to Yucatan.

The only two Germans south of Campeche that we heard of, say as far south as the eastern side of the Bahia de Terminos are employed on this plantation. One Adolf Raab is the manager in Kosbiel's absence, and the other Gustav Walker is his assistant. Raab is described to me as a clever and able fellow. As both are being employed by an American firm their discharge can easily be procured at that end if you deem the matter of sufficient importance to take it up. Raab has been in Progreso during the past week.

Kosbiel once asked me to go out to Saccacal with him and see some ruins that were on the place, and if I hear anything further about this alleged Champoton wireless plant I will take an archaeological pasear out that way before we leave.

Champoton was our "fartherest south" on the west coast of the Peninsula of Yucatan and after reaching there we turned back.

(Copy of S. G. Morley's report, File 20977–14A. O.N.I.)

Appendix 3

Report No. 22: "Detailed Report of Coast Reconnaissance from Champoton, Campeche to Frontera, Tabasco"

South of Champoton (No. 96) the coast continues low and flat. The hills gradually draw away from the shore, and as the coast swings more and more away to the southwest they finally disappeared inland. There are no streams or arms of the sea until the eastern end of the Laguna de Terminos is reached, i.e., La Aguada (No. 109).

No. 99 Chankon. 8 leagues south of Champoton, pop. about 6 [?]. This is the landing or "paso" of the large American owned plantation "San Pablo" (The San Pablo Development Co., Philadelphia) which figured in our courts five years ago, and whose promoters, Martley and Miller, were sentenced to prison for misuse of the United States Mails in connection with the same. Formerly there was a wharf, but this has now fallen into disrepair. There is a telephone-line connecting this landing with San Pablo, 10 kilometers inland, and also a Decauville tram-line thereto. A small stream "El Rampida" enters the sea at this point; it has $1^{1}/_{2}'$ at the bar at high tide, and is only navigable for a short distance even by the smallest canoes. It is used chiefly in getting out lumber.

No. 100 San Pablo. Pop. 200 to 300. Headquarters of the San Pablo Development Co. The only work now going on here is the cultivation of sisal. The present manager is an Italian, Felipe Beltramo. The lands of this company extend south to within 2 miles of Varadero (No. 102).

No. 101 Niche. Few fishermens huts only occupied occasionally during the fishing season. It is on the lands of the San Pablo Development Co.

No. 102 Varadero. A few deserted huts on the mainland behind the Estero de Sabanuey. This arm of the sea commences in the neighborhood of Varadero and parallels the sea from here southwest to La Aguada opening into the eastern end of the Laguna de Terminos. There is a short tram-line from Varadero across the intervening strip of land down to the beach. The owner is a Yucatecan named Aceret.

No. 103 Paso de Sabancuy. Pop. 6–8. There is a government telegraph station on the beach here the first south of Champoton and three or four huts.

No. 104 Sabancuy. Pop. 400 all Mexican. This is a mile from the preceding and back from the shore on the Estero de Sabancuy. It is a fishing village.

No. 105 Las Palmas. Pop. 8–10 large cocoanut plantation owned by a Mexican, Emilio Acosta living at Ciudad del Carmen.

No. 106 Tichel. Pop. 8–10 just behind the preceding on the Estero de Sabancuy, a lime and cattle plantation also owned by Acosta. Mr. Robert Boyd of Ciudad del Carmen, an American citizen, holds a mortgage on this and the preceding.

No. 107 Cubos. Pop. 8–10, large cocoanut plantation owned by the widow of a Mexican named Manuel Pinto now living in Campeche.

No. 108 Puerto Escondido. This mouth of the Laguna de Terminos is closed now, and indeed most of the time. It is only open during rare intervals of exceptionally high water. No one lives here.

No. 109 La Aguada. Pop. 330, all Mexican. Government telegraph station and lighthouse. It is chiefly a fishing village. It is located on the mainland at the eastern entrance of the Laguna de Terminos.

The Laguna de Terminos

The Laguna de Terminos is a large body of salt-water approximately 30 miles long (east and west) and 15 miles wide (north and south). It is separated from the sea by the long narrow island of Carmen (No. 115) and Point Xicalango (No. 124) 4 miles wide; and the smaller and eastern one—just west of La Aguada (No. 109) a quarter of a mile wide.

Formerly there was a third and very much smaller entrance at Puerto Escondido, (No. 108). This is incorrectly shown on Chart No. 1295 of the Hydrographic Office as being open and having 2 fathoms of water, but as a matter of fact as already noted, it is now closed practically all of the time.

The eastern entrance has 10' of water at all times and 12' at high tide. With a skilled local pilot who knows the courses, it is possible to pick a 10' channel on the inside i.e., through the laguna, clear around to Ciudad del Carmen at the western extremity of the island. This should not be attempted however without such a pilot, as the channel is tortuous and the laguna filled with shoals; 6' depths are found almost everywhere.

The western and larger entrance has a 13' channel right up to the wharf at Ciudad del Carmen. The official depth of this channel is 12' 6," but loaded vessels with drafts not exceeding 13' 1" or 2" can dock. The Captain of the "Wheeling" claims to have found a new 15' channel but I was told he went aground in following it. The safe maximum for this channel would seem to be 13'.

There are 7' to 9' channels from Ciudad del Carmen to various points within the laguna, but as the secondary bars i.e., those of the rivers opening into the laguna, are all under 5', for inland navigation i.e., for river-boats, the maximum usable draft is 4' to 5'.

The shores are low, flat and marshy, mango swamps and mudflats forming the margin of the laguna. The water near the shores is very shallow, and in the rainy season the shores themselves are under water for a long distance back. There is a 2' difference in the tides.

Beginning at the eastern end of the laguna the following tributaries empty into it: Rio Chivoja, bar 5', no settlement at the mouth, navigable for boats drawing not more than 5' up as far as Chivoja (No. 110) where the Campeche Laguna Corporation (see No. II in the following list of American corporations owning property in this region) have a settlement of laborers. There is another settlement 12 miles farther up the river belonging to this same company, Pop. 100.

Rio Mamantel, 5' at bar, a fisherman's hut west bank at the mouth, navigable for boats drawing not more than 5' of water for 20 miles up as far as Pital (No. 112), the headquarters of the Campeche Laguna Corporation. Pop. About 300. There is an American named Hobart in charge at Pital. Between Pital and the mouth there are no settlements. East of Pital there are some 60 kilometers of Decauville tram-line, 8 kilometers from Pital to San Isidro (No. ?) and 12 kilometers from San Isidro to Chivoja (No. 110).

Rio Candelaria runs into the Rio Mamantel from the south 3 miles from the mouth of the latter. The Mexican Gulf Land and Lumber Co. and the Campeche Timber and Fruit Co., Nos. I and III in the following list own properties along this river.

Rio Chumpan, bar 3', settlement on the west side at the mouth Balchaca (No. 113). La Encantada (No. 114), the headquarters of the Campeche Timber and Fruit Co., is also on the west bank 20 miles above the mouth.

Rio Palisada or the Boca Chica of the Rio Usumacintla, bar 5'. A light-house marks the entrance of the channel. There is a small island in the mouth of the river, the main channel passing to the east of this. There are a few houses on the west bank just above the mouth, and scattering ranches on both sides up to the Rio Usumacintla. The only large settlement is Palizada (No. 116) on the west bank, 25 miles above the mouth. Pop. 800. There is a government telegraph station here; the chief industry is stock raising.

The Rio Palizada leaves the main branch of the Usumacintla 12 miles above—i.e., south of Palizada—at the Boca de Amatitan. At this point the main stream turns west, and 3 miles below on the north side of the main stream is the village of Jonuta (No. 117), Pop. 500. There is a government telegraph station here also. From this point the Usumacintla bears northwest to Tres Bocas (No. 128) where it is joined by the Rio Grijalva and Rio Tulida, 5 miles above Frontera (No. 127); and below here the three flowing together empty into the sea 3 miles below Fontera. There are no villages between Jonuta and Frontera but scattering ranches on both sides of the river.

The Rio Usumacintla is the largest river entering either the Gulf of Mexico or the Caribbean Sea from the Rio Grande down to the Isthmus of Panama. It has three different mouths as follows: the Rio Palizada just described, the Rio San Pedro and San Pablo and the Rio Usumacintla, the last being the largest. The intervening country is a vast network of shallow lagoons connected during the rainy season but separated during the dry months; a great part of the region is under water all of the time.

There are two steamship lines running from San Juan Bautista, now called Villahermosa (No. 129) down the Grijalva River to Frontera, thence back up through the Usumacintla River to the Palizada and Usumacintla to Monte Cristo (No. 118), Balancan (No. 199) as far south as Tenosique (No. 120), the end of steam navigation.

There are 6 or 7 boats in the two lines, all wood-burning side-wheelers drawing not more than 4'. These do a considerable river freighting business.

Returning to the Laguna de Terminos there is but one tributary on the west side, the Estero de Atasta, 3' to 4' at the bar. This gives access to a series of shallow connecting lagoons.

The village of Atasta (No. 121) is on the west side of the lagoon of the same name. It is a farming and cattle settlement all Mexican. Pop. about 100. Just west of Atasta is Pom (No. 122), a cattle and cocoanut plantation belonging to a Mexican named Manuel Repetto. Pop. 75.

Cerrillos (No. 123) is a cattle ranch owned by a Mexican named Tomas Riquena of Ciudad del Carmen. Pop. 50.

No. 115   Ciudad del Carmen. Pop. About 5000. Government telegraph and light-house. No wireless. Presidente de Municipalidad: Onesimo Cahuicho. The town is located on the western extremity of the Island of Carmen. Vessels drawing up to 13' can lay alongside of the wharf although the official depth of the channel is 6" less, i.e., 12' 6."

The government telegraph coming from Campeche and Merida crosses under the eastern entrance to the laguna to the island and thence west to Ciudad del Carmen, and thence under the western entrance across to Point Xicolango (No. 124) 4 miles. The place where the cable leaves the island—on the southern side of the town—is marked by a buoy.

In addition to the river-boats already mentioned as plying between Tenosique, Balancan, Monte Cristo, Palizada, Jonuta, Frontera and Villahermosa there are about 50 power-boats at Ciudad del Carmen ranging from small cayucas equipped with Evinrude engines to 50 ton motor-canoes, which cruise east as far as Campeche and Progreso and west as far as Frontera, Puerto Mexico and Vera Cruz. About 20 belong to our nationals the rest to Mexicans.

There are two regular steamship lines calling at Ciudad del Carmen: The Compania de Fomento del Sureste de Mexico, which maintains a more or less regular tri-monthly service and the Mexican Gulf and Fruit Co. a more regular bi-monthly service. In the season mahogany tramps frequently call here for lumber.

The following countries have consular representatives:

France, Jose Cue, a Spaniard.

England, George Ludivig (German descent but said to be loyal to the allies) now in the United States

Norway, Jose Rivas, a Spaniard, has taken out his first papers for American citizenship.

The foreign colony is composed roughly of the following nationals:

75 Syrians, 50 Chinese, 40 Spaniards, 8 Americans and 2 Germans.

The Syrians are overwhelmingly pro-ally. They have collected money for the French Red Cross and can be counted upon as on our side. Unhappily they are technically Turkish citizens and as such, are subject to the rulings against alien enemies, particularly in regard to drafts. If some special dispensation could be granted them in this particular, it would not be a bad idea, for they are really our friends.

The Spaniards as nearly as I can find out are about neutral.

The two Germans are George Goldsmith and Alfred Lehmann. The first has already figured in a previous report (No. 21). He was formerly employed by the Mexican Gulf Land and Lumber Co. being an old friend of the resident manager, C. W. Woodruff. Recently he was discharged, I believe at the instance of Consul Marsh. He is an able fellow and the active head of the German propaganda work in this region. He has no visible means of support and yet spends plenty of money. Finally he is known to be the distributor of the German "war literature" in Ciudad del Carmen. Agent Watkins will keep an eye upon him and his activities.

The other German, Alfred Lehmann, is still working for the Laguna Campeche Corporation in spite of the fact that they are aware of his nationality. He is a book-keeper. The resident manager, Mr. Thomas Ward, told me he was harmless, but I heard from other Americans there, that Lehmann had been actively engaged in German propaganda work.

And now about our own nationals at Ciudad del Camen, and the large American corporations they severally represent there.

The southern half of the state of Campeche, as you will see by a glance at Mr. Held's map, is for the most part held by 6 or 7 American corporations engaged in the lumber and chicle business. The resident managers of these live at Ciudad del Carmen and constitute the American colony there. For the general location of their respective holdings see the accompanying map A where they have been outlined in yellow and given Roman numerals. No. VI is not located on the map.

No. I.   The Mexican Gulf Land and Lumber Co., Davenport, Iowa.
Resident Manager, C. W. Woodruff

No. II.   The Campeche Laguna Corporation, New York City.
Resident Manager, Thomas Ward

No. III.   The Campeche Timber and Fruit Co., Boston, Mass.
Resident Manager, Leslie Moore

No. IV.   The Hearst Estate, New York City.
Resident Manager, W. M. Ferris

No. V.   The Pennsylvania Campeche Land and Lumber Co., Williamsport, Penn.
Resident Manager, Robert Boyd

No. VI.   Campeche Land and Development Co., Chicago, Ill.
           Resident Manager, Robert Boyd

No. VII.   The San Pablo Development Co., Philadelphia, Penn.
           Resident Manager, Felipe Beltramo, an Italian. He lives
           at San Pablo.

Of these companies the holdings of Nos. II, V and VII are very
extensive, ranging between 600,000 and 800,000 acres each.

In addition to the foregoing the following chicle companies
maintain buying offices at Ciudad del Carmen:

The William Wrigley Jr. Co.—agent, Robert Boyd

The Mexican Exploitation Co., a branch of the American
Chicle Co.—agent, Alfonso Echeverria.

You will note that these properties pretty effectually dominate
the eastern end of the Laguna de Terminos and that Ciudad del
Carmen commands the western end so that it would be difficult if
not practically impossible for the Germans to utilize this body of
water against us in any way without news thereof quickly reaching one or other of our nationals at Ciudad del Carmen and being
immediately forwarded by them to Consul Marsh at Progreso, the
speediest channel for transmission to the outside.

All own, or control, motor-boats, and I arranged that if any
trouble should arise, and use of the government telegraph should
be found impracticable or forbidden, they are to get word to
Consul Marsh by motor-boat at once, a matter of 24 hours.

Such a contingency, however, all agree, appears extremely
remote; the absence of Germans in the region, the vigilance of our
own nationals who have little to do but look out for just such activities, and finally the physiographic unfitness of the Laguna de
Terminos, i.e., its shallow depths and marshy shores, practically
preventing its manipulation against us in any way.

Continuing the coast reconnaissance the next point is:

No. 124.   Point Xicalango. Western boundary of the Laguna de Terminos.
            Pop. about 50 all Mexican. This is a cocoanut and cattle planta-
            tion owned by Tomas Riquena, who lives at Ciudad del Carmen.
            The government telegraph cable from Carmen emerges here, and
            there is a station. There is also a light-house. There are no settle-
            ments on the coast between here and the mouth of the San Pedro
            and San Pablo River.

No. 125.   San Pedro. At the mouth of the San Pedro and San Pablo River on
            the east side, the last settlement owned by a Spaniard, Manuel
            Gutierrez, said to be strongly pro-ally.

The bar of the San Pedro and San Pablo River is 6' to 7'. The river is now somewhat choked up with vegetation, but with very little clearing could be made navigable for boats up to that draft, as far as the main channel of the Rio Usumacintla, of which it is one of the mouths.

No. 126.   Victoria. Small village about 20 people all Mexican.

No. 127   Frontera. The town is on the east bank of the Usumacintla River about 3 miles above the mouth. Pop. 5000, chiefly Mexican. The Spaniards and Syrians are the most numerous of the foreigners. The sympathies of most of them are pro-ally, particularly the latter. Although there are only three Germans in the place plenty of German propaganda finds its way down here. We have a consulate here and there is a government telegraph and at the mouth of the river on the east bank there is a light-house.

Formerly boats drawing up to 12' and 14' were able to get over the bar and up the river to the town docking alongside of the wharf, but some years ago another channel was opened up west of the old channel and before the breakwater at the mouth was finished so that it would remain open, the project was discontinued and the work stopped. This had the unfortunate result of shallowing both channels the old channel now being reduced to 5' to 9' and the new channel to 3 1/2' at the bars. Even the small 800 to 1000 ton boats of the Compania de Fomento del Sureste de Mexico are obliged to anchor outside and load and discharge cargo from lighters.

Formerly Frontera divided with Ciudad del Carmen all the large export business of the Rio Usumacintla and the Rio Grijalva, the chicle, mahogany and dye-woods coming out through the former and the coffee and bananas out through the latter.

The exorbitant export duties imposed on bananas by the present Government of Mexico have killed the fruit business at Frontera and the town is very dead, Ciudad del Carmen now being almost twice as large.

The Compania de Fomento del Sureste de Mexico has boats call here tri-monthly, and the Mexican Gulf and Fruit Co. boats bi-monthly. In addition there are occasional mahogany tramps in the season.

Appendix 4

"Office of Naval Intelligence Designations"

NAME	NUMBER	REMARKS
A.	77	
Adolph, Henry F.	205	
Allen, S.	234	
Andrews, Roy Chapman	241	
Baker, Virgil	125	Lt. (Castleman)
Ballantine, J. W.	83	
Barry, Jasper	179	
Bayless, Samuel E.	87	
Beare, C. L.	225	
Beers, G. K.	51b	
Beers, W. L.	51	
Behn, H.	150	also 108 ?
Behn, Hernand	108	also 150 ?
Benane, D.	257	
Benkert, A. W.	228	

Bennett, S. Alfred	188	
Bohlen, F. H., Jr.	198	
Bourland, G. B.	230	
Bowling, H. H.	156	
Boyd, George W.	131	
Boyd, W. Y.	258	
Breck, E.	61	(Dorsey, Geo A.)
Brown, W. P.	233	
Browne, Thomas	193	
Bullitt, W. C.	63	
Burgess, Edward A.	204	
Burgoyne, A. G.	251	
Bryan, H. F.	36	Capt. 2 N.D.
Camara, J. J.	88	
Caminetti, A. B.	253	
Caperton, W. B.	38	Rear Adm. Com Pac.
Carpentier, E.	159	
Carminati, A. A.	160	
Carrigan, W. L.	232	
Carver, C. N.	195	
Casarico, C.	158	
Castberg, Biarne	167	
Catlin, W. H.	247	
Chandler, C. L.	223	
Cherrie, George K.	245	
Cicero, Charles S.	221	

Clark, George R.	28	Capt.
Clark, L. C., Jr.	166	
Cole, Eli K.	122	Brig. Gen.
Cone, H. I.	46	Comdr.
Connor, J. A.	238	originally No. 218
Coontz, R. E.	37	Capt. 13 N.D.
Cooper, G. F.	34	Capt. 4 N.D.
Costa, E. S.	97	
Costa, Jos. F.	137	
Crampton, Henry Edward	270	
Crosley, W. S.	113	Capt.
Cusachs, C. V.	25	Prof.
Dana, C. B.	11	
Davis, George S.	110	
De Booy, Theodoor [*sic*]	142	
De Brun, A. S.	184	
De Bullett, W. J.	187	
Decker, B. C.	118	Capt. (Crosley; Wells)
DeKnight, C. W.	92	
Director of Naval Intelligence	1	
Dodson, R. I.	134	
Dorton, F. T.	30	Lt. Sec. 1, 5 N.D.
DuBois, A. W.	140	
Duhn, J.	79	
Dunn, Herbert O.	111	Adm.
Dunn, W. E.	168	

Eastman, C. R.	139	
Edie, J. R.	20	Capt.
Edwards, T. E.	151	
Eisler, W. I.	259	
Eustis, G. P.	65	
Evans, George R.	31	Capt.
Executive Officer	2	
Felder, Thomas J.	267 & 272	
Fielding, F. H.	89	
Fish, A. R.	67	
Flanders, Paul A.	265	Lt. USNR (inactive)
Fowler, O. W.	21	Lt. Comdr.
Fullam, W. F.	175	Rear Adm.
Funk, J. Clarence	252	
Gade, John A.	60	
Gann, Thomas	242	
Gardiner, C. E.	206	
Gibbons, J. H.	181	Capt.
Gillis, I. V. G.	22	Comdr. (Hutchins, C.)
Gittings, J. S., Jr.	148	
Goetchius, I. S.	235	
Goldsmith, C. A.	207	
Gonzalez Lamas, A.	138	
Graham, W. C.	256	
Hale, Arthur	244	
Hall, D. P.	6	Maj.

Hamilton, W. P.	124	Lt. (j.g.)
Hampson, H. S.	199	
Hatch, J. F.	123	Paymaster
Havemeyer, Frederick C.	202	
Haworth, B. C.	171	
Haxtun, S. R.	62	
Held, John, Jr.	154	
Henderson, R. W.	23	Comdr.
Henry, W. B.	153	
Higbee, Robert	271	
Hill, F. K.	112	Capt. Rio
Hines, H. K.	44	Capt.
Hodges, H. M.	24	Capt.
Holm, Fritz	149	
Homer, A. P.	68	
Horn, R. E.	128	
Horne, F. J.	115	Lt. Comdr. (Watson, E.)
Hough, F. P. W.	196	U.S.N.
Howard, John G.	208	
H. S. H.	129	
Huffnagel,	237	Lt.
Hughes, William P.	189	
Hutchins, C. T.	120	Lt. Comdr.
Iseman, J. E.	5	
Irving, Duer	75	[ensign]
Johnson, James L.	210	

Jordan, M. A.	82	
Judson, T. M.	59	
Jukes, E. W.	135	
Kear, C. R.	26	Lt. Comdr.
Kelley, Edward J.	177	
Kennedy, W. J.	90	
Kerner, H. P.	73	
Kimm, S. H.	72	
King, John	76	
Kirk, W. B.	239	
Kittredge, Tracy Barrett	290	
Klein,	8	Lt.
Knapp, H. S.	101	(Sims) [& 49?]
Knapp, H. S.	49	Rear Adm. San Dom. [& 101?]
Knott, Charles H.	197	
Knox, D. W.	40	Comdr. Guantanamo
LaBlache, Armand	211	
Lane, Rella M.	213	
Langford, Lucien John	172	
Langworthy, E. D.	87a	Lt.
Levis, F. A.	48	6 N.D.
Lewis, F. A.	243	
Little, L. McC.	121	Maj.
Lloyd, Edward, Jr.	269	
Lockman, D. M.	78	
Loots, B.	260	

Lothrop, Samuel Kirkland	173	
McAfee, R. A.	224	
McBride, L. B.	103	Nav Constr.
McCormick, E. D.	32	Lt. (j.g.) (Bagley)
McDougall, W. D.	100	Capt.
McIntosh, H. P.	17	Lt.
McIntyre, Frank P.	203	
McLean, W.	43	Adm. 5 N.D.
Magie, W. F.	250	
Mahoney, Julia	220	Miss
Mahony, W. [?] F.	98	
Marqued, R. E.	236	
Marshall, George	212	
Mason, John Alden	157	
Mayo, H. T.	248	Adm.
Mechling, William Hubbs	52	
Meyer, Agnes	261	Miss
Meyerheim, A. H.	227	
Miles, Muriel	209	
Milne,	7	Lt. Comdr.
Miscellaneous Accounts	200	
Mitchell, J. D.	96	
Martinek, P. V.	185	
Moffett, W. A.	27	
Morgan, Harry C.	186	
Moore, James	130	

Morley, Sylvanus Griswold	53	
Neilson, John	86	
Nelson, H.	226	(Civil Service Clerk)
Nelson, V. S.	42	Comdr. 8 N.D.
Nicholson, R. F.	180	Rear Adm. (Durell, E. H.)
Norman, Maxwell	117	Boston
Northrup, A. S.	85	
O'Bleness, F. B.	136	
Oliver, J. H.	41	Rear Adm. Virgin Isl.
O'Laughlin, J. C.	70	
Parsons, Frank B.	215	
Pender, B. D.	71	
Perdomo, Joseph J.	93	
Pfund, Richard	95	
Piper, James	29	
Pleadwell, F. L.	102	Surgeon
Plunkett, Charles	164	
Popenoe, Wilson	219	
Pratt, P. R.	162	
Preuschen, Franz	262	
Proskauer, Samuel	178	
Pruett, R. L.	74	
Purcell, John F.	174	
Quilty, Joseph A.	214	
Ramsey, F. A.	183	Capt.
Redles, W. L.	116	Capt.

Riis, S. M.	13	
Robinette, E. Burton	182	
Robinson, Phillip E.	249	
Rodgers, W. L.	263	Rear Adm.
Rosencrans, W. P.	143	
Rothrock, H. E.	264	Lt., USMC
Rowe, G. E.	128a	[also 201?]
Rowe, George E.	201	[also 128a?]
Roys, J. H.	9	Lt. Comdr.
Runnells, Olive	119	
Rush, W. R.	35	Capt. 1 N.D.
Russell,	4	Lt. Col.
Russell, L. B.	191	
Russell, R. L.	45	Capt. 12 N.D.
Rynzel, S. R.	163	
S	144	E. M. Sasse
Sard, R. E.	194	
Sargent, L. R.	176	Comdr.
Sayles, W. R.	106	Lt. Comdr. (Long)
Scully, W. A.	190	
Seraphic, Alcibiades Antoine	94	
Sheldon, Charles	246	
Shepardson, Whitney Hart	291	
Simone, G. D.	141	
Siqueland, T. A.	170	
Smith, B. L.	107	1st Lt.

Smith, Ch. H.	216	
Sneed, J. A.	169	
Spinden, Herbert Joseph	56	
Stafford, A. B.	254	
Stevenson, W. L.	50	
Stolpe, E. R. S.	132	
Stone, Louis D.	222	
Sturgeon, W. F.	192	
Terhune, W. J.	39	Comdr. Key West
Tobey, E. C.	104	Paymaster
Todd, F. C.	133	
Townsend, O. C.	55	
Train, C. R.	10	Lt. Comdr. (Reeves, J. M.)
Travis, G. B.	161	
Usher, N. R.	33	Rear Adm. 3 N.D.
Van Antwerp, W. C.	80	
Vander Kley, J. G.	229	
W	145	
Wales, Edward	266	Lt. Comdr. USNRF (inactive)
Wales, E. H.	54	
Watkins, Lewis Hunt	99	
Watts, Joseph Henry	84	
Weinberger, E.	231	
White, J. F.	64	
Whittlesay, H. H.	18	Lt. Comdr.
Whyte, A. O.	155	

Wicker, Cyrus	165	
Williams, G. W.	255	Capt.
Wood, Warren D.	268	
Woodrome, J. E.	152	
Wright, R. K.	47	
Wurm, W. [?]	91	
X	81	
Y	146	
Z	147	Mrs. H. K. Henry
	105	(Jackson)

Appendix 5

"General Instructions."

Report all urgent information by telegram in code.

Report information which is not urgent, or which will not be affected by delay, by letter.

When a question arises which is not covered by your instructions, use your discretion. It is impossible to cover all contingencies in these instructions and it will be necessary for you to adapt them to local and temporal conditions and to use your best endeavor to carry out the purpose of your mission in the most efficient manner possible.

Use plain language only when code messages are not permitted and then only when information is urgent and no knowledge of importance can be obtained by an outsider by reading the plain (language) message.

Number all letters and written reports in sequence so that any missing may be detected.

Sign all written communications with your number.

Use number or name under which you are working in signing telegrams.

Do not use the number if it is apt to create suspicion.

When practicable to do so without disclosing or affecting your mission endeavor to meet influential persons in the district to which you are assigned, especially those who are in authority and who might be of assistance in obtaining information.

News regarding the movements of enemy naval or merchant vessels can often be obtained by visiting ships arriving in port; making the acquaintance of ships officers, passengers and crews on these ships, and by cultivating the acquaintance of residents, American and foreign, when it is safe to do so.

Valuable information can be obtained from newspapers, and through conversation with business men.

Do not make a report on suspicion alone, but obtain all evidence from facts.

Give your confidence to no one.

Acknowledge no connection with O.N.I. to anyone.

Make reports only to the persons or addresses specified.

Always have in mind that your actions are being observed.

Do not correspond with O.N.I. direct or with any United States Government department or official. Send personal correspondence only as specified.

Be sure that the marks on your clothes, luggage, etc., correspond with your name.

Guard carefully your code and information.

Destroy same by burning if there is danger of their loss from any cause.

Your luggage or room may be searched at any time; therefore destroy or guard carefully everything which might be incriminating.

You may be subjected to search at any time, either officially, by deception or by attack.

You may be followed or under observation at any time.

Your letters may be opened; therefore be sure to mail them yourself; call for them in person; and destroy letters after you have read them.

Always have a good reason for being anywhere.

In case of arrest call on or refer to _____.

Divulge to him only sufficient information to obtain your release and demand his confidence.

Obey instructions received from O.N.I. implicitly.

Carry no mail or documents except as absolutely necessary and then only in an entirely safe place.

Trust as far as possible to your memory.

Avoid any action which might bring you under suspicion or affect your mission unfavorably.

In employing natives or residents to obtain information the greatest care must be used. Be sure that your man is reliable and do not disclose anything whatever to him of your true identity, mission, knowledge, circumstances, or the circumstances under which you are working.

On the first of each month, if practicable, forward a statement of your expenses to date enclosing receipts covering all important items. Where obtaining the receipts was impracticable forward your certificate covering the amount expended.

If not practicable to forward a statement of your accounts on the first of the month forward such a statement at the earliest opportunity.

Immediately upon your arrival at your destination or base report your mail and telegraphic address by cable.

Copies to No.
     Accounts,
     File.

Notes

Preface

1. The Fairview Cemetery is located on Cerrillos Road. Although Cerrillos Road is the most heavily traveled road in Santa Fe, the cemetery, located on the south side of the street directly across from the New Mexico Highway Department headquarters, is screened by a fence, and only older Santa Fe residents know where the cemetery is located. In its day the cemetery was where most of Santa Fe's most distinguished citizens were buried, including governors and prominent businessmen and their wives. However, the cemetery filled up and an adjacent annex contains only a few burial plots. By the 1960's the cemetery had fallen into disuse, and Santa Fe County was forced to take over management of the burial ground. Morley is buried alongside his second wife, Frances.

2. The most recent version, which no longer bears Morley's name, is the fifth edition, published in 1994; it bears only Robert J. Sharer's name. According to Norris Pope, Director of the Stanford University Press, whom the present authors thank for compiling these numbers, the fourth and fifth editions alone have sold almost 30,000 hardbound and paperback copies. For a scholarly work that first appeared over fifty years ago, this is remarkable. Another of Morley's contributions has stood the test of time. Morley wrote the introduction to and Delia Goetz translated from the Spanish the *Popul Vuh: The Sacred Book of the Ancient Quiché Maya*, which the University of Oklahoma Press published in 1952. According to John N. Drayton, Director of the Press, whom the authors thank for compiling these numbers, the *Popul Vuh* is in its seventeenth printing, having sold a total of some 40,000 copies. For a listing of Morley's publications see Boaz Long, ed., *Morleyana: A Collection of Writings in Memoriam Sylvanus Griswold Morley—1883–1948*. (Santa Fe: The School of American Research and the Museum of New Mexico, 1950), pp. 73–84.

3. Brian M. Fagan, ed. *The Oxford Companion to Archaeology*. New York: Oxford University Press, 1996.

4. Michael D. Coe, *The Maya*. 5th ed. rev. and expanded (New York: Thames and Hudson, 1993), p. 11. See also Richard A. Wertime and Angela M. H. Schuster, "Written in the Stars: Celestial Origin of Maya Creation Myths," *Archaeology*, XL, no.4 (July/August 1993), pp. 26–32, where it is noted that Morley and his colleague Herbert J. Spinden had long ago suggested "that the Maya creation myth was linked in deep ways to Maya astronomy" (p. 28), a belief that is now back in vogue.

5. Marian F. Love, "Vignette, Sylvanus Morley," *The Santa Fean Magazine*, vol. 11, no. 2 (March, 1983), p. 13.

6. Robert L. Brunhouse, *Sylvanus G. Morley and the World of the Ancient Mayas* (Norman: University of Oklahoma Press, 1971), pp. 112–147.

7. Wyman H. Packard, *A Century of U.S. Naval Intelligence* (Washington, D.C.: Office of Naval Intelligence and the Naval Historical Center, 1996), pp. 41, 56 n. 21.

8. On "Operation Sunrise" see Allen Dulles, *The Secret Surrender*. New York: Harper and Row, 1966. See also Bradley F. Smith and Elena Agrossi, *Operation Sunrise*. New York: Basic Books, 1979; Peter Gross, *Gentleman Spy: The Life of Allen Dulles*. (Boston: Houghton Mifflin, 1994), pp. 221–254, and James Srodes, *Allen Dulles: Master of Spies*. (Washington: Regnery Publishing, 1999), pp. 342–349.

9. Jeffrey Dorwart, *The Office of Naval Intelligence: The Birth of America's First Intelligence Agency 1865–1918*. Annapolis: Naval Institute Press, 1979, and *Conflict of Duty: The Navy's Intelligence Dilemma 1919–1945*. Annapolis: Naval Institute Press, 1983. See also James R. Green, "The First Sixty Years of the Office of Naval Intelligence," M.A. thesis, American University, Washington, D.C., 1963.

10. Rhodri Jeffreys-Jones and Andrew Lownie, eds. *North American Spies: New Revisionist Essays* (Lawrence: University Press of Kansas, 1991), p.245.

11. Welles to Director of Naval Intelligence, November 14, 1919, in "Memorandum for the Chief of Naval Operations," December 23, 1919, 3809–846:13, Records of the Office of the Chief of Naval Operations, Record Group 38, National Archives and Records Service, Washington, D.C.

12. Paul Sullivan, *Unfinished Conversations: Mayas and Foreigners Between Two Wars* (New York: Alfred A. Knopf, 1989), pp. 132–134, 240–241.

Chapter 1

1. Meirion and Susie Harries, *The Last Days of Innocence: America at War, 1917–1918* (New York: Random House, 1997), 73.

2. See, for example, David F. Trask, *Captains and Cabinets: Anglo-American Naval Relations, 1917–1918* (Columbia: University of Missouri Press, 1972), 44–60.

3. See Link's excellent analytical foreword in Reinhard R. Doerries, *Imperial Challenge: Ambassador Count Bernsdorff and German-American Relations, 1908–1917* (Chapel Hill: University of North Carolina Press, 1989), xiv.

4. For a survey of this topic, see Jules Witcover, *Sabotage at Black Tom: Imperial Germany's Secret War in America: 1914–1917* (Chapel Hill: Algonquin Books of Chapel Hill, 1989). See also Captain Henry Landau, *The Enemy Within: The Inside Story of German Sabotage in America* (New York: G. P. Putnam's Sons, 1937).

5. As Gerhard L. Weinberg has noted in *A World at Arms: A Global History of World War II* (Cambridge: Cambridge University Press, 1994), 559 n., there is a "veil of obfuscation" surrounding this whole topic. The best analysis to date is Doerries, *Imperial Challenge*, 189, 344. The first mention of germ warfare in print was by a World War I British Secret Service agent, Captain Henry Landau, *Enemy Within*, 168–70; incontrovertible evidence can be found in the intercepted and cryptanalyzed telegrams the British provided to the United States. See the Mixed Claims Commission, United States and Germany, VII, Exhibit 320, Record Group 76, National Archives and Records Service, College Park, Md. In 1997, a vial of anthrax was discovered in a Danish museum. It had been seized during World War I by local authorities from a German. A chemical analysis determined that it was indeed anthrax and still potent. This incident is described by Stephen Jay Gould, "This View of Life: Above All Do No Harm," *Natural History* 107, no. 8 (October 1998): 16–22; *International Herald Tribune*, June 26, 1998. The anthrax

attacks via mail of October 2001 have obviously focused recent attention on the use of anthrax as a biological warfare weapon. This past history (of which no one in the United States government seemingly has any knowledge) might suggest to someone in Washington that it is occasionally useful to study the past.

6. A competent institutional history of the United States Secret Service has yet to be written. However, James Bamford, the author of *The Puzzle Palace: A Report on NSA, America's Most Secret Agency* (Boston: Houghton Mifflin, 1982), reportedly is writing one. Bamford's most recent study of the NSA is *Body of Secrets: Anatomy of the Ultra-Secret National Security Agency from the Cold War through the Dawning of a New Century* (New York: Doubleday, 2001). William R. Corson, *The Armies of Ignorance: The Rise of the American Intelligence Empire* (New York: Dial Press, 1977), 581–83, covers this time frame.

7. The most recent scholarship on American counterintelligence during the Spanish-American War suggests that the U.S. Secret Service was not as successful as earlier accounts reported. The present authors suggest that the new scholarship is somewhat overblown. See Graeme S. Mount, "The Secret Operations of Spanish Consular Officials within Canada during the Spanish-American War," in Jeffreys-Jones and Lownie, *North American Spies*, 31–48. For earlier scholarship, see Rhodri Jeffreys-Jones, *American Espionage from Secret Service to CIA* (New York: Free Press, 1977), 30–36; George J. A. O'Toole, *The Spanish War: An American Epic—1898* (New York and London: W. W. Norton and Co., 1984), 232–35.

8. Joe Priest to Chief, U.S. Secret Service, Dec. 8, 12, 19, 1910, Records of the U.S. Secret Service, Daily Reports of Agents, 1875 through 1936, Daily Reports from San Antonio, vol. 12, Microcopy no. 3157, RG 87, NA.

9. See, for example, Captain Franz von Rintelen, *The Dark Invader: War-Time Reminiscences of a German Naval Intelligence Officer* (New York: Penguin Books, 1939), passim; Francis MacDonnell, *Insidious Foes: The Axis Fifth Column and The American Home Front* (New York: Oxford University Press, 1995), pp. 13–19; Frank J. Rafalko, ed., *A Counterintelligence Reader*, 3 vols. (Langley, Va.: National Counterintelligence Center, 1997), 1:89–102; and Witcover, *Sabotage at Black Tom*, 76–133.

10. Joan M. Jensen, *The Price of Vigilance* (Chicago: Rand McNally, 1968), 91–123; Corson, *Armies of Ignorance*, 585–92.

11. Unfortunately, a pre-John Edgar Hoover history of the Federal Bureau of Investigation remains to be written. There are two studies that deal competently with the Bureau during this period. See Sanford J. Ungar, *FBI: An Uncensored Look Behind the Walls* (Boston: Little Brown, 1975), 39–40; and Corson, *Armies of Ignorance*, 583–85. Ungar quotes from Attorney General George W. Wickersham's Congressional testimony in 1910, noting that the Bureau's most important work dealt with violations of the "national banking laws, peonage laws, the bucket-shop law, the laws relating to fraudulent bankruptcies, the impersonation of government officials with intent to defraud, thefts and murders committed on government reservations, offenses against government property, and those committed by federal court officials and employees, Chinese smuggling, customs frauds, internal revenue frauds, post office frauds, violations of the neutrality laws . . . land frauds and immigration and naturalization cases." The White Slave Traffic Act, or so-called Mann Act, was passed later in 1910.

12. Occasional references to "White Slave Officers" may be found in various rolls of the Old Mexican Files, microcopy 232 (reels 1–24), Records of the Federal Bureau of Investigation, Record Group 65, National Archives and Records Service, Washington, D.C., hereafter cited as BI. See, for example, "Special Employee Marshall" report of Mar. 8, 1912, conducting a census of houses of prostitution on Delaware and D. Street in Washington, D.C., in reel 1, BI. The Miscellaneous Files, some 145 rolls of microfilm,

also have numerous references to White Slave Officers. Although it is academically fashionable to ignore Don Whitehead's *The FBI Story* (New York: Random House, 1956), 24–27, his discussion of the Bureau's role in enforcing the Mann Act is the best available.

13. See, for example, Case No. 232, Dec. 1, 1910, p. 494, reel 4, BI. The Old Mexican Files, formerly called "The Old Mexican 232" files, exist only on microfilm. There are twenty-four reels—an estimated eighty thousand pages—and the documents were destroyed after filming.

14. The penetration agent was W. C. Chamberlain. His reports are in reel 3, Nov. 29–30, 1911, BI. For a discussion of the Reyes Conspiracy, see Charles H. Harris III and Louis R. Sadler, "The 1911 Reyes Conspiracy: The Texas Side," *Southwestern Historical Quarterly* 82 (April 1980): 325–48.

15. Charles H. Harris III and Louis R. Sadler, "The 'Underside' of the Mexican Revolution: El Paso, 1912," *The Americas: A Quarterly Review of Inter-American Cultural History* 39 (July 1982): 69–83. The standard biography for Orozco is Michael C. Meyer, *Mexican Rebel: Pascual Orozco and the Mexican Revolution, 1910–1915* (Lincoln: University of Nebraska Press, 1967).

16. See, for example, Special Agent H. A. Thompson report from Douglas, Ariz., Mar. 4, 1913, and Special Agent E. M. Blanford, also from Douglas, Mar. 14, 1913, both in reel 3, BI; Rafalko, *Counterintelligence Reader*, 1:109. According to Whitehead, *FBI Story* (14), by 1915 the Bureau had increased its agent roster to 219. See numerous reports in reels 3, 4, 5, and 9 (March 1913-June 1914), BI.

17. Charles H. Harris III and Louis R. Sadler, "The Plan of San Diego and the Mexican-United States War Crisis of 1916: A Reexamination," *Hispanic American Historical Review* 58 (August 1978): 381–408.

18. Ibid. The source and quotation on the killing of Mexican-Americans in south Texas is U.S. Secret Service Agent Edward Tyrell, who was based in San Antonio and reported on Nov. 25, 1915: "There has [*sic*] been over 300 or more Mexicans killed in this vicinity [Brownsville] most of them shot down in cold blood." Tyrell to Chief, U.S. Secret Service, Microcopy no. 3.158, Record Group 87, Records of the U.S. Secret Service, Daily Report of Agents, 1875 through 1936, Daily Reports from San Antonio, Vol. 12, NA.

19. Charles H. Harris III and Louis R. Sadler, *The Border and the Revolution: Clandestine Activities of the Mexican Revolution: 1910–1920*, 2d rev. ed. (Silver City, N.M.: High Lonesome Books, 1990), 79–80.

20. There is a plethora of histories of the Columbus raid and the Punitive Expedition. See, for example, Colonel Frank Tompkins, *Chasing Villa: The Last Campaign of the U.S. Cavalry* (Harrisburg, Pa.: Military Service Publishing Company, 1934; Silver City, N.M.: High Lonesome Books, 1996); Friedrich Katz, "Pancho Villa and the Attack on Columbus, New Mexico," *American Historical Review* 83, no. 1 (February 1978): 101–30, and Katz, *The Life and Times of Pancho Villa* (Stanford, Calif.: Stanford University Press, 1998), 560–614; Herbert Malloy Mason, *The Great Pursuit* (New York: Random House, 1970); Clarence C. Clendenen, *Blood on the Border: The United States and the Mexican Irregulars* (New York: Macmillan, 1969); Alberto Salinas Carranza, *La Expedición Punitiva* (México, D.F.: Ediciones Botas, 1936); Harris and Sadler, *Border and the Revolution*, 7–23; James W. Hurst, *The Villista Prisoners of 1916–17* (Las Cruces, N.M.: Yucca Tree Press, 2000); Alberto Calzadíaz Barrera, *Por Qué Villa Atacó Columbus: Intriga Internacional* (México, D.F.: Editores Mexicanos Unidos, 1972); and Haldeen Braddy, *Pancho Villa at Columbus: The Raid of 1916* (El Paso: Texas Western Press, 1965).

21. State Department Special Agent George C. Carothers made a cursory examination of the so-called "Villa saddlebag documents," following the raid and reported on their contents

to the secretary of state. See his letter to the Secretary of State, Mar. 11, 1916. A copy is in reel 6, BI, and was sent from the State Department to BI Director Bruce Bielaski. On the Bureau's response to the raid, see Special Agent E. B. Stone, El Paso, report to Robert L. Barnes, San Antonio, quoted in Barnes's March 9 telegram to Bielaski, reel 7, BI. Stone learned of the raid from Brigadier General John J. Pershing, the El Paso Patrol District commander, based at Fort Bliss outside El Paso. Barnes, Stone's superior, telegraphed him to go immediately to Columbus, (Barnes report, Mar. 10, 1916, reel 9, BI); also, see Stone telegram to Bielaski, Mar. 9, 1916. Stone estimated (probably incorrectly, although there was not a count of Villista casualties by the 13th Cavalry) that "around two hundred Villa soldiers killed . . . were lying on the streets . . . and afterwards piled up . . . and burned," in reel 7, BI. By March 13 Barnes was en route to El Paso, where he ordered Stone to meet him and examine the Villista documents after they had been translated. See Barnes report, Mar. 13, 1916, reel 6, BI. Special Agent Stone's interrogation of Maud Hawk Wright, who was captured by Villa before the Columbus raid, and a précis of Villista documents recovered after the raid can be found in Stone reports, Mar. 18, 19, 1916, El Paso, reel 7, BI. The search for Morris Nordhouse involved a respectable number of Bureau agents who tracked him down. See, for example, Special Agent V. L. Farbershaw, Chicago, Mar. 18, 1916, reel 11, BI. For a report on the interview with Nordhouse, see Special Agent Arthur T. Bagley, Mar. 18, 1916, Kansas City, Missouri, in reel 11, BI. For a later and more complete inventory, see Bagley's report, Nov. 15, 1916, in reel 11, BI. During World War II, United States intelligence agencies set up special teams to follow troops capturing enemy installations in an effort to exploit captured documents. See, for example, Packard, *Century of U.S. Naval Intelligence*, 45–49. On the Office of Strategic Services (OSS) Oral Intelligence Unit, see Tom Moon, *This Grim and Savage Game: The OSS and U.S. Covert Operations in World War II* (New York: Da Capo Press, 2000).

22. On the "Bureau Special," see Ungar, *FBI*, 660. One of the present authors, as a reporter, covered the Major Bureau Special of all Major Bureau Specials (next to the Kennedy assassination): the 1964 murders of civil rights workers Michael Schwerner, Andrew Goodman, and James Chaney near Philadelphia, Mississippi. Obviously the events of September 11, 2001, and the subsequent anthrax attacks in October 2001 have superseded the previous Major Bureau Specials.

23. Special Employee Tom Ross report for June 1916, dated July 7, 1916, reel 13, BI. See also Harris and Sadler, *Border and the Revolution*, 89, 94–95.

24. Special Employee C. N. Idar, Reports, July 2, 14, 1916, reels 7 and 13, BI. See also *Laredo Weekly Times*, July 2, 1916. Tom Ross to Bielaski, Aug. 3, 1916, reel 13, BI. The Bielaski letter to Ross dated July 29, 1916, is not in the file; the cover letter is. Ross's response suggests that the warning was about drinking: "Yours of the 29th in hand and contents noted. Thanking you for the confidential warning and I assure you that you won't have to take it up with me anymore." Ross apparently continued to drink. See A. Smith to Chief, Bureau of Investigation, Sept. 26, 1916: "Capt. Ross' conduct at the present time, and for some time passed, is a disgrace to himself and to the Department he represents; he remains constantly under the influence of liquor." Reel 13, BI. See also Willard Utley report, San Antonio, Feb. 2, 1917, and Barnes telegram to Breniman, Dec. 30, 1916, quoted in Barnes report, Jan. 2, 1917, San Antonio, reel 15, BI.

25. The operations of the Japanese agents hired by the BI/El Paso office are recounted in detail in a chapter of Harris and Sadler, "Termination With Extreme Prejudice: The United States Versus Pancho Villa," in *Border and the Revolution*, pp. 7–23. The Bureau of Investigation records upon which the account is based are found in reels 7, 13, 14, BI.

26. See Special Agent E. B. Stone Report, Brownsville, Texas, Oct. 31, 1915, reel 8, BI. The chronology appears to be as follows: Special Agent in Charge Barnes traveled to Brownsville following the Plan of San Diego attack on a train a few miles north of that city on October 19, 1915, which resulted in the death of several individuals. In Brownsville

he talked with U.S. Army officials and interviewed Louis Laulon, a former U.S. Customs mounted inspector who had earlier been involved in smuggling ammunition into Mexico. Laulon apparently suggested to Barnes that for $5,000 each, or $10,000 total, he would deliver Luis de la Rosa and Aniceto Pizaña (presumably dead) to the U.S. side of the Rio Grande. Barnes reported this in a telegram to the director of the Bureau of Investigation on Oct. 28, 1915. See Attorney General T. W. Gregory to John E. Green, Jr., U.S. Attorney for the Southern District of Texas, Nov. 6, 1915, 90755–2461, in the Records of the Department of Justice, Record Group 60.

27. In addition, one of Captain McCoy's subordinates, a Captain Scott, had a secret agent who had spent time at Pizaña and de la Rosa's camp who stated his willingness to try to capture the two Plan of San Diego leaders and deliver them to the United States side of the Rio Grande. See Stone Report, Oct. 31, 1915, Brownsville, Texas, reel 8, BI.

28. Stone Report, Nov. 5, 1915, quoting Bielaski telegram to Barnes, reel 6, BI.

29. U.S. Attorney John E. Green, Jr., to the Attorney General, Nov. 2, 1915, Houston, Tex., 90755–2461, Department of Justice, RG 60.

30. Attorney General T. W. Gregory to Green, Nov. 6, 1915, 90755–2461, Department of Justice, RG 60.

31. Ibid.

32. Major W. H. Hay, Chief of Staff, Southern Department, Fort Sam Houston, San Antonio, Tex., to Captain Frank McCoy, Oct. 28, 1915, Box 79, Frank McCoy Papers, Library of Congress, Washington, D.C.

33. The standard work on the American Protective League (APL) is Jensen, *Price of Vigilance.* Jensen estimated that the APL had between 300,000 and 350,000 members at its height. See p. 251. See also Ungar, *FBI*, 41–43. The official APL history is Emerson Hough, *The Web* (Chicago: Reilly and Lee, 1919).

34. On Cuba, see, for example, Special Agent L. M. Cantrell's report from Havana, Mar. 13, 1916, reel 11, BI. Cantrell went to investigate gunrunning to Mexico and ties to the Mexican revolutionary faction headed by General Félix Díaz. See Cantrell report, same date, BI. On Mexico, see Harry Brolaski to Bielaski, Mar. 17, 1916 from Eagle Pass, Tex., reel 11, BI. Brolaski also took photographs secretly and sent them to Bielaski. Brolaski spent more than a week in Mexico, including a visit to Mexico City, before he returned to the United States. The purpose of the trip was to collect intelligence. In late May 1916, as tensions built up on the U.S.-Mexican border, J. P. S. Mennett was sent to Saltillo and Monterrey in northeastern Mexico. During his week-long intelligence collection journey, Mennett observed a military buildup by the Carranza government and sought to gauge whether or not the Mexican government planned to go to war with the United States. See Mennett Report, June 5, 1916, "Confidential," San Antonio, Tex., reel 14, BI. Another BI undercover operative dispatched to Mexico in 1917 was William Neunhoffer, a San Antonio newsman who posed as a draft dodger (or "slacker," as they were called in World War I) in Mexico City. See testimony of Neunhoffer in U.S. War Department Record of the Court Martial of Lothar Witzke, VIII, Exhibit 3212, Mixed Claims Commission, United States and Germany, RG 76, National Archives, College Park, Md. These records were previously housed at the Federal Records Center, East Point, Ga. On Central America, see reels 15 and 16, BI, for Berliner, who, in January and February 1917, was based for a time in Puerto Limón and San José, Costa Rica. A Bureau special employee, one J. García, was sent into Mexico, in December 1916, to investigate munitions smuggling. See reel 16, BI. In addition, the Bureau recruited Richard Levering, an oil company executive, and sent him to Tampico to report in 1917. See reel 17, BI. Levering was replaced by a veteran BI agent, J. P. S. Mennett, who had been based on the U.S.-Mexico border for several years. See his reports, principally from Tampico, in 1918, in reel 18, BI.

35. A. Bruce Bielaski, former director, Bureau of Investigation to L. L. Winslow, Bureau of Secret Intelligence, Department of State, June 16, 1919, A. B. Fall Papers, MS 8, Rio Grande Historical Collections, Branson Library, New Mexico State University, Las Cruces, N.M. (hereafter cited as RGHC, NMSU). Bielaski wrote Winslow, "This note will introduce to you . . . Charles Jones. During the time I was with the Department of Justice Mr. Jones was a very valuable source of information . . . especially with regard to Mexico and Central America. I think someone in your office once told me that he [Jones] turned in a greater amount of correct information regarding those countries than any other individual. . . . You will find that the reports were in the name of Cresse." Jones also used the Newspaper Service Company as a front. The chief investigator for the so-called Fall Committee, the U.S. Senate committee investigating Mexican affairs, was one William Martin Hanson, who had acquired a certain reputation as one who was au courant on Mexican affairs and had been the senior Texas Ranger captain. Hanson reported to Fall, "Jones has made a lot of money by furnishing arms and ammunition to Mexico and South America but I understand it was always with the acquiescence of our government." See W. M. Hanson to Senator A. B. Fall, Dec. 2, 1919; see also Bielaski to Jones, June 28, 1916, both in Fall Papers, RGHC, NMSU. See also Michael Stone, "The Fall Committee and Double Agent Jones," *Southern New Mexico Historical Review* (hereafter cited as *SNMHR*) 6, no. 1 (January 1999): 45–49.

36. Charles H. Harris III and Louis R. Sadler, "United States Government Archives and the Mexican Revolution," *New World: A Journal of Latin American Studies* 1, no. 2 (1986): 108–16; "Cresse" reports in reels 20, 22, and 23, BI. Some of this material is reproduced in *Investigation of Mexican Affairs*, Senate Document 285, 66th Cong., 2d sess., 2 vols. (Washington, D.C.: Government Printing Office, 1920), 2:2994–3117.

37. "Cresse" reports, New Orleans, Feb. 19 and May 25, 1918, reel 20, BI. Jones had, with the knowledge of the Bureau, been employed by Mexican Foreign Minister Cándido Aguilar as a confidential agent and public relations director in the United States. See Jones to Hanson, Dec. 31, 1919: " . . . due to my previous connections with the Mexican government as confidential agent in the United States of its foreign office." Fall Papers, RGHC, NMSU.

38. Forrest C. Pendleton, Division Superintendent, BI to "whom it may concern," May 28, 1919, in *Investigation of Mexican Affairs*, 2:2894. A copy is in the Fall Papers, RGHC, NMSU. On Jones's reason for severing his connection with the BI, see his testimony in *Investigation of Mexican Affairs*, 2:2890.

39. Kearful to Fall, Dec. 8, 1919, A. B. Fall Papers, RGHC, NMSU.

40. *Investigation of Mexican Affairs*, 2:3223–49. See also Stone, "Fall Committee and Double Agent Jones," 45–49.

41. Barnes to Major S. W. Anding, Intelligence Officer, Nogales, Ariz., Dec. 10, 1917, 51–45, Records of the War Department General and Special Staffs, Military Intelligence Division, Record Group 165, National Archives (hereafter cited as MID).

42. For the early history of MI, see Corson, *Armies of Ignorance*, 593–95; O'Toole, *Spanish War*, 353–54; Nathan Miller, *Spying for America: The Hidden History of U.S. Intelligence* (New York: Paragon House, 1989), 161–70, 176–81.

43. Ralph E. Weber, ed., *The Final Memoranda: Major General Ralph H. Van Deman, USA Ret. 1865–1952 Father of U.S. Military Intelligence* (Wilmington, Del.: Scholarly Resources Books, 1988), 15–22. Given the fact that Van Deman was eighty-four years old when he wrote the final memoranda, the present authors are somewhat skeptical about the specific accuracy of a number of Van Deman's "war stories," which on their face appear to be embroidered at the very least. After all, Van Deman, in some cases, was writing about incidents that occurred more than forty years previously. That said, the Weber edition is useful in pulling together Van Deman's correspondence.

44. See, for example, Captain Frank R. McCoy, June 14, 1906, telegram to Lt. Poillon, Zamboanga, Mindanao. McCoy informed Poillon that it was unnecessary to account for the secret service funds in his possession. The fund was principally used to pay informants. He also informed the lieutenant that additional funds were available. See "Secret Service Fund, 1906–1908," in Vol. 69, Tasker H. Bliss Papers, Library of Congress.

45. Weber, *Final Memoranda*, 11–13, 17–18.

46. For a survey of army intelligence gathering operations in Cuba, see Joan M. Jensen, *Army Surveillance in America, 1775–1980* (New Haven, Conn.: Yale University Press, 1991), 84–87.

47. Jeffreys-Jones, *American Espionage*, 33.

48. Captain William S. Scott to the Adjutant General, Aug. 26, 1907, in Numerical and Minor Files of the Department of State, Microcopy M-862, file numbers 5026 and 5028, National Archives. See also Charles H. Harris III and Louis R. Sadler, *Bastion on the Border: Fort Bliss, 1854–1943* (Historic and Natural Resources Report Number 6, Cultural Resources Management Program, Directorate of Environment, United States Army Air Defense Artillery Center, Fort Bliss, Tex., 1993), 13, 17.

49. Captains Rhodes and Malone to the Chief of Staff, U.S. Army, "Confidential," Oct. 27, 1911, 5761–308, RG 165, MID.

50. Colonel John Biddle to 1st Lieutenant W. E. W. MacKinley, Dec. 15, 1911, "Confidential," 6931-1-30, Army War College, General Correspondence, MID.

51. Harris and Sadler, "1911 Reyes Conspiracy," 325–48. The most important U.S. Army intelligence document cited is File No. 5761–358, MID; Lt. Charles Braden, ed., Supplement, vol. 5 (1900–1910), to George Washington Cullum, ed., *Biographical Register of the Officers and Graduates of the United States Military Academy* (Saginaw, Mich.: Seeman and Peters, 1910), 436.

52. Burnside's reports are cited in Harris and Sadler, "'Underside,'" pp. 69–83. The specific citations are File Nos. 5761–532, July 24, 1912, and 5384–16, MID.

53. Harris and Sadler, "'Underside,'" 56–58. The BI documents cited are found in reels 1–3, BI.

54. The standard work on this subject is Robert E. Quirk, *An Affair of Honor: Woodrow Wilson and the Occupation of Veracruz* (New York: W. W. Norton, 1967).

55. The details of this particular incident, as we know it from available sources, should probably be viewed with some skepticism. See William Manchester, *American Caesar: Douglas MacArthur, 1880–1964* (Boston: Little Brown, 1978), 73–76. For the occupation of Veracruz, see Michael C. Meyer, "The Arms of the *Ypiranga*," *Hispanic American Historical Review* 50 (1970): 543–56; and Meyer, *Huerta: A Political Portrait* (Lincoln: University of Nebraska Press, 1972), 196–203.

56. For MacKinley, see Harris and Sadler, "Plan of San Diego," 388. For McCoy, see Boxes 5, 14, and 79, Frank R. McCoy Papers, Library of Congress, particularly "Commendation" from Brigadier General James Parker, Mar. 17, 1917; McCoy "was in charge of the work of military intelligence, for which he is remarkably well fitted." This document is in Box 79. In a very brief period (July-October 1915), McCoy put together a rather unique intelligence collection network along the Rio Grande south of Laredo. He recruited young women schoolteachers (principally Anglos) who spoke Spanish. McCoy, who was a dashing, handsome (and single) cavalry officer soon had these school marms (also single) producing prodigious and accurate intelligence reports identifying the Plan of San Diego raiders. They obtained this information very simply—by interrogating their students and listening to their conversations about the raids. For example, see Miss E. B. Baldridge, Oct. 5, 1916, to McCoy in Box 79, Frank R. McCoy Papers.

57. Harris and Sadler, *Border and the Revolution*, 12.

58. For the 1913 Japanese War Crisis, see William Reynolds Braisted, *United States Navy in the Pacific, 1909–1922* (Austin and London: University of Texas Press, 1971), 123–40. For the best account of Campanole's career during this period, see John J. Pershing Papers, General Correspondence, 1904–1948, Box 38, Colonel Nicolas W. Campanole File, Library of Congress.

59. Harris and Sadler, *Border and the Revolution*, 12–14.

60. This account is derived from the debriefing of the four Japanese spies, apparently by Campanole. There is also mute evidence that one of Pershing's intelligence officers succeeded in planting a story in a Chihuahua City newspaper that a Japanese doctor had poisoned Villa. This rather sophisticated ploy would have deflected blame from the United States to a third-country national—nominally from a country that was pro-Mexican—had the poison plot succeeded. See Harris and Sadler, *Border and the Revolution*, 15–17.

61. Ibid., 17–23.

62. John Patrick Finnegan, *Military Intelligence*, Army Lineage Series, Center for Military History, United States Army (Washington, D.C.: Government Printing Office, 1998), 18–19.

63. Harris and Sadler, *Border and the Revolution*, 12–13.

64. David Kahn, *The Codebreakers: The Story of Secret Writing* (New York: Macmillan, 1967).

65. Signal Security Agency, *Mexican Cryptographic Systems Prior to 1929* (SPSIS-1, May 23, 1945), 9, hereafter cited as *Mexican Cryptographic Systems*. The *Magonista* codes were technically monoalphabetic substitutions using arbitrary symbols as cipher equivalents.

66. Ibid.; Harris and Sadler, "United States Government Archives," 138–39. The *Reyista* code was actually a cipher that was also a monoalphabetic substitution.

67. See, for example, Lieutenant Colonel Samuel Reber to Captain Parker Hitt, Jan. 4, 1915, Parker Hitt Papers (courtesy of David Kahn). This letter is reproduced in Harris and Sadler, *Border and the Revolution*, 132.

68. *Mexican Cryptographic Systems*, 9–10; Harris and Sadler, *Border and the Revolution*, 14–15 n. 33.

69. The U.S. Army Signal Corps School at Fort Leavenworth, Kansas, was actually closed down because all the faculty and students were sent to the Punitive Expedition to assist in maintaining communications and monitoring Mexican Army radio and telegraphic traffic. Harris and Sadler, *Border and the Revolution*, 137–38; Major General John J. Pershing, Commanding General, Punitive Expedition, to the Adjutant General of the Army, May 1, 1917, "Report of operations, Punitive Expedition, from July 1,1916 to February 5, 1917." Pershing noted in his report, "This department took up the study of code messages and soon was able to decipher any code used in Northern Mexico. Thereafter, by tapping the various telegraph and telephone wires and picking up wireless messages we were able to get practically all the information passed between the various leaders in Mexico" (16). Found in Record Group 407, Records of the Adjutant General's Office, 1917- ; Central Decimal Files—Project Files, 1917–1925; 470. Mexican Border to 580.81 Mexican Border, Box 1373, NA. An excellent report on tapping telegraph lines on the border is Commanding General, Nogales, Ariz., to the Commanding General Southern Department, "Special Report on Tapping Telegraph Wires," May 6, 1916, found in 8536–83, Office of the Chief of Staff, War College Division, RG 165.

70. Kahn, *Codebreakers*, 370 ff.; John Michell, *Who Wrote Shakespeare?* (London: Thames and Hudson, 1996), pp. 144 ff.

71. David Alvarez, *Secret Messages: Codebreaking and American Diplomacy, 1930–1945* (Lawrence: University of Kansas Press, 2000), 17 passim; Captain Luke McNamee, Director, Office of Naval Intelligence, Sept. 18, 1922, to William J. Burns, Director, Bureau of Investigation, in Loose Papers, Box 91, Confidential Correspondence, 1913–1924,

21500—, RG 65, NA. It should be noted that McNamee stated that William F. Friedman "is a Jew" but "there is nothing to indicate . . . [that Friedman] is disloyal." The officer corps of the U.S. Navy and thus ONI was also notoriously anti-Semitic during World War I. See Dorwart, *Office of Naval Intelligence*, 119.

72. *Mexican Cryptographic Systems*, 10–11; Harris and Sadler, *Border and the Revolution*, 138.

73. Army Security Agency, *Historical Background of the Signal Security Agency*, vol. 2: *World War II* (Assistant Chief of Staff, G-2: Apr. 12, 1946), 2:3, 10, 24, 166–67, 180, and 218. See also SRH-004/NA, *The Friedman Lectures*, Department of Defense, April 1963, 106–8.

74. Army Security Agency, *Historical Background*, 3:58, 66, 70, 204. For an excellent discussion of U.S. Navy communications intelligence during this period, see John Prados, *Combined Fleet Decoded: The Secret History of American Intelligence and the Japanese Navy in World War II* (New York: Random House, 1995), 75–77.

75. Unfortunately, a history of the Department of State's Bureau of Secret Intelligence has not yet been written. See Robert Lansing's autobiography, *War Memories of Robert Lansing: Secretary of State* (Indianapolis: Bobbs-Merrill Company, 1935), 318–29. See also Jeffreys-Jones, *American Espionage*, 42–48.

76. John F. Chalkley, *Zach Lamar Cobb: El Paso Collector of Customs and Intelligence during the Mexican Revolution, 1913–1918,* Southwestern Studies no. 103 (El Paso: Texas Western Press, 1998), 30–31.

77. Doerries, *Imperial Challenge*, 167–68; Von Rintelen, *Dark Invader*, 110–12; Chalkley, *Zach Lamar Cobb*, 30–31. Chalkley suggests that Cobb at the time Huerta was arrested was not aware of the German connection. Although the documentation is lacking it can at the very least be speculated that the El Paso Collector of Customs had some level of awareness that Huerta was being backed by the German government. See also United States Senate, *Brewing and Liquor Interests and Bolshevik Propaganda*, Senate Document 62, 66th Cong., 1st sess., III (Washington, D.C.: Government Printing Office, 1919); Michael C. Meyer, "The Mexican-German Conspiracy of 1915," *The Americas* 23 (July 1966): 76–89.

78. Chalkley, *Zach Lamar Cobb*, 45, 77–78. Domestic Contacts Officers would identify themselves as CIA personnel, and they carried a genuine credential with their correct names. On the other hand, the Foreign Resources Division (FR) operated covertly in the United States. Ronald Kessler, *Inside the CIA: Revealing the Secrets of the World's Most Powerful Spy Agency* (New York: Pocket Books, 1992), 18–19.

79. Chalkley, *Zach Lamar Cobb*, 59, 63, 77–78.

80. Ibid., 61, 77–78, 80–81.

81. Ibid., 64–66. Cobb did suggest, just prior to the raid, that one of his sources had informed him that Villa planned to cross the border peacefully near Columbus. This was a story an Associated Press reporter, George Seese, who was in Columbus at the time of the raid, was floating, and he is the probable source.

82. General John J. Pershing Papers, Library of Congress.

83. The best account of Kalamatiano's career is Colonel Richard S. Friedman's unclassified nineteen-page article: "The American Spy: Xenophon Dmitrievich deBlumenthal Kalamatiano," (Langley, Va.: Central Intelligence Agency Counterintelligence and Security Program, 1997).

84. Record Group 59, General Records of the Department of State, Classified Records of the Office of the Counselor 1916–27, National Archives, College Park, Md. For reports of agents of the Bureau of Secret Intelligence, see Boxes 209, 217, 218, 222, 224, 226, 237, 238.

85. Ibid.; Lansing, *War Memories*, 318–29.

Chapter 2

1. The best account of this period is Dorwart, *Office of Naval Intelligence*, 12–37.

2. Packard, *Century of U.S. Naval Intelligence*, 58–59; Dorwart, *Office of Naval Intelligence*, 46–58.

3. The question of how effective the European-based naval attachés were in recruiting agents or suborning Spanish officials is unclear. Dorwart suggests that the agents recruited were not very effective. See Dorwart, *Office of Naval Intelligence*, 64–65. However, Captain Herbert E. Cocke, who in 1930 was assistant director of Naval Intelligence, authored a fifty-page unpublished history of ONI in which he states that the Spanish-American war reports by ONI agents were "destroyed after the war [because] . . . the reports contained much data that would have been compromising to the special agents, some of whom were of high position in Spain." See Cocke, "History of the Intelligence Division of Naval Operations," 10, Operational Archives Branch, Naval Historical Center, Washington, D.C. See also O'Toole, *Spanish War*, 227–28; and Packard, *Century of U.S. Naval Intelligence*, 59–60. For an account of William S. Sims's activities as naval attaché based in Paris, see Elting E. Morison, *Admiral Sims and the Modern American Navy* (Boston: Houghton Mifflin, 1942), 54–55.

4. Dorwart, *Office of Naval Intelligence*, 80–85; Also, see Charles J. Weeks, *An American Naval Diplomat in Revolutionary Russia: The Life and Times of Vice Admiral Newton A. McCully* (Annapolis: Naval Institute Press, 1993), 17–73. Weeks incorrectly states, "In 1904, the United States possessed only one agency exclusively concerned with the gathering of intelligence, the Office of Naval Intelligence" (17). What Army Intelligence was doing was apparently a mystery to the author.

5. Huntington Wilson, Acting Secretary of State, to U.S. Ambassador to Mexico Henry Lane Wilson, Feb. 17, 1911, 209–168, Confidential Files, Navy Personnel Office, Office of Naval Intelligence, RG38, National Archives and Records Service, Washington, D.C., hereafter cited as ONI. The letter introduced Lt. Commander McCully, "who is about to proceed to Mexico under confidential orders from the Secretary of the Navy. You will give . . . McCully all possible assistance to enable him to accomplish the object of his mission." Also, see Weeks, *American Naval Diplomat*, 74–75, 292–93. ONI's inability to deploy secret agents on short notice during this period is illustrated by Navy Secretary Daniels's account in his memoirs of Rear Admiral Frank Fletcher being forced to informally recruit in 1914 in Veracruz a Marine Corps officer, Smedley Butler (later a famous Marine Corps general) to travel to Mexico City on an intelligence-gathering mission. See Josephus Daniels, *The Wilson Era: Years of Peace, 1910–1917* (Chapel Hill: University of North Carolina Press, 1944), 204–7.

6. See Dawson, U.S. Consul, Tampico (via Naval Radio) to Secretary of State, June 6, 1916, and J. B. Rogers, Special Employee, Bureau of Investigation, Brownsville, Tex., to Bielaski, Washington, D.C., June 10, 1916, both in reel 13, BI. These telegrams have an interesting history. Dawson's telegram to the secretary of state quotes a letter he received that morning, dated June 4, presumably from Ciudad Victoria: "Kindly get . . . off by wireless as quickly as possible. It is urgent. . . . It is mooted that the Carranza forces are going to open the ball not later than the tenth." The letter was signed by the figure seven. Agent No. 7 on the secret agent list of the Office of Naval Intelligence was Lt. Commander Macgillivray Milney. The enclosure read in part: "Yellow heads today's train. Red heads later. Nigger referred to should be looked after. Letter confirming tomorrow." The Bureau special employee in Brownsville, Rogers, responding to a telegram from Bielaski, informed him: "Yellow Heads means troops moving by train. Red heads hot times for grego (gringo) here."

7. Packard, *Century of U.S. Naval Intelligence*, 13. Packard makes an excellent point that this appropriation gave ONI "new authority for confidential collection of information."

8. Dirk A. Ballendorf and Merrill L. Bartlett, *Pete Ellis: An Amphibious Warfare Prophet 1880–1923* (Annapolis: Naval Institute Press, 1997), 155–58; Weber, *Final Memoranda*, 9–10, 12, 14.

9. William Reynolds Braisted, *The United States Navy*, 123–40.

10. Ibid.; Brian McAlister Linn, *Guardians of Empire: The U.S. Army and the Pacific, 1902–1940* (Chapel Hill: University of North Carolina Press, 1997), appendix, p. 253; Braisted, *United States Navy*, 125–40.

11. [Josephus] Daniels to Captain J. H. Oliver, Director, ONI, Nov. 20, 1916, responding to a memorandum from Oliver dated Nov. 14, 1916, 20961–616, Records of the Office of the Chief of Naval Operations, Office of Naval Intelligence, Confidential General Correspondence 1913–24, RG 38, National Archives.

12. Major John H. Russell, USMC, to Director, ONI, "Historical data relating to the Office of Naval Intelligence during the war," Aug. 7, 1919 in Historical Section, ONI. This document is cited in Packard, *Century of U.S. Naval Intelligence*, 56.

13. For example, see Confidential Files No. 20944–976, Navy Personnel, Office of Naval Intelligence, Joseph H. Watts. Watts began work as an ONI secret agent on Feb. 1, 1917, although he did not sign his official secrecy oath until Feb. 19, 1917. Watts subsequently was called to active duty in March 1917, before being assigned to Guatemala.

14. The classic work on the subject is Barbara Tuchman, *The Zimmermann Telegram* (New York: Viking Press, 1958).

15. Captain Roger Welles, Director of Naval Intelligence, to the Navy Department, July 7, 1917, Josephus Daniels Papers, Manuscript Division, Library of Congress, Washington, D.C.

16. Dorwart, *Office of Naval Intelligence*, 94. Also, see Packard, *Century of U.S. Naval Intelligence*, 65, 67.

17. Townsend Hoopes and Douglas Brinkley, *Driven Patriot: The Life and Times of James Forrestal* (New York: Vintage Books, 1992), 136. Hoopes and Brinkley's excellent description of the Navy Department prior to the American entry into World War II applies equally to the period prior to and during World War I.

18. Braisted, *United States Navy*, 124; Josephus Daniels, *Wilson Era: Years of Peace*, 117.

19. Morison, *Admiral Sims*, 435–60.

20. Josephus Daniels, *The Wilson Era: Years of War and After, 1917–1923* (Chapel Hill: University of North Carolina Press, 1946), passim.

21. Captain Edward McCauley report, "U.S. Naval Intelligence Before and During the War," ONI.

22. Dorwart, *Office of Naval Intelligence*, 97, 102–5; Packard, *Century of U.S. Naval Intelligence*, 40–41. Among the first ONI agents to be deployed in the run up to World War I was A. S. Northrup, who was assigned to the Colombian coast in February 1917. Navy Intelligence Service, WX-8 (Neutrals—South America) box 892, RG 45.

23. See, for example, "Diagram Illustrating the method of obtaining Information from Commercial Sources regarding the movements of Enemy Naval Vessels." Also, see "Diagram Representing the Method of Transmission of Other Information from Commercial Sources," March 1915, ONI. The diagrams have an attached buckslip that reads as follows: "Plans for intelligence service in peacetime through commercial concerns . . . *should be kept by ONI or destroyed. Should not go to the National Archives* (italics by the authors). Dorwart has an excellent discussion of the Vacuum Oil episode. See Dorwart, *Office of Naval Intelligence*, 104–5; Packard, *Century of U.S. Naval Intelligence*, 249. Also, see Cocke, "History," 28.

24. Major John H. Russell, USMC, to the Director of Naval Intelligence, Aug. 7, 1919, Historical Section, ONI. See undated but, by internal content, a 1917 organizational chart

in file E-9, 11334A, ONI. Also, see Cocke, "History," 18–33.

25. Undated Organization Chart of Section "A." From internal evidence it probably was drafted in May 1917, ONI.

26. Undated ONI organizational chart, probably July 1917, ONI. See Cocke, "History," 27; Packard, *Century of U.S. Naval Intelligence*, 249.

27. "Lists of ONI Agents and Informants Residing in Foreign Countries during the Period 1917–1925." See also "Numerical Identification List of Personnel 1917–1918 of the Office of Naval Intelligence." Both are in ONI.

28. This statement is based on our reading of Bureau of Investigation, Military Intelligence Division, and the Bureau of Secret Intelligence of the Department of State records during the period 1898–1942. The Office of Naval Intelligence had thirteen agents recruited and posted overseas during the period June 1940-Oct. 1, 1941, before they were merged into the Coordinator of Information (COI), the precursor to the Office of Strategic Services (OSS). We would also suggest that it was not until late 1942 that even OSS had recruited, trained, and deployed overseas eighty-five agents under cover.

29. A number of examples of agent evaluations ("Useless") can be found in "Lists of ONI Agents and Informants Residing in Foreign Countries During the Period 1917–1925," ONI.

30. See Office of Naval Intelligence, General File, Secret Lists of Agents (1917–1920), ONI.

31. Ibid.

32. Lt. (j.g.) John F. White, "Memorandum to the Director of Naval Intelligence," Dec. 4, 1919, ONI.

33. "Taro" to Morley, Nov. 3, 1917, ONI.

34. Oliver C. Townsend file, 21500/597, ONI.

35. See, for example, Sylvanus G. Morley to Taro, Aug. 17, 1917, Report no. 9, ONI.

36. Sims to Secretary of the Navy, Sept. 4, 1917, Naval Records Collection of the Office of Naval Records and Library, Area File/Caribbean Area, 1911–1927, RG 45, NA; hereafter cited as Naval Records Collection, NA.

37. Mayo to Benson, Sept. 5, 1917, Naval Records Collection, NA.

38. Madrid to Berlin, No. 205, Intercepted Telegrams, Room 40, British Office of Naval Intelligence, Records of the U.S.-German-Austro-Hungarian Mixed Claims Commission, RG 76, NA; hereafter cited as Records of U.S.-German Claims. There is an article on Kurt Jahnke which propounds a case that he was not only a German spy but also a British double agent who teamed up with the ubiquitous British spy Sidney Reilly to carry out two major sabotage operations at Black Tom Island, New Jersey and at Kingland, New Jersey to force the United States into declaring war on Germany. The authors agree with a review which suggests that this thesis is "so highly circumstantial that it must be read with extreme caution." The article is Richard B. Spence, "K. A. Jahnke and the German Sabotage Campaign in the United States and Mexico, 1914–1918," *Historian* 59, no. 1 (1996): 89–112.

39. See Admiral Sir W. Reginald Hall Affidavit with annexed copies of 327 Intercepted German Telegrams, particularly telegrams: Madrid to Berlin, Dec. 17, 1917; Berlin to Madrid, Jan. 4, 1918; Madrid to Berlin, Mar. 18, 1918; Madrid to Berlin (No. 178 of March 26), Mar. 18, 1918; Madrid to Berlin, No. 1367, Apr. 3, 1918; Madrid to Berlin, No. 402, Apr. 9, 1918; Madrid to Berlin, (No. 1357 of April 13), Apr. 15, 1918; and Berlin to Madrid, No. 203, Apr. 23, 1918, Records of U.S.-German Claims.

40. Nauen to Mexico, No. 7 of June 8, 1918, "Most Secret," Intercepted German Telegram in Records of U.S.-German Claims. The telegram reads: "The Legation in Mexico is to instruct Jahnke, . . . to prepare as rapidly as possible a point d'appui (stutzpunkt) for submarines on the Mexican coast. . . . The transport of oil and fresh provision for the

submarines should be effected by means of a sailing vessel with auxiliary motor. . . . Absolute reliability and security against use as a submarine trap is necessary. The officers should . . . as possible be Germans and the crew Mexican-Germans, who should be well paid." Friedrich Katz, *The Secret War in Mexico: Europe, The United States and the Mexican Revolution* (Chicago and London: University of Chicago Press, 1981), 425–26.

41. Maxwell Stevenson to Commander Edward McCauley, Jr., Aug. 1, 1916, "Conditions in Tampico Oil Regions," 20959/125A, ONI.

42. William R. Rosenkrans personnel file, 20944/531; Instructions for Rosenkrans, July 2, 1917, both in ONI.

43. Rosenkrans personnel file, 20944/531, ONI.

44. Frank Polk to Captain Edward McCauley, Jr., "Confidential," Jan. 29, 1918, in Rosenkrans personnel file, 20944/531, ONI. See Rosenkrans report received by ONI on Oct. 10, 1917, Navy Intelligence Service, WX-7, Subject File, 1911–27, box 887, RG 45.

45. Paul M. Kennedy, "Great Britain Before 1914," in Ernest R. May, ed., *Knowing One's Enemies: Intelligence Assessment Before the Two World Wars* (Princeton, N.J.: Princeton University Press, 1984), 187–88; Brayton Harris, *The Navy Times Book of Submarines: A Political, Social and Military History*, ed. Walter J. Boyne (New York: Berkeley Books, 1997), 160.

46. Paul G. Halpern, *A Naval History of World War I* (Annapolis: Naval Institute Press, 1994), 33; Harris, *Navy Times Book*, 180.

47. See Clay Blair's excellent World War I introduction in his *Hitler's U-Boat War: The Hunters, 1939–1942* (New York: Random House, 1996), 12.

48. Paul König, *Voyage of the Deutschland: The First Merchant Submarine* (New York: Hearst's International Library Co., 1917); Harris, *Navy Times Book*, 210, 214–22.

49. Halpern, *Naval History*, 336; Harris, *Navy Times Book*, 206–7.

50. Trask, *Captains and Cabinets*, 43–45.

51. The copy of the Zimmermann Telegram furnished to the United States government is found in File No. 123, Box 200, General Records of the U.S. Department of State, Classified Records of the Office of the Counselor, RG 59, NA. There are several copies of the original British cryptanalyzed Zimmermann Telegram; they can be found in HW 7/8 Records Created and Inherited by Government Communications Headquarters (GCHQ): Room 40 German decrypts: diplomatic telegrams including Zimmermann message of Jan. 16, 1917, in Public Record Office, Kew, England (hereafter cited as PRO).

52. Burton J. Hedrick, ed., *Life and Letters of Walter Hines Page*, 3 vols. (London: William Heinemann, 1926), 3:328.

53. Confidential File, "German Sub-Bases on Mexican Coast," General Correspondence Files, 1913–1924, 20961–583, ONI.

54. Cornelius C. Smith, Jr., *Don't Settle for Second: The Life and Times of Cornelius C. Smith* (San Rafael, Calif.: Presidio Press, 1977), 135–41.

55. Major General Fredrick Funston to the Adjutant General, forwarded by Colonel C. W. Kennedy, Acting Chief, War College Division, to Captain James H. Oliver, Director, Office of Naval Intelligence, Dec. 15, 1916, 20961–583, ONI.

56. See, for example, Special Agent Alfred S. Northrup report, Nogales, June 14, 1918; C. E. Breniman report, San Antonio, Aug. 21, 1918; Branch Babcock report, Charleston, South Carolina, June 15, 1918; Special Informant Ibs, New Orleans, Jan. 15, 1918; E. T. Needham, San Antonio, July 9, 1918; E. Kosterlitsky, Los Angeles, June 4, 1918; Clarence Parker, Los Angeles, July 9, 1918; J. J. Lawrence, Laredo, June 11, 1918; W. A. Wiseman, San Antonio, June 10, 1918; Northrop report, Nogales, July 25, 1918; Lawrence report, Laredo, Aug. 30, 1918, reel 19, BI.

57. B. C. Baldwin report, San Antonio, June 20, 1918, reel 19, BI.

58. Secretary of War to Secretary of the Navy, Nov. 10, 1916, 20276/2/3/4, including CNO Benson to Commanding Officer USS *Illinois* (undated); 20276/5A; 2d endorsement, Nov. 29, 1916, Commanding Officer Edward Watson, USS *Wheeling* to the Senior Officer Present, Mexican Atlantic Waters, all found in "Confidential File," "German Sub-Bases on the Mexican Coast," ONI.

59. "German Sub-Bases on Mexican Coast," 20961–583, ONI.

60. Commanding Officer, USS *Illinois*, Dec. 10, 1916, Veracruz, to the Director of Naval Intelligence, 20962–583, ONI.

61. Commanding Officer USS *Wheeling* Progreso, Mexico, to Navy Department (Operations), Mar. 24, 1917, "German Sub-Bases on Mexican Coast," 20615, 8C, ONI. The USS *Wheeling* had steamed from the Honduran coast, along the cays off British Honduras, and northward along the coast of Yucatán the previous week. Port calls were made and potential submarine bases (rivers, etc.) were examined by the crew of the warship. See Commanding Officer, USS *Wheeling* to the Navy Department (Operations), Mar. 22, 1917, "Investigation of possible existing submarine bases—Cape Gracias a Dios to Progreso [*sic*]," 20615/8. Also, see Watson reports, Mar. 11 and 14, 1917, 20491, all in ONI. See also Commanding Officer, USS *Wheeling* to Navy Department (Operations), Mar. 24, 1917, Progreso, Mexico, in Naval Records Collection, NA.

62. Brigadier General Joseph E. Kuhn, Chief of War College Division, Office of the Chief of Staff, War Department, Apr. 5, 1917 to Commander Edward McCauley, Jr., Acting Director, Office of Naval Intelligence, "German Sub-Bases on the Mexican Coast," 20961–583: 20276, ONI.

63. The best account of German submarines operating in U.S. coastal waters is a Navy Department monograph, *German Submarine Activities on the Atlantic Coast of the United States and Canada*, Office of Naval Records and Library, Historical Section, publication No. 1 (Washington, D.C.: Government Printing Office, 1920).

Chapter 3

1. "An article on the Office of Naval Intelligence by Rear Admiral Roger Welles, U.S.N., 1919," 21, in "Memorandum for the Chief of Naval Operations," Dec. 23, 1919, file 3809–846:13, Records of the Office of the Chief of Naval Operations, RG 38, National Archives and Records Service, Washington, D.C.

2. Edwin M. Shook, *Incidents in the Life of a Maya Archaeologist*, as told to Winifred Veronda. (Guatemala City: Southwestern Academy Press, 1998), 199, 204.

3. Long, *Morleyana*, 4–5.

4. Brunhouse, *Sylvanus G. Morley*, 14.

5. Sylvanus Griswold Morley, *An Introduction to the Study of the Maya Hieroglyphs*, 2d ed. (New York: Dover Publications, 1975), vi. It is extraordinary that sixty years after it was first published that Morley's 1915 description of Mayan hieroglyphs remains a standard work today.

6. Long, *Morleyana*, 94–99; Chris Wilson, *The Myth of Santa Fe: Creating a Modern Regional Tradition* (Albuquerque: University of New Mexico Press, 1997), 117–20.

7. Edgar L. Hewett, *Pajarito Plateau and Its Ancient People*, 2d rev. ed. (Albuquerque: University of New Mexico Press and the School of American Research, 1953), 67 ff.

8. Wilson, *Myth of Santa Fe*, 121–37; Long, *Morleyana*, 162–73; Harry Moul and Linda Tigges, "The Santa Fe 1912 City Plan: A 'City Beautiful' and City Planning Document," *New Mexico Historical Review* 71, no. 2 (April 1996): 135–55.

9. Morley to Boaz Long, May 1 and July 21, 1939, Boaz Long Papers, New Mexico State Records Center and Archives, Santa Fe.

10. John A. Garraty and Edward T. James, eds., *Dictionary of American Biography, Supplement Four, 1946–1950* (New York: Scribner's, 1974), 605–6; Brunhouse, *Sylvanus G. Morley*, 49.

11. Shook, *Incidents in the Life*, 200–202.

12. Frederick W. Hodge to R. S. Woodward, Dec. 17, 1912; Jacob Gallinger to same, Dec. 18, 1912; Morley to same, Mar. 15, 1913; [R. S. Woodward] to Morley, July 29, 1914, all in the Sylvanus G. Morley File, Carnegie Institution of Washington (hereafter cited as Morley File, CIW). In March 1913, Morley published his first article in *National Geographic*, "Excavations at Quiriguá, Guatemala."

13. Brunhouse, *Sylvanus G. Morley*, 63–64.

14. [R. S. Woodward] To Whom It May Concern, Jan. 21, 1916; Morley to Woodward, Apr. 9, 1916, both in Morley File, CIW; *Carnegie Institution of Washington Year Book No. 15, 1916* (Washington, D.C.: The Carnegie Institution, [1917]), 337–39.

15. See, for example, Brunhouse, *Sylvanus G. Morley*, 319; Long, *Morleyana*, 102.

16. Long, *Morleyana*, 21.

17. Ibid., 22.

18. Ibid., 23–48.

19. Morley to Sam[uel Lothrop], June 19, [1916], Samuel K. Lothrop and Joy Mahler Lothrop Archive, 996–20, Peabody Museum Archives, Harvard University, Cambridge, Mass. (hereafter cited as LP).

20. G. Grindle to Foreign Secretary, June 8, 1916, FO 371/2641, PRO; George H. Lewis to Colonial Secretary, May 20, 1916, FO 371/2641, PRO; Wilfred Collet to Colonial Secretary, June 1, 1916, FO 371/2641, PRO; Alban Young to Sir Edward Grey, June 5, 1916, FO 371/2641, PRO; Same to Luis Toledo Herrarte, June 1, 1916, FO 371/2641, PRO; R. Walter to Colonial Secretary, July 4, 1917, FO 252/526, PRO.

21. Long, *Morleyana*, 65–66.

22. Morley to Taro, Jan. 18, 1918, Report no. 17, Confidential File 20977–14, Record Group 38, Records of the Office of the Chief of Naval Operations, Office of Naval Intelligence, Confidential General Correspondence 1913–24 (hereafter cited as ONI), National Archives and Records Service, Washington, D.C.; Brunhouse, *Sylvanus G. Morley*, 112. During his first tour of duty Morley submitted twenty-two reports to ONI. Of these, numbers 6, 13, and 15 are missing from ONI Confidential File 20977–14. However, a copy of Report no. 15 is found in Military Attaché at Tegucigalpa, Honduras, to Chief, Military Intelligence Division, General Staff, Washington, D.C., Jan. 24, 1919, 2357–37, MID.

23. William H. Mechling file, 20944–918, and Sylvanus Morley file, 21500–552, ONI.

24. Neil B. Carmony and David E. Brown, eds., *The Wilderness of the Southwest: Charles Sheldon's Quest for Desert Bighorn Sheep and Adventures with the Havasupai and Seri Indians* (Salt Lake City: University of Utah Press, 1993), xiii–xv.

25. Ibid., xvi–xxii.

26. Ibid., xxii–xxx.

27. Ibid., xxxii–xxxv.

28. Ibid., xxxvi–xxxviii.

29. 186 [H. C. Morgan] to Lothrop, May 21, 1918, LP.

30. Roy Chapman Andrews, *Under a Lucky Star: A Lifetime of Adventure* (New York: Viking Press, 1943), 147.

31. *Membership of the Cosmos Club (1878–1968)* (Washington, D.C.: n.p., 1968), 84.

32. Morley file, 21500–552; "Name List of Persons Considered (ca. 1914–18) as Potential Sources of Information—Paid Agents," unnumbered (hereafter cited as Paid Agents)—both in ONI; *Membership of the Cosmos Club*, 106.

33. Herbert J. Spinden file, Special Files 827 and 906, Department of Library Services, Archives, American Museum of Natural History, New York, N.Y. (hereafter cited as American Museum).

34. Clark Wissler to F. A. Lucas, Apr. 27 and May 14, 1915; [President Henry Fairfield Osborn] to the Minister at Salvador, May 14, 1915. Both are in Herbert J. Spinden, Special File 906, American Museum.

35. Paid Agents; Herbert J. Spinden files 20996–3228 and 21500–581. Both are in ONI.

36. Clark Wissler to F. A. Lucas, Apr. 4, 1917; [Lucas] to Wissler, Apr. 4, 1917; Osborn to Lucas, Apr. 6, 1917; [Osborn] To Whom It May Concern, Apr. 12, 1917, Spinden Special File 906, American Museum.

37. William Hubbs Mechling file, Archives, Harvard University, Cambridge, Massachusetts. Mechling's Ph.D. dissertation, "The Social and Religious Life of the Malectites and Micmacs" is found in the Harvard Archives; *Malectite Tales* was published in 1914 by the Canadian Government Printing Bureau.

38. William Hubbs Mechling file, 20944–918; Paid Agents. Both are in ONI.

39. *Who Was Who among North American Authors, 1921–1939* (Detroit, Gale Research Co., c. 1976), 977; John Alden Mason file, 20944–917, and Paid Agents, both in ONI; Mason to Major Sherman Miles, Dec. 8, 1920, 51–320, MID.

40. Daniels, *Wilson Era: Years of War and After,* 126–28.

41. Roger Welles to Navy Department, July 7, 1917, Josephus Daniels Papers, container 521, Manuscript Division, Library of Congress, Washington, D.C.

42. Brunhouse, *Sylvanus G. Morley,* 119–20; John A. Garraty, ed., *Dictionary of American Biography, Supplement Six, 1956–1960* (New York: Scribner's, 1980), 287–88; *The Most of John Held Jr.* (Brattleboro, Vt.: The Stephen Greene Press, 1972), 144; Chronology of Held's life prepared by his widow, Margaret Held, John Held, Jr., Papers (1889–1958), (microfilm), Archive of American Art, Smithsonian Institution, Washington, D.C.

43. Morley to R. S. Woodward, June 21, 1917, Morley File, CIW.

44. Paid Agents; Held file, 20944–8, both in ONI. Held's reports were infrequent. See his undated report from Puerto Barrios, Guatemala, and one on Feb. 1, 1918, Navy Intelligence Service, WX-8, Subject File, 1911–27, Central America, folder 3/4, Box 891, RG 45.

45. George W. Stocking, Jr., *The Shaping of American Anthropology, 1883–1911: A Franz Boas Reader* (New York: Basic Books, 1974), 309; [Franz Boas] to John Swanton, Jan. 15, 1920, reel 20, "The Professional Correspondence of Franz Boas," microfilm edition, Wilmington, Del., Scholarly Resources, 1972 (hereafter cited as BP). The correspondence itself is at the American Philosophical Society, Philadelphia.

46. Ross Parmenter, "Zelia Nuttall and the Recovery of Mexico's Past," vol. 3, "Casa Alvarado (1917–1933)," unpublished MS ed. Kornelia Kurbjuhn, 1051.

47. Mechling and Mason files, 20944–918 and 20944–917, ONI.

48. Mason file, 20944–17, ONI; Mason to Major Sherman Miles, Dec. 8, 1920, 51–320, MID.

49. Mason to Mrs. John Held Jr., Jan. 3, 1967, Held Papers.

50. Parmenter, "Zelia Nuttall," 1050.

51. Woodward became a member in 1885, Gilbert in 1906. *Membership of the Cosmos Club,* 84, 132, 44.

52. M. S. Brown to Carnegie Institution, Apr. 12, 1917, Morley File, CIW.

53. [R. S. Woodward] to Morley, Jan. 23, 1917; Morley to John L. Wirt, Aug. 31, 1918, both in Morley File, CIW.

54. [R. S. Woodward] to Morley, Apr. 21, 1917; President [R. S. Woodward] To Whom It May Concern, Apr. 21, 1917, both in Morley File, CIW.

55. C. Sheldon to Mrs. S. K. Lothrop, May 15, 1918, LP.

56. "Diary of Sylvanus Griswold Morley, 1917," Vol. 9, Pt. 1: Apr. 26, 1917. It should be noted that the Diary contains occasional lacunae, in which Morley simply noted and dated his itinerary. The original Diary is in the Peabody Museum of Archaeology and Ethnology at Harvard University. In 1959, Morley's widow bequeathed a typescript of the Diary to the American Philosophical Society, Philadelphia. The present authors have utilized a copy of this typescript. See Robert H. Lister and Florence C. Lister, eds. *In Search of Maya Glyphs: From the Archaeological Journals of Sylvanus G. Morley* (Santa Fe: Museum of New Mexico Press, 1970), v.

57. Morley to R. S. Woodward, Apr. 24, 1917, Morley File, CIW.

58. New Orleans *Times-Picayune*, May 6, 1917.

59. Morley to Taro, Feb. 1, 1918, Report no. 19.

Chapter 4

1. Morley to Kato, Apr. 26, 1917, Report no. 1, ONI. Who Kato was remains unclear. He may have been Captain Edward McCauley, Jr., Assistant Director of ONI. Or—Morley may just have gotten his Japanese names confused, using "Kato" instead of "Taro."

2. Since 1981, British Honduras has been the Republic of Belize. Belmopan is the capital.

3. Lt. Col. E. L. Cowie to the Acting Governor, Aug. 3, 1917, CO 123/288, PRO; Thomas Gann, *Ancient Cities and Modern Tribes: Exploration and Adventure in Maya Lands* (London: Duckworth, 1926), 21–24.

4. "Medical Report for the Year 1916," CO 123/287, PRO; R. Walter to Walter H. Long, Aug. 15, 1917, CO 123/288, PRO; Governor of British Honduras to Secretary of State for the Colonies, May 17, 1916, CO 123/284, PRO. As of 1918, Gann's salary was $2,916, plus a house and a consulting practice on the side. Sir William H. Mercer, A. E. Collins, and J. R. W. Robinson, *The Colonial Office List for 1918* (London: Waterlow and Sons, 1918) 125.

5. Robert L. Brunhouse, *Frans Blom, Maya Explorer* (Albuquerque: University of New Mexico Press, 1976), 35; Robert l. Brunhouse, *Pursuit of the Ancient Maya: Some Archaeologists of Yesterday* (Albuquerque: University of New Mexico Press, 1975), 82; Elizabeth Carmichael, *The British and the Maya* (London: Trustees of the British Museum, 1973), 34.

6. See, for example, Gann's "Mounds in Northern Honduras," Smithsonian Institution, Bureau of American Ethnology, *Annual Report 19* (Washington, D.C.: Government Printing Office, 1900), 655–92.

7. *Carnegie Institution of Washington Year Book No. 15, 1916*, 337–39; Morley to R. S. Woodward, Apr. 9, 1916, Morley File, CIW; Morley to Taro, Feb. 1, 1918, Report no. 19; Same to same, May 8, 1917, Report no. 2; Herbert J. Spinden to Mrs. John Held, May 15, 1958, Held Papers.

8. J. Eric Thompson, *Maya Archaeologist* (Norman: University of Oklahoma Press, 1963), 206–7.

9. Hubert Herring, *A History of Latin America from the Beginnings to the Present* (New York: Alfred A. Knopf, 1957), 439–40; Lester D. Langley and Thomas Schoonover, *The Banana Men: American Mercenaries and Entrepreneurs in Central America, 1880–1930* (Lexington: The University Press of Kentucky, 1995), 58–59, 61.

10. Morley to Gilbert, Feb. 6 [1917], Morley File, CIW.

11. Christopher Winters, gen. ed. *International Dictionary of Anthropologists* (New York: Garland Publishing, 1991), 424–25; Morley to R. S. Woodward, Apr. 9, 1916; W. H. Holmes to same, Apr. 13, 1916, both in Morley File, CIW; Boaz Long, *Morleyana*, 126–29.

12. "Name List of Persons Considered (ca. 1914–1918) as Potential Sources of Information–Paid Agents," unnumbered, ONI; Samuel K. Lothrop files 20977–25 and 20977–25a, both in ONI; Morley to Taro, May 8, 1917, Report no. 2.

13. Morley to Taro, May 8, 1917, Report no. 2.

14. Ibid.

15. Morley to Kato, [May 13, 1917], Report no. 3.

16. *Register of the Commissioned and Warrant Officers of the United States Navy and U.S. Naval Reserve Force National Naval Volunteers Marine Corps Medical Reserve Corps and Dental Reserve Corps January 1, 1918* (Washington, D.C.: Government Printing Office, 1918), 362; *Register of the Commissioned and Warrant Officers of the United States Navy U.S. Naval Reserve Force and Marine Corps January 1, 1919* (Washington, D.C.: Government Printing Office, 1919), 717, 740.

17. Langley and Schoonover, *Banana Men*, pp. 3, 4, 38, 158; Herbert J, Spinden to Mrs. John Held, May 15, 1958, and Roy Hebard to same, July 7, 1958, both in the Held Papers.

18. Morley to Taro, June 13, 1917, Report no. 4; *Carnegie Institution of Washington Year Book No. 16, 1917* (Washington, D.C.: Carnegie Institution, 1918), 285–89.

19. Morley to Taro, June 13, 1917, Report no. 4.

20. *New York Herald*, Apr. 4, 1917.

21. R. Walter to Secretary of State for the Colonies, Apr. 3 and 7, 1917, CO 123/287, PRO.

22. H. H. Fawcett to Under Secretary of State, Colonial Office, Apr. 9, 1917, WO 106/868; [R. Walter] to Secretary of State for the Colonies, May 7 and June 8, 1917, WO 106/868; G. Grindle to Secretary of State for the Colonies, Nov. 19, 1917, CO 123/288; Lloyd Hirsch[?] to G. Grindle, Nov. 19, 1917, CO 123/288; Walter H. Long to Governor of British Honduras, Oct. 18, 1917, CO 123/288; [R.] Walter to Secretary of State for the Colonies, Sept. 18, 1917, CO 123/288; Colonial Office to R. Walter, Sept. 18, 1917, CO 123/288; Lt. Col. E. L. Cowie to Acting Governor, May 14, June 15, Aug. 3, 1917, CO 123/288; [R.] Walter to Walter H. Long, Aug. 15, 1917, CO 123/288, all in PRO.

23. Morley to Taro, June 13, 1917, Report no. 4.

24. Ibid.

25. Ibid.

26. Unless otherwise indicated, this account of Morley's journey to San Salvador is based on his Diary, June 13–15, 1917.

27. Brunhouse, *Sylvanus G. Morley*, 125, n. 1; Long, *Morleyana*, 117–20.

28. Spinden to "Gustav Koch," June 14, 1917; [ONI] to Spinden, June 16, 1917; Long to [State Department], July 6, 1917, all in Spinden personnel file 20996–3228, ONI.

29. Morley to Taro, June 25, 1917, Report no. 5. Spinden also wrote an account of the earthquake and volcanic eruption. He mentioned that the last time the volcano had erupted was in 1674, and the last earthquake to hit San Salvador was in 1873. Spinden to George H. Sherwood, June 15, 1917, Spinden Special File 906, American Museum. By August, Spinden was in Costa Rica. See his report from Puerto Limón, Aug. 20, 1917, and on December 14 he was again in San Salvador. Navy Intelligence Service, WX-8, Central America, folder 3/4, box 891, RG 45.

30. American Minister to Secretary of State, June 16, 1917, Morley File CIW.

31. Alvey A. Adee to Gustav Vioch, June 20, 1917, Morley File, CIW.

32. [R. S. Woodward] to Secretary of State, July 10, 1917; [Woodward] to Henry F. Osborn, July 10, 1917; Osborn to Woodward, July 17, 1917; Adee to Woodward, July 17, 1917, all in Morley File, CIW. Woodward to Osborn, July 10, 1917; [Osborn] to Woodward, July 17, 1917, and a copy of the telegram, all in Spinden Special File 906, American Museum. See also Brunhouse, *Sylvanus G. Morley*, 125, and Long to Secretary of State,

June 16, 1917, 816.48/17, Records of the Department of State Relating to the Internal Affairs of El Salvador, 1910–1929, microcopy 658, reel 12.

33. Braisted, *United States Navy*, 231–45.

34. David McCreery, "Wireless Empire: The United States and Radio Communications in Central America and the Caribbean, 1904–1926," *Southeast Latin Americanist* 33 (Summer 1993): 29. Carranza was convinced that Estrada Cabrera was aiding General Félix Díaz's cause in the state of Chiapas, which borders Guatemala. The evidence would indicate that he probably was.

35. Morley to Taro, June 25, 1917, Report no. 5.

36. Ibid.

37. Secretary of State to Secretary of War, July 2, 1919, and enclosures, 87–21, MID; Brigadier General Marlborough Churchill to W. L. Hurley, Jan. 13, 1920, General Lee Christmas File, Department of State, Classified Records of the Office of the Counselor, 1916–27, Box 2, Record Group 59, National Archives.

38. A[lban] Young to A. J. Balfour, Oct. 7, 1918, FO 252/542, PRO.

39. Morley to Taro, July 10, 1917, Report no. 7.

40. Ibid.

41. Ibid.

42. Morley to Taro, July 31, 1917, Report no. 8.

43. Morley to Taro, July 10, 1917, Report no. 7.

44. Morley to Taro, July 31, 1917, Report no. 8.

45. Ibid.

46. Boaz Long to Secretary of State, July 22, 1917, 20606–13, ONI. See also Long to Mrs. John Held, May 5, 1959, Held Papers. A copy of the offending enciphered cablegram is in the H. J. Spinden personnel file 20996–3228, ONI.

47. Morley to Taro, July 31, 1917, Report no. 8.

48. Joseph L. Walter to C. Alban Young, Feb. 3, 1918, FO 252/546, PRO.

49. Laposso to American Forwarding, June 15, 1918, LP. See Stormont's dispatches: Feb. 3, 5, 8, and 15, Mar. 10, 11, April 9, 19, May 4, 28, 1918, FO 252/546, PRO.

50. A. Young to A. J. Balfour, Oct. 7 and Dec. 10, 1918, FO 252/542, PRO.

51. Morley to Taro, July 31, 1917, Report no. 8; Same to same, Aug. 17, 1917, Report no. 9.

52. Morley to Taro, July 31, 1917, Report no. 8. In the same report, Morley stated: "A minor matter in the same connection is the fact that the third daughter, Marguerite, is more or less infatuated with a German, Hans Wencel [sic], who calls on her at the Legation daily, and the younger daughter, Janet, is in love with a Hondureno, Agurcia, whose firm here, American Minister Price of Panama, wired to Mr. Belt the other day, was about to be placed on the British blacklist. In fact this Agurcia is hand in glove with the Rossner and Kohncke firms at Amapala, and is moreover violently pro-German."

53. Copy of a letter from Mrs. Ewing to her daughter, Jan. 3, 1918, LP.

54. A[lban] Young to A. J. Balfour, Oct. 19, 1918, FO 252/542, PRO.

55. Robert Lansing to President [Woodrow Wilson], Aug. 24, 1917 and attachments, Woodrow Wilson Papers, reel 90, Manuscript Division, Library of Congress, Washington, D.C. See also Morley to Taro, Nov. 27, 1917, Report no. 16.

56. Joseph Walter to C. Alban Young, Jan. 20, 1918, FO 252/546, PRO; A[lban] Young to A. J. Balfour, Oct. 19, 1918, FO 252/542, PRO.

57. Morley to Taro, July 31, 1917, Report no. 8; Same to same, Aug. 17, 1917, Report no. 9.

58. A copy of this article, in *El Nuevo Tiempo*, Aug. 15, 1917, is in the Morley File, CIW.

59. Morley to Taro, Aug. 17, 1917, Report no. 9.

60. Ibid.

61. Morley to Taro, July 31, 1917, Report no. 8.
62. Lothrop to Taro, June 20, 1917, Aug. 1, 1917, Sept. 14, 1917, and Nov. 9, 1917, 20977–25a, all in ONI.
63. Morley to Taro, July 31, 1917, Report no. 8.
64. Ibid.; Morley to R. S. Woodward, June 21, 1917, Held Papers.
65. Morley to Taro, July 31, 1917, Report no. 8.
66. Ibid; Same to same, Aug. 17, 1917, Report no. 9.
67. Morley to Taro, Aug. 17, 1917, Report no. 9.

Chapter 5

1. Unless otherwise indicated, this account of Morley's activities is based on his Diary, August 18-October 23, 1917.
2. Langley and Schoonover, *Banana Men*, 40.
3. Morley to Taro, Sept. 8, 1917, Report no. 10.
4. Ibid.
5. Ibid.
6. Ibid.
7. Ibid.
8. Ibid.
9. Ibid.
10 Samuel Eliot Morison, *Admiral of the Ocean Sea: A Life of Christopher Columbus,* 2 vols. (New York: Time Incorporated, 1962), 2:588.
11. Morley to Taro, [Oct. 11, 1917], Report no. 11.
12. Ibid.
13. Ibid.
14. Morley to Taro, Oct. 12, 1917, Report no. 12.
15. Ibid.
16. Morley to Taro, Nov. 11, 1917, Report no. 14.
17. There have been several editions of Stephens's works. See, for example, *Incidents of Travel in Central America, Chiapas and Yucatan,* 2 vols. (New York: Dover Publications, 1969); and *Incidents of Travel in Yucatan,* 2 vols. (New York: Dover Publications, 1963).
18. Wicker became a member in 1915, Spinden in 1917. *Membership of the Cosmos Club,* 111, 129.
19. Morley to Taro, Oct. 12, 1917, Report no. 12. See Wicker's instructions, July 23, 1917, and his report, Aug. 23, 1917, Navy Intelligence Service, WX-8, Subject File, 1911–27, Central America, folder 3/4, box 891, RG 45.
20. Swan Island, or, more properly, Great Swan Island, was one of two miserable guano islands some one hundred miles off the coast of Honduras, with uninhabited Little Swan being the other. Swan Island was a mile and a half long by half a mile wide. The islands were reportedly named for a seventeenth-century pirate whose base they were. Swan Island gained notoriety in the 1960s as the site of a covert CIA radio station. Radio Swan, with a fifty-kilowatt transmitter, was established in 1960 by the CIA and was "owned" by a front company. Prior to and during the Bay of Pigs debacle, Radio Swan ostensibly broadcast as the voice of Cuban exiles. As late as 1964, the CIA beamed radio broadcasts to Mexico, Cuba, Central America, and northern South America from Swan Island. David Wise and Thomas B. Ross, *The Invisible Government* (New York: Bantam Books, 1965), 15, 350–60; David Atlee Phillips, *The Night Watch* (New York: Ballantine Books, 1982), 113–14, 121, 124–25. The United States and Honduras disputed sovereignty over the islands until 1971, when the United States acknowledged Honduran ownership.

21. Morley to Taro, Nov. 11, 1917, Report no. 14.

22. [Henry Fairfield Osborn] to Spinden, Mar, 18, 1918, Spinden Special File 906, American Museum; Aid for Information to Navintel, July 24, 1918, Spinden personnel file 20996–3228, ONI; Spinden to Charles Sheldon, July 30, 1918, 10987–182, MID; Spinden to Mrs. John Held, May 15, 1958, Held Papers; Museum News Letters No. 5, Oct. 31, 1918, and Dec. 20, 1918, American Museum.

23. Morley to Taro, Nov. 11, 1917, Report no. 14.

24. Shook, *Incidents in the Life*, 204–5.

25. Morley to R. S. Woodward, Apr. 9, 1916, Morley file, CIW; Long, *Morleyana*, 22–23.

26. Morley to Taro, Nov. 11, 1917, Report no. 14.

Chapter 6

1. Morley to Taro, Nov. 11, 1917, Report no. 14.

2. Ibid.

3. Unless otherwise indicated, the following account of Morley's activities is based on his Diary, Nov. 2-Dec. 3, 1917.

4. Long, *Morleyana*, 4–5.

5. Morley to Taro, Nov. 11, 1917, Report no. 14; Long, *Morleyana*, 230–33.

6. [Taro] to Morley, Nov. 3, 1917, 20977–4, ONI.

7. Morley to Taro, Nov. 11, 1917, Report no. 14.

8. New Orleans *Times-Picayune*, May 6, 1917. For a scholarly treatment of this topic, see William J. Williams, *The Wilson Administration and the Shipbuilding Crisis of 1917: Steel Ships and Wooden Steamers* (Lewiston, Queenston, Lampeter: Edwin Mellen Press, 1992).

9. [Morley] to [Taro], Nov. 22, 1917, Report no. 15. This report is missing from ONI Confidential file 20977–14, but a copy is in Military Attaché at Tegucigalpa, Honduras, to Chief, Military Intelligence Division, General Staff, Washington, D.C., Jan. 24, 1919, 2357–37, MID, Record Group 165, National Archives and Records Service, Washington, D.C. See also Morley to Taro, Nov. 27, 1917, Report no. 16.

10. Morley to Taro, Nov. 27, 1917, Report no. 16.

11. Ibid.

12. Ibid.

13. Ibid.

14. Langley and Schoonover, *Banana Men*, 37–38.

15. Morley to Taro, Nov. 27, 1917, Report no. 16.

16. Ibid. Morley told ONI that he could be reached by cable through the legation in Guatemala City until December 12; after that date by letter in care of the American consulate in Belize.

17. Ibid.

18. Ibid.

19. Ibid.

20. Ibid.

Chapter 7

1. Unless otherwise indicated, the following account of Morley's activities is based on his diary, Dec. 4, 1917–Jan. 6, 1918. There is a gap in the Diary from Jan. 7 through Feb. 1, 1918.

2. Morley to Taro, Jan. 18, 1918, Report no. 17.

3. Ibid.

4. Jack Armstrong to Wireless Press, Dec. 6, 1917, FO 252/537, PRO.

5. Bureau of Investigation report, May 12, 1919, in Joseph H. Watts file, 20944–976, ONI; McCreery, "Wireless Empire," 28. In 1912, at the request of the Guatemalan government, a U.S. Signal Corps sergeant was assigned to give radio instruction in that country. When, in 1913, the Signal Corps was unable to continue providing this service, the navy detailed J. H. Watts as advisor in what would be the first of several tours of duty; see "Memorandum for Captain McCoy," Apr. 20, 1912, 814.74/3; R. Bengochea to Secretary of State, Apr. 15, 1912, 814.74/3; Joaquín Méndez to Secretary of State, Apr. 24, 1913, 814.74/14; F. D. Roosevelt to Secretary of State, July 19, 1913, 814.74/20, Records of the Department of State Relating to Internal Affairs of Guatemala, 1910–29, Microcopy No. 655, National Archives and Records Service, Washington, D.C.

6. Joseph H. Watts file, 20944–976, ONI.

7. Ibid; Josephus Daniels to Secretary of State, June 8, 1917, 5023–31, ONI.

8. For example, in June 1918, one P. W. Schufeldt, an American businessman, became Watts's subagent in the Petén region of Guatemala. H. Henneberger to Charles Sheldon, June 25, 1918, 21115, ONI.

9. Morley to Taro, Feb. 1, 1918, Report no. 19.

10. Jack Proby Armstrong was an experienced diplomat, having served in the Ivory Coast, the Congo, Cameroons, Honduras, and in Guatemala City since 1914. Godfrey E. P. Herstlet, Percy C. Rice, and Leslie G. Brown, *The Foreign Office List and Diplomatic and Consular Year Book for 1917* (London: Harrison and Sons, 1917), 187.

11. Long, *Morleyana*, 4.

12. Wilson Popenoe file, 20944–362, and file 20996–1, both in ONI. Charles Morrow Wilson, *Empire in Green and Gold: The Story of the American Banana Trade* (New York: Henry Holt, 1947), 215.

13. *Membership of the Cosmos Club*, 94.

14. Perdomo later stated that the president was amenable to any arrangement that would end the long-standing boundary dispute between Guatemala and Honduras, and that he welcomed the help of the United States in this matter. Commander L. R. Sargent to Lt. Commander O. W. Fowler, Jan. 19, 1918, 21115, ONI. File 21115, containing many of the 15th Naval District's intelligence records, is in Box 86.

15. Morley to Taro, Jan. 18, 1918, Report no. 17.

16. Besides his Immigration Bureau salary of $1,400 a year, Perdomo received $5 a day and expenses while under ONI orders. Perdomo file, 20996–461, ONI.

17. Morley, Diary, Dec. 13, 1917.

18. Alban Young to A. J. Balfour, Aug. 30 and Oct. 28, 1918, FO 252/542, PRO.

19. Morley to Taro, Jan. 28, 1918, Report no. 18.

20. Morley to Taro, Jan. 18, 1918, Report no. 17.

21. Ibid.

22. Brunhouse, *Sylvanus G. Morley*, 113, is incorrect on this point.

23. Morley to Taro, Jan. 28, 1918, Report no. 18.

24. Ibid.

25. Stephen J. Whitfield, "Strange Fruit: The Career of Samuel Zemurray," *American Jewish History* (March 1994), 307–23; Langley and Schoonover, *Banana Men*, 38–39.

26. Morley to Taro, Jan. 28, 1918, Report no. 18.

27. Ibid.

28. Ibid.

29. Ibid; Office of Naval Intelligence to Chief of Naval Operations, Dec. 29, 1917, 20977–14, 87–4, MID; Same to same, Jan. 23, 1918, 87–5, MID.

30. Morley to Taro, Jan. 18, 1918, Report no. 17.

31. Hermann B. Deutsch, *The Incredible Yanqui: The Career of Lee Christmas* (London, New York, Toronto: Longmans Green and Co., 1931), 219, 52–53; Langley and Schoonover, *Banana Men*, 69, 72.

32. Deutsch, *Incredible Yanqui*, 190–91; [William H.] Leavell to Secretary of State, Mar. 1, 1918, General Lee Christmas File, Department of State, Classified Records of the Office of the Counselor, 1916–27, Box 2, Record Group 59 (hereafter cited as Christmas File), National Archives and Records Service, Washington, D.C.

33. Walter C. Thurston to Secretary of State, Jan. 19, 1918 and Feb. 5, 1918, Christmas File.

34. [Leland Harrison] to William H. Leavell, Mar. 13, 1918, Christmas File.

35. [Lt. Commander] O. W. Fowler to State Department, Mar. 1, 1918, Christmas File.

36. William H. Leavell to Leland Harrison, Apr. 19, 1918, Christmas File; Deutsch, *Incredible Yanqui*, 234–37.

37. Ibid.

38. Robert Lansing to Lee Christmas, May 17, 1918; Walter C. Thurston to Secretary of State, Nov. 4, 1918, both in Christmas File. In the Thurston letter there is an obvious error, for Thurston states that Christmas took the oath on *November* 25. See Thurston to Secretary of State, Oct. 26, 1918, Christmas File.

39. Robert Lansing to Lee Christmas, May 17, 1918; [Leland Harrison] to William H. Leavell, June 3, 1918, both in Christmas File.

40. [Leland Harrison] to William H. Leavell, June 3, 1918, Christmas File.

41. [Robert] Lansing to American Legation, Guatemala, Sept. 4, 1918, Christmas File.

42. Deutsch, *Incredible Yanqui*, 193, 241, 236–37.

43. [William H.] Leavell to Secretary of State, July 5 and 13, 1918; [Robert] Lansing to American Legation, Guatemala, July 2 and 10, 1918, Christmas File.

44. [Alban] Young to A. J. Balfour, Oct. 28, 1918, FO 252/542, PRO. For another case of intelligence agents tripping over each other, see Charles H. Harris III and Louis R. Sadler, "The Witzke Affair: German Intrigue on the Mexican Border, 1917–1918," *Military Review*, 59, no. 2 (February 1979), 36–49.

45. Morley to Taro, Jan. 18, 1918, Report no. 17.

46. Ibid.

47. Ibid.

48. Ibid.

49. Ibid.

50. Morley to Taro, Jan. 28, 1918, Report no. 18.

51. Ibid. See also the "Guatemala-Honduras Boundary Dispute" file in Department of State, Classified Records of the Office of the Counselor, 1916–27, Box 2.

Chapter 8

1. This summary of Morley's activities is based on Morley to Taro, Feb. 1, 1918, Report no. 19.

2. See reports by G. M. Shaw, Feb. 15, 1918, and H. D. Scott, Feb. 10, 1918, Navy Intelligence Service, WX-8, Central America, folder 3/4, box 891, RG 45.

3. Sir Cecil Spring-Rice to Foreign Secretary, May 25, 1916, FO 371/2641, PRO; W. Graham Greene to the Foreign Secretary, July 11, 1916, FO 371/2641, PRO.

4. D.N. Cuitt[?] to Foreign Secretary, June 28, 1916, FO 371/2641, PRO.

5. Foreign Office to Sir Cecil Spring-Rice, July 22, 1916, FO 371/2641, PRO; Spring-Rice to Foreign Office, July 24, 1916, FO 371/2641, PRO.

6. The present writers have been unable to determine whether such letters were ever sent.

7. Morley to Taro, Jan. 28, 1918, Report no. 18.

8. Thomas Gann, *In an Unknown Land* (New York: Charles Scribner's Sons, 1924), 19; a photograph of Hubert's passport "photo" is found between 14 and 15.

9. Morley to Taro, Mar. 31, 1918, Report no. 20.

10. Ibid; British Honduras *Government Gazette*, No. 11, Feb. 2, 1918, p. 45, No. 19, Mar. 9, 1918, 85, and No. 26, Apr. 6, 1918, 127, CO 127/18, PRO. Although Gann was along in an intelligence capacity, Morley charged Gann's salary of $100 a month and expenses to the Carnegie Foundation. Morley to John Wirt, Sept. 16, 1918, Morley File, CIW.

11. Morley to Taro, Mar. 31, 1918, Report no. 20.

Chapter 9

1. *Fifty Years of Naval District Development, 1903–1953* (Washington, D.C.: Naval History Division, Office of the Chief of Naval Operations, 1954), 4–5.

2. Ibid., 9–10, 15.

3. Ibid., 17–18.

4. Ibid., 26.

5. "Historical Narrative of Activities of Fifteenth Naval District," 5, Historical Section, Archives, Operations, Navy Department, RG 38, National Archives and Records Service, Washington, D.C.

6. Marine Superintendent to Navintel, Aug. 19, 1917, 20598–14, Records of the Office of the Chief of Naval Operations, Office of Naval Intelligence, Disbursing Officer, 1916–29, RG 38, National Archives and Records Service, Washington, D.C.

7. [Lt. Commander O. W. Fowler] to Commander L. R. Sargent, Oct. 18, 1917, 21115, ONI.

8. Fowler to Sargent, Dec. 2, 1917, 21115, ONI.

9. Sargent to Director of Naval Intelligence, Nov. 30, 1917, 21115, ONI.

10 Sargent to Fowler, Jan. 19, 1918, 21115, ONI.

11. Sargent to Fowler, Nov. 12, 1917, 21115; Sargent to Director of Naval Intelligence, Nov. 30, 1917, 21115, ONI.

12. Oliver C. Townsend personnel file, 21500–597, ONI.

13. Sargent to Director of Naval Intelligence, Nov. 30, 1917, and Apr. 1, 1918, 21115, ONI. A. A. Seraphic's mailing address was in care of Commander Sargent. He used code A-16, and his key word was SANDY. Seraphic file, 20996–1, ONI; Perdomo file, 20996–1, ONI. See Perdomo report, Jan. 12, 1918, Navy Intelligence Service, WX-8, Subject File, 1911–27, Central America, folder 3/4, Box 891, RG 45.

14. Secnav to Commander, Naval Forces, Canal Zone, Apr. 3, 1918, 21115, ONI.

15. Sargent to Director of Naval Intelligence, Apr. 1, 1918, 21115, ONI.

16. "Historical Narrative of Activities," 10.

17. Sargent to Fowler, Jan. 19, 1918, 21115, ONI.

18. Wicker file, 20944–971; "Secret Lists of Agents (1917–1920)"; Sargent to Director of Naval Intelligence, Apr. 1, 1918, 21115, ONI.

19. H. Henneberger to Charles Sheldon, June 25, 1918, 21115, ONI.

20. Aide for Information to Commandant, 15th Naval District, Mar. 14, 1918, 21115. In June 1918, ONI inquired of the 15th Naval District: "Can you use Agent whose cover is dealing in hides?" The answer was a prompt "Yes." Commandant 15th Naval District to Navintel, June 9, 1918, 21115, ONI.

21. H. Henneberger to Director of Naval Intelligence, May 22, 1918, 75004, ONI.

22. Sargent to Director of Naval Intelligence, Apr. 1, 1918, 21115; Same to Fowler, Jan. 18, 1918, 21115, ONI.

23. Sargent to Director of Naval Intelligence, Apr. 1, 1918, 21115, ONI.

24. Sargent to Director of Naval Intelligence, Nov. 30, 1917, and Dec. 24, 1917, 21115; Pullen Personnel File, 21069–651; [Sargent] to Burnav [Bureau of Navigation], Sept. 28, 1918, 21996–987, ONI. As vice-consul in Puerto Limón, Pullen had been reporting to the 15th Naval District as early as October 1917. See Pullen to Secretary of State, Oct. 21, 1917, and to American Forwarding Company, Oct. 20, 1917, Navy Intelligence Service, WX-8, Central America, folder 3/4, box 891, RG 45.

25. Commandant 15th Naval District to Burnav, Sept. 28, 1918, 21996–987, ONI.

26. Albert B. Pullen to Dr. W. R. Pullen, Apr. 19, 1918, U.S. Postal Censorship, Apr. 30, 1918, 21069–651, ONI.

27. Leland Harrison to Captain Edward McCauley, Jr., May 18, 1918, 21069–651, ONI.

28. Commandant 15th Naval District to Navintel, Oct. 15, 1918, no file number [21996–987?], ONI.

29. Commandant, 15th Naval District to Navintel, Oct. 15, 1918, no file number [21996–987 ?]; William C. Van Antwerp to Director of Naval Intelligence, Sept. 9, 1918, 21996–987, both in ONI.

30. Van Antwerp to Director of Naval Intelligence, Sept. 9, 1918, 21996–987, ONI.

31. Ibid.

32. Ibid; Aide for Information, 15th Naval District to Burnav, Sept. 19, 1918, 21115; Same to Navintel, Sept. 21, 1918, 21115; Director of Naval Intelligence to Commandant, 15th Naval District, Nov. 1, 1918, 21996–987, ONI.

33. Commandant, 15th Naval District to Navintel, Sept. 18, 1918, 21996–987; Navintel to Commandant, 15th Naval District, Sept. 16, 1918, 21996–987; [Sargent] to Charles Sheldon, Oct. 8, 1918, 21996–987, ONI.

34. Dunn's ONI file, as of Jan. 23, 1920, read: "Served under the office of Naval Intelligence in Central America, Mexico and Venezuela from August 1917 to February 1919. Is now contemplating a trip to Mexico and Central America as editor of the Latin-American Section of the New York Sun. Will make periodical trips of this character. Is authorized to collect information principally on ports; has seen a list containing information desired. Has no cable address. Will submit reports on return. Will sign reports under old number—168. Desires no remuneration whatever but is authorized upon his return to submit vouchers covering expenditure of money for maps, photographs, stenographic work, covering these reports, same to be approved by the Director of Naval Intelligence. Total amount allowed for these expenses during any one trip not to exceed $100. "Address—New York Sun, N.Y. City."

35. Sargent to Director of Naval Intelligence, Nov. 30, 1918, 21115, ONI.

36. Laposso to Wilberjohn, Jan. 22, 1918, LP. Lothrop did report once by mail to "Taro" on Mar. 4, 1918, and he also mailed reports to the "American Forwarding Co."—i.e., 15th Naval District, LP.

37. Lothrop to American Forwarding Co., Mar. 4, 1918, LP.

38. S. H. Barker to Lt. Manly, Mar. 13, 1918, LP.

39. J. J. Perdomo to Lothrop, Nov. 9, 1917, LP.

40. W. H. Holmes to Robert S. Woodward, Apr. 13, 1916, CIW; Rachel Lothrop to [Charles] Sheldon, Feb. 27, [1918]; Charles Sheldon to Mrs. S. K. Lothrop, Mar. 4, 1918, both in S. K. Lothrop personnel file, ONI.

41. "Plan for Organization of Costa Rica," April 1918, LP; Rear Admiral Roger Welles to Lt. Commander Spencer Eddy, Nov. 21, 1918, 20975–25, ONI.

42. Lothrop to American Forwarding, Apr. 13, 1918, LP.

43. "Plan for Organization of Costa Rica," April 1918; Laposso to Steele, July 1, 1918, LP.

44. Andoran to Wilber, May ___, 1918, LP.

45. Laposso to [John] Steele, June 9, 1918, LP.

46. H. Henneberger to Charles Sheldon, June 25, 1918, 21115, ONI.

47. Wicker to Rear Admiral Roger Welles, Oct. 22, 1918, Wicker file, 21500–570, ONI. In fairness to Wicker it should be pointed out that Lt. Commander O. W. Fowler sometimes made verbal arrangements with agents without informing the Director of Naval Intelligence. See [Rear Admiral Roger Welles] to Captain George W. Williams, Apr. 17, 1919, Container 3, Roger Welles Papers, Manuscript Division, Library of Congress, Washington, D.C.

48. S-32 report, "Costa Rica, German Activities," May 8, 1918, LP.

49. Agent No. 173 report, "Review of the Tinoco Administration," Apr. 22, 1918, LP.

50. J. Steele to Lothrop, May 24, 1918, LP.

51. Laposso to American Forwarding, June 15, 1918; 173 report, "Relations of U.S. Chargé d'Affaires to the Gomez Revolution," June 25, 1915 [*sic*—1918], both in LP.

52. Steele to Lothrop, June 27, 1918, LP. See also Aide for Information to Director of Naval Intelligence, Mar. 30 and Aug. 14, 1918; Director of Naval Intelligence to Commandant, 15th Naval District, July 31 and Sept. 6, 1918, Paymaster files, ONI.

53. Laposso to Steele, July 1, 1918, LP.

54. Agent No. 173 report, "Relation of U.S. Chargé d'Affaires to the Gomez Revolution," July 13, 1918; Lothrop report, Aug. 10, 1918, LP.

55. Lothrop report, July 19, 1918; John Steele to Mrs. S. K. Lothrop, Aug. 12, 1918, LP.

56. Wilbur to Laposso, Aug. 20, 1918, LP; Navintel to Commandant 15th Naval District, Aug. 22, 1918, 21115, ONI.

57. S-32 report, "Re Johnson," Sept. 14, 1918, LP.

58. Lt. Commander Spencer Eddy to Director of Naval Intelligence, Nov. 8, 1918; Rear Admiral Roger Welles to Lt. Commander Spencer Eddy, Nov. 21, 1918, 20975–25, ONI.

59. Navintel to Commandant, 15th Naval District, Aug. 24, 1918; Commandant, 15th Naval District to Opnav, Aug. 24, 1918, 21115, ONI; John M. Keith to Lothrop, Dec. 13, 1918, LP.

60. Navintel to Aid[e] for Information, 15th Naval District, Sept. 27, 1918; Same to Lt. (j.g.) J. Vining Harris, Oct. 14, 1918, 21115, ONI; C. Sheldon to Lothrop, Oct. 19, 1918, LP.

61. W. H. Holmes To Whom It May Concern, Sept. 27, 1918; Adjutant General of the Army to S. K. Lothrop, Oct. 24, 1918, LP.

62. Sargent to Director of Naval Intelligence, Apr. 1, 1918, 21115, ONI.

Chapter 10

1. Gann, *In an Unknown Land.*

2. Ibid., 21–22, 107, 70–71.

3. Ibid., 28.

4. See, for example, Michel Peissel, *The Lost World of Quintana Roo* (New York: E. P. Dutton & Co., 1963), pp. 50–51.

5. Nelson Reed, *The Caste War of Yucatán* (Stanford, Calif.: Stanford University Press, 1964), vii, ix, 53ff, 226.

6. Ibid., 229, 238–42.

7. Long, *Morleyana*, 126–29.

8. Unless otherwise indicated, this account of Morley's activities is based on his Diary, Jan. 1-Feb. 28, 1918.

9. Gann, *In an Unknown Land*, 20; Reed, *Caste War*, 252.

10. A photograph of the dapper General Solís is in Gann, *In an Unknown Land*, between 20 and 21.

11. Ibid., 22–23.

12. Ibid., 21–22.

13. Morley to Taro, Mar. 31, 1918, Report no. 20.

14. Gann, *In an Unknown Land*, 23.

15. Reed, *Caste War*, 243–44; Gann, *In an Unknown Land*, 27.

16. Sullivan, *Unfinished Conversations*, 227, states that Gann did not accompany Morley and Held on this trip. Gann was indeed a member of Morley's party. See Morley's Diary, Feb. 9 and 10, 1918.

17. Reed, *Caste War*, 245–50; Gann, *In an Unknown Land*, 30–34.

18. Gann, *In an Unknown Land*, 29–30.

19. Ibid., 40.

20. Morley to Taro, Mar. 31, 1918, Report no. 20.

21. Dr. Gann commented unfavorably on the swarm of federal officials at Cozumel who, in his opinion, were there primarily to prey financially on travelers. Gann, *In an Unknown Land*, 62–63.

22. *Carnegie Institution of Washington, Year Book No 17, 1918* (Washington, D.C.: Carnegie Institution, 1919), 271, 275.

23. Morley had visited the area in 1913 and again in 1916. Morley to R. S. Woodward, Mar. 15, 1913, and Apr. 9, 1916, both in Morley File, CIW.

24. Gann, *In an Unknown Land*, 142.

25. Sullivan, *Unfinished Conversations*, 136.

26. Roger Welles to Captain V. H. Haggard, Apr. 24, 1918; Haggard to Welles, May 1, 1918, 20977–14, ONI.

27. Franklin D. Roosevelt to Secretary of State, Oct. 20, 1917; Josephus Daniels to same, Dec. 7, 1917 and Jan. 12, 1918, 8480–28, ONI.

Chapter 11

1. Gann, *In An Unknown Land*, 170, says they arrived on February 6, which is incorrect.

2. Ibid., 172, 176.

3. Ibid., 173.

4. Ibid., 179.

5. Morley, Diary, Feb. 25–28, 1918; Gann, *In an Unknown Land*, 178–79.

6. Alvarado was allegedly motivated by two considerations: (1) revolutionary ideology's concern for the oppressed, in this case including the rebel Maya, and (2) he didn't want to leave several battalions of troops, who might become hostile, so far from his immediate control. Reed, *Caste War*, 249–50.

7. The foregoing account is based on Morley to Taro, Mar. 31, 1918, Report no. 20.

8. Gann, *In an Unknown Land*, 179–80.

9. Carnegie Institution of Washington, *Year Book No. 17, 1918*, 271; Gann, *In an Unknown Land*, 238 ff.

10. Gann, *In an Unknown Land*, 181–253.

11. Except where otherwise noted, the following account is based on Morley to Taro, Apr. 20, 1918, Report no. 21.

12. Allen Wells and Gilbert M. Joseph, *Summer of Discontent, Seasons of Upheaval: Elite*

Politics and Rural Insurgency in Yucatán, 1876–1915 (Stanford, Calif.: Stanford University Press, 1996), 286.

13. For an excellent discussion of German propaganda in Mexico and Allied countermeasures, see Katz, *Secret War in Mexico*, 441–59.

14. Sidney Charles Burnett file, FO 372/1144, PRO.

15. Alan Judd, *The Quest for C: Mansfield Cumming and the Founding of the Secret Service* (London: Harper Collins, 1999), 302–3.

16. Not yet having personally investigated conditions in Tabasco, Morley grossly overestimated German presence in that state. In his later Report no. 22 of June 1, 1918, he stated that there were probably not more than twenty-five Germans in Tabasco.

Chapter 12

1. The following account of Morley's activities is based on Morley to Taro, June 1, 1918, Report no. 22. Into "Taro's" office flowed the reports of several agents in Area No. 2, among them Morley, Thomas Gann, John Held, Samuel Lothrop, Wilson Popenoe, Herbert J. Spinden, Lewis H. Watkins, and Joseph H. Watts. Handwritten but undated and unnumbered list of agents in records of Disbursing Officer, ONI.

2. The report is found in B. C. Decker to MID, June 14, 1918, 20969-28, 87-9, MID.

3. See Harry Thayer Mahoney and Marjorie Locke Mahoney, *Espionage in Mexico: The 20th Century* (San Francisco, London, Bethesda: Austin and Winfield, 1997), 107-11.

4. For Altendorf's career, see Harris and Sadler, "Witzke Affair," 36-49.

5. Morley to Walter M. Gilbert, Apr. 3, 1918; [Gilbert] to Morley, Apr. 19, 1918, Morley File, CIW.

6. Fowler to Morley, June 11, 1918, Sylvanus G. Morley Papers, Laboratory of Anthropology, Office of Cultural Affairs, State of New Mexico, Santa Fe.

7. Captain E. W. McCauley to Morley, June 26, 1918; Ensign C. S. Fairbanks to same, July 9 and Aug. 7, 1918, ibid.

8. Morley to Captain E. McCauley, Jr., July 5, 1918, Morley file, 21500-552, ONI.

Chapter 13

1. H. Henneberger to Charles Sheldon, June 25, 1918, 21115, ONI.

2. Navintel to Commander, Naval Forces, I.C.Z., Aug. 10, 1918, 21115, ONI.

3. Navintel to Commandant, 15th Naval District, Sept. 18, 1918, Morley file, 21500-552, ONI.

4. "Paid Agents—Cards Kept by Milne and Capt. McCauley personally," unnumbered, ONI.

5. Commandant 15th Naval District to Navintel, Aug. 24, 1918, 21115, ONI.

6. Morley to Assistant Director of ONI, Aug. 2, 1918; Same to Bureau of Navigation, Aug. 31, 1918, Morley file, 21500-552, ONI. See also Morley to John Wirt, Aug. 31, 1918, Morley File, CIW.

7. The DNI's first endorsement to Morley's request for promotion, Aug. 31, 1918, Morley File, CIW.

8. Acceptance and Oath of Office, Aug. 18, 1918; Bureau of Navigation to Morley, Dec. 10, 1918, both in ONI.

9. Morley to R. S. Woodward, Sept. 3 and 16, 1918, Morley File, CIW.

10. Morley to Woodward, Sept. 16, 1918, ibid.

11. Morley to Woodward, Sept. 16 and 26, 1918, ibid.

12. Morley to Woodward, Oct. 18, 1918, ibid.

13. T. S. Jones to Secretary of State, Nov. 4, 1918, Morley file, 21500–552, ONI.

14. Morley File, CIW.

15. Walter M. Gilbert to Director of Naval Intelligence, Oct. 21, 1918, 21115, ONI.

16. Mrs. B. F. Morley to [R. S.] Woodward, Oct. 27, [1918]; [Woodward] to Mrs. Morley, Oct. 29, 1918. See also [John Wirt] to Morley, Oct. 30, 1918, Morley File, CIW.

17. Commandant 15th Naval District to Navintel, Nov. 18, 1918; Same to Director of Naval Intelligence, Nov. 30, 1918, 21115, ONI.

18. Morley submitted six reports (nos. 23–28) during his second tour of duty. Of these, only nos. 26 and 27 were located, in file 20969–130, ONI.

19. A[lban] Young to A. J. Balfour, Dec. 10, 1918, FO 252/542, PRO.

20. A. M. Medhurst to Alban Young, Feb. 14 and 22, July 12, Oct. 15, 1918, FO 252/542, PRO.

21. Except where otherwise indicated, the following account is based on Morley to Gitaro, Dec. 28, 1918, Report no. 26.

22. Commander L. R. Sargent to Director of Naval Intelligence, Nov. 30, 1918, 21115, ONI. Huber had evidently been a subordinate agent of Pullen's. Director of Naval Intelligence to Commandant, 15th Naval District, Oct. 31, 1918, ONI.

23. A. M. Medhurst to Alban Young, Feb. 22, 1918, with a copy of the president's speech enclosed, FO 252/542, PRO.

24. The British consul believed that Meléndez could easily secure reelection notwithstanding the constitution's limiting the president to a four-year term. A short Act could be rushed through the National Assembly; Meléndez was so popular that there would be little opposition to this course. Medhurst to Alban Young, Oct. 15, 1918, FO 252/542, PRO.

25. A[lban] Young to A. J. Balfour, Dec. 10, 1918, FO 252/542, PRO.

26. A. M. Medhurst to Alban Young, Oct. 15, 1918, FO 252/542, PRO.

27. The following account is based on Morley to Gitaro, Jan. 6, 1919, Report no. 27. Morley signed it "53," his agent number.

28. [T. S.] Jones to Secretary of State, Jan. 4, 1919; Roger Welles to Leland Harrison, January 8, 1919; ___ Arnold to Secretary of State, Jan. 13, 1919, 20977–14, ONI; Rear Admiral A. P. Niblack, Director of Naval Intelligence, "Report upon the Current Political Situations in the Five Republics of Central America," July 21, 1919, Papers as Assistant Secretary of the Navy, 1913–1920—Office of Naval Intelligence, Manuscript Collection, Franklin Delano Roosevelt Library, Hyde Park, N.Y.

29. Acting Director of Naval Intelligence to Commandant, 15th Naval District, Feb. 19, 1919; Navintel to same, Feb. 27, 1919; Commandant, 15th Naval District to Navintel, Jan. 17, 1919, 21115, ONI.

30. Morley to Wilbur, Feb. 1, 1919, 21115, ONI.

31. Chief of Naval Operations to Commandant, 12th Naval District, undated, 28550–923, General Records of the Navy, Secretary of the Navy, General Correspondence, 1916–1926, RG 80, National Archives and Records Service, Washington, D.C.; Sylvanus G. Morley service record, Freedom of Information Act release, National Personnel Records Center (Military Personnel Records), St. Louis, Mo.

32. Morley to Taro, Nov. 27, 1917, Report no. 16.

33. Morley to Taro, Feb. 1, 1918, Report no. 19.

Chapter 14

1. Lyle Rexer and Rachel Klein, *American Museum of Natural History: 125 Years of Expedition and Discovery* (New York: Harry N. Abrams, 1995), 31–34.

2. Boas, "Scientist as Spies," *The Nation*, Dec. 20, 1919.

3. Stocking, *Shaping of American Anthropology*, 309; David Price, "Anthropologists as Spies," *The Nation* (Nov. 20, 2000), 24–27. Price could have profited by consulting the Boas papers.

4. Boas to A. L. Kroeber, Feb. 28, 1914; William Hubbs Mechling to Boas, Mar. 11, 1914; Boas to J. Alden Mason, Mar. 30 (?), 1914; Same to Alfred Tozzer, Apr. 17, May 4, and Sept. 24, 1914; Same to Edward M. Painter, Nov. 13, 1914; Alfred Tozzer to Boas, Nov. 29, 1914; Boas to Mason, Dec. 1, 1914; Same to F. R. Hoisington, Dec. 1, 1914; Same to William H. Mechling, Dec. 4, 1914, reel 15, BP.

5. Berthold Laufer to Boas, July 31, 1917; [Boas] to A[lfred] Tozzer, Aug. 3, 1917; Tozzer to Boas, Aug. 4, 1917, all in reel 18, BP.

6. Boas to Goddard, Aug. 7, 1917, reel 18, BP.

7. Berthold Laufer to Boas, Aug. 10 and 11, 1917, reel 18, BP.

8. Boas to Manuel Gamio, Aug. 14 and 15, 1917, reel 18, BP.

9. Boas to Berthold Laufer, Aug. 16, 1917, reel 18, BP.

10. [Boas] to Aureliano M. Espinoza, Aug. 17, 1917, and to Ezequiel A. Chávez, Aug. 21, 1917, reel 18, BP.

11. Manuel Gamio to Boas, Aug. 23, 1917, reel 18, BP.

12. Boas to Robert H. Lowie, Dec. 3, 1917, reel 18, BP.

13. Stocking, *Shaping of American Anthropology*, 308.

14. The letter is reprinted in ibid., 331–35.

15. W. H. Holmes to [Samuel Lothrop], Dec. 26, 1919, LP.

16. Tozzer to Military Intelligence Branch, Executive Division, May 20, 1918, 2338–87; Same to Major C. H. Mason, June 11, 1918, 2338–128, MID.

17. For Saville, see: Marshall Saville to Colonel M. Churchill, July 17, 1918, 10681–18/1; Same to Major C. H. Mason, May 20, 1918, 2338–189; Same to General [Marlborough] Churchill, Feb. 22, 1920, 87–26/1; Colonel Sherman Miles to Saville, Mar. 15, 1920, 87–26/3, MID.

18. *American Anthropologist* (New Series) 22 (1920): 93–94; Morley to Boaz Long, July 28, [1925], Box 36, folder 174, Boaz Long Papers, New Mexico State Records Center and Archives, Santa Fe (hereafter cited as BLP).

19. George W. Stocking, Jr. *Race, Culture, and Evolution: Essays in the History of Anthropology* (New York: The Free Press, 1968), 273. Stocking gives an excellent account of the personal and factional animosities involved in this affair, 273–93; Boas to Chairman of the Committee of Nominations of the American Anthropological Association, Dec. 29, 1919, reel 20, BP.

20. He sent in his Report no. 30 on Mar. 11, 1919, and no. 31 on Apr. 3, 1919. [Morley] to "Ando," Report no. 32, July 16, 1919, 813.00/956, Records of the Department of State Relating to the Internal Affairs of Central America, 1910–1929, Microcopy 670, National Archives and Record Service, Washington, D.C.

21. Ibid.

22. "Strictly Confidential" memorandum from [J. Herbert] Stabler to [L. L.] Winslow, July 16, 1919, Christmas File.

23. Col. John M. Dunn to Morley, Mar. 17, 1919, 2338–1034; Col. F. L. Dengler to same, June 18, 1919, 2338–1185; Lt. Commander R. S. Field, "Memorandum for Lieutenant-Colonel Campanole," Jan. 17, 1920, 11021–97/3; Major Fred T. Cruse to Assistant Chief of Staff, G2, Mar. 29, 1922, 10989-D-8/84, MID.

24. Brunhouse, *Sylvanus G. Morley*, 165–69.

25. Ibid., 170 ff.

26. Ibid., 175–78; Antoinette May, *Passionate Pilgrim: The Extraordinary Life of Alma Reed* (New York: Marlowe and Company, 1994), 72, 74, 82, 92, 103–4, 109.

27. Brunhouse, *Sylvanus G. Morley*, 201–4.

28. Ibid., 211–12.

29. Ibid., 205–48.

30. Ibid., 261–69. Morley's complex relations with these Maya are treated at length in Sullivan, *Unfinished Conversations*. See also Judith Hancock de Sandoval, "The Virgin of Tabi," *Américas* 32, no. 4 (April 1980): 50–56.

31. Brunhouse, *Sylvanus G. Morley*, 280–81.

32. Ibid., 285.

33. Morley's diary, Yaxchilán Expedition, Mar. 22-May 14, 1931, 123, Dorothy Rhoads/Morley Papers, L. Tom Perry Special Collections Library, Brigham Young University Library, Provo, Utah.

34. Shook, *Incidents in the Life of a Maya Archaeologist* as told to Winifred Veronda (Guatemala City: Southwestern Academy Press, 1998), 203; for Morley's love letters to Anne Bucher, see her papers in RGHC at NMSU.

35. Ibid., 203–4.

36. Brunhouse, *Sylvanus G. Morley*, 298–300.

37. "1918 Spring," Held Papers.

38. *Most of John Held, Jr.*, 144.

39. Ibid., 19, 144.

40. Ibid., 144; Thomas Craven, ed., *Cartoon Cavalcade* (New York: Simon and Schuster, 1943), 103, 105, 172–73.

41. They were:

245	Cherrie, G. K.
134	Dodson, R. I.
168	Dunn, W. E.
206	Gardiner, C. E.
148	Gittings, J. S.
242	Gann, Thomas
154	Held, J.
173	Lothrop, S. K.
53	Morley, S. G.
215	Parsons, F. B.
219	Popenoe, W.
143	Rosenkrans, W. R.
56	Spinden, H. J.
55	Townsend, O. C.
99	Watkins, L. H.
84	Watts, J. H.

Handwritten but undated and unnumbered agents' list in the Disbursing Officer's records, ONI. See also Aide for Information to Director of Naval Intelligence, June 3, 1918, 21115, ONI.

42. Sheldon to [George] Grinnell, Apr. 25, 1919, Charles Sheldon Collection, Folder 6, Box 1, Archives, University of Alaska, Fairbanks. The authors wish to thank Archivist Caroline Atuck for locating this document.

43. Johnson [?] to Commander, Battleship Division One, May 15, 1919, Container 3, Roger Welles Papers, Manuscript Division, Library of Congress, Washington, D.C.

44. Boaz Long Diaries, July 11, 1919, Box 37, folder 327, BLP.

45. Carmony and Brown, *Wilderness of the Southwest*, xxviii, xl, xli.

46. George Bird Grinnell and Charles Sheldon, eds., *Hunting and Conservation: The Book of the Boone and Crockett Club* (New Haven, Conn.: Yale University Press, 1925; repr., New York: Arno Press and the New York Times, 1970).

47. Carmony and Brown, *Wilderness of the Southwest*, xxviii, xl–xlii, xxxvi.

48. J. Alden Mason to Franz Boas, Feb. 18, 1920; Boas to Mason, Mar. 1, 1920; Mason to Boas, Mar. 7, 1920, all in reel 21, BP.

49. Long, *Morleyana*, 151–53.

50. Biographical sketch in *The Ancient Civilizations of Peru*, rev. ed. (London: Penguin Books, 1991); *National Directory of Latin Americanists: Biobibliographies of 1,884 Specialists in the Social Sciences & Humanities*, Hispanic Foundation Bibliographical Series No. 10 (Washington, D.C.: Library of Congress, 1966), 200–201.

51. Major George C. Butte to Lothrop, Mar. 5, 1919, LP.

52. "Memorandum for Captain Wilkins," Feb. 18, 1919; Lothrop's discharge certificate, LP.

53. D. L. Hazard to Lothrop, Mar. 11, 1919, LP.

54. Marshal Saville to Lothrop, May 6, 1919; Henry Cabot Lodge to same, May 6 and 20, 1919; John Belt to same, May 17, 1919; Lothrop to J. J. Rogers, Dec. 4, 1919, LP.

55. Joyce Kelly, *An Archaeological Guide to Mexico's Yucatán Peninsula* (Norman and London: University of Oklahoma Press, 1993), 312, 318, 320, 327, 329, 335; *National Directory of Latin Americanists*, 184–85.

56. Carmichael, *British and the Maya*, 35.

57. Thomas Gann, *Ancient Cities and Modern Tribes: Exploration and Adventure in Maya Lands* (London: Duckworth, 1926), pp. 176–184, 208–234; J. Eric Thompson, *Maya Archaeologist* (Norman: University of Oklahoma Press, 1963), p. 42; Thomas Gann, *Maya Cities: A Record of Exploration and Adventure in Middle America* (New York: Charles Scribner's Sons, 1928), 168ff; Brunhouse, *Pursuit of the Ancient Maya*, 80–82; F. A. Mitchell-Hedges, *Danger My Ally* (London: Elek Books, 1954), 172–73, 174–80, 181–84; Kelly, *Archaeological Guide*, 308.

58. Brunhouse, *Frans Blom*, 34–35, 78–79; Douglas R. Givens, "Sylvanus G. Morley and the Carnegie Institution's Program of Mayan Research," in Jonathan E. Reyman, ed., *Rediscovering Our Past: Essays on the History of American Archaeology* (Aldershot: Avebury Publishers, 1992), 142–43.

59. Carmichael, *British and the Maya*, 35; Kelly, *Archaeological Guide*, 330; Brunhouse, *Sylvanus G. Morley*, 210–11.

60. Smithsonian Institution, Bureau of American Ethnology, Bulletin 64 (Washington, D.C.: Government Printing Office, 1918).

61. Spinden file, 21500–581, ONI; Spinden service record, Freedom of Information Act release, National Personnel Records Center (Military Personnel Records), St. Louis, Mo.; Museum Letter No. 8, Jan. 30, 1919, American Museum.

62. Charles Wissler to Dr. [H. C.] Bumpus, Mar. 11, 1909; Director to Spinden, Apr. 22, 1909; Spinden to Bumpus, May 6, 1909; Wissler to same, Sept. 1, 1909, Herbert J. Spinden Special File 827, American Museum.

63. Spinden to F. A. Lucas, June 21, 1920; Minor C. Keith to same, July 2, 1920, File 551, American Museum.

64. Kelly, *Archaeological Guide*, 322, 323.

65. Dr. Herbert Joseph Spinden obituary, American Museum. A chronological list of Spinden's works is in Brunhouse, *Pursuit of the Ancient Maya*, 225–33.

66. L. H. Watkins file, 20966–3229, ONI.

67. Three telegrams from Riverbank Laboratories to Leland Harrison, Nov. 21, 1917, Christmas File.

68. [William H.] Leavell to Secretary of State, Oct. 10 and 14, 1918, Christmas File.

69. Lansing to American Legation, Oct. 16, 1918; Synopsis for [Leland] Harrison of a telegram from the American Legation in Guatemala City, Oct. 18, [1918]; J. H. Burton to General Christmas, Oct. 22, 1918; Thurston to Secretary of State, Oct. 26, 1918; J. H. Burton & Co. to J. M. Nye, Oct. 29, 1918, Christmas File.

70. Deutsch, *Incredible Yanqui*, 195; F. C. Pendleton BI report, Nov. 6, 1918, Christmas File.

71. Three handwritten and undated reports by Christmas, Christmas File.

72. [Robert] Lansing to American Legation, Jan. 19, 1919, Christmas File.

73. "Strictly Confidential" memorandum from [J. Herbert] Stabler to [L. L.] Winslow, July 16, 1919, Christmas File.

74. [Herbert Stabler] to [L. L.] Winslow, Aug. 11, 1919; Memo, L. L. W[inslow] to Bo[az Long], Aug. 13, 1919, Christmas File.

75. Deutsch, *Incredible Yanqui*, 195–97.

76. J. Edgar Hoover to Brigadier General A. E. Nolan, Feb. 3, 1921, with two enclosures, 87–34, MID.

77. Deutsch, *Incredible Yanqui*, 198–205.

78. Langley and Schoonover, *Banana Men*, photo between 126–27.

79. Admiral A. P. Niblack to Wilson Popenoe, Sept. 10, 1919; Memo by Admiral A. P. Niblack, Sept. 11, 1919, 977–38, ONI.

80. Popenoe personnel file, 20944–362, ONI.

81. Long, *Morleyana*, 208–9; Langley and Schoonover, *Banana Men*, 170.

82. Lt. (j.g.) John F. White, "Memorandum for Director of O.N.I.," July 21, 1919; Director of Naval Intelligence to Chief, Bureau of Navigation, May 28, 1919, Watts file, 20944–976, ONI.

83. Consul E. M. Lawton to Secretary of State, June 2, 1919; Acting Secretary of State to Secretary of the Navy, June 16, 1919, Watts file, ONI; Captain William B. Osgood Field, "Memorandum for Colonel Martin," Mar. 14, 1919, 87–19, MID.

84. Bureau of Investigation reports, May 8 and 12, 1919; W. E. Allen, Acting Chief, Bureau of Investigation to Rear Admiral Roger Welles, May 17, 1919; Rear Admiral A. P. Niblack to W. E. Allen, May 26, 1919, Watts file, ONI.

85. Joseph H. Watts to State Department, June 1, 1919, Watts file, ONI.

86. Bureau of Navigation to 9th Naval District, June 17, 1919; Bliss Morton to W. E. Allen, June 18, 1919; G. M. B. to J. T. Suter, Acting Chief, Bureau of Investigation, June 25, 1919, Watts file, ONI.

87. Director of Naval Intelligence to Bureau of Navigation, July 16, 1919; Rear Admiral A. P. Niblack to J. T. Suter, Acting Chief, Bureau of Investigation, July 16 and 18, 1919, Watts file, ONI.

88. Rear Admiral A. P. Niblack to Ensign A. P. Madden, July 22, 1919; Assistant Director of Naval Intelligence to Chief of Police, Fall River, Mass., July 22, 1919; Ensign A. P. Madden, "Memorandum for Comdr. Baum," July 25, 1919, Watts file, ONI; "Expense Account in Connection with Return of J. H. Watts from Fall River, Mass., to Washington, D.C.," unnumbered, ONI.

89. Rear Admiral A. P. Niblack to Chief of Police, Fall River, Mass., July 25, 1919, Watts file, ONI.

90. Frank Burke to Rear Admiral A. P. Niblack, July 30, 1919; Ensign H. E. Ruisseau to Director of Naval Intelligence, July 30, 1919; Copies in English and Spanish of the con-

tract between Luis F. Mendizábal, Guatemalan Secretary of the Interior and Joseph H. Watts, Feb. 7, 1919, Watts file, ONI.

91. Commander Frank F. Rogers to Mrs. Leroy Harris, Sept. 2, 1919; Same to Bureau of Navigation, Sept. 2, 1919, Watts file.

92. Commander F. W. Hoffman to Commandant, 3rd Naval District, Oct. 9, 1919; [Rear Admiral A. P. Niblack] to Intelligence Officer, 3rd Naval District, Oct. 31, 1919, Watts file.

93. Rear Admiral A. P. Niblack to L. Lanier Winslow, Nov. 12, 1919; Same to Joseph H. Watts, Dec. 16, 1919; Director of Naval Intelligence to Commandant, 3rd Naval District, Dec. 15, 1919; Joseph H. Watts to Rear Admiral A. P. Niblack, Dec. 16, 1919, Watts file.

94. McCreery, "Wireless Empire," 39 n. 29. As of December 1923, Watts was in Guatemala City engaged in electrical and automobile repair work. He was acknowledged as the leading authority on the radio situation in Guatemala, and he was keeping the American legation apprised of recent activities by German radio engineers in that country. Clarence B. Hewes to Secretary of State, "Strictly Confidential," Dec. 18, 1923, with an enclosed Watts memorandum, 814.74/86, Records of the Department of State Relating to Internal Affairs of Guatemala, 1910–29, Microcopy No. 655, National Archives and Records Service, Washington, D.C.

95. Roger Welles to Dr. Fritz Holm, Apr. 16, 1919, Container 3, Welles Papers.

96. John E. White, "Memorandum for the Director of Naval Intelligence," Sept. 27, 1920, ONI.

97. In January 1920, ONI's Confidential Fund was allocated as follows:

12 naval attachés	$94,764.94
13 intelligence officers in the Naval Districts	$25,196.74
10 "agents and special intelligence officers"	$8,945.94

"Memorandum for the Director of Naval Intelligence," Jan. 19, 1920, ONI.

98. Commander Fred F. Rogers to Director of ONI, May 29, 1919, ONI.

99. Kittridge personnel file, Nov. 11, 1920, ONI.

100. Biographical sketch of Andrews, Jan. 2, 1931, American Museum. For a recent popularly written biography, see Charles Gallenkamp, *Dragon Hunter: Roy Chapman Andrews and the Central Asiatic Expeditions* (New York: Viking, 2001).

101. Andrews, *Under a Lucky Star*, 146–47, 149.

102. Ibid., 153. For an overview of Andrews's espionage career, see Gallenkamp, *Dragon Hunter*, 71–76, 208.

103. Mrs. Roy Chapman Andrews to Mrs. Franklin Brandreth, Dec. 1, 1918, 156–48, MID.

104. Mrs. Roy Chapman Andrews to Mrs. George Barton French, Dec. 1, 1918; Navintel to [Naval Attache, Peking], Jan. 24, 1919, Confidential file 21012–9.3, ONI.

105. Roy Chapman Andrews to Col. Sherman Miles, May 11, 1920, 51–206–3, MID.

106. "Lists of Agents and Informants Residing in Foreign Countries, 1917–25," undated, ONI; Museum Letter, [July 6, 1918], File 1069, American Museum; Confidential file 21012–9.3, ONI.

107. Andrews conveyed his intense dislike of Japan's foreign policy in China in a personal letter to former president Theodore Roosevelt. Noting that he arrived in China in 1918 with a pro-Japanese attitude, he reported that, based on what he had seen, "Japan has absolutely no political morality," and suggested that Japanese policy was "China for the Japanese." See Andrews to Roosevelt, Dec. 26, 1918, Navy Subject File 1910–1927, WA 7, China (Japanese Intrigue), RG 45, National Archives and Records Service, Washington, D.C.; Andrews, *Under a Lucky Star*, 153–56.

108. "Lists of Agents and Informants," ONI. Andrews said his headquarters were at Urga, Mongolia. *Under a Lucky Star*, 158. Urga is today Ulân Bator, capital of the Mongolian Republic.

109. Roy Chapman Andrews to Col. Sherman Miles, Apr. 5, 1920, 51–206, MID.

110. Maynard Owen Williams to Lt. Col. N. W. Campanole, Mar. 27, 1920, 2338-NN-20, MID.

111. Col. Sherman Miles to Dr. Frederick A. Lucas, Apr. 1, 1920, 51–206-7; Capt. F. M. Barrows, "Memorandum for Colonel Campanole," Apr. 5, 1920, 51–206-9; Roy Chapman Andrews to Col. Sherman Miles, Apr. 5, 1920, 51–206-8, MID.

112. Col. C. H. Mason, "Memorandum for Colonel Miles," Apr. 13, 1920, 51–206-1; [Lt. Col.] N. W. Campanole, "Memorandum for Captain Barrows," Apr. 20, 1920, 51–206-10; undated questionnaire, 51–206-2; Col. Sherman Miles to Roy Chapman Andrews, Apr. 21, 1920, 51–206-11; Roy Chapman Andrews to Col. Sherman Miles, May 11, 1920, 51–206-3, MID.

113. Major F. M. Barrows to Dr. Frederick A. Lucas, Oct. 22, 1920, 51–206; 1st Lt. F. B. Butler to Commanding General, U.S. Army Forces in China, Oct. 16, 1925, 2055–632, MID.

114. Andrews to Lt. Col. [Nelson E.] Margetts, Sept. 13, 1930, 2483–466-5, MID.

115. "Report of Travel with the Central Asiatic Expedition, Summer of 1930," Aug. 8, 1930, 2055–682-1; "Memo to Dr. Andrews," undated, 2055–682-2; 1st Lt. Willard G. Wyman to Military Attaché, Nov. 22, 1930, 2055–682-2, MID.

116. Col. William H. Wilson to C. G. Abbott, Apr. 1, 1931, 2055–682-3, MID.

117. Capt. Parker G. Tenney to Assistant Chief of Staff, G-2, May 20, 1932, 2657-D-935-4, MID.

118. Rexer and Klein, *American Museum of Natural History*, 53; between 52 and 66 there is a good overview of the Gobi expeditions.

119. *The Boston Globe*, June 8, 1989.

120. Lynne Hale to Charles Gallenkamp, Apr. 20, 1995, American Museum.

121. Ballendorf and Bartlett, *Pete Ellis*, 139–41.

122. Dorwart, *Conflict of Duty*, 30–37, 56; Joseph E. Persico, *Roosevelt's Secret War: FDR and World War II Espionage* (New York: Random House, 2001), 11–13.

123. Thomas E. Mahl, *Desperate Deception: British Covert Operations in the United States, 1939–1944* (Washington, D.C.: Brassey's, 1998), 26.

124. Office of Naval Intelligence, General File, Secret Lists of Agents (1917–1920), Group 4: Volunteer Agents: Mr. Roosevelt's Friends. Interestingly, of this group of "Mr. Roosevelt's friends," William Bullitt was the sole individual who was given an ONI special agent number.

125. The date of Shepardson's resignation from the CIG was provided by Michael Warner of the CIA's Historical Office. Shepardson's other career moves can be found in his *Who's Who in America* listing. For his OSS career, see, among others, Thomas Troy, ed., *Wartime Washington: The Secret OSS Journal of James Grafton Rogers, 1942–1943* (Washington, D.C.: University Publications of America, 1987), 81, 124; Max Corvo, *The OSS in Italy, 1942–1945: A Personal Memoir* (New York: Praeger, 1990), 169, 201, 273, 276, 278, 279; and R. Harris Smith, *OSS: The Secret History of America's First Central Intelligence Agency* (Berkeley: University of California Press, 1972), 54.

126. Thomas F. Troy, *Donovan and the CIA: A History of the Establishment of the Central Intelligence Agency* (Frederick, Md.: Aletheia Books, 1981), 2–6; John Gade, *Experiences of a Naval Intelligence Officer in Europe* (New York: Scribner's, 1942).

127. Office of Naval Intelligence (Special Intelligence Section), OP-16-F-9 and Op-16-Z, NND 883021 files, June 17, 1940-Oct. 1941, ONI; Dorwart, *Conflict of Duty*, 123; Burton

Hersh, *The Old Boys: The American Elite and the Origins of the CIA* (New York: Charles Scribner's Sons, 1992), 18–19, 28–29, 34–45, 87–88. On ONI agent numbers, see Srodes, *Allen Dulles*, 222.

128. Shook, *Incidents in the Life*, 79–84; Price, "Anthropologists as Spies," 24–25.

129. Karl E. Meyer and Shareen Blair Brysac, *Tournament of Shadows: The Great Game and the Race for Empire in Central Asia* (Washington, D.C.: Counterpoint, 1999), 509–28.

130. David W. King to Colonel _____ Smith, Feb. 14, 1941, 51–205/12, MID.

Chapter 15

1. Nancy Mitchell, *The Danger of Dreams: German and American Imperialism in Latin America* (Chapel Hill and London: University of North Carolina Press, 1999), states: "There was no German threat" (217). Her book, however, ends in May 1914. Mitchell was apparently unaware that Kaiser Wilhelm II of Germany, in 1897 authorized the drafting of plans for an invasion of the United States and continued to plan for an amphibious assault on several East Coast cities. It was not until 1906 that the invasion planning was finally dropped. n.a. "The Kaiser's Naval Dreams," *MHQ : The Quarterly Journal of Military History Review* (Autumn 2002), 6. For a detailed discussion of German economic policy in Central America during World War I, see Thomas Schoonover, *Germany in Central America: Competitive Imperialism, 1821–1929* (Tuscaloosa and London: University of Alabama Press, 1998), 154–72, 210.

2. Sullivan, *Unfinished Conversations*, 134–36.

3. Quoted in ibid., xxiv.

4. See Robin Winks, *Cloak & Gown: Scholars in the Secret War, 1939–1961* (New York: William Morrow and Co., 1987).

5. Price, "Anthropologists as Spies," 26–27.

6. "A Tribe at War," *The Wall Street Journal*, Nov. 17, 2000, W19; John Leo, "Open Warfare Erupts in Academic World of Anthropology," *Albuquerque Journal*, Dec. 5, 2000, A8; Clifford Geertz, "Life among the Anthros," *The New York Review of Books*, Feb. 8, 2001, 18–22; Samuel M. Wilson, "Informed Consent," *Natural History* (March 2001), 90; Terence S. Turner, "Life among the Anthros," *The New York Review of Books* (Apr. 26, 2001), 69.

Bibliography

Primary Sources

Archives and Manuscript Collections

Scholarly Resources, Wilmington, Delaware
"The Professional Correspondence of Franz Boas" (microfilm)

Harvard University, Cambridge Massachusetts
Archives
William Hubbs Mechling File
Peabody Museum Archives
Samuel K. Lothrop and Joy Mahler Lothrop Archive

Carnegie Institution of Washington, Washington, D.C.
Sylvanus Morley File

American Philosophical Society, Philadelphia, Pennsylvania
Diary of Sylvanus Griswold Morley (typescript)

Archive of American Art, Smithsonian Institution, Washington, D.C.
John Held, Jr., Papers (microfilm)

Archives, Department of Library Services, American Museum of Natural History, New York, N.Y.
Herbert J. Spinden File
Roy Chapman Andrews File

State Records Center & Archives, Santa Fe, New Mexico
Boaz Long Papers

Office of Cultural Affairs, Laboratory of Anthropology, Santa Fe, New Mexico
Sylvanus G. Morley Papers

National Personnel Records Center (Military Personnel), St. Louis, Missouri
Freedom of Information Act Release, Service Records of:
Sylvanus G. Morley
Herbert J. Spinden

Manuscript Division, Library of Congress, Washington, D.C.,
Papers of:
Tasker H. Bliss
Josephus Daniels
Frank R. McCoy
John J. Pershing
Roger Welles
Woodrow Wilson

Rio Grande Historical Collections, New Mexico State University, Las Cruces, New Mexico
Anne Bucher Papers
A. B. Fall Papers

Manuscript Collection, Franklin D. Roosevelt Library, Hyde Park, New York
Papers as Assistant Secretary of the Navy, 1913–1920—Office of Naval Intelligence

British Public Record Office, Kew (PRO)
Admiralty (ADM): 137 (American Submarine Intelligence); 223 (Room 40, British Office of Naval Intelligence—German decrypts)
Colonial Office (CO): 123; 126; 127; 348 (British Honduras).
Foreign Office (FO): 252 (Guatemala; Honduras; El Salvador; Nicaragua)
340 (Guatemala)
371 (Central America)
372 (Mexico)

Records Inherited by the Government Communications Headquarters (GCHQ) (HW): 7/8 (Zimmermann Telegram); 7/17 (Intercepts of American Diplomatic Dispatches).
War Office (WO): 106 (Caribbean)

National Archives and Records Service, Washington, D.C.

Record Group 38—Records of the Office of the Chief of Naval Operations, Office of Naval Intelligence, Confidential General Correspondence, 1913–24

Record Group 45—Naval Records Collection of the Office of Naval Records and Library, Area File/Caribbean Area, 1911–1927

Record Group 60—Records of the Department of Justice

Record Group 65—Records of the Federal Bureau of Investigation

Record Group 80—General Records of the Navy, Secretary of the Navy, General Correspondence, 1916–1926

Record Group 165—Records of the War Department General and Special Staffs, Military Intelligence Division

Record Group 395—Records of the U.S. Army Overseas Operations and Commands, Mexican Punitive Expedition

Record Group 407—Records of the Adjutant General's Office, 1917–1941

National Archives and Records Service, College Park, Maryland:

Record Group 59—Department of State, Classified Records of the Office of the Counselor, 1916–27

Record Group 76—Mixed Claims Commission, United States and Germany

Record Group 87—Records of the U.S. Secret Service, Daily Reports of Agents, 1875 through 1936, Microcopy 3.158

Records of the Department of State Relating to the Internal Affairs of Central America, 1910–1929, Microcopy 670

Records of the Department of State Relating to the Internal Affairs of El Salvador, 1910–1929, Microcopy No. 658

Records of the Department of State Relating to Internal Affairs of Guatemala, 1910–29, Microcopy No. 655

Numerical and Minor Files of the Department of State, Microcopy M-862

Operational Archives Branch, Naval Historical Center, Washington, D.C.
        Cocke, Captain Herbert E. "History of the Intelligence Division of Naval Operations."

L. Tom Perry Special Collections Library, Brigham Young University Library, Provo, Utah
        Dorothy Rhoads/Morley Papers

Archives, University of Alaska, Fairbanks
        Charles Sheldon Collection

Published Primary Sources
Government Documents

British Honduras Government Gazette, Feb. 2, Mar. 9, and Apr. 6, 1918.

Fifty Years of Naval District Development, 1903–1953. Washington, D.C.: Naval History Division, Office of the Chief of Naval Operations.

Finnegan, John Patrick. *Military Intelligence*. Army Lineage Series. Center for Military History, United States Army. Washington, D.C.: Government Printing Office, 1998.

Friedman, Richard S. "The American Spy: Xenophon Dmitrievich deBlumenthal Kalamatiano." Langley, Va.: Central Intelligence Agency Counterintelligence and Security Program, 1997.

Gann, Thomas. *The Maya Indians of Southern Yucatan and Northern British Honduras*. Smithsonian Institution. Bureau of American Ethnology. Bulletin 64. Washington, D.C.: Government Printing Office, 1918.

———. "Mounds in Northern Honduras." Smithsonian Institution. Bureau of American Ethnology. *Annual Report 19*, 655–92. Washington, D.C.: Government Printing Office, 1900.

Harris, Charles H. III and Louis R. Sadler. *Bastion on the Border: Fort Bliss, 1854–1943*. Historic and Natural Resources Report Number 6, Cultural Resources Management Program, Directorate of Environment, United States Army Air Defense Artillery Center, Fort Bliss, Tex., 1993.

Rafalko, Frank J., ed. *A Counterintelligence Reader*. 3 vols. Langley, Va.: National Counterintelligence Center, 1997.

Register of the Commissioned and Warrant Officers of the United States Navy and U.S. Naval Reserve Force National Naval Volunteers Marine Corps Medical Reserve Corps and Dental Reserve Corps January 1, 1918. Washington, D.C.: Government Printing Office, 1918.

Register of the Commissioned and Warrant Officers of the United States Navy U.S. Naval Reserve Force and Marine Corps January 1, 1919. Washington, D.C.: Government Printing Office, 1919.

United States. Navy Department. *German Submarine Activities on the Atlantic Coast of the United States and Canada*. Office of Naval Records and Library, Historical Section, publication No. 1. Washington, D.C.: Government Printing Office, 1920.

———. Senate. *Brewing and Liquor Interests and Bolshevik Propaganda*. Senate Document 62, 66th Cong., 1st sess., III. Washington, D.C.: Government Printing Office, 1919.

———. Senate. *Investigation of Mexican Affairs*. Senate Document 285, 66th Cong., 2d sess. 2 vols. Washington, D.C.: Government Printing Office, 1920.

———. *Signal Security Agency*. Mexican Cryptographic Systems Prior to 1929. SPSIS-1, May 23, 1945.

Books

Andrews, Roy Chapman. *Under a Lucky Star: A Lifetime of Adventure*. New York: Viking Press, 1943.

Carmony, Neil B., and David E. Brown, eds. *The Wilderness of the Southwest: Charles Sheldon's Quest for Desert Bighorn Sheep and Adventures with the Havasupai and Seri Indians*. Salt Lake City: University of Utah Press, 1993.

Carnegie Institution of Washington Year Book No. 15, 1916. Washington, D.C.: Carnegie Institution, [1917].

Carnegie Institution of Washington Year Book No. 16, 1917. Washington, D.C.: Carnegie Institution, 1918.

Carnegie Institution of Washington, Year Book No. 17, 1918. Washington, D.C.: Carnegie Institution, 1919.

Corvo, Max. *The OSS in Italy, 1942–1945: A Personal Memoir.* New York: Praeger, 1990.

Daniels, Josephus. *The Wilson Era: Years of Peace, 1910–1917.* Chapel Hill: University of North Carolina Press, 1944.

———. *The Wilson Era: Years of War and After, 1917–1923.* Chapel Hill: University of North Carolina Press, 1946.

Dulles, Allen. *The Secret Surrender.* New York: Harper and Row, 1966.

Gade, John. *Experiences of a Naval Intelligence Officer in Europe.* New York: Scribner's, 1942.

Gann, Thomas. *Ancient Cities and Modern Tribes: Exploration and Adventure in Maya Lands.* London: Duckworth, 1926.

———. *In An Unknown Land.* New York: Charles Scribner's Sons, 1924.

———. *Maya Cities: A Record of Exploration and Adventure in Middle America.* New York: Charles Scribner's Sons, 1928.

Grinnell, George Bird and Charles Sheldon, eds. *Hunting and Conservation: The Book of the Boone and Crockett Club.* New Haven, Conn.: Yale University Press, 1925. Reprint: New York: Arno Press and the New York Times, 1970.

Hedrick, Burton J., ed. *Life and Letters of Walter Hines Page.* 3 vols. London: William Heinemann, 1926.

Hewett, Edgar L. *Pajarito Plateau and Its Ancient People.* 2d rev. ed. Albuquerque: University of New Mexico Press and the School of American Research, 1953.

König, Paul. *Voyage of the Deutschland: The First Merchant Submarine.* New York: Hearst's International Library Co., 1917.

Landau, Henry. *The Enemy Within: The Inside Story of German Sabotage in America.* New York: G. P. Putnam's Sons, 1937.

Lansing, Robert. *War Memories of Robert Lansing: Secretary of State.* Indianapolis: Bobbs-Merrill Company, 1935.

Lister, Robert H., and Florence C. Lister, eds. *In Search of Maya Glyphs: From the Archaeological Journals of Sylvanus G. Morley.* Santa Fe: Museum of New Mexico Press, 1970.

Long, Boaz, ed. *Morleyana: A Collection of Writings in Memoriam Sylvanus Griswold Morley—1883–1948.* Santa Fe: The School of American Research and the Museum of New Mexico, 1950.

Membership of the Cosmos Club (1878–1968). Washington, D.C.: n.p., 1968.

Mercer, Sir William H., A. E. Collins, and J. R. W. Robinson. *The Colonial Office List for 1918.* London: Waterlow and Sons, 1918.

Mitchell-Hedges, F. A. *Danger My Ally.* London: Elek Books, 1954.

Morley, Sylvanus Griswold. *An Introduction to the Study of the Maya Hieroglyphs.* 2d ed. New York: Dover Publications, 1975.

Packard, Wyman H. *A Century of U.S. Naval Intelligence.* Washington, D.C.: Office of Naval Intelligence and the Naval Historical Center, 1996.

Peissel, Michel. *The Lost World of Quintana Roo.* New York: E. P. Dutton and Co., 1963.

Phillips, David Atlee. *The Night Watch*. New York: Ballantine Books, 1982.

Sharer, Robert J. *The Ancient Maya*. 5th ed. Stanford, Calif.: Stanford University Press, 1994.

Shook, Edwin M. *Incidents in the Life of a Maya Archaeologist*. As told to Winifred Veronda. Guatemala City: Southwestern Academy Press, 1998.

Thompson, J. Eric. *Maya Archaeologist*. Norman: University of Oklahoma Press, 1963.

Tompkins, Frank. *Chasing Villa: The Last Campaign of the U.S. Cavalry*. Harrisburg, Pa.: Military Service Publishing Company, 1934. Reprint, Silver City, N.M.: High Lonesome Books, 1996.

Troy, Thomas, ed. *Wartime Washington: The Secret OSS Journal of James Grafton Rogers 1942–1943*. Washington, D.C.: University Publications of America, 1987.

Von Rintelen, Franz. *The Dark Invader: War-Time Reminiscences of a German Naval Intelligence Officer*. New York: Penguin Books, 1939.

Weber, Ralph E., ed. *The Final Memoranda: Major General Ralph H. Van Deman, USA Ret. 1865–1952 Father of U.S. Military Intelligence*. Wilmington: Scholarly Resources Books, 1988.

Secondary Sources
Books

Alvarez, David. *Secret Messages: Codebreaking and American Diplomacy, 1930–1945*. Lawrence: University of Kansas Press, 2000.

Ballendorf, Dirk A. and Merrill L. Bartlett. *Pete Ellis: An Amphibious Warfare Prophet 1880–1923*. Annapolis: Naval Institute Press, 1997.

Bamford, James. *The Puzzle Palace: A Report on NSA, America's Most Secret Agency*. Boston: Houghton Mifflin, 1982.

———. *Body of Secrets: Anatomy of the Ultra-Secret National Security Agency from the Cold War through the Dawn of a New Century*. New York: Doubleday, 2001.

Blair, Clay. *Hitler's U-Boat War: The Hunters, 1939–1943*. New York: Random House, 1996.

Braddy, Haldeen. *Pancho Villa at Columbus: The Raid of 1916*. El Paso: Texas Western Press, 1965.

Braden, Lt. Charles, ed. Supplement, vol. 5 (1900–1910), to *Biographical Register of the Officers and Graduates of the United States Military Academy*. Edited by George Washington Cullum. Saginaw, Mich.: Seeman and Peters, 1910.

Braisted, William Reynolds. *The United States Navy in the Pacific, 1909–1922*. Austin and London: University of Texas Press, 1971.

Brunhouse, Robert L. *Frans Blom, Maya Explorer*. Albuquerque: University of New Mexico Press, 1976.

———. *Pursuit of the Ancient Maya: Some Archaeologists of Yesterday*. Albuquerque: University of New Mexico Press, 1975.

———. *Sylvanus G. Morley and the World of the Ancient Mayas*. Norman: University of Oklahoma Press, 1971.

Calzadíaz Barrera, Alberto. *Por Qué Villa Atacó Columbus: Intriga Internacional*. México, D.F.: Editores Mexicanos Unidos, 1972.

Carmichael, Elizabeth. *The British and the Maya*. London: Trustees of the British Museum, 1973.

Chalkley, John F. *Zach Lamar Cobb: El Paso Collector of Customs and Intelligence during the Mexican Revolution, 1913–1918*. Southwestern Studies no. 103. El Paso: Texas Western Press, 1998.

Clendenen, Clarence C. *Blood on the Border: The United States and the Mexican Irregulars*. New York: Macmillan, 1969.

Coe, Michael D. *The Maya*. 5th rev. and expanded ed. New York: Thames and Hudson, 1993.

Corson, William R. *The Armies of Ignorance: The Rise of the American Intelligence Empire*. New York: Dial Press, 1977.

Craven, Thomas, ed. *Cartoon Cavalcade*. New York: Simon and Schuster, 1943.

Deutsch, Hermann B. *The Incredible Yanqui: The Career of Lee Christmas*. London, New York, Toronto: Longmans Green and Co., 1931.

Doerries, Reinhard R. *Imperial Challenge: Ambassador Count Bernsdorff and German-American Relations, 1908–1917*. Chapel Hill: University of North Carolina Press, 1989.

Dorwart, Jeffrey. *Conflict of Duty: The Navy's Intelligence Dilemma 1919–1945*. Annapolis: Naval Institute Press, 1983.

———. *The Office of Naval Intelligence: The Birth of America's First Intelligence Agency 1865–1918*. Annapolis: Naval Institute Press, 1979.

Fagan, Brian M., ed. *The Oxford Companion to Archaeology*. New York: Oxford University Press, 1996.

Gallenkamp, Charles. *Dragon Hunter: Roy Chapman Andrews and the Central Asiatic Expeditions*. New York: Viking, 2001.

Garraty, John A., ed. *Dictionary of American Biography, Supplement Six, 1956–1960*. New York: Scribner's, 1980.

Garraty, John A., and Edward T. James, eds. *Dictionary of American Biography, Supplement Four, 1946–1950*. New York: Scribner's, 1974.

Gross, Peter. *Gentleman Spy: The Life of Allen Dulles*. Boston: Houghton Mifflin, 1994.

Halpern, Paul G. *A Naval History of World War I*. Annapolis: Naval Institute Press, 1994.

Harries, Meirion and Susie. *The Last Days of Innocence: America at War, 1917–1918*. New York: Random House, 1997.

Harris, Brayton. *The Navy Times Book of Submarines: A Political, Social and Military History*. Edited by Walter J. Boyne. New York: Berkeley Books, 1997.

Harris, Charles H. III, and Louis R. Sadler. *The Border and the Revolution: Clandestine Activities of the Mexican Revolution*. 2d rev. ed. Silver City, N.M.: High Lonesome Books, 1990.

Herring, Hubert. *A History of Latin America from the Beginnings to the Present*. New York: Alfred A. Knopf, 1957.

Hersh, Burton. *The Old Boys: The American Elite and the Origins of the CIA*. New York: Charles Scribner's Sons, 1992.

Herstlet, Godfrey E. P., Percy C. Rice, and Leslie G. Brown. *The Foreign Office List and Diplomatic and Consular Year Book for 1917*. London: Harrison and Sons, 1917.

Hoopes, Townsend, and Douglas Brinkley. *Driven Patriot: The Life and Times of James Forrestal*. New York: Vintage Books, 1992.

Hough, Emerson. *The Web*. Chicago: Reilly and Lee, 1919.

Hurst, James W. *The Villista Prisoners of 1916–17*. Las Cruces, N.M.: Yucca Tree Press, 2000.

Jeffreys-Jones, Rhodri. *American Espionage from Secret Service to CIA*. New York: Free Press, 1977.

Jeffreys-Jones, Rhodri, and Andrew Lownie, eds. *North American Spies: New Revisionist Essays*. Lawrence: University Press of Kansas, 1991.

Jensen, Joan M. *The Price of Vigilance*. Chicago: Rand McNally, 1968.

———. *Army Surveillance in America, 1775–1980*. New Haven, Conn.: Yale University Press, 1991.

Judd, Alan. *The Quest for C: Mansfield Cumming and the Founding of the Secret Service*. London: Harper Collins, 1999.

Kahn, David. *The Codebreakers: The Story of Secret Writing*. New York: Macmillan, 1967.

Katz, Friedrich. *The Life and Times of Pancho Villa*. Stanford, Calif.: Stanford University Press, 1998.

———. *The Secret War in Mexico: Europe, The United States and the Mexican Revolution*. Chicago and London: University of Chicago Press, 1981.

Kelly, Joyce. *An Archaeological Guide to Mexico's Yucatan Peninsula*. Norman and London: University of Oklahoma Press, 1993.

Kessler, Ronald. *Inside the CIA: Revealing the Secrets of the World's Most Powerful Spy Agency*. New York: Pocket Books, 1992.

Langley, Lester D., and Thomas Schoonover. *The Banana Men: American Mercenaries and Entrepreneurs in Central America, 1880–1930*. Lexington: The University Press of Kentucky, 1995.

Linn, Brian McAlister. *Guardians of Empire: The U.S. Army and the Pacific, 1902–1940*. Chapel Hill: University of North Carolina Press, 1997.

MacDonnell, Francis. *Insidious Foes: The Axis Fifth Column and the American Home Front*. New York: Oxford University Press, 1995.

Mahl, Thomas. *Desperate Deception: British Covert Operations in the United States, 1939–1944*. Washington, D.C.: Brassey's, 1998.

Mahoney, Harry Thayer and Marjorie Locke Mahoney. *Espionage in Mexico: The 20th Century*. San Francisco, London, Bethesda: Austin and Winfield, 1997.

Manchester, William. *American Caesar: Douglas MacArthur, 1880–1964*. Boston: Little Brown, 1978.

Mason, Herbert Malloy. *The Great Pursuit*. New York: Random House, 1970.

May, Antoinette. *Passionate Pilgrim: The Extraordinary Life of Alma Reed*. New York: Marlowe and Company, 1994.

Meyer, Karl E., and Shareen Blair Brysac. *Tournament of Shadows: The Great Game and the Race for Empire in Central Asia*. Washington, D.C.: Counterpoint, 1999.

Meyer, Michael C. *Mexican Rebel: Pascual Orozco and the Mexican Revolution, 1910–1915*. Lincoln: University of Nebraska Press, 1967.

————. *Huerta: A Political Portrait*. Lincoln: University of Nebraska Press, 1972.

Michell, John. *Who Wrote Shakespeare?* London: Thames and Hudson, 1996.

Miller, Nathan. *Spying for America: The Hidden History of U.S. Intelligence* New York: Paragon House, 1989.

Mitchell, Nancy, *The Danger of Dreams: German and American Imperialism in Latin America*. Chapel Hill and London: University of North Carolina Press, 1999.

Moon, Tom. *This Grim and Savage Game: The OSS and U.S. Covert Operations in World War II*. New York: Da Capo Press, 2000.

Morison, Elting E. *Admiral Sims and the Modern American Navy*. Boston: Houghton Mifflin, 1942.

Morison, Samuel Eliot. *Admiral of the Ocean Sea: A Life of Christopher Columbus*. 2 vols. New York: Time Incorporated, 1962.

The Most of John Held Jr. Brattleboro, Vt.: The Stephen Greene Press, 1972.

National Directory of Latin Americanists: Biobibliographies of 1,884 Specialists in the Social Sciences & Humanities. Hispanic Foundation Biographical Series No. 10. Washington, D.C.: Library of Congress, 1966.

O'Toole, George J. A. *The Spanish War: An American Epic—1898*. New York and London: W. W. Norton and Co., 1984.

Persico, Joseph E. *Roosevelt's Secret War: FDR and World War II Espionage*. New York: Random House, 2001.

Prados, John. *Combined Fleet Decoded: The Secret History of American Intelligence and the Japanese Navy in World War II*. New York: Random House, 1995.

Quirk, Robert E. *An Affair of Honor: Woodrow Wilson and the Occupation of Veracruz*. New York: W. W. Norton, 1967.

Reed, Nelson. *The Caste War of Yucatan*. Stanford, Calif.: Stanford University Press, 1964.

Rexer, Lyle and Rachel Klein. *American Museum of Natural History: 125 Years of Expedition and Discovery*. New York: Harry N. Abrams, 1995.

Salinas Carranza, Alberto. *La Expedición Punitiva*. México, D.F.: Ediciones Botas, 1936.

Schoonover, Thomas. *Germany in Central America: Competitive Imperialism, 1821–1929*. Tuscaloosa and London: University of Alabama Press, 1998.

Smith, Bradley F., and Elena Agrossi. *Operation Sunrise*. New York: Basic Books, 1979.

Smith, Cornelius C., Jr. *Don't Settle for Second: The Life and Times of Cornelius C. Smith*. San Rafael, Calif.: Presidio Press, 1977.

Smith, R. Harris. *OSS: The Secret History of America's First Central Intelligence Agency*. Berkeley: University of California Press, 1972.

Srodes, James. *Allen Dulles: Master of Spies.* Washington, D.C.: Regnery Publishing, 1999.

Stocking, George W., Jr. *Race, Culture, and Evolution: Essays in the History of Anthropology.* New York: The Free Press, 1968.

———. *The Shaping of American Anthropology, 1883–1911: A Franz Boas Reader.* New York: Basic Books, 1974.

Sullivan, Paul. *Unfinished Conversations: Mayas and Foreigners Between Two Wars.* New York: Alfred A. Knopf, 1989.

Trask, David F. *Captains and Cabinets: Anglo-American Naval Relations, 1917–1918.* Columbia: University of Missouri Press, 1972.

Troy, Thomas F. *Donovan and the CIA: A History of the Establishment of the Central Intelligence Agency.* Frederick, Md.: Aletheia Books, 1981.

Tuchman, Barbara. *The Zimmermann Telegram.* New York: Viking Press, 1958.

Ungar, Sanford. *FBI: An Uncensored Look Behind the Walls.* Boston: Little Brown, 1975.

Weeks, Charles J. *An American Naval Diplomat in Revolutionary Russia: The Life and Times of Vice Admiral Newton A. McCully.* Annapolis: Naval Institute Press, 1993.

Weinberg, Gerhard. *A World at Arms: A Global History of World War II.* Cambridge: Cambridge University Press, 1944.

Wells, Allen and Gilbert M. Joseph. *Summer of Discontent, Seasons of Upheaval: Elite Politics and Rural Insurgency in Yucatan, 1876–1915.* Stanford: Stanford University Press, 1996.

Whitehead, Don. *The FBI Story.* New York: Random House, 1956.

Who Was Who among North American Authors, 1921–1939. Detroit: Gale Research Co., c. 1976.

Williams, Vernon L. *Lieutenant Patton and the American Army in the Mexican Punitive Expedition, 1915–1916.* Dubuque, Iowa: Kendall/Hunt Publishing Co., 1992.

Williams, William J. *The Wilson Administration and the Shipbuilding Crisis of 1917: Steel Ships and Wooden Steamers.* Lewiston, Queenstown, Lampeter: Edwin Mellen Press, 1992.

Wilson, Charles Morrow. *Empire in Green and Gold: The Story of the American Banana Trade.* New York: Henry Holt, 1947.

Wilson, Chris. *The Myth of Santa Fe: Creating a Modern Regional Tradition.* Albuquerque: University of New Mexico Press, 1997.

Winks, Robin. *Cloak & Gown: Scholars in the Secret War, 1939–1961.* New York: William Morrow & Co., 1987.

Winters, Christopher, gen. ed. *International Dictionary of Anthropologists.* New York: Garland Publishing, 1991.

Wise, David and Thomas B. Ross. *The Invisible Government.* New York: Bantam Books, 1965.

Witcover, Jules. *Sabotage at Black Tom: Imperial Germany's Secret War in America: 1914–1917.* Chapel Hill: Algonquin Books of Chapel Hill, 1989.

Periodicals and Articles

American Anthropologist. New Series, 22 (1920): 93–94.

Boas, Franz. "Scientists as Spies," *The Nation* (Dec. 20, 1919).

Givens, Douglas R. "Sylvanus G. Morley and the Carnegie Institution's Program of Mayan Research," 137–44. In *Rediscovering Our Past: Essays on the History of American Archaeology*, edited by Johnathan E. Reyman. Aldershot: Avebury Publishers, 1992.

Geertz, Clifford. "Life among the Anthros," *The New York Review of Books* (Feb. 8, 2001): 18–22.

Gould, Stephen Jay. "This View of Life: Above All Do No Harm," *Natural History* 107, No. 8 (October 1998): 16–22.

Hancock de Sandoval, Judith. "The Virgin of Tabi." *Américas* 32, no. 4 (April 1980): 50–56.

Harris, Charles H. III, and Louis R. Sadler. "The Plan of San Diego and the Mexican-United States War Crisis of 1916: A Reexamination." *Hispanic American Historical Review* 58 (August 1978): 381–408.

———. "The Witzke Affair: German Intrigue on the Mexican Border, 1917–18." *Military Review* 59, no. 2 (February 1979): 36–49.

———. "The 1911 Reyes Conspiracy: The Texas Side." *Southwestern Historical Quarterly* 82 (April 1980): 325–48.

———. "The 'Underside' of the Mexican Revolution: El Paso, 1912." *The Americas: A Quarterly Review of Inter-American Cultural History* 39 (July 1982): 69–83.

———. "United States Government Archives and the Mexican Revolution." *New World: A Journal of Latin American Studies* 1, no. 2 (1986): 108–16.

Katz, Friedrich. "Pancho Villa and the Attack on Columbus, New Mexico." *American Historical Review* 83, no. 1 (February 1978): 101–30.

Kennedy, Paul M. "Great Britain before 1914." In *Knowing One's Enemies: Intelligence Assessment before the Two World Wars*, edited by Ernest R. May. Princeton. N.J.: Princeton University Press, 1984.

Leo, John. "Open Warfare Erupts in Academic World of Anthropology." *Albuquerque Journal* (Dec. 5, 2000): A8.

Love, Marian F. "Vignette, Sylvanus Morley." *The Santa Fean Magazine* 11, no. 2 (March 1983): 10–13.

McCreery, David. "Wireless Empire: The United States and Radio Communications in Central America and the Caribbean, 1904–1926," *Southeast Latin Americanist* 33 (Summer 1993): 23–41.

Meyer, Michael C. "The Mexican-German Conspiracy of 1915." *The Americas* 23 (July 1966): 76–89.

———. "The Arms of the *Ypiranga*." *Hispanic American Historical Review* 50 (1970): 543–56.

Moul, Harry, and Linda Tigges. "The Santa Fe 1912 City Plan: A 'City Beautiful' and City Planning Document." *New Mexico Historical Review* 71, no. 2 (April 1996): 135–55.

Mount, Graeme S. "The Secret Operations of Spanish Consular Officials within Canada during the Spanish-American War." In *North American Spies: New Revisionist Essays*, edited by Rhodri Jeffreys-Jones and Andrew Lownie. Lawrence: University Press of Kansas, 1991.

n. a. "The Kaiser's Naval Dreams." *MHQ: The Quarterly Journal of Military History Review* (Autumn 2002), 6.

Price, David. "Anthropologists as Spies." *The Nation* (November 20, 2000), 24–27.

Spence, Richard B. "K. A. Jahnke and the German Sabotage Campaign in the United States and Mexico, 1914–1918." *Historian* 59, no. 1 (1996), 89–112.

Stone, Michael. "The Fall Committee and Double Agent Jones." *Southern New Mexico Historical Review* 6, no. 1 (January 1999).

Turner, Terence S. "Life among the Anthros." *The New York Review of Books* (Apr. 26, 2001): 69.

Wertime, Richard A., and Angela M. H. Schuster. "Written in the Stars: Celestial Origin of Maya Creation Myths." *Archaeology* 40, no. 4 (July–August 1993), 26–32.

Whitfield, Stephen J. "Strange Fruit: The Career of Samuel Zemurray." *American Jewish History* (March 1994): 307–23.

Wilson, Samuel M. "Informed Consent." *Natural History* (March 2001): 90.

Unpublished Material

Green, James R. "The First Sixty Years of the Office of Naval Intelligence." Master's thesis, American University, Washington, D.C., 1963.

Mechling, William Hubbs. "The Social and Religious Life of the Malectites and Micmacs." Ph.D. diss., Archives, Harvard University, Cambridge, Mass.

Parmenter, Ross. "Zelia Nuttall and the Recovery of Mexico's Past," vol. 3, "Casa Alvarado (1917–1933)." Unpublished MS edited by Kornelia Kurbjuhn.

Newspapers

Albuquerque Journal. December 5, 2000.

The Boston Globe. June 8, 1989.

International Herald Tribune. June 26, 1998.

Laredo Weekly Times. July 2 and 16, 1916.

New Orleans Times-Picayune, May 6, 1917.

New York Herald. April 4, 1917.

The Wall Street Journal. November 17, 2000.

Index

Fig 22. At 50 years of age, Sylvanus G. Morley still worked as an archaeologist in the Yucatán peninsula. This photograph was taken in 1933 or 1934, from Robert H. Lister and Florence C. Lister, editors, In Search of Maya Glyphs: From the Archaeological Journals of Sylvanus G. Morley. *(Santa Fe : Museum of New Mexico Press, 1970), p. 11.*